Peace-Building by, between, and beyond Muslims and Evangelical Christians

Peace-Building by, between, and beyond Muslims and Evangelical Christians

Edited by
Mohammed Abu-Nimer and
David Augsburger

LEXINGTON BOOKS

A division of
ROWMAN & LITTLEFIELD PUBLISHERS, INC.
Lanham • Boulder • New York • Toronto • Plymouth, UK

LEXINGTON BOOKS

A division of Rowman & Littlefield Publishers, Inc.
A wholly owned subsidiary of The Rowman & Littlefield Publishing Group, Inc.
4501 Forbes Boulevard, Suite 200
Lanham, MD 20706

Estover Road
Plymouth PL6 7PY
United Kingdom

British Library Cataloguing in Publication Information Available

Library of Congress Cataloging-in-Publication Data

Peace-building by, between, and beyond Muslims and Evangelical Christians / [edited by] Mohammed Abu-Nimer and David Augsburger.
p. cm.
Includes index.
ISBN 978-0-7391-3521-1 (cloth : alk. paper) — ISBN 978-0-7391-3523-5 (ebook)
1. Islam—Relations—Christianity. 2. Christianity and other religions—Islam. I. Abu-Nimer, Mohammed, 1962- II. Augsberger, David, 1938-
BP172.P345 2009
261.2'7—dc22 2009001770

Printed in the United States of America

™ The paper used in this publication meets the minimum requirements of American National Standard for Information Sciences—Permanence of Paper for Printed Library Materials, ANSI/NISO Z39.48-1992.

Contents

Acknowledgments

We wish to express our gratitude to the following persons who contributed to the Conflict Transformation Program of Dialogue with Muslim and Evangelical Christians. We are indebted in some way to all of the following for their contribution that has resulted, along with many other events and resources, in this publication.

Congressmen Frank Wolfe of Virginia and Adam Schiff of California for their assistance and support. Fuller Seminary President Richard J. Mouw and his staff, particularly Fred Messick, for guidance and counsel.

Mohammed Abu-Nimer, Salam Institute for Peace and Justice, our co-partners in this dialogue, for their peace training and constructive networking and active staff, Ayse Kadayifci, Ashleigh Zimmerman, Diana Bandak, Fait A. Muedini, and Melinda Witter.

Sayyid Syeed and the Islamic Society of North America and his associates Dr. Louy Safi, Mohamad El-Sanousi, and Dr. Muhammad Shafiq. Professor Said Abdul Aziz, the chair of Mohammad Said Farsi Islamic Peace Endowment at American University, contributed to the Christian–Muslim dialogue meetings. Also Ahmed Alwani, director of the Graduate School of Islamic and Social Sciences, generously offered his support and network of contacts in different phases of this project.

Yahia Abdul Rahman and the Islamic Shura Council of Southern California and Los Angeles leaders Maher Hathout, Hassan Hathout, and Najeeba Sayeed-Miller.

Jared Holton and Robin Basselin, project directors for Fuller Seminary's Grant Staff, and Lynn Kunkle, project director for Salam Institute.

And the Conflict Transformation Team at Fuller, Dudley Woodberry, Glen Stassen, Al Dueck, Evelyne Reisacher, Wilbert Shenk, Ronald Kernaghan, Kevin Reimer, and David Augsburger.

This publication was supported by Award No. 2003-DD-BX-1025 awarded by the U.S. Department of Justice, Office of Justice Programs. The opinions, findings, and conclusions or recommendations expressed in this publication are those of the authors and do not necessarily reflect the views of the Department of Justice.

Many other participants made lasting contributions, obviously including the authors of the chapters and responses in this volume, the Muslim and Evangelical Christian participants in the scholarly and dialogical consortia, and the many persons who wrote, both in support and criticism of this effort at lowering walls that can be reduced, removing those that can be broken down, and renewing conversation on the vital agreements and disagreements that we bring to our abiding friendship.

Introduction

Mohammed Abu-Nimer and David Augsburger

When Evangelical Christian and Muslim scholars meet to dialogue, to explore the interface between their perspectives, and to deepen the shared understandings, common resources, and relationships, they discover that they have much to talk about.

There is much that is shared in common. Both take their Scriptures seriously. Both care deeply about peacemaking. Both believe that it is God's will that we work for justice for all. Both believe in the power of prayer.

And there are differences. True dialogue does not seek to avoid or to evade differences. On the contrary, it facilitates the discovery of meaningful differences. Openness to conversation and firmness in belief are both necessary to meaningful dialogue. Our differences make our conversations rich and surprising. Meeting, learning to know each other, increasing our shared resources for peace-building, coming to common understandings of effective peacemaking, and jointly acting or taking a stand against injustice are the most crucial tasks of this century.

This book contains scholarly chapters written by Muslims and Christians shared in dialogue with each other—a dialogue that requires clear statements of one's own faith and convictions and open recognition and response to the stance and perspectives of the other. These conversations were conducted over the period of 1 year beginning with the first consultation on April 22–23, 2005, Washington, DC, and concluding with a second consultation on April 22–23, 2006, Pasadena, California.

Convened by Fuller Theological Seminary, Salam Institute of Peace & Justice, and the Islamic Society of North America (ISNA), these conversations have produced a set of documents that can be the basis for ongoing dialogue—a stimulation to seek the next steps in understanding, mutual respect, and collaboration.

Fuller, Salam, and ISNA have been collaborating for three years in a two-level project—scholarly and practitioner levels—to seek common practices, patterns, and pathways for conflict reduction, resolution, and transformation between faiths as well as to learn how to better resolve differences within our individual faith communities. The scholarly level has brought Muslim and Christian thinkers together to jointly write and now publish these materials that will be a basis for education on practices of peacemaking and the resulting understanding of each other's values, vision, and faith. On the community leadership level, the group collaborated in bringing key leaders together for training events of dialogue, conversation, and exploration of joint work in our communities that can build bridges of understanding that reduce tension and increase respect. We believe that we can work together to strengthen our mutual understandings of living in secure and productive relationships.

Fuller Theological Seminary, Pasadena, California, is a nondenominational evangelical seminary. Each year students from more than ninety language and ethnic groups and as many different Christian denominations gather to study in three schools, a School of Theology, a School of Psychology, and a School of Intercultural Studies. It serves as a convening center for Evangelical groups to gather and explore both within their historic Christian communities and across boundaries in dialogue and interfaith conversations.

Salam Institute of Peace & Justice is a Muslim research and practice center offering training and mediation expertise, and doing conflict mediation and intervention around the world. Located at American University, with its renowned Farsi Chair of Islamic Peace, it brings experience in creative peacemaking and commands high respect for its convening power to gather the various leading organizations of Islamic thought throughout the nation for Muslim dialogue and theory building within the Muslim community and across faith boundaries in interfaith dialogue.

The ***Islamic Society of North America***, the umbrella organization of several hundred Muslim community and professional organizations of North America, publishes a magazine, *Islamic Horizons*, with a circulation of more than 70,000, and holds conferences, conventions, interfaith initiatives, and training programs throughout the year attracting the largest number of Muslims and people of other faiths in North America.

This book, *Peace-Building by, between, and beyond Muslim and Evangelical Christians*, brings together the best of the conversations between these two groups. The key issues of diversity and pluralism, interfaith and intrafaith dialogue, peace building in nonviolent action and constructive conflict resolution, and the challenge of preserving basic human rights in war and conflict areas and a shared ethic of civilizational discourse are addressed by voices from one or the other religious perspective and then reconsidered from another point of view. This offers a basis for Christian and Muslim groups to frame their initial conversations and then see where dialogue leads them in exploring their own steadfast convictions and their unstinting commitment to understand and prize the other as a fellow traveler on the road toward just and peaceful community relations.

We recognize that in both Christian and Muslim groups there exist wide spectra of beliefs and practices. We came together as Muslim and Christian scholars who are profoundly persuaded that it is the responsibility of groups such as our own to point out and pursue those paths toward nonviolent resolution of our differing values and visions. We see our task as seeking for a larger vision of peace-building that we can share and promote to our particular communities of faith and practice as well as to the larger common of the world community. We hope that our humble experience and each of the following articles contribute to the much needed conversation between Muslims and Christians on all levels.

I

PEACE-BUILDING, NONVIOLENCE, AND CONFLICT RESOLUTION

1

The Practices of Forgiveness and Reconciliation in Conflict Transformation

David Augsburger

What do we mean when we use the concepts of *forgiving, reconciling,* and *transforming relationships*? These words have greatly varied usages in theological, ritual, spiritual, social, psychological, and political contexts. In interfaith dialogue, in multicultural contexts, in intercultural and interreligious mediation, one may easily assume a common coinage that does not actually exist when speaking of forgiving or reconciling.

This chapter offers a set of paradigms drawn from an analysis of Christian usage for critique, comparison, conversation between groups, and their heritages of meaning.

The following three sections of self-analysis of Christian beliefs and practices are offered as a basis for conversation and interfaith dialogue on the nature and practice of forgiving and reconciling where there are injuries, significant alienation, or historical atrocities dividing individuals or groups. The strong tendency to soften the meanings of words, reduce the demands of a moral or theological concept such as forgiving, and erode the definitions into a common sand of civility and tolerance is visible in Christian thought and practice. It is necessary to constantly return to the radical—or root—meaning of central concepts and recover the soul of reconciliation. Is this tendency specific to one religion or does it occur in others as well? What are the meanings that cluster around the concepts of forgiving and reconciling in Muslim thought? Is there a parallel attrition of their significance in popular culture or in the faith community of Islam?

The understandings of forgiveness vary greatly within and between both cultures and virtually all religious groups. Thus it is not possible to speak of a single and common "Christian understanding" of forgiving or reconciling. The same impossibility may well be present in the diverse cultural, communal, and theological variation of the wider Muslim world. However, in spite of the impossibility of constructing unified definitions of our practices in either the Muslim or the Christian communities, dialogue on our thought and action in forgiving and reconciling is basic and central to our work in transforming conflict from the negative spirals of alienation to the positive directions of healing, growth, and the rejoining of what has been severed or broken.

In his excellent monograph, *Nonviolence and Peace Building in Islam*, Mohammed Abu-Nimer (2003) affirms forgiveness as a central value in Islamic and Arab culture, indeed one of the major values making dispute resolution possible (p. 177). He offers an intriguing spectrum of references to the value and practice of forgiveness in Muslim practices that move from the virtues of forgiveness and mercy as expressions of tolerance that recognize the dignity and rights of others (p. 39). At times he speaks of an attitudinal forgiveness that is equivalent to kindness and mercy (p. 67), then couples it with practices of forgiveness that break the chain of retribution and revenge in authentic reconciliation (p. 68). He offers a case study that ends with the offenders offering remorse and requesting forgiveness from the victims through the appeal to and the ritual of quoting a powerful series of texts from the Qur'an (42:37, 40, 43; 45:14). He connects apology and the request for forgiveness to the process of reconciliation (p. 108). He argues that forgiveness is one of the most powerful values that strengthens the pursuit of justice by means of nonviolent resistance to evil (p. 174).

There are a wide range of forgiveness practices and rituals in both religious communities. Some are similar, perhaps parallel; others unique in character and practice. In their description of rituals of reconciliation, Irani and Funk (2001, p. 187) portray the powerful rituals of *sulh* (settlement), *musalaha* (reconciliation), *musafaha* (exchange of handshakes), and *mumalaha* (breaking bread together) that demonstrate forgiveness and further reconciliation with the language of bitter coffee shared and bread broken together. Each group possesses a vocabulary and sets of practices that facilitate the offering and reception of remorse, repentance, and a desire to return to relationship in reconciliation. Dialogue on the nature of these practices and their unique strengths to resolve injury is a central task of interfaith conversation on peacemaking.

Thus the following propositions, the diagrammatic spectrum, and the most frequently cited definitions used in the Christian community will be set forth to serve as one end of the bridge of dialogue, providing a basis for contrast or discovery of similarity, as ground for growth in either or both communities or a basis for building increased mutual understanding.

1. PROPOSITIONS FOR DIALOGUE ON FORGIVENESS AND RECONCILIATION

The following eleven propositions for the practice of forgiving and its inextricable relation to reconciliation are offered from a Christian perspective. They are affirmed with the awareness that propositions from Muslim theology and practice will express similar concerns but in differing and distinct formulations. These are put forward as an invitation for the discovery of parallel or contrasting perspectives from Muslim theology and practice. In what ways do they agree with or vary from the understandings used by Muslim peacemakers in bringing people together after alienation or injury? What are the Muslim guidelines that challenge or confirm, sharpen or negate, these affirmations about the nature of forgiveness?

1. Accepting and forgiving are different processes.
   We accept persons for the good that they are or do.
   We forgive people for the evil that they did or caused.
   (The first is love of neighbor, the second, love of enemy.)
2. Tolerating and forgiving are different processes.
   We tolerate what another has done when we overlook or ignore.
   We forgive what we cannot tolerate, will not overlook, and dare not ignore.
   (When we reduce forgiving to tolerating, we choose denial instead of reality.)
3. Excusing and forgiving are different processes.
   We excuse people when we no longer hold them accountable.
   We forgive persons when we hold them accountable but do not excuse.
   (When we excuse, we condone; when we forgive we confront yet conciliate.)
4. Forgetting and forgiving are different processes.
   We do not need to forgive if we can simply forget—deny, detach, and dismiss.
   We forgive when we face injury and pain yet seek to reframe, restore, and rebuild.
   (To equate forgiving with forgetting is to exchange healing for memory fatigue.)
5. Forgiving is not an arbitrary, unilateral act of mercy received as good fortune.

Such "forgiving" bypasses the actual injury and offers no truly moral contact.
Such "forgiveness" requires no moral response to the offender.
(There is a place for generous pardon; it also places the other in debt or denial.)

6. Forgiving requires an ethical context of moral values and categories.
Forgiving outside of a moral universe is meaningless and empty.
(When we forgive we are not avoiding but addressing moral injury and injustice.)
7. Forgiving is not a moral victory for the offended that judges, controls, or obligates.
Forgiving seeks to confront, challenge, rework, and transform the relationship.
(When used as a strategy for superiority, it is self-defeating and alienating.)
8. Forgiving is based on a prior step of restoring an attitude of mercy for the other.
Forgiving requires the practice of empathy that continues to see co-humanity.
(When empathy breaks through one's hurt, love can penetrate the hate.)
9. Forgiveness is the practice of the virtue of love for neighbor and enemy.
Reconciliation is practice of the virtues of forgiving, self-giving, and love-giving.
(Both practices are grounded in these virtues that offer inner, not outer, rewards.)
10. True reconciliation occurs when violence is renounced, justice sought, victims heard, innocence honored, guilt and responsibility admitted, repentance expressed, rapprochement risked, and relationship opened.
(It is costly. Both sides must open, both yield, both move, and both change.)
11. Religion that is on the side of reconciliation, healing, and peace is not false.
Religion that is on the side of estrangement, alienation, and destruction is not true.
(A bias toward reconciliation, a disposition toward constructive relationships, a commitment to work toward the renewal and rejoining of alienated parties, and a desire to see estranged persons or groups reconnect is essential religion.)

(Augsburger 1996, pp. 165–68)

A SPECTRUM OF PERSPECTIVES ON FORGIVING AND RECONCILING

The following table offers a spectrum of positions taken by persons or groups in the practice of forgiving and seeking reconciliation.

As a basic working assumption in Christian theology, it is understood that "conciliation is our work, reconciliation is God's work." We are responsible to do the most effective conciliation possible that invites persons to open their attitudes and their memories to each other and before God. When reconciliation occurs, we recognize that it was not our achievement, not a result of our work, but a sign of God's presence in effecting the mystery of rekindling compassion, reawakening empathy, and reopening closed attitudes and intentions. It is God who is the ground of all redemptive interhuman bridge building. We do the wall-destroying work that creates a new community, but it is God who renews connections between peoples.

Out of this assumption that our task is to work toward restoration of the broken relationships, the theologically informed mediator is strongly inclined toward the right side of the following diagram, to reach beyond civility and tolerance to reopen relationships and to seek to move persons toward authentic contact and communion.

This distinction between conciliation and reconciliation is central to Christian peacemaking. How is this interrelationship between human effort and Divine intervention expressed in Muslim thought? Is this assumption shared in Muslim faith and practice? How does it influence your thought, faith, and practice in conciliation?

The following paradigm offers a range of goals that stretch from peaceful coexistence to reconciled interdependence in constructive community. The left end focuses on social acceptance of diversity and the harmonious fabric of a free society that invites interchange and mutual respect with security and liberty for all participants. The right end is directed toward a deeper peace of resolved conflicts, reconciled differences, restored privileges, reopened conversations, and a common though richly diverse reality.

This paradigm offers a summary of the wide variation in Christian thought and practice. The most common understandings in "The Christian Culture of North America" tend toward columns one and two. Most Christian practice strives for columns one through three at best. Mediators and peacemakers speak for columns four through seven, but find that popular culture and media construe their efforts in the language of the first three columns. Christian theology has not effectively taught or practiced the values of columns five through seven.

What is the experience of Muslim peacemakers? Can this be a basis for effective conversation on methods and practices as well as our goals and ends?

Table 1.1. Practices of Forgiving and Reconciling

Civility	*Acceptance*	*Co-humanity*	*Pardon*	*Process*	*Contact*	*Restitution*
Politeness Courtesy	Unconditional positive regard	Equal regard for other Restitution of the human	Unilateral release	Reach out	Reconnect Reconcile	Restore Repay
Overlook insult or injury by refusing all judgment, ignoring guilt or responsibility	Accept the other as fallible yet of worth although morally in the wrong or socially challenged in behavior	Acknowledges the other as another human being in spite of hurtful acts or injurious actions	Release of demands vs. offender setting self free of review or resentment, for grieving hurt or loss	Work through validating repentance by one or both in mutual intention and action	Mutually recognize repentance as genuine and right, relationships restored or achieved	Return to full moral community by returning what was usurped, repaying the injury
Goals:						
Tolerance, openness, accepting diversity, human fallibility	Affirm self-esteem, other-regard, neighbor-love and mutual value	Extend empathy, reciprocity, mutuality, co-humanity, compassion	Offer remission of punishment, release of revenge or retaliation	Caringly work at relating, deal with hurt, guilt, and shame	Authentically risking trust, opening future, discern reality, settle for less, reward self	Justly seeking to restore the loss or repay the hurt done as possible
Virtues:						
Civility	Grace	Mercy	Relinquishment	Agape	Shared reality	Justice

FREQUENTLY CITED DEFINITIONS OF FORGIVING

The following definitions extend the brief notes on the table above by citing definitions frequently used by Christian thinkers. They are offered as an invitation for comparison with Muslim parallels or contrasts.

(1) *Forgiveness* as Civility and Tolerance

Forgiveness is enlightened social tolerance, civility, and politeness that excuses an offender or an offense by offering immediate, automatic tolerance without consideration of responsibility or guilt. Forgiveness is memory fatigue, as time passes and "heals all" and one chooses to "put it behind in forgetfulness, in what is popularly called 'closure.'" One evicts the event, refuses to be held hostage by memory or resentment, and "gets on with life."

(2) *Forgiveness* as Acceptance

Forgiveness accepts the other in spite of the painful actions suffered, generously and benevolently—from a position of superiority—offers inclusion and some degree of relationship through excusing, covering, overlooking, ignoring, or denying in unselfish reframing of the event.

Forgiveness is an increase in our internal motivation to repair and maintain a relationship after it has been damaged by the hurtful actions of the other (McCullough, Sandage, and Worthington 1997, p. 22).

(3) *Forgiveness* as Cohumanity

Forgiveness is the restitution of the human, the recognition of cohumanity. One human being chooses to see and accept another—in spite of a terrible past—as a fellow human being (Yevtushenko 1964, p. 26; Mueller-Fahrenholz 1997).

Forgiveness [as cohumanity] is morally possible because of the inherent value of all persons. The moral status of the offender may be in question, but this does not diminish the person's inherent worth as a human being. Forgiveness is a relational stance of accepting the inherent worth of another person even after judging the wrong action (Kellenberger 1995, p. 407).

(4) *Forgiveness* as Pardon

Forgiveness is not something you do, it is something you discover: you discover you are in no position to forgive; you are more like than unlike the one who hurt you (Patton 1985).

Forgiveness is breaking free from bondage. An act of transgression locks the perpetrator to the victim; every offense creates human bondage; evil acts create chains—largely unconscious—of debt, guilt, and obligation. Forgiveness is a complex process of "unlocking" painful bondage, of individual or mutual liberation (Mueller-Fahrenholz 1997, p. 24).

(5) *Forgiveness* as Process

Forgiveness is a process that includes both perpetrator and victim, occurring when the offender asks and the offended grants it, not unilaterally but in an appropriate measure of mutuality. It may be reciprocal, with both sides recognizing failure, owning responsibility, moving toward each other, changing offensive behavior, releasing anger demands, healing resentments, redeeming the past, renewing the present, and opening the future to a more just relationship.

(6) *Forgiveness* as Contact

Forgiveness is the mutual recognition that repentance is genuine and right relationships have been restored or achieved (Frank Kimper 1972).

Forgiveness is an act of recognizing remorse and repentance in the perpetrator(s), and granting the person(s) release. In repenting, one returns to the point of time—the evil act—feels the shame of victimizing or of victimization, owns the hatred, cancels the wish for revenge, and relinquishes actual and illusory power. In reciprocal repentance, both return, recognize, express remorse, pledge change in future actions and both release demands on the event and on the other.

(7) *Forgiveness* as Restitution

Forgiveness is completed by the mutual search for justice that is retributive where possible, so that the stolen is returned, the injured is cared for, the loss is recompensed; where the loss is irreparable, redemptive and transformative justice seeks to change the relationship as well as the system around it to promote justice in the future, work for parity, mutuality, and security in both relationships and systemic practice of fairness and respect for diversity in social solidarity.

(8) *Forgiveness* as Practice

Forgiveness is a habit, a practice, a craft. It is not simply an action, an emotional judgment, or a declarative utterance—though Christian forgiveness includes all of these dimensions. Rather forgiveness is a habit that must be practiced over time within the disciplines of Christian community. Forgiveness is a habit, a practice alongside other practices including . . . confession, repentance, excommunication, prayer, and healing (Jones 1995, pp. 163–66).

QUESTIONS FOR MUSLIM–CHRISTIAN EXPLORATION:

1. How do they parallel or differ from those used by Muslim thinkers?
2. The most thoughtful Christian theology, ethics, and psychology focus on the three central columns of the continuum. Is there a similar pattern in Muslim practice?
3. Most Christian practice falls toward the left end of the continuum—civility, tolerance, denial, acceptance, and private one-way pardon. Is there a parallel tendency in Muslim practice?
4. Constructive Christian theology that takes the biblical texts seriously presses toward the two right columns of constructive process and authentic reconciliation and renewed contact. How does this emerge in Muslim thought and practice?

BIBLIOGRAPHY

Abu-Nimer, Mohammed. 2003. *Nonviolence and peacebuilding in Islam.* Gainesville: University of Florida.

Augsburger, David. 1986. *Helping people forgive.* Louisville, Ky.: John Knox Press.

———. 2004. *Hate-work: Working through the pain and pleasures of hate.* Louisville, Ky.: Westminster John Knox Press.

Irani, George, and Nathan Funk. 2001. Rituals of reconciliation. In *Peace and conflict resolution in Islam,* ed. A. Said, N. Funk, and A. Kadayifci. New York: University Press of America.

Jones, L. Gregory. 1995. *Embodying forgiveness.* Grand Rapids, Mich.: Eerdmans.

Kellenberger, James. 1995. *Relationship morality.* University Park: Pennsylvania State University Press.

Kimper, Frank. 1972. Lecture notes. Claremont, Calif.: Claremont School of Theology. Unpublished.

McCullough, Michael, Steven Sandage, and Everett Worthingon. 1997. *To forgive is human.* Downer's Grove, Ill.: Intervarsity Press.

Mueller-Fahrenholz, Geiko. 1997. *Vergebung macht frei: Vorschlaege fuer eine Theologie der Versoehnung.* Frankfurt: Otto Lembeck.

Patton, John. 1985. *Is human forgiveness possible?* Nashville, Tenn.: Abingdon.

Said, Abdul Aziz, Nathan C. Funk, and Ayse S. Kadayifci, eds. 2001. *Peace and conflict resolution in Islam.* New York: University Press of America.

Yevtushenko, Yevgeny. 1967. *Yevtushenko's Reader.* New York: Avon.

2

Forgiveness in Muslim Thought and Practice

Response to Augsburger's "The Practices of Forgiveness and Reconciliation in Conflict Transformation"

Karim Douglas Crow

> In the name of God, merciful and beloved, the lord of sunrise and sunset and everything in between.

I want to thank David Augsburger for his invitation; in a way he has offered a challenge, for a Muslim, to respond to this very central issue of forgiveness and reconciliation. And I thank him for his insistence from the beginning to return to the radical root meaning of "concepts," which is something that I think is also very much needed in the Muslim context. He is only offering one end of the dialogue; he wants someone to take up the other end and have a meaningful exchange. I do not know about my ability to do that meaningfully, but I will offer some ideas and some specific responses to the points he raises in his interesting chapter.

He offers eleven propositions on forgiveness and reconciliation. The two that resonated most with me are number 5: "Forgiving is not an arbitrary, unilateral act of mercy received in good fortune. Such forgiveness is bypassing actual injury and requires no more response to the offender." And number 10: "True reconciliation occurs when violence is renounced, justice sought, and guilt and responsibility are admitted, and it is costly." I think that those two are most directly relevant to the Islamic perspective.

First, forgiveness may be valid and concrete only when repentance and atonement are sincerely manifested by the perpetrator, or by the offender. It cannot be something that is hidden from sight. In fact, in the Muslim context it is usually done in a public way so that there is a communal context and it has a message and weight to the larger group, not just an individual act but part of everyone's concern. We have this perennial emphasis in the Islamic context on the role of the community and the identity of the individual within the community; these two are inescapable when you deal with Islamic responses or concepts. The emphasis on justice is also welcome from the Islamic perspective. Without genuine remorse and recognition of offense and harm, what would forgiveness be? It would be foolhardy and ignorant to forgive an unrepentant offender. Do you forgive Timothy McVeigh for his Oklahoma bombing? He was unrepentant until the day he was executed. And he was laughing at you. So it is hard to be forgiving to someone like that. A Muslim might agree with that.

Second, there are established modes and avenues to express this repentance. Who knows the secrets of the heart? You can feed poor people. You can liberate slaves. You can pay money. You can make amends in some public way. Islam has provided a number of concrete ways that will ratify and guarantee that you have indeed recognized your responsibility and owned up to it in the public domain. I think that is the useful, more practical thing; it may have to be reinterpreted or reapplied in our modern concept. I do not think I can free many slaves, but I might be able to liberate myself from certain enslavements that I have. I mean, I can see someone saying, "If you really are repentant, give up drinking coffee for one year. You love it so much." That would be a genuine suffering on my part, and a sacrifice on my part. It would be a payment. So the question becomes, "What price are we willing to pay?" It is not simply the individual who's being held responsible, but it is also the individual who is going to recognize and accept that a person has met the conditions that validate his being worthy of forgiveness.

Now Islam has, as I said, a spectrum. Some people are not able to be big enough of heart to forgive unilaterally without demanding payment of some kind. Islam recognizes that. For example, in the case of murder, and the rules and legal literature on Qisas, you could insist, "My brother was killed unjustly by this man." He is the culprit. "I want him put to death in exchange." Of course, through the legal means and judgments authorized for capital punishment. But someone might come to you and say, "Please. . . . He has children. Why? Why do you want to put his life to an end just for retaliation? Aren't you big enough to accept, for example, a blood money payment, or something of this kind? Can you not accept some repayment in view of his life? And Islam provides, in the traditional legal context, that if someone was mean-spirited and minimalist enough to insist on blood in exchange . . . that on the other hand, *al-husna,* the best, the more elevated, the higher response, closer to the prophetic practice, would be to forgive or to accept an intermediate, partial payment, offer a partial forgiveness or something. So there is a spectrum here, which is pragmatic. It says that human beings are not all angels but they have something angelic in them! And yet we have to aid that response, somehow, and accommodate it.

Now in the comments made in interpreting the spectrum of forgiveness practices, when you say that the Christian center of gravity falls in the middle, I get the feeling you are dancing around the deeper issue. Which is this: something we will call theological, but it is the basic human issue of suffering and loss. Now I think from what I understand, for you as a Christian, suffering is at the center of your faith. The whole symbolism of your faith deals with a man who is suffering in extremity, and in a very cruel manner. Some might find it strange that a religion worships the image of a man being put to death in an extremely brutal way. And if you see some of the crucifixes that are painted very realistically, with blood and gore, it is a bit gruesome from an outsider's perspective. On the other hand, the message is clear, that the ultimate sacrifice and suffering that this man, "Jesus, the son of Mary," offered in his example stands at the core of the message of Christian faith: that is to say, suffering done consciously, not mechanically or passively like most of our suffering (being stuck in a traffic jam, for example) but voluntary suffering, given as an offering, a payment. This is something that makes him truly human. I know that Christians believe that he is the Son of God. But in a way, the mystery of his divinity, from what I understand, is that he also has this "human side" to him. So I would say that Islam understands the message of suffering. Some Sufis say that Christians have the cross, but we have the meaning of the cross. I do not want to interpret that beyond just the repetition of it, but the higher ideal of the willingness to sacrifice, to suffer and thereby set an example and to teach the virtue of suffering done consciously for a higher purpose, is a tremendous and extremely valuable idea that I think Christians and Muslims, in the deepest level, will not argue about.

When we go back to the life of the Prophet, we know that for the first fifteen years of his mission, out of the twenty-two and a half years, he operated solely in a peaceable manner. I do not want to say nonviolent, although his manner approaches it. And this was the original meaning of jihad, by the way, which is found in the early Meccan chapters of the Qur'an, before the battles began in Medina and also afterwards; the original meaning behind jihad is "the suffering." I want to mention one example, one of the earliest converts was a slavewoman, Sumayya, her son 'Ammar and her husband Yasir. They were being tortured by their Meccan Quraysh because they had adopted Islam, and they were being forced to abjure Islam, and the prophet would pass by in the midst of this very severe torture of theirs and exclaim, "Be patient. Be long suffering. Do not give in to this form of jihad. This form of striving. Your rendezvous is paradise." In fact, in the case of Sumayya, her owner put a spear into her private parts and killed her! And these were the kind of provocations and suffering that Muslims were asked

to endure; this is an extreme case, of course, of those who suffered before they were given leave, so to speak, to respond to the hostility and oppression and violence against them through a military option.

But suffering cuts two ways, it is not just that a person is setting an example for others. Conscious suffering is a path for the education of your own self. It operates as an inner grace for a person; it initiates forgiveness. So in an ultimate sense, in the finest way, it is the best kind of selfishness. I forgive you not because I want to be nice to you or because you have manifested the objective signs of repentance and remorse, but because it is good for me. And it brings me closer to my Lord.

You say in conclusion that "conciliation is our work, reconciliation is God's work." I do not know. I suppose that is a doctrinal statement. Is everything God's work? Or do humans have a role to play, too? And I am more of a free-will person and we do not want to get into that in this debate. But I think there is a synergy. God works through people, so to always say, "Well, that is up to God and that is God's will" can also be a way of copping out, by saying "I am not going to pull my weight." But we really have to be willing to pay the price and to suffer, for our own sake and for the sake of our brothers and our fellows. And in that dynamic, forgiveness has real meaning. Otherwise it is taken at a very simple level, in a kind of sentimental, mawkish way. I think that it actually is destructive, and self-defeating. You cannot just forgive everyone, just because you want to be seen as forgiving. But there has to be a real basis for it.

"Does the Qur'an give specific guidance on forgiving?" The Qur'an has many statements that guide us. God is, of course, compassionate and just, and the reason why humans emulate these divine qualities is part of the basis of Islamic ethics. But because of the nature of interpretation and the variety of interpretive communities within Islam, to say yes or no in a simplistic way is difficult. So I now shift to the other canonical, or revelation-based, body of teaching in Islam, which is the historical record, the example of the prophet. And here we have a clear sign.

At the conquest of Mecca, the opponents of the prophet who had fought him for about seventeen years were now cornered, and unwillingly and reluctantly had to embrace Islam. It became clear that there were certain people among their leaders whom the prophet, his heart, was not inclined to welcome; he even made his position clear to his followers X, Y, and Z. "Someone does something to them; I do not know what I would do." And yet these opposing people were brought before the prophet by relatives and friends, and they made their allegiance to the new faith. And the prophet accepted it. But, his companions noted, he was not necessarily happy. But he accepted it, and these ringleaders of the opposition to the prophet were then called "those people whose hearts were reconciled" to Islam. In fact they were treated very well and generously, and they were paid handsome amounts of booty in the immediately following military engagements.

So there is an answer there. Some of those people were known for their antipathy to Islam years after that event; one leader even went and put his foot on the grave of some of his former Muslim enemies after they had been buried, and then he boasted, "We have conquered you! We the leadership of Quraysh who opposed the prophet now control Islam!" There is always a discussion among the Muslims about how sincere or superficial their acceptance of Islam was. Nevertheless, the Prophet showed an acceptance of and forgiveness to his opposition.

So there is an answer there. Now Muslims need to look at that. They need to see their own tradition and their own models and use the indications and the guidance they can find there to respond to these questions. The fact is, many Muslims today, even well-educated professionals, do not know that much about their own Prophet's history, they are not that up on the details of their own Prophet's career and mission in life. We find this especially among young Muslims; I think it is very alarming. That is my own worry.

But there is an answer, and we should give it. Muslims should be in a position to say, "In fact, we do have a position on this." Recognizing that there is a spectrum within the interpretive community, there may be variations and more than one way of understanding these events. Nevertheless, we have the historical material to guide ourselves to a position on the issue of forgiveness.

I apologize if my response is not adequate. But I think we have touched on some important things, and there is a lot more to explore, to squeeze out of your chapter. Perhaps we should have a scholarly response written, specifically trying to fill in the other side?

3

Muslim Perspectives on War and Peace[1]

S. Ayse Kadayifci-Orellana

All you who believe! Enter fully into peace. (Q2:208)

Use and abuse of religion to justify war or encourage peace is not a novel phenomenon. On the contrary, religion has been a powerful tool in the hands of political leaders since time immemorial. This is because religion as a system of beliefs and practices relating to the sacred, and uniting its adherents in a community, has a powerful hold on people's way of thinking, acting, and perception of interests.[2] Consequently, even though the main reasons and issues may not be of a religious character, religion plays a significant role at times of conflict, especially when different religious systems encounter each other. In such cases, political leaders do not hesitate to resort to religious myths and sacred documents of their religion to justify their acts and policies to get the support of their communities and reinforce their power.[3] Simultaneously, the same religious traditions that have been used to justify violence have also been an inspiration for peacemaking and nonviolent struggles for establishing justice.

The relationship between violence and religion, in general, and Islam, in particular, became a central concern for scholars and politicians, especially after the heinous attacks on the World Trade Center and the Pentagon on September 11, 2001. Islam, like other religious traditions, is deeply implicated in individual and social conceptions of peace and conflict, because it addresses some of the most profound existential issues of human life, such as freedom and inevitability, fear and security, right and wrong, and sacred and profane among others, because it is "a powerful constituent of cultural norms and values" and "embodies and elaborates upon its highest morals, ethical principles and ideals of social harmony."[4] Consequently, it has a direct impact on when war is justified, the way peace is conceptualized, and the way conflicts are resolved in Islamic societies. Based on this observation, this chapter explores different Muslim perspectives of war and peace and introduces some of the basic principles that underpin the Islamic perspective on conflict resolution and peace-building.

ISLAMIC CONCEPTION OF PEACE

Muslim perspectives on peace, war, and traditions of peace-building are based on the Islamic conception of peace, which is derived from the Qur'an, the Hadith (Prophet Mohammed's sayings), and the Sunna (Prophet Mohammed's deeds). Many references to peace (e.g., *salam, silm, sulh*) in the Qur'an suggest that peace together with justice is the central theme in the Islamic discourse.[5] Based on the centrality of peace in the Qur'an, Muslims, irrespective of the Islamic tradition they adhere to, agree that Islam is a religion of peace and that application of Islamic principles will bring justice, harmony, order, and therefore peace.[6] Indeed even the word *Islam* is derived from the Arabic word *salam/silm* (peace) suggesting peace through submission (*taslim*) to the will of God.

Islamic concept of peace is wider than absence of war, oppression, and tyranny. Peace in Islam suggests a condition of internal and external order. According to Qur'anic discourse, peace in Islam begins with God, since *as-Salam* (peace) is one of the Most Beautiful ninety-nine names of God (Q59:23). The Qur'an refers to peace as the greeting, language, and condition of Paradise (Q10:10, Q14:23, Q19:61–63, Q36:58) and God calls believers to the "abode of peace" (Q10:25). These uses recommend that peace is a positive state of safety or security, which includes being at peace with oneself, with fellow human beings, nature, and God.[7] Based on these and other verses, peace in Islam is associated with a wide range of concepts. These concepts include, but are not limited to, justice and human development, wholeness, salvation, perfection, and harmony,[8] and peace is defined as a *presence* (e.g., of justice, harmony, conditions for human development, and security).[9]

In addition to these Qur'anic verses, the Islamic stance on peace is derived from Prophet Mohammed's diplomacy and basic attitude toward peace, which can be summarized in his slogan "reconciliation of hearts" that he issued at the capture of Mecca in 630 (cf. Q9:60).[10] Moreover, Troger observes that "coming to terms with adversaries and enemies and the contractual guaranteeing of agreements were corner-stones of Mohammed's policy" and that he preferred peaceful regulation of conflicts and peaceful resolution of enmity.[11] These policies are evident in both the *Hudaybiya* Treaty, signed by Mohammed to end the hostilities with Meccans, and also in the contractually regulated relations between Muslims and non-Muslims, which ensured peaceful coexistence of people with different ethnic and religious backgrounds. During his prophethood, Mohammed also concluded twenty-three treaties and agreements between groups and tribes, advocated tolerance to others, and strictly enforced compliance to treaties.

Pillars of Islamic Conception of Peace

Qur'anic verses and Prophet's *sunna* regarding peace and peace-building rest on certain Islamic values and principles. Although various ethical principles and values underpin the concept of peace in Islam, certain notions are particularly important. These notions, which can be called the pillars of Islamic conception of peace, include *tawhid* (Unity of Being), *fitrah* (original constitution of human beings), *adl* (justice), *afu* (forgiveness), *Rahmah* (compassion), and *Rahim* (mercy). Some of the other Islamic values and principles that underpin Islamic understanding of peace include pursuit of love, kindness, mercy, benevolence, compassion, wisdom and knowledge, service, social empowerment, universality and dignity of human life, sacredness of human life, equality, quest for peace and harmony, creativity and innovation, individual responsibility and accountability, patience, collaboration and solidarity, inclusion and participation, and diversity and unity among others.[12]

Tawhid

The central principle, which the Islamic understanding of peace is derived from, is the "Principle of Unity of God and all being" (*tawhid*). The principle of *tawhid* expresses the fundamental unity of all humankind and all life and rejects a vision of human rooted in exclusiveness.[13] It is all-Oneness, the One who transcends all duality and plurality, embraces all diversity and multiplicity.[14] The concept of *tawhid* mediates the direct personal relations to the Absolute (which is Absolute Peace) and the maintenance of harmony with all of God's creation, including other fellow human beings and nature that surrounds us.[15] *Tawhid* is the basis of Islamic universalism, tolerance, and inclusivity as everything emanates from God, and everything is part of his creation irrespective of species, race, nationality, creed, or gender. The Islamic universality based on the notion of *tawhid* is best expressed in the Qur'anic verses:

> Oh mankind! We created you from a single (pair) of a male and female, and made you peoples (or nations) and tribes that you may know one another. (49:3)

> To each among you have We prescribed a Law and an Open Way. If Allah had so willed, He would have made you a single People, but (His Plan is) to test you in what He hath given you: so strive as in a race in all virtues. (5:48)

"*Tawhid* allows for reconciliation within multiplicity at cosmic as well as microcosmic (human) levels, and affirms that the manyness of reality is itself a pattern of connectedness."[16] Therefore, Unity of Being, God's One reality is the source of harmony, order and peace and from the Islamic point of view recognizing Unity of all Being and obedience to God's wishes will lead Muslims to work toward creating harmony and peace on earth.

However, the Islamic notion of *tawhid* is not limited to relations within and between human beings only but among all of God's creation, including animals and plants as "human disobedience results in even consequences for the whole of creation."[17] Conflict and war between mankind results in the corruption and ruin of the earth and all that inhabits it. Therefore, Islam calls upon Muslims to actively pursue unity and harmony because according to Islamic theology, when God created human beings, He made them His vicegerents or representatives on earth (Q2:30 and 33:72). Thus each individual as a representative of God on earth (*khilafat Allah fi l-Ard* Q2:30) is responsible for the order thereof[18] and to contribute toward bringing all creatures under the sway of equilibrium and harmony and to live in peace with creation.[19]

Fitrah

Derived from the concept of *tawhid*, upholding peace becomes a responsibility of every Muslim. The individual responsibility to uphold peace emerges out of the original constitution of human beings (*fitrah*), which, according to Islam, is good and *muslim* in character.[20] Islam holds that every human being is created in accordance with the form and image of God and Divine Names or Qualities, which are manifested in their entirety in the human form.[21] According to Islam, every human being is created "innocent, pure, true and free, inclined to right and virtue and endued with true understanding about . . . his [or her] true nature."[22] This belief is based on the Qur'anic verse "verily, we have honored every human being" (Q17:70). It is also stated in the Qur'an that every human being is worthy of respect because they are made "in the best of molds" (Q95:4), and they possess the faculty of reason, which distinguishes them from the rest of the creation (Q2:30–34). According to the Qur'anic tradition, this faculty enables human beings to accept the "trust" of freedom of will, which no other creature is willing to accept (Q33:72).

The quality of *fitrah* furnishes each individual with the prospect of being perfect (*insan-i kamil*) as it "suggests both the possibility and the desirability of harmony within human beings and with God, leading to harmony among human beings and, ultimately, with the cosmos."[23] The Islamic notion of *fitrah* indicates that individuals can choose to follow the path of God as their stewardess on earth and *strive* to bring justice, harmony, and peace and thus perfect their humanity, or they can choose their egos (*al-nafs*), and follow their own interests.[24] Human *reason* or the individual *will* plays a crucial role in making this choice. Within this context, as vicegerents of God on earth, "the greater *jihad* [struggle] (*jihad al-akbar*) in the Islamic tradition has always been the inner struggle to purify the self and behave in a manner which furthers rather than disrupts the divine harmony."[25]

As Sharify-Funk states, "*Fitrah* provides not only the foundational premise for a constructive politics of human potential and value maximization, but also a safeguard against dehumanizing 'the other' within the context of a conflict situation."[26] Therefore, the notion of *fitrah* is critical for the Islamic conception of peace since recognition of the goodness of each and every human being is a precondition for peaceful, constructive, and harmonious relations between human beings and human communities despite their religious, ethnic, or ideological differences.

Justice

Al-Adl (justice), like *As-Salam* (Peace), is one of the most beautiful names of God according to Islamic tradition. God is the Ultimate Judge (*Hakam*) and Absolute Justice. Justice is an integral aspect of the Islamic discourse of peace, since the Qur'an clearly states that the aim of religion is to bring justice: "We sent aforetime Our messengers with Clear Signs and sent down with them the Book and the Balance (of Right and Wrong), that men May stand forth in justice" (Q57:25). Without justice, there can be no peace. Therefore justice is the essential component of peace according to this Qur'anic message. Such interpretation of the Islamic understanding of peace suggests that justice is the overriding principle.[27]

The Qur'anic notion of justice is universal and valid for all human beings; for that reason it transcends any consideration of religion, animosity, race, or creed.[28] Universality of justice is clearly expressed in the Qur'anic verses "O ye who believe! Stand out firmly for justice as witnesses to Allah even as against yourselves, your parents or your kin, and whether It be (against) the rich and poor" (Q4:135); "To fair dealing, and let not the hatred of others to you make you swerve to wrong and depart from justice. Be just for it is Next to Piety" (Q5:8); "God commands justice and good-doing . . . and He forbids indecency, dishonor, and insolence" (Q16:90); and "O ye who believe! The law of equality is prescribed to you" (2:178). The Prophet calls Muslims to mobilize and act against injustice, even if a Muslim originates the injustice.[29] The universality of justice for all, not only for Muslims, is critical for resolution of conflicts and developing peaceful relations as it calls upon Muslims to be self-reflexive, self-critical, and humble and to accept responsibility for one's actions.

Qur'anic discourse also emphasizes social and economic justice as central to social harmony and peace. Many Islamic institutions, such as the institution of *zakah* (alms giving), aim to establish justice in the social and economic realms.[30] Moreover, there is a consistent and recurrent message in the Qur'an and the Hadith to resist and correct the conditions of injustice, which are seen as a source for conflict and disorder on earth. Pursuing justice is not only a responsibility of the Muslims as vicegerents of God on earth but also a divinely ordered command.[31] For that reason, from an Islamic point of view, every Muslim must pursue justice for all in order to establish the Islamic ideal of harmony and peace.

Forgiveness

In addition to the notions of *tawhid, fitrah,* and *adl,* forgiveness (*afu*) is also a critical notion in the Islamic understanding of peace. Many verses in the Qur'an emphasize the importance of forgiveness. Although there are verses in the Qur'an that permit war as a legitimate conduct to correct injustice and overthrow tyranny and oppression, various Qur'anic verses indicate that "there is a clearly articulated preference in Islam for nonviolence over violence, and for forgiveness (*afu*) over retribution"[32] Qur'an stresses that forgiveness is a higher value than to maintain hatred, as the believers are urged to forgive when they are angry (Q42:37). The verse "the recompense of an injury the like thereof: but whosoever forgives and thereby brings about a reestablishment of harmony, his reward is with God; and God loves not the wrongdoers" (Q42:40) advocates sincere forgiveness as the preferred option to establish God's harmony on earth. Even the Prophet himself was told by God to forgive in the verse "Keep to forgiveness (O Mohammed) and enjoin kindness, and turn away from the ignorant" (Q7:99).

Centrality of forgiveness was illustrated by the Prophet himself when he forgave all those persecuted and fought him when he entered Mecca and stated, "There is no censure from me today on you (for what has happened is done with), may God, who is the greatest amongst forgivers, forgive you."[33] This attitude of forgiveness was the basis of his reconciliation efforts to establish peace between the Muslims and the Meccans, who fought them, which allowed him to win over friends among his former enemies; it made possible the peaceful building up of the Islamic community and did away with the desire for revenge.[34]

Compassion and Mercy

The values *rahmah* (compassion) and *rahim* (mercy) underpin the Islamic tradition of peace. Closely related to each other, these words are invoked by every Muslim before they take any action by reciting "*Bi Ism-i- Allah al-Rahman al-Rahim*" (i.e. begin in the name of Allah Who is Compassionate and Merciful). Centrality of compassion and mercy are evident in the Qur'an as almost all chapters start with this recitation and as God states "My Mercy extends to all things" (Q7:156) and "To be one of those who believe and urge each other to steadfastness and urge each other to compassion. Those are the Companions of the Right" (Q17:18). Moreover, according to a famous Hadith, God states: "Without doubt My Mercy precedes My Wrath,"[35] which is one of the crucial principles of Islamic thought. Qur'an also refers to the Prophet Mohammed as "Mercy of the World" (Q21:107); thus, as the messenger of God, he represents Universal Mercy.

Based on these and other Qur'anic verses as well as the Hadith, a true Muslim must be merciful and compassionate to all human beings, irrespective of their ethnic and religious origins or gender. In fact, Islam urges Muslims to show mercy and compassion to all of God's creation, including all forms of animal and plant life. Values of compassion and mercy connote that a true Muslim cannot be insensitive to the suffering of other beings (physical, economic, psychological, or emotional), nor can he be cruel to any creature. Thus, torture, inflicting suffering or willfully hurting another human being or another creature, is not allowed according to Islamic tradition.[36]

ISLAMIC CONCEPTION OF WAR[37]

Qur'anic verses also deal with the initiation and termination of hostilities, conduct during war, and nature and duration of treaties.[38] For example, in verse Q2:190, the Qur'an commands, "Fight in the way of Allah against those who fight against you; but begin not hostilities." Another verse states, "Go forth, light armed or heavy armed, and strive with your wealth and your lives in the Way of Allah" (Q9:41). The Islamic provisions regarding war and relations with non-Muslims were articulated as part of Islamic law under the title *Siyar*. "Although originally it was applied to the Prophet's conduct in war" *Siyar* was formalized to encompass Islamic laws on the conditions for peace and neutrality in the eighth century by Imam Abu Hanifa in a lecture series titled "The Muslim Laws of War and Peace."[39] These lectures were later compiled by his student Shaybani under the title "Introduction to the Law of Nations."[40]

Siyar, which is the plural of *Sirat*, means "ways" and in the early Islamic history referred to the ways the Prophet dealt with war and peace.[41] Sources of *Siyar* include the Qur'an, the Hadith, the Sunna, and the practices of the first four Caliphs (head of the Muslim community). More specifically, *siyar* deals with initiation and termination of hostilities, treatment of prisoners and relations with non-Muslims, and nature and duration of treaties. *Siyar* deals with *jihad* within this context.

Contrary to the general belief, *jihad*, which is often mistranslated as "holy war" against external forces, does not mean war with weapons, but literally means "striving" or "struggle" and refers to a commitment to "strive in the cause of God" (Q22:78). More specifically, it refers to struggling for the cause of God by means of speech, property, wealth, or life. However, it also was understood to exert effort to repel the enemy. Based on these different connotations, *jihad* is applicable in three distinct ways: to strive against a visible enemy, against the Devil, or against one's ego or selfish interests. The Islamic tradition holds that the most difficult and greater *jihad* (*jihad al-akbar*) has always been the inner struggle to purify the self and behave in a manner that furthers rather than disrupts the divine harmony.[42] This tradition is based on the Hadith after a military expedition: "We have returned from the minor *jihad* (war) to the major *jihad* (against the self),"[43] which has been the basis of differentiating between these levels of *jihad* in the Islamic literature. In the context of *siyar*, *jihad* means repulsion of aggression, protecting the faith, and defending the *Ummah* (the Muslim community). In this sense, minor *jihad* becomes no different from fighting (*qital*) and war (*harb*) to defend the Muslim faith and community against its enemies.

Qur'anic discourse considers war an odious measure and an instrument that ought never to be used for individual aggrandizement or sport.[44] Nevertheless, Qur'anic discourse also recognizes that under extreme conditions war may become a necessity. Islamic Just-War Theory, as articulated in *Siyar* in the eighth century considers war just only when it is commenced and prosecuted in accordance with the necessary formalities required under the Islamic system of law, or waged for justifiable reasons in accordance with the tenets of the religion or the mores of the Muslim society.[45] Islamic tradition emphasizes that war can only be justified if it is in accordance with the sanction of religion and the implied orders of God, and launched by a legitimate Islamic leader. Similar to the Just-War Theory of St. Augustine, which was articulated later on, the Islamic doctrine of Just War (*Jus ad bellum*) includes both a justifiable reason and the necessary formalities for prosecuting war. Therefore Islam outlaws all war but the war that God permits, *jihad*, and the most obvious just cause according to Islam is self-defense.

Siyar also lays down strict regulations regarding acts that were not allowed during war (*Jus im bello*). Based on the Qur'anic injunctions, sayings, and the practice of the Prophet and the first four Muslim leaders, *Siyar* clearly articulates that killing of noncombatants, such as women, children, the blind, the old, monks and hermits, the insane or delirious, those who are physically incapable of actual fighting, and servants, is absolutely forbidden according to Islam. Moreover, torturing by fire and burning of prisoners is strictly prohibited, as well as the execution of prisoners of war. Severing the heads of fallen enemies and sending them to higher authorities and mutilating the enemy and animals are also firmly forbidden. *Siyar* also records that Islam forbids using enemy prisoners as shields or compelling them to fight their own army, or using poison. *Siyar* also states that Islam does not allow violating agreements with the enemy on what they have mutually agreed to avoid in war, as well as retaliation against the enemy when they kill Muslim women, children, the aged and hostages, and for acts of mutilation. *Siyar* is also clear that adultery and fornication with female captives, killing hostages as well as massacring innocent people, even if the enemy has resorted to such actions, is not allowed. *Siyar* also enunciates that unnecessary devastation of the enemy lands, destruction of animal stocks, harvesting and cutting trees, especially fruit trees, are not permissible.[46]

Transformation of the Concepts of Peace and War in Islamic History

Islam, like many other living traditions, has a repertoire of precepts and practices that in some sense has a universal meaning and a particular form. Even where ideals converge into a single tradition, styles of practice often diverge, which leads to manifold ways of relating essential precepts and values to social life."[47] History of Muslim communities reflects the tension between precept and practice, as Muslim leaders and scholars attempted to apply the ideals of their religious tradition to the realpolitik of their era. This is true also regarding the Islamic ideals of peace and peace-building, as there are different interpretations concerning war and peace among the Muslims. Although there are certain fundamental ethical principles and moral values that united Muslim peacemaking traditions across cultures and historical periods, as they are all derived from the Qur'an, Hadith, and the Sunna, it has not been possible to develop a single Islamic tradition of peace and war.

There are various reasons for this. Many of the Qur'anic verses and Hadiths refer to particular historical events, and at times they seem to contradict each other. Local traditions and geopolitical conditions have also affected the evolution of the Islamic traditions of peace and peacemaking. Consequently, similar to secular discourses, there are various approaches to peace and peacemaking in the Muslim world. Furthermore, the Qur'an and Hadith are compiled in medieval Arabic, which is different than the Arabic used by many Arabs today, and also the majority of Muslims live in non-Arabic-speaking societies.

Examination of the evolution of the concepts of war and peace and how Islamic precepts were adapted to the lifeworld of the Muslim communities suggests that geographical, historical, cultural, and sociopolitical contexts of these societies had a deep impact on the way religious texts were interpreted. The geographical and temporal context in which Islam was revealed illuminates why peace was valued to such a great extent and elucidates various verses in the Qur'an that deal with "war" (*harb*) and "fighting" (*qital*). In the pre-Islamic Arab society, war, which was seen as a normal aspect of life, played a central role and a "state of war" was assumed to exist between one's own tribe and all others, unless a particular treaty or agreement had been reached with another tribe establishing amicable relations."[48] The arts of fighting were rewarded with the highest social respect, next to the virtues of loyalty, among the seminomadic Arab tribes. Additionally, conflicts between the neighboring superpowers of the time, Sassanian, Persian, and Byzantine empires and the Samaritan revolt in Palestine that took place at the time also influenced the Islamic understanding of war.[49] Also, as Islam expanded to different geographical regions, people with different cultural and traditional practices, such as Turks, Moguls, Indians, Africans, and Indonesians among others, embraced Islam. Each cultural group brought different attitudes toward peace and war and interpreted the legal doctrines from their own historical and traditional experiences.

In addition to the geographical and temporal context of their time, Muslim attitudes regarding war was also influenced by the increasing hostility and persecution toward them as their numbers grew. Initially Prophet Muhammad resorted to complete nonviolence and refused to engage in any form of hostility against the Meccans. "In 615, in an effort to spare some of his followers from further persecution, Muhammad recommended that they seek haven in Abyssinia (modern day Ethiopia)."[50] Even when the persecution of Muslims became unbearable, he chose to emigrate to Yathrib (later on called Madina), a city to the north of Mecca, where he had secured the well-being of Muslims. Here, Muhammad laid the foundations of the first Islamic state and entered into treaties with various Jewish clans. Mohammed allowed fighting in self-defense when the Meccans laid siege to and attacked Madina in 627, but in 628 the truce of *Hudaybiya* was inked between the Muslims and the Meccans for a duration of ten years. This treaty, known as the *Sulh of Hudaybiyah*, has become the model for Muslims. Wahiduddin observes that during his twenty-three-year Prophetic career Mohammed had actively engaged in three Battles (Battles of *Badr*, *Uhud*, and *Hunayn*), for a total of one and a half days,[51] but signed twenty-three agreements and treaties with his enemies and various tribes.[52] Thus, *sunna* of Prophet Mohammad insinuates that the preferred method for resolving conflicts in the initial years of the Muslim state was nonviolence and that war was permissible only under the extreme conditions of self-defense.

Nevertheless, as political and tribal competition between the Muslim rulers in the aftermath of the four rightly guided caliphs (the first four Islamic rulers after the Prophet) surfaced and as the military power of Muslim rulers increased, war came to be employed as an aggressive tool under the rubric of *jihad* to expand Islam. Many Qur'anic verses were reinterpreted to justify the offensive form of *jihad*, based on the argument that Islam is a universal message and therefore it was the *ummah*'s duty to establish the order of God on earth. Evolution of Prophet's attitude was interpreted as supporting the evolution of the concept of *jihad* from nonviolent struggle to offensive wars to spread the power of Muslim rulers.[53] As the conditions in which the Islamic entities interacted changed, so did the interpretation of the doctrine of *jihad*. Accordingly, Muslim jurists reevaluated the verses of the Qur'an regarding *jihad*, war, and peace in relation to the way they perceived the interest of the Islamic world and at times under the pressure of the Muslim rulers.

Current-Day Muslim Perspectives of Peace and War

The Islamic understanding of war and peace went through another transformation during the nineteenth and twentieth centuries. Various factors contributed to this transformation. First of all, by the nineteenth century, Muslim states lost their military and economic power, while European states flourished in the sciences, military technology, and economic power. Second, the majority of Muslims fell under the colonial rule of European states, which was marked with exploitation, humiliation, and thus resentment. Furthermore, in the twentieth century, many Muslim states, such as the Ottomans and the Moguls, disintegrated due to independence wars and emergence of nationalism. During this period, the Muslim world has been influenced by the discourses of nationalism, communism, secularism, and liberalism. Colonialism and exploitation became the main targets of revolutionary movements that were trying to establish the legitimacy of their rule. Due to this colonial experience, *jihad* took the form of resistance to Western invasion of Islamic lands. With this shift in emphasis, *jihad* has once again become mainly a doctrine of defense. Moreover, failure of new—*secular and modern*—states to satisfy the basic needs of their people, combat poverty, degradation, and corruption, and restore their previous esteem and glory created more turmoil in Muslim lands.

Various Muslim leaders and scholars blamed the decline of Muslim power in the world on the rulers' deviating from the *right path of Islam*. This led to a growing demand for reinstitution of Islamic rule and religiously motivated violence among Muslims.[54] Modern activists and scholars began to reinterpret the Islamic texts to address the problems of the Muslim communities in the modern world. Within this context all kinds of resistance movements adopted *jihad* as an ideological framework, and as a political rhetoric. The notion of *jihad* acquired a new momentum while some of the concepts of *Siyar* are rethought.

Modern-day interpretations of the Qur'an concerning war and peace can be grouped under three main trends in the Islamic world: "offensive Islamic interpretation of war," "defensive Islamic interpretation of war," and "nonviolent Islamic interpretation of war." The roots of these interpretations can be traced back to the formative years of Islam; they all operate within the Islamic discursive field, and take the Qur'an, Hadith, and Sunna as their sources. Sympathizers and followers of these trends who read the same texts interpret them and come out with completely different conclusions.

Offensive Islamic Perspective of Peace and War

The offensive Islamic perspective of peace and war holds that Muslims have an obligation to expand Islam, as it is the true path to bring justice, freedom, and peace. This perspective is advocated mostly by militant fundamentalists. As Bessam Tibi notes, in the Muslim world, "fundamentalism as a mass movement dates back to the 1970s, though its intellectual and organizational roots can be traced to 1928, when the Muslim Brotherhood (al-ikhwan al-Muslimun) was created in Egypt."[55] Fundamentalist activists and ideologues such as Sayyed Qutb argue that the current political, economic, and international system that dominates the world only breeds oppression, injustice, and exploitation, which therefore must be removed and replaced by God's governance. Freedom of choice (i.e., freedom of religion based on the Qur'anic verse (Q2:256), "there is no compulsion in religion," can only come after these forces of oppression and tyranny, represented by the West and modernity, are eradicated, and where it is possible for people to adhere to and appreciate God's vision for humanity. Ignoring more than seventy verses that prohibit war, they decontextualize two verses that are coined unconditional (Q2:244 and Q9:123)—"Then fight in the cause of Allah, and know that Allah hearth and knoweth all things" and "O ye who believe! Fight the unbelievers who are near to you and let them find harshness in you: and know that Allah is with those who fear Him"—to argue that now it is each and every Muslim's duty to spread God's rule on earth. They add that Islamic understanding of peace, war, and jihad evolved from the nonviolent to the defensive because Muslims were not strong enough then. Yet it is important to note that not all Islamic terrorist groups fit into this category of offensive Islam. Groups such as the Hamas argue that Islam permits war only for defensive reasons and also justify the use of terror as a legitimate means to defend Islam. Therefore, it becomes important to distinguish between those groups who purport an offensive perspective of

Islam that support terrorism and advocates of defensive Islam that support terrorism.

Defensive Islamic Perspective of Peace and War

Majority of Muslims agree that Islam permits war and violence only under certain dire circumstances such as in self-defense, which is considered a legitimate tool. This perspective views jihad as a comprehensive effort in the path of God that requires "utilizing all the physical, mental, and spiritual faculties of human beings" and "of course, it also includes actual participation in war but only as a last resort, with those non-Muslims who actively oppose and hinder the deen [religion] of Allah and wish to subvert it."[56] Thus, minor jihad or war is permitted purely for defense purposes and aggression is totally forbidden.[57] This perspective holds that in the face of oppression and persecution, Islam calls Muslims to defend themselves and to fight in order to establish justice and restore harmony. Regarding the Qur'anic verses on war, scholars like Chiragh Ali add: "All the defensive wars, and the verses of the Qur'an relating to the same, were strictly temporary and transitory in their nature."[58] In regards to those "unconditional" verses used by those who adopt an offensive perspective of war and peace, Ali argues that "the law of interpretation, the general scope and tenor of the Qur'an, and the context of the verses and parallel passages, all show that those few verse which are not conditional should be construed as conditional in conformity with other passages more clear, expressive, and conditional, and with the general laws of scriptural interpretation."[59]

However, the defensive perspective can be further divided into two categories, depending on what they consider permissible in a just war. These are, respectively a moderate defensive and an extremist defensive Islamic perspective.

Moderate Defensive Islamic Perspective of War. The moderate defensive perspective holds that not only the ends but also the means of *jihad* must be based on ethical grounds, and that although war is permitted, it is also limited.[60] Proponents of this perspective argue that the Qur'an permits Muslims to fight to protect their faith, their freedom, and their lands and property. Nevertheless, they add that Qur'an insists that Muslims must be strong advocates of peace,[61] and if war is necessary it must be fought as humanely as possible. For example, based on the verse "And fight them until persecution is no more, and religion is for Allah. But if they desist, then let there be no hostility except against wrongdoers" (Q2:193), Muqtedar Khan argues that Qur'an limits retaliation against all except those who are directly responsible for wrongdoing and also suggests that persecution could mean religious persecution.[62] Only those who actively persecute must be retaliated. Moreover, this perspective upholds the regulation of *pacta sunt*

servanda, honoring the treaties. According to this regulation, treaties contracted with non-Muslims need to be respected as long as the other party does not violate them.

This perspective also calls for strict distinction between combatants and noncombatants. In that line, Jamilah Jitmoud refers to the Hadith where the Prophet, after learning about it, criticizes the killing of a non-Muslim woman and prohibits the killing of women and children and innocent people during wars, and argues that such strict regulations and restrictions rooted in the Qur'an and Hadith "keep it from becoming an act of violence."[63] Furthermore, she adds that if non-Muslims are prepared to live with Muslims peacefully, then *jihad* would not be necessary, for Muslims have been urged to treat others with fairness.[64]

"The authoritative textbooks of Al-Azhar University (the oldest and most prestigious Islamic University) also adopt moderate defensive Islamic perspective of peace and war."[65] The official view of Al-Azhar suggests that offensive wars are not permitted, and in the modern age, communication networks offer a much better medium than armed conflict.[66] One of the most well-recognized sheikhs, Sheikh Mahmut Schaltut, argues that Islam allows pluralism and rejects the claim that Islam must resort to war to spread its beliefs by quoting the verse "Had Allah wanted, all people of the earth would have believed in Him, would you then dare force faith upon them" (Q10:99) and also the verse "We have created you as peoples and tribes to make you know one another" (Q49:13). Interpreting the Qur'anic idea of war and peace in the light of these two verses, he concludes, "War is an immoral situation," and therefore it is not the right method.[67]

Extremist Defensive Islamic Perspective of War. The extremist defensive Islamic perspective, on the other hand, also holds that Islam permits defensive wars, but adds that Islam allows Muslims to utilize all the necessary means to win it. Consequently, all the weapons of the opponent, which could also include nuclear weapons, and those weapons that cannot distinguish between combatants and noncombatants can be employed, as long as the opponent also employs them.[68] This perspective argues that under the current war system, where distinguishing between the civilian and military targets is increasingly difficult, Islam allows all that is "necessary," including suicide (or as they prefer to call "martyrdom") attacks to "defend" the Muslims against their enemies.

Supporters of this perspective recognize that in the Islamic tradition there is a clearly articulated regulation, in the Hadith and the practices of the four rightly guided caliphs as well as in the *Siyar* tradition, concerning ethical conduct during the battle. The *Siyar* tradition of conduct during war (*jus im bello*) introduces two categories of restrictions. The first one concerns the permitted targets (e.g., civilian targets vs. military targets). The second category concerns the right methods and weapons that are permitted during the

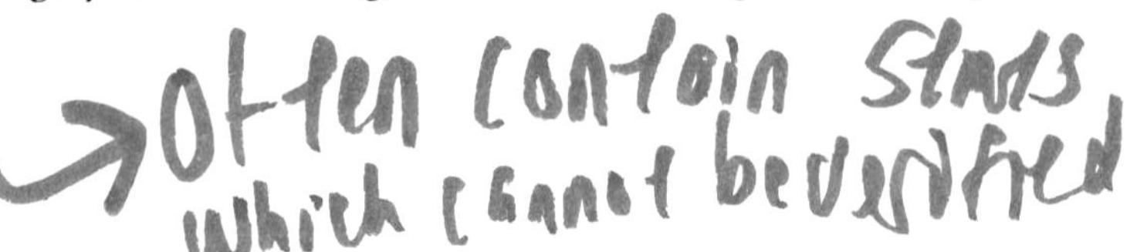

war (e.g., conventional weapons vs. mass destruction weapons, including nuclear, chemical, and biological weapons). Proponents of this perspective attempt to justify their position by arguing that under extreme conditions, some of these restrictions can be set aside.[69] Justification for this is sought in the Islamic precept "necessity overrides the forbidden," which allows moral constraints to be overridden in emergencies, although the criteria for determining whether an emergency exists are vague.[70] This line of thinking is employed to justify terrorist attacks on civilians on the grounds that the adversary is also killing Muslim civilians.

Nonviolent Islamic Perspective of Peace and War. In addition to the offensive and defensive perspectives, nonviolent perspective is also an authentic tradition rooted in the Qur'an, Sunna, and Hadith. "From the nonviolence perspective, peace is defined as a process in which human beings can establish foundations for interacting with each other and with nature in harmony and to institute just social-economic structures, where human beings can flourish and fulfill their potentials."[71] Such a conceptualization of peace rests "on the acknowledgment of dignity and worth of each and every human being, the recognition of the needs and interests of all those involved and addressing social, political and economic injustices."[72] "Nonviolence implies an active commitment to social change that would ultimately result in a fair distribution of world resources, a more creative and democratic cooperation between peoples, and a common pursuit of those social, scientific, medical, and political achievements that serve to enhance the human enterprise and prevent warfare."[73] And employing nonviolent active resistance becomes crucial for building peace that can be sustained.

Islamic nonviolence perspective holds that nonviolent struggle is the preferred response to injustice, conflict, and war according to Islam. Islamic holy texts emphasize values and principles that promote nonviolence and peaceful resolution of conflicts. Although in the Qur'an there are verses that seem to allow war, there are also stringent rules that govern use of violence under extreme conditions. Moreover, according to these rules if violence cannot discriminate between combatants and noncombatants, it is not acceptable in any form or shape. This is based on the Hadith that states:

> "Go in God's name trusting in God, and adhering to the religion of God's messenger. Do not kill a decrepit old man, or a young infant, or a woman: do not be dishonest about booty, but collect your spoils, do right and act well, for God loves who do well."[74]

Moreover, the speech of the first Caliph before a battle states:

> Stop, O, people, that I may give you ten rules for your guidance in the battlefield. Do not commit treachery or deviate from the right path. You must not mutilate dead bodies. Neither kill a child, or a woman, or an aged man. Bring

> no harm to the trees, nor burn them with fire, especially those, which are fruitful. Slay not the enemy's flock, save for your food. You are likely to pass people who have devoted their lives to monastic services, leave them alone.[75]

Accordingly, because the modern technology of destruction renders discrimination virtually impossible, Muslims cannot use violence in the contemporary world.[76] In that respect Jawdat Sa'id states:

> What is in the order of the world is that it has reached an extent that world problems can no longer be solved by violence (*bi-l-'unf*). The evidence for this that the great powers themselves cannot use violence anymore to solve their conflicts. As for the weak and the oppressed (*al-mustad 'afun*) among small states, their violence will only turn in favor of the great powers whenever they attempt to solve their problems by such means.
>
> With the advent of the nuclear bomb, nonviolence has become an historical destiny—not just a choice as it was before. Those who do not accept this as true will only expose themselves to repeated suffering and losses. History does not change its course, people are the ones who adopt to it.[77]

Proponents of nonviolence emphasize values such as patience, forgiveness, and kindness among others that are central to the Qur'anic narrative. For example Maulana Wahiduddin Khan observes that patience (*sabr*) is the focus of about 200 verses of the Qur'an and is referred to indirectly in many others. Thus he argues that patience is set above all other Islamic virtues with the exceptional promise of reward beyond measure (Q39:10).[78] He furthermore states that the entire spirit of the Qur'an is in consonance with the concept of patience. To support this view he invokes the Qur'anic verse "perform *jihad* with this [the word of the Qur'an] most strenuously" (Q25:52). He concludes that since the Qur'an is not a sword or a gun, but a book of ideology, performing *jihad* could only mean an ideological struggle to conquer people's hearts and minds through Islam's superior philosophy.[79]

Qur'an also conveys a preference for kindness, forgiveness, and nonviolence as it is evinced in the following verses:

> Whenever they kindle the fire of war, God extinguishes. They strive to create disorder on earth and God loves not those who create disorder (5:64); God commands you to treat (everyone) justly, generously and with kindness (16:90); Repel evil (not with evil) but something that is better (*Ahsan*)—that is with forgiveness and amnesty. (13:22)

Jawdat Sa'id also asserts that armies and governments have lost their traditional role in protecting the populace, while people have re-sorted their role in protecting themselves.[80] In our current system, war no longer solves the problem, nor does it even bring the needed ease of conscience. Referring to Qur'anic verse, "God does not change the condition of a people until they change what is within themselves," Sa'id states that "as soon as we cease to place our trust in a Napoleon or a Hitler to make peace and unity, and as soon as we trust in ourselves being able to change what is within ourselves,"[81] we will be able to establish peace. In that sense, referring to the verses "God forbids you not respecting those who have not fought against you on account of your religion, and who have not driven you out from your homes, that you be kind to them and deal equitably with them" (Q60:8), and "if they withdraw from you but fight you not, and (instead) send you (guarantees of) peace, then Allah hath opened no way for you (to war against them)" (Q4:90), he argues that "sacred struggle," *jihad*, cannot mean violence and aggression but a nonviolent struggle to establish justice and peace.

More specifically, Sa'id argues that the true message of Islam is nonviolence. To support his view he highlights the story of Adam's sons Abel and Cain stated in the Qur'an, arguing that this story clearly illustrates God's preference for nonviolence. According to the Qur'anic story, Cain, jealous of his brother Abel, attempted to kill Abel. In response to his attack, Abel told Cain, "if you stretch your hand to slay me, it is not me to stretch my hand against you to slay you for I fear Allah" (Q2:28). The Qur'an goes on to say "if any one slew a person unless it be for Murder or for spreading Mischief in the land, it would be as if he slew the whole people. And if anyone saved a life it would be as if he saved the life of the whole people" (Q2:32). For that reason, he states that "it is obligatory upon us—people of understanding—and it is within our grasp, to continually maintain nonviolent peaceful contacts with other understanding people in the world, without waiting for the politicians."[82]

In that line Chaiwat Satha-Anand articulates eight theses on Muslim nonviolent action that are rooted in the original vision of Islam and "true" meaning of peace thereof.[83] The first thesis is that for Islam, the problem of violence is an integral part of the Islamic moral sphere. Violence, if used by Muslims, must be governed by the rules prescribed in the Qur'an and the Hadith. If violence cannot discriminate between combatants and noncombatants, it is not acceptable according to Islam. Modern technology of destruction renders discrimination virtually impossible. Therefore Muslims cannot use violence in the modern world. Islam teaches Muslims to fight for justice with the understanding that human life is—as is all of God's creation—sacred and has a purpose. For that reason, being true to Islam requires Muslims to use nonviolent action as the mode of struggle. Moreover, Islam itself is a fertile soil for nonviolence because of its potential for disobedience, strong discipline, sharing and social responsibility, perseverance, self-sacrifice, the belief in the unity of the Muslim community, and the oneness of mankind.[84]

Satha-Anand also suggests that principles of nonviolence in Islam are derived from the five pillars of Islam: to obey God and His Prophet only and disobey the others if necessary; practice discipline through prayers; solidarity and support of the poor through *zakat*; self-sacrifice, suffering, and patience through fasting; and unity and brotherhood through pilgrimage.[85] These pillars also become the basis to undertake nonviolent acts of resistance such as civil disobedience, vigils, protests, and refusal to pay taxes among others. Others, such as Johansen and Crow, Grant, and Ibrahim,[86] identify various Islamic rituals and traditions as effective sources of nonviolent action in Islam. These include "fasting rituals, which are excellent training for hunger strikes; ritualistic prayers, for the habituated formation of worshipers into parallel lines to prepare people for engagement in disciplined actions; religious chanting, which can become an outlet for peaceful marches, meetings and sit-ins."[87]

The nonviolent Islamic perspective is not a modern approach to peace and war. On the contrary, it has been an integral part of Islamic practice from the very inception of Islam. For example, as stated earlier, Prophet Mohammed adopted a strictly nonviolent approach while he was in Mecca and Madina. He allowed fighting only when Meccans sieged Madina, and he himself was engaged in battle only three instances and for the duration of a day and a half. Nonviolent persuasion was also used as a conflict resolution tool by Lala Aziza in fourteenth-century Morocco.[88] Nonviolent resistance was also employed by the Pashtun leader Ghaffar Khan against the British colonial rule in India.[89] More recently, an Islamic perspective of nonviolence was also used widely during the First Palestinian Intifada, which was initially a nonviolent resistance.[90]

CONFLICT RESOLUTION AND PEACE-BUILDING IN ISLAM

Although there are different interpretations regarding peace and war, and although different Muslim communities have differing practices, Islamic tradition on peace and peacemaking rests on various core Islamic concepts, principles, and values that if consistently and systematically applied, can transcend all levels of conflict. In addition to the four core notions of *tawhid, fitrah, Adl* (justice), and *afu* (forgiveness) mentioned earlier, some of the other values include helping the poor, wisdom and knowledge, compassion, pursuit of love, kindness, mercy, benevolence, service, social empowerment, universality and dignity of human life, sacredness of human life, equality, quest for peace and harmony, creativity and innovation, individual responsibility and accountability, patience, collaboration and solidarity, inclusion and participation, and diversity and unity among others.[91] These values and principles instruct Muslims with a wide range of attitudes and behavior models applicable in different situations.[92]

Islamic teachings emphasize the importance of common good, social and divine harmony, justice, social responsibility, and accountability. Islamic tradition conceptualizes the individual in terms of his or her place within the divine project and network of social relations not as an autonomous and self-regulating agent. There is a strong sense of community, solidarity of people, and a collaborative understanding of freedom that is embedded in the notion of *Ummah*, the community of Muslims. The society and the common good comes before the individual, and consequently the individual has obligations toward the community. The freedom of the individual exists only within the limits of the community traditions and well-being. Existence of all being is the reflection of the Supreme Being itself. As the reflection of God, who is complete freedom and complete necessity, the human being participates in both freedom and necessity. Personal freedom lies in surrender to the Divine Will, and this must be sought within oneself.

Because conflict is viewed as harmful to both divine and communal harmony, Islam instructs Muslims to take action to resolve conflicts and restore harmony. This perspective is based on Qur'anic verses such as the following: "If two parties among the believers fall into a fight, make ye peace [*sulh*] between them [. . .] make peace between them with justice, and be fair; for Allah loves those who are fair (and just)" (Q49:9). According to the Qur'an, the disputes among Muslims have to be judged according to the guidelines in the Qur'an, based on clear proof:

> But no by thy Lord they can have no (real) faith until they make thee [Muhammad] judge in all disputes between them. And find their souls no resistance against thy decision, but accept them with the fullest conviction. (Q4:65)
>
> We have sent down to thee [Muhammad] the Book in truth, that tough mightiest judge between people by that which Allah has shown thee; so be not an advocate for those who betray their trust. (Q4:105)

Sulh or *sulha* refers to the Islamic peacemaking tradition and means conciliation. Based on various Qur'anic verses Islamic law states, "The purpose of *sulh* is to end conflict and hostility among believers so that they may conduct their relationship in peace and amity." [93] Based on the Islamic emphasis on harmony, Islamic conflict resolution models emphasize restoration of social and divine harmony. Conflict is considered to be harmful to both divine and communal harmony. As stated earlier, justice is central to any Islamic conflict resolution model. For that matter, Islamic conflict resolution practices must restore social and economic justice, as injustice is seen to be one of the major causes of conflict. Therefore both the parties and third parties must seek justice as well as equality to restore balance and harmony among the community members. In restoring justice and harmony, both the interveners and parties must consider the common good rather than their ego and personal interests.

Based on the values and principles highlighted in the Qur'an, Hadith, and Sunna, in Islamic conflict resolution practices, group affiliation is the primary concern; therefore the conflict resolution technique must be directed at protecting this affiliation. Invoking acknowledgment, apology, compensation, forgiveness, and reconciliation are crucial to resolving conflicts. Qur'an especially is a very important source for comprehending conflict resolution and reconciliation processes. Unity of the social group and restoration of harmony are ultimate goals in Islamic conflict resolution traditions.

Religious leaders who know the parties, the history of the conflict, and the Islamic tradition well are legitimate authorities to intervene, either upon being called to do so or on their own. These religious leaders play the roles of arbitrators, mediators, facilitators, and educators of the parties toward the resolution of the conflict. They recite Qur'anic sagas and stories, messages of the Prophets, Hadiths, and Sunnas of Prophet Mohammed, as well as historical examples drawn from Islamic history that emphasize the importance of resolving conflicts peacefully and justly and restoring harmony among God's creatures. "As Muslims aspire to model their behaviors after Qur'an and Sunnah, it becomes a task of Muslim conflict interveners to replicate the process of restoring Islamic principles by clarifying to conflicted parties the misperceptions and negative practices that for long have influence their lives."[94]

Another important aspect of Islamic conflict resolution traditions is the binding nature of peace agreements or arrangements, as observance of treaties and oaths is considered crucial and a religious duty from the Islamic point of view. This is based on the Qur'anic verse "Fulfill the Covenant of Allah when ye have entered into it, and break not your oaths after ye have confirmed them; indeed ye have made Allah your surety; for Allah knoweth all that ye do" (Q16:91). Because *sulh* is a form of contract (*'aqd*), it is legally binding both at the individual and community levels.[95]

Derived from the tradition of *sulha,* one form of Islamic conflict reconciliation model is *musalaha* (reconciliation). Although particular practices differ, the tradition of *musalaha* is usually a ritualistic tradition that aims to restore harmony and peace, aided by facilitation efforts of a third party, such as a religious leader or leaders.[96] Like all other conflict resolution practices it is built upon the Islamic values and principles regarding peace. "According to Jordanian judge Abu-Hassan there are two types of *sulh* processes: *public sulh* and *private sulh.*"[97] Private *sulh* takes place when there is a conflict between the members of a community who know each other. The aim of private *sulha* is to avoid revenge and to restore harmony within a community. The outcome of *sulha* can be a total peace where two parties of the conflict forgive each other, forget what happened, and do not hold any resentment toward each other. The outcome of *sulha* can also be partial or conditional, where the conflict between two parties ends according to the agreed conditions set in the peace process. Public *sulh*, on the other hand, can be compared to a peace treaty between two countries to end conflict for a period of time. It takes place to resolve conflicts between tribes, or communities, or different religious groups.[98] This is also referred to as *Hudna* (cease-fire) and is based on the *Hudaybiya* Treaty signed between prophet Mohammed and the Meccans.[99]

CONCLUSION

Like many other religious traditions, the goal of Islam is peace. However, every religious scripture is communicated through words, and the meaning of words may change over time. Therefore, although one might believe that God revealed guidelines to humanity, one must also realize that its meaning can only be communicated through words and symbols, which are subject to human interpretation in the face of ever-changing conditions. Islamic Scriptures too have to go through the filter of human interpretation, which is influenced by the historical, cultural, sociopolitical, and personal experiences of the interpreting agent. As a consequence, Islamic sources of peace and conflict resolution have been interpreted to contain contesting approaches and these different interpretations have been employed by different groups to pursue particular ends.

In our current world, where religion in general and Islam in particular has come to be seen as a propellant of conflict and violence, we need to recognize that each religious tradition can also be a source of peace and conflict resolution. There is also an urgent need to understand under what conditions (i.e., historical, cultural, and sociopolitical experiences) religious traditions come to be used and abused to justify violence and conflict, in order to develop tools to prevent this from occurring.[100] Moreover, religious people have the duty and responsibility to reflect on their belief systems, contribute maximally to understanding the meaning of life, and to implement the highest values of their religion.

As presented in this chapter, even though Islamic tradition encompasses different perspectives, there are some core values and principles that underline the Islamic understanding of peace and conflict resolution practices. Islamic sources, namely the Qur'an, Hadith, and Sunna, emphasize the importance of peace based on a universal conception of justice for all, irrespective of creed, ethnicity, race, or gender. These sources urge Muslims to resolve conflicts peacefully and justly, put forth values and principles to preserve harmony among all God's creation, and peaceful relations among human communities. Based on these values and principles, which include unity of God and all being, goodness of human constitution, justice, forgiveness, helping the poor, wisdom and knowledge, compassion, pursuit of love, kindness, mercy, benevolence, service, social empowerment, universality and dignity of human life, sacredness of human life, equality, quest for peace and harmony, creativity and innovation, individual responsibility and accountability, patience, collaboration and solidarity, inclusion and participation, diversity and unity, the Islamic notion of peace is wider than *absence of war* and is conceptualized as *presence of justice, harmony,* and *security.*

In addition, Qur'an urges Muslims to resolve their conflicts peacefully and nonviolently and articulates a preference for forgiveness and patience, rather than revenge and retaliation. Accordingly, based on these values and principles, Islamic conflict resolution practices give priority to common good, social and economic justice, communal and divine harmony, and social responsibility. It is clear, then, that these core values and principles render it the responsibility of each Muslim, and particularly Muslim leaders, to uphold these values that promote peace and nonviolent resolution of conflicts in a world stained by religious violence, to work toward establishing harmony, justice, and security for all irrespective of religion, race, ethnicity, or gender. And finally, it is the responsibility of scholars and practitioners in social sciences, like conflict resolution, to understand when and under what conditions religious traditions are used and abused to promote either peace or violence.

NOTES

1. This chapter was presented at the First Annual Conference of the Mahatma Gandhi Center for Global Nonviolence at James Madison University, Harrisonburg, Virginia, on "Religion: Conflict and Peace," April 11, 2005. A revised version of this chapter will be published by the Mahatma Gandhi Center. For further information, please contact the Mahatma Gandhi Center at GandhiCenter@jmu.edu.
2. S. Ayse Kadayifci-Orellana, "Religion, Violence and the Islamic Tradition of Nonviolence," *Turkish Yearbook of International Relations,* no. 34 (2003): 26.
3. S. Ayse Kadayifci-Orellana, *Standing on an Isthmus: Islamic Narratives of War and Peace in Palestine* (Lanham, Md.: Lexington, forthcoming), 303.
4. Abdul Aziz Said and Nathan C. Funk, "The Role of Faith in Cross-Cultural Conflict Resolution," *Peace and Conflict Studies* 9, no. 1 (May 2002): 37–50.
5. Kadayifci-Orellana, "Religion, Violence and the Islamic Tradition," 43.
6. Kadayifci-Orellana, *Standing on an Isthmus,* 101.
7. Kadayifci-Orellana, *Standing on an Isthmus.*

8. Qur'an, footnote 2512 states: "*Salam*, translated 'Peace,' has a much wide signification. It includes (1) a sense of security and permanence, which is unknown to this life; (2) soundness, freedom from defects, perfection as in the word *salim*; (3) preservation, salvation, deliverance, as in the word *sallama*; (4) salutation, accord with those around us; (5) resignation, in the sense we are satisfied and not discontented; besides (6) the ordinary meaning of Peace, *i.e.* freedom from any jarring element." All these shades of meaning are implied in the word *Islam*.

9. See Said and Funk, "The Role of Faith," 42; see also Kadayifci-Orellana, "Religion, Violence and the Islamic Tradition."

10. See Karl-Wolfgang Troger, "Peace and Islam: In Theory and Practice," *Islam and Christian Muslim Relations* no. 1 (1990): 17.

11. Troger, "Peace and Islam," 16.

12. Mohammed Abu-Nimer, *Nonviolence and Peace-building in Islam* (Florida: University Press of Florida, 2003).

13. Abdul Aziz Said and Nathan Funk, "Peace in the Sufi Tradition: An Ecology of the Spirit," in *Peace and Conflict Resolution in Islam: Precept and Practice*, ed. Abdul Aziz Said, Nathan C. Funk, and Ayse S. Kadayifci (Lanham, Md.: University Press of America, 2001), 247–62.

14. Meena Sharify-Funk, "Peace and the Feminine in Islam," in *Peace and Conflict Resolution in Islam* (Lanham, Md.: University Press of America, 2001), 277–98.

15. See Said and Funk, "Peace in the Sufi Tradition."

16. Sharify-Funk, "Peace and the Feminine in Islam," 279.

17. William C. Chittick, "The Theological Roots of Peace and War According to Islam," *The Islamic Quarterly* 34, no. 3 (3rd Quarter 1990): 145–63.

18. Kadayifci-Orellana, *Standing on an Isthmus*, 102.

19. Chittick, "Theological Roots of Peace and War," 156.

20. Said, Funk, and Kadayifci, *Peace and Conflict Resolution in Islam* (Lanham, Md.: University Press of America, 2001), 7.

21. Suad Al Hakim, "Islam and Peace," trans. Tara Aziz and Karim Crow (paper presented at the symposium Islam and Peace in the 21st Century, February 1998), 5.

22. Cited in Sharify-Funk, "Peace and the Feminine in Islam," 279.

23. Sharify-Funk, "Peace and the Feminine in Islam," 279.

24. Kadayifci-Orellana, *Standing on an Isthmus*, 103.

25. Cited in Said, Funk, and Kadayifci, *Peace and Conflict Resolution in Islam* (Lanham, Md.: University Press of America, 2001), 7.

26. Sharify-Funk, "Peace and the Feminine in Islam," 279.

27. Kadayifci-Orellana, *Standing on an Isthmus*.

28. Kadayifci-Orellana, *Standing on an Isthmus*.

29. See Abu-Nimer, *Nonviolence and Peace-building in Islam*.

30. For more examples see Abu-Nimer, *Nonviolence and Peace-building in Islam*.

31. Abu-Nimer, *Nonviolence and Peace-building in Islam*.

32. Said, Funk, and Kadayifci, *Peace and Conflict Resolution in Islam* (Lanham, Md.: University Press of America, 2001), 8. These verses are presented under the "Nonviolent Islamic Perspective" section of this chapter.

33. Based on *Ibd Sad Al Tabaqa al Kubra* II: 142 (Beirut, 1957), cited in K. G. Saiyidain, *Islam: The Religion of Peace*, 2nd ed. (New Delhi: Har Anand, 1994), 93.

34. Troger, "Peace and Islam," 17.

35. See Bukhari, Tawhid 15, 22, 28, 55, Badi'ul'-Halk 1; Muslim, Tawba 14 (2751); Tirmidhi, Daawat 109 (3537). Cited in Fethullah Gulen, *Toward a Global Civilization of Love and Tolerance* (New Jersey: Light, 2004), 39.

36. For more information on these see Ralph H. Salmi, Cesar Adib Majul, and George K. Tanham, *Islam and Conflict Resolution: Theories and Practices* (Lanham, Md.: University Press of America, 1998), and Majid Khadduri, *Islamic Law of Nations: Shaybani's Siyar* (Baltimore: Johns Hopkins University Press, 1966).

37. The fourteen hundred years of Islamic literature is rich with debates regarding this issue. Various prominent jurist-philosophers such as Ibn Khaldun, Ibn Taymmiyya, Al Ghazali, and Al Farabi among many others dealt with war and peace in Islam. However, acknowledging this vast literature, this chapter uses only more recent sources and debates.

38. Salmi, Majul, and Tanham, *Islam and Conflict Resolution*.

39. Thomas Troy, "Prisoners of War in Islam: A Legal Inquiry," *The Muslim World* 87, no. 1 (January 1997): 44–53.

40. Troy, "Prisoners of War in Islam."

41. Troy, "Prisoners of War in Islam," 65.

42. Said, Funk, and Kadayifci, *Peace and Conflict Resolution in Islam* (Lanham, Md.: University Press of America, 2001), 7.

43. Muhammad Abdul Lateef al Sobki, "Al Jihad in Islam," *The Fourth Conference of the Academy of Islamic Research* (Cairo: Al Azhar Academy of Islamic Research, 1968), 158. Cited in Salmi, Majul, and Tanham, *Islam and Conflict Resolution*, 67.

44. Salmi, Majul, and Tanham, *Islam and Conflict Resolution*, 68.

45. See also Khadduri, 1955, 57.

46. See Salmi, Majul, and Tanham, *Islam and Conflict Resolution*; Kadayifci-Orellana, and Khadduri for more information.

47. Abdul Aziz Said, Nathan C. Funk, and Ayse Kadayifci, "Islamic Approaches to Conflict Resolution and Peace," *The Emirates Occasional Papers No. 48* (The Emirates Center for Strategic Studies and Research, 2002).

48. Fred M. Donner, "The Sources of Islamic Conceptions of War," in *Just War and Jihad: Historical and Theoretical Perspectives on War and Peace in Western and Islamic Traditions*, ed. John Kelsay and James Turner Johnson (New York: Greenwood, 1991), 31–69.

49. For more information see Kadayifci-Orellana, *Standing on an Isthmus*, and Donner, "Sources of Islamic Conceptions of War."

50. Salmi, Majul, and Tanham, *Islam and Conflict Resolution*, 23.

51. Maulana Wahidduddin Khan, "Nonviolence and Islam" (paper presented at the symposium Islam and Peace in the 21st Century, American University, Washington, DC, February 6–7, 1998).

52. Troger, "Peace and Islam," 17.

53. For more information on transformation of the concept of war and peace in the Islamic tradition, see Kadayifci-Orellana, *Standing on an Isthmus*, chap. 4.

54. For a more detailed discussion, see Kadayifci-Orellana, *Standing on an Isthmus*.

55. Bessam Tibi, "War and Peace in Islam," in *The Ethics of War and Peace: Religious and Secular Perspectives*, ed. Terry Nardin (Princeton, N.J.: Princeton University

Press, 1996), 137. For the definitions of *fundamentalism* and *fundamentalist* used here, see Kadayifci-Orellana, *Standing on an Isthmus*.

56. M. M. Qurashi, "The Concept of Islamic Jehad," *Islamic Thought and Scientific Creativity* 2, no. 1 (1991): 57–71.

57. Muhammad Asad, *The Principles of State and Governance in Islam* (Berkeley: University of California Press, 1961).

58. Asad, *The Principles of State*, 72.

59. Asad, *The Principles of State*, 73.

60. For more information, see Kadayifci-Orellana, *Standing on an Isthmus*, chap. 4.

61. Khan, "Nonviolence and Islam," 5.

62. Mohammed A. Muqtedar Khan, "Peace and Change in the Islamic World" (paper presented at the conference Islam and Peace in the 15/20th Century, Washington, DC, February, 1997), 2.

63. Jamilah Jitmoud, "Principles of *Jihad* in the Qur'an and Sunnah," in *State Politics and Islam*, ed. Mumtaz Ahmad (Burr Ridge, Ill.: American Trust Publications), 133–46.

64. Jitmoud, "Principles of *Jihad*," 142.

65. Kadayifci-Orellana, *Standing on an Isthmus*, 129.

66. Tibi, "War and Peace in Islam," 137.

67. Tibi, "War and Peace in Islam," 136.

68. See Kadayifci-Orellana, *Standing on an Isthmus*, chap. 4.

69. Tibi, "War and Peace in Islam," 133.

70. Tibi, "War and Peace in Islam," 133.

71. Kadayifci-Orellana, "Religion, Violence and the Islamic Tradition," 38.

72. Kadayifci-Orellana, "Religion, Violence and the Islamic Tradition," 38.

73. Daniel L. Smith-Christopher, *Subverting Hatred: The Challenge of Nonviolence in Religious Tradition* (Cambridge, Mass.: Boston Research Center for the 21st Century, 1998), 10.

74. Chaiwat Satha-Anand, "The Nonviolent Crescent: Eight Thesis on Muslim Nonviolent Action," in *Peace and Conflict Resolution in Islam* (Lanham, Md.: University Press of America, 2001), 198.

75. Satha-Anand, "The Nonviolent Crescent," 199.

76. Jawdat Sa'id, "Peace—or Nonviolence—in History and with the Prophets" (paper written for conference on Islamic Values for Change, Bi'r Ajam, Qunaytra, Syria, April 3, 1997, trans. Dr. Abduhu Hammud al-Sharif, revised with notes by Dr. Karim Crow), 1.

77. Sa'id, "Peace—or Nonviolence—in History."

78. Maulana Wahiduddin Khan, "Non-Violence and Islam," 1.

79. Khan, "Non-Violence and Islam," 2.

80. Sa'id, "Peace—or Nonviolence—in History," 4.

81. Sa'id, "Peace—or Nonviolence—in History."

82. Sa'id, "Peace—or Nonviolence—in History," 8.

83. Satha-Anand, "The Nonviolent Crescent," 209.

84. Satha-Anand, "The Nonviolent Crescent," 209.

85. Satha-Anand, "The Nonviolent Crescent."

86. Robert C. Johansen, "Radical Islam and Nonviolence: A Case Study of Religious Empowerment and Constraint among Pashtuns," *Journal of Peace Research* 34,

no. 1 (1997): 53–71; Ralph Crow, Philip Grant, and Saad Eddin Ibrahim, eds., *Arab Nonviolent Struggle in the Middle East* (Boulder, Colo.: Lynne Rienner, 1990).

87. See Abu-Nimer, *Nonviolence and Peace-building in Islam*, 83.

88. See M. Elaine Combs-Schilling, "Sacred Refuge: The Power of a Muslim Female Saint" *Fellowship* 60, no. 5–6 (May/June 1994).

89. See Eknath Easwaran, *A Man to Match His Mountains: Badshah Khan: Nonviolent Soldier of Islam* (Petaluma, Calif.: Nilgiri Press, 1984); Johansen, "Radical Islam and Nonviolence"; and Kadayifci-Orellana (2002).

90. See Abu-Nimer, *Nonviolence and Peace-building in Islam.*

91. Abu-Nimer, *Nonviolence and Peace-building in Islam.*

92. Amr Abdalla, "Principles of Islamic Interpersonal Conflict Intervention: A Search within Islam and Western Literature," *Journal of Law and Religion* 15, no. 1–2 (2000–2001): 151–84.

93. M. Khadduri, "Sulh," in *The Encyclopedia of Islam*, vol. 9, ed. C. E. Bosworth, E. van Donzel, W. P. Heinrichs, and the late G. Lecomte (Holland: Brill. Leiden, 1997), 845–46.

94. Khadduri, "Sulh," 171.

95. Khadduri, "Sulh."

96. For more information on *Sulha*, see Mohammed Abu-Nimer, "Conflict Resolution Approaches: Western and Middle Eastern Lessons and Possibilities," *The American Journal of Economics and Sociology* 55, no. 1 (1996): 35–55; "Conflict Resolution in an Islamic Context: Some Conceptual Questions," *Peace and Change* 22–40 (1996); George Irani, "Reconciliation and Peace: Rituals For the Middle East," *Middle East Insight* (September–October 1998): 24–26; George Irani, "Islamic Mediation Techniques for Middle Eastern Conflicts" *MERIA (Middle East Review of International Affairs) Journal* 3, no. 2 (June 1999), at www.bui.ac.il/SOC/meria/journal/1999/issue2/jv3n2a1.html (accessed January 2000); George E. Irani and Nathan C. Funk, "Rituals of Reconciliation: Arab-Islamic Perspectives" *Arab Studies Quarterly* 20, no. 4 (Fall 1998), 64.

97. Irani and Funk, "Rituals of Reconciliation," 64.

98. Irani and Funk, "Rituals of Reconciliation," 64.

99. For more information, see Gideon Weigert, "A Note on Hudna: Peacemaking in Islam," in *War and Society in the Eastern Mediterranean 7th and 15th Centuries*, ed. Yaacov Lev (New York: Brill, 1997), 399–405; Salmi, Majul, and Tanham, *Islam and Conflict Resolution*; Troger, "Peace and Islam"; and Kadayifci-Orellana, *Standing on an Isthmus.*

100. See Kadayifci-Orellana, *Standing on an Isthmus.*

BIBLIOGRAPHY

Abbad, Abdul Rahman. "Peace and Pacifism in Islam." *International Journal of Nonviolence* 3 (1996), 60–71.

Abdalla, Amr. "Principles of Islamic Interpersonal Conflict Intervention: A Search Within Islam and Western Literature." *Journal of Law and Religion* 15, no. 1/2 (2000–2001): 151–84.

Abu-Nimer, Mohammed. *Nonviolence and Peace-building in Islam.* Florida: University Press of Florida, 2003.

———. "Conflict Resolution, Culture, and Religion: Toward a Training Model of Interreligious Peace-building." *Peace Research* 38, 6 (2001), 685–704.

Abu-Nimer, Mohammed. "Conflict Resolution in an Islamic Context: Some Conceptual Questions." *Peace and Change* (January 1996), 22–40.

al Banna, Hasan. *Majmu'at Rasa'I al-Imam al-Shahid Hasan al-Banna,* new legal ed. Cairo: Dar al Da'wa, 1990.

———. *Five Tracts of Hasan al-Banna (1906–1949).* Translated by Charles Wendell. Berkeley: University of California Press, 1978.

al Hakim Suad. "Islam and Peace." Paper presented at the symposium Islam and Peace in the 21st Century, February 1998. Translated by Tara Aziz and Karim Crow.

Asad, Muhammad. *The Principles of State and Governance in Islam.* Berkeley: University of California Press, 1961.

Chittick, William C. "The Theological Roots of Peace and War According to Islam." *The Islamic Quarterly* 34, no. 3 (3rd Quarter, 1990): 145–63.

Combs-Schilling, M. Elaine. "Sacred Refuge: The Power of a Muslim Female Saint." *Fellowship* 60, no. 5–6 (May/June, 1994).

Crow, Ralph, Philip Grant, and Saad Eddin Ibrahim, eds. *Arab Nonviolent Struggle in the Middle East.* Boulder, Colo.: Lynne Rienner, 1990.

Easwaran, Eknath. *A Man to Match His Mountains: Badshah Khan: Nonviolent Soldier of Islam.* Petaluma, Calif.: Nilgiri Press, 1984.

Hashmi, Sohail. "Interpreting the Islamic Ethics of War and Peace." In *Ethics of War and Peace: Religious and Secular Perspectives.* Edited by Terry Nardin. Princeton, N.J.: Princeton University Press, 1996.

Iftikhar, Malik H. "Islamic Discourse on Jihad, War and Violence." *Journal of South Asian and Middle Eastern Studies* 21, no. 4 (Summer 1998), 47–78.

Irani, George. "Reconciliation and Peace: Rituals for the Middle East." *Middle East Insight* (September–October 1998): 24–26.

———. "Islamic Mediation Techniques for Middle Eastern Conflicts." *MERIA (Middle East Review of International Affairs) Journal* 3, no. 2 (June 1999) at www.bui.ac.il/SOC/meria/journal/1999/issue2/jv3n2a1.html (accessed January 2000).

Irani, George E., and Nathan C. Funk. "Rituals of Reconciliation: Arab-Islamic Perspectives." *ASQ* 20, no. 4 (Fall 1998), 64.

Jamilah, Jitmoud. "Principles of *Jihad* in the Qur'an and Sunnah." In *State Politics and Islam.* Edited by Mumtaz Ahmad, 133–46. Burr Ridge, Ill.: American Trust Publications.

Johansen, Robert C. "Radical Islam and Nonviolence: A Case Study of Religious Empowerment and Constraint Among Pashtuns." *Journal of Peace Research* 34, no. 1 (1997), 53–71.

Kadayifci-Orellana, S. Ayse. "Religion, Violence and the Islamic Tradition of Nonviolence." *Turkish Yearbook of International Relations,* no. 34 (2003).

———. *Standing on an Isthmus: Islamic Narratives of War and Peace in Palestine.* Lanham, Md.: Lexington, forthcoming.

Khadduri, Majid. *War and Peace in the Law of Islam.* Baltimore: Johns Hopkins University Press, 1955.

———. *Islamic Law of Nations: Shaybani's Siyar.* Baltimore: Johns Hopkins University Press, 1966.

———. "The Islamic Theory of International Relations and Its Contemporary Relevance." *Islam and International Relations.* Edited by J. Harris. Greenwood, Conn.: Praeger, 1965.

———. "Sulh." In *The Encyclopedia of Islam,* vol. 9. Edited by C. E. Bosworth, E. van Donzel, W. P. Heinrichs, and the late G. Lecomte, 845–46. Holland: Brill. Leiden, 1997.

Khan, Inamullah. "Nuclear War and the Defense of Peace: The Muslim View." *International Peace Research Newsletter* 23, no. 2 (April 1985), 9–11.

Khan, Maulana Wahiduddin. "Non-Violence and Islam." Paper prepared for the symposium Islam and Peace in the 21st Century, Washington, DC, February 6–7, 1998.

Khan, Mohammed A. Muqtedar. "Peace and Change in the Islamic World." Paper presented at the conference Islam and Peace in the 15/20th Century, Washington, DC, February 1997.

Kishtani, Khalid. *Towards Nonviolence.* Amman: Dar al Karmil, 1984.

Moulavi Chiragh Ali. "War and Peace: Popular Jihad." In *Contemporary Debates in Islam: An Anthology of Modernist and Fundamentalist Thought.* Edited by Mansoor Moaddel and Kamran Talattof, 71–94. New York: St. Martin's, 2000.

M. M. Qurashi. "The Concept of Islamic Jehad." *Islamic Thought and Scientific Creativity* 2, no. 1 (1991): 57–71.

Paige, Glenn D., Chaiwat Satha-Anand, Sarah Gilliatt, eds. *Islam and Nonviolence.* Honolulu: Center for Global Nonviolence, 2001.

Qutb Sayyid. "War, Peace and Islamic Jihad." In *Contemporary Debates in Islam: An Anthology of Modernist and Fundamentalist Thought.* Edited by Mansoor Moaddel and Kamran Talattof, 223–45. New York: St. Martin's, 2000.

Said, Abdul Aziz, Nathan C. Funk, and Ayse S. Kadayifci. *Peace and Conflict Resolution in Islam: Precept and Practice.* Lanham, Md.: University Press of America, 2001.

Said, Abdul Aziz, and Nathan C. Funk. "The Role of Faith in Cross-Cultural Conflict Resolution." *Peace and Conflict Studies* 9, no. 1 (May 2002): 37–50.

Said, Abdul Aziz, and Nathan Funk. "Peace in the Sufi Tradition: An Ecology of the Spirit." *Peace and Conflict Resolution in Islam.* Edited by Abdul Aziz Said, Nathan C. Funk, and Ayse S. Kadayifci, 247–62. Lanham, Md.: University Press of America, 2001.

Said, Abdul Aziz, Nathan C. Funk, and S. Ayse Kadayifci, eds. *Peace and Conflict Resolution in Islam: Precept and Practice.* New York: University Press of America, 2001.

Said, Abdul Aziz, Nathan C. Funk, and S. Ayse Kadayifci. "Islamic Approaches to Conflict Resolution and Peace." *The Emirates Occasional Papers,* no. 48, Abu Dhabi: The Emirates Center for Strategic Studies and Research, 2002.

Sa'id, Jawdat. *The Doctrine of the First Son of Adam: The Problem of Violence in Islamic Practice,* 5th ed. Damascus: Dar al Fikr, 1993.

———. "Peace—or Nonviolence—in History and with the Prophets." Paper written for conference on Islamic Values for Change, Bi'r Ajam, Qunaytra, Syria, April 3, 1997. Translated by Dr. Abduhu Hammud al-Sharif, revised with notes by Dr. Karim Crow.

———. "Law, Religion and the Prophetic Method of Social Change." *Journal of Law and Religion* 15, no. 1-2 (2000–2001): 83–149.

Satha-Anand, Chaiwat. "Core Values for Peacemaking in Islam: The Prophet's Practice as Paradigm." In *Building Peace in the Middle East: Challenges for the States and Civil Society*. Edited by Elise Boulding. Boulder, Colo.: Lynne Reinner, 1993.

Saiyidain, K. G. *Islam: The Religion of Peace*, 2nd ed. New Delhi: Har Anand, 1994.

Satha-Anand, Chaiwat. *Nonviolent Crescent: Two Essays on Islam and Nonviolence*. Alkmaar, Netherlands: International Fellowship of Reconciliation, 1996.

———. "The Nonviolent Crescent: Eight Thesis on Muslim Nonviolent Action." In *Peace and Conflict Resolution in Islam: Precept and Practice*. Edited by Abdul Aziz Said, Nathan C. Funk, and Ayse S. Kadayifci, 195–211. Lanham, Md.: University Press of America, 2001.

Salmi, Ralph H., Cesar Adib Majul, and George K. Tanham. *Islam and Conflict Resolution: Theories and Practices*. Lanham, Md.: University Press of America, 1998.

Sharify-Funk, Meena. "Peace and the Feminine in Islam." In *Peace and Conflict Resolution in Islam: Precept and Practice*. Edited by Abdul Aziz Said, Nathan C. Funk, and Ayse S. Kadayifci, 277–98. Lanham, Md.: University Press of America, 2001.

Smith-Christopher, Daniel L. *Subverting Hatred: The Challenge of Nonviolence in Religious Tradition*. Cambridge, Mass.: Boston Research Center for the 21st Century, 1998.

Muhammad Abdul Lateef al Sobki. "Al Jihad in Islam." Paper presented in the Fourth Conference of the Academy of Islamic Research, Al-Azhar Academy of Islamic Research, Cairo, 1968.

Terri-Harris, Rabia. "Nonviolence in Islam: The Alternative Community." In *Subverting Hatred: The Challenge of Nonviolence in Religious Traditions*. Edited by Daniel L. Smith-Christopher, 95–113. Boston: Boston Research Center for the 21st Century, 1998.

Tibi, Bassem. "War and Peace in Islam." In *The Ethics of War and Peace: Religious and Secular Perspectives*. Edited by Terry Nardin. Princeton, N.J.: Princeton University Press, 1996.

Troger, Karl-Wolfgang. "Peace and Islam: In Theory and Practice." *Islam and Christian Muslim Relations*, no. 1 (June 1990): 12–24.

Troy, Thomas. "Prisoners of War in Islam: A Legal Inquiry." *The Muslim World* 87, no. 1 (1997): 44–53.

Weigert, Gideon. "A Note on Hudna: Peacemaking in Islam." In *War and Society in the Eastern Mediterranean 7th and 15th Centuries*. Edited by Yaacov Lev, 399–405. New York: Brill, 1997.

4

Response to S. Ayse Kadayifci-Orellana's "Perspectives on War and Peace"

Glen Stassen

I am excited that Ayse Kadayifci-Orellana has identified so many specific practices of peacemaking in the Qur'an and Hadith, and that she has written of them with such concreteness and definiteness. They create the possibility for envisioning important cooperative work together with those of us Christians who worked to gather a list of peacemaking practices similar to Ayse's list.

We have found among Christians that often they say they are in favor of peace but are so vague and indefinite about what they actually mean to do about it that it amounts to very little in actual practice. In fact, it can amount to self-deception and false consciousness, like the alcoholic who can talk at length about being in favor of sobriety but is doing nothing one day at a time about living a life that leads to sobriety. Ayse Kadayifci-Orellana is not vague and indefinite; she identifies concrete practices of actual peacemaking in the heart of Muslim faith and practice.

I am also excited because Ayse bases these peacemaking practices not merely in some vague humanitarian argument but in the heart of the character of God and the central teachings of Islam. As Christians who have caught the vision say, this is not about peripheral matters, it is about the heart of faith. "By their fruits you know them" (Matthew 7:20).

I am excited, thirdly, because in what Ayse has written, there are many similarities to the just-peacemaking ethic that many of us have been developing for the last twenty years, and that is gathering increasing attention. If we can produce something like parallel just-peacemaking ethics—one

Muslim and one Christian—we can strengthen each other in the cause of peacemaking greatly—not merely peacemaking as a nice word but peacemaking as an actual practice. Ayse wrote independently from what we wrote, based on the Qur'an, Hadith, and Muslim tradition, but the results have many similarities. The similarities suggest we could work to strengthen each others' hands. There is only one God. What God has revealed, what God has spoken through our prophets, has a consistency to it. We can see similarities. Of course that should not be greatly surprising, since the Qur'an gives proper respect to what God has said through Moses and Jesus, and since we are all children of Abraham. Thank God for this!

THE PRACTICE OF RESPECTING TREATIES AND INTERNATIONAL COOPERATION

Ayse Kadayifci-Orellana writes:

> Another important aspect of Islamic conflict resolution traditions is the binding nature of peace agreements or arrangements as observance of treaties and oaths is considered crucial and a religious duty from the Islamic point of view. This is based on the Qur'anic verse "Fulfill the Covenant of Allah when ye have entered into it, and break not your oaths after ye have confirmed them; indeed ye have made Allah your surety; for Allah knoweth all that ye do."

Furthermore, she cites what Troger has observed: "Coming to terms with adversaries and enemies and the contractual guaranteeing of agreements were corner-stones of Mohammed's policy." Mohammed made twenty-three treaties and agreements with other groups and "strictly enforced compliance to treaties." This includes the *Hudaybiya* Treaty that he signed, ending the hostilities with Meccans.

Here Muslims may have an advantage over Christians, since Mohammed had the ability to make actual treaties. By contrast, Jesus had only a small band of disciples, and was soon crucified, so he did not have the ability to make treaties with other groups. Therefore, Muslims have very concrete guidance from Mohammed—twenty-three concrete guidances!—where Christians need to point to the prophet Amos's affirmation of treaty obligations and to Jesus' teaching that even enemies should be included in the community of neighbors, as God gives rain and sunshine to the just and unjust alike (Matthew 5:43–48).

I believe all Muslim nations have joined the United Nations, and have supported international treaties. I do not mean that any of us is perfect in our ethics, whether Muslim, Christian, or of other faith or no faith. But to respect international treaties, to work together cooperatively with other nations, and to participate in the United Nations and regional organizations is Muslim practice grounded in the teachings and practices of Mohammed. I do not claim to be a Muslim scholar, but I see this also taught in Q9:1–8, Q4:90, and Q16:91–92.

Mohammed Abu-Nimer has pointed out that

> Muslim countries have not hesitated to join or cooperate with the United Nations, the Universal Postal Union, the International Civil Aviation Organization, the International Monetary Fund and numerous other international bodies. Some of them have been willing to bring their disagreements and suits against non-Muslim countries to the International Court of Justice for resolution. Even conflict between Muslim states has not prevented them from heeding to and, in most cases, honoring UN resolutions. For example, Iran was the first country to seek arbitration in the international court over territorial claims of the former Soviet Union; Egypt did not hesitate to bring its dispute with Israel over Taba to the World Court; and, more recently, Kuwait was quick to call on the United Nations Security Council when she fell victim to Iraq's aggression.[1]

Muhammad Taalat Al Ghunaimi points out that "under normal conditions the Islamic principle of adherence to treaties . . . ought to be respected since God is the third party in any treaty entered into by Muslims."[2] Abdullahi Ahmed An-Na'im argues for "strict adherence to the Islamic principle of the sanctity of treaties between Muslims and non-Muslims, the acceptance of methods for peaceful international dialogue, and the settlement of disputes through arbitration or other diplomatic means.[3]

The practice of respecting treaties, of international cooperation, and of support for the United Nations and other regional organizations, is also echoed in the *Just Peacemaking* paradigm for the ethics of peace and war. Furthermore, political science data show that nations that engage in a greater amount of international cooperation, as well as nations that welcome more United Nations organizations into their countries, make war less often and have war made against them less often.[4]

PRACTICES OF JUSTICE, INCLUDING SOCIAL AND ECONOMIC JUSTICE AND HUMAN RIGHTS

Both the Qur'an and Muslim practice have a strong and central emphasis on practicing justice and on having rules and laws of justice. Ayse writes:

> Without justice, there can be no peace. Therefore justice is the essential component of peace according to the Qur'anic message. Such interpretation of the Islamic understanding of peace suggests that justice is the overriding principle. . . . Qur'anic discourse also emphasizes social and economic justice as central to social harmony and peace. Many Islamic institutions, such as the

institution of *zakah* (alms giving) aim to establish justice in the social and economic realms.

Because working to support human rights means resisting and correcting the conditions of injustice, I take it that Ayse is affirming human rights for all people, and that Muslims have this responsibility as a crucial means for working toward peace:

> Moreover, there is a consistent and recurrent message in the Qur'an and the *Hadith* to resist and correct the conditions of injustice, which are seen as a source for conflict and disorder on earth. Pursuing justice is not only a responsibility of Muslims as vicegerents of God on earth, but also a divinely ordered command. For that reason, from an Islamic point of view, every Muslim must pursue justice for all in order to establish the Islamic ideal of harmony and peace.

Riffat Hassan has written of the practice of human rights in Islam. It was Riffat who first taught me the Qur'an, and I want especially to credit her research and writing on human rights, although of course numerous other Muslim scholars have written similarly. The key feature of the practice of supporting human rights is that human rights belong to every person universally because all are created by God. And human rights focus our attention especially on those whose rights are being violated. They direct our compassion and our action toward the victims. So Ayse writes:

> Based on these and other Qur'anic verses as well as the *Hadith*, a true Muslim must be merciful and compassionate to all human beings, irrespective of their ethnic, religious origins, or gender. In fact, Islam urges Muslims to show mercy and compassion to all God's creation, including all forms of animal and plant life. Values of compassion and mercy connote that a true Muslim cannot be insensitive to suffering of other beings (physical, economic, psychological, or emotional), nor can he be cruel to any creature. Thus, torture, inflicting suffering or willfully hurting another human being or another creature is not allowed according to Islamic tradition.

Doing justice is the first principle that Abu-Nimer mentions for Muslim peacebuilding. And he writes that justice must include human rights, religious liberty, and democracy as a needed part of Muslim peacemaking and essential for overcoming authoritarian systems.[5]

I wonder whether the emphasis on justice is greater in Islam than in Christianity, although the four words for justice appear 1,060 times in the Bible. God is a God of compassion who cares deeply for the powerless, and who wills that justice flow down like a mighty stream (Amos 5:24). Here is a place where I believe Christians should repent and deepen our practice of the faith.

At the working conference of Christian scholars held at the Abbey of Gethsemani, to develop our ethic of just peacemaking, most insisted that justice must be an essential practice of peacemaking. Some realists, however, pointed out that full justice is never achieved on this earth, and if people insist on achieving justice in the full sense before they are willing to make peace, they will never be ready to make peace. The danger is that insisting that justice is necessary before we can make peace is that this insistence can become a source of anger and war, which then leads to enormous killing and enormous injustice. The perfect ideal becomes the enemy of the achievable real. We reached agreement that justice should be understood as a practice, not as a perfect ideal. A practice is what you work on, what you actually do; it is not an absolute ideal that must be completely realized before we can make peace. The difference between actually working on a process that leads toward justice and much present defense of injustice is dramatic. We all then agreed that justice is crucial for peacemaking. The difference between justice as an absolute ideal and justice as a practice we are working on could be a fruitful question for discussion among Muslims and Christians.

Political science data show decisively that nations that respect human rights, and especially democracies that respect human rights, are much less likely to make wars against other democracies, and much less likely to have civil war and rebellions and insurgencies in them.[6]

THE PRACTICE OF FORGIVENESS AND ACCEPTING RESPONSIBILITY FOR ONE'S ACTIONS

Ayse Kadayifci-Orellana writes:

> Forgiveness (*afu*) is also a critical notion in the Islamic understanding of peace. Many verses in the Qur'an emphasize the importance of forgiveness. Although there are verses in the Qur'an that permit war as a legitimate conduct to correct injustice and overthrow tyranny and oppression, various Qur'anic verses indicate that "there is a clearly articulated preference in Islam for nonviolence over violence, and for forgiveness (*afu*) over retribution." The Qur'an stresses that forgiveness is a higher value than to maintain hatred as the believers are urged to forgive when they are angry (Q42: 37).
>
> Centrality of forgiveness was illustrated by the Prophet himself when he forgave all those who persecuted and fought him when he entered Mecca and stated "There is no censure from me today on you (for what has happened is done with); may God, who is the greatest amongst forgivers, forgive you." This attitude of forgiveness was the basis of his reconciliation efforts to establish peace between the Muslims and the Meccans, who fought them, which allowed him to win over friends among his former enemies, it made possible

the peaceful building up of the Islamic community, and did away with the desire for revenge.

Forgiveness is also a crucial teaching of Christian faith as well, of course. Even from the cross, Jesus said of those who were crucifying him, "Father, forgive them, for they know not what they are doing."

Additionally, Christian faith teaches that we must acknowledge responsibility for our own wrong actions, and repent, which means to turn around, let our loyalties to selfish or idolatrous causes be replaced by loyalty to God, change our wrong practices, and ask forgiveness. So Jesus' central message is "The kingdom of God is at hand; *repent* and believe the good news." It seems logical that the Qur'an's central emphasis on God as merciful and compassionate would make us feel welcomed by God when we accept responsibility for our own wrong actions. And I do find verses in the Qur'an which say exactly that. Ayse says similarly: "The universality of justice for all, not only for Muslims, is critical for resolution of conflicts and developing peaceful relations as it calls upon Muslims to be self-reflective, self-critical, humble and to accept responsibility for one's actions." I wonder whether this is a place where Christian faith puts more emphasis, although the character of God and the Qur'an do encourage great emphasis here by Muslims as well. This would be an interesting question for dialogue among Muslims and Christians. I predict we all could learn from each other.

NONVIOLENT RESISTANCE

Ayse points out that "nonviolent resistance was employed by the Pashtun leader Ghaffar Khan against the British colonial rule in India. More recently, the Islamic perspective of nonviolence was also used widely during the First Palestinian *Intifada*, which was initially a nonviolent resistance." Here she points to the hugely insightful study by Mohammed Abu-Nimer, comparing the first or popular intifada with the second intifada.[7]

I add that the practice of nonviolent direct action was employed by the people of Iran when millions demonstrated against the regime of the Shah and successfully toppled his rule. This despite the fact that under the Shah, Iran was importing more military weapons each year than all of the NATO countries combined were importing per year. The Shah had a hugely powerful army, but it was unable (or unwilling) to keep him in power in the face of determined nonviolent action by the people. In fact, his overspending for military weapons and therefore depriving the people of the benefits of Iran's wealth were a factor in persuading the people to withdraw their consent from his authoritarian rule and to engage in nonviolent direct action against his regime. The practice of nonviolent resistance is spreading throughout the world, toppling dictators nonviolently, and producing greater justice for people while avoiding the violence of rebellion and war. All these practices of peacemaking that Ayse articulates are not merely wished-for ideals; they are actually being practiced in specific incidents in real history, and they are in fact achieving a significant amount of justice while preventing war that was otherwise likely to erupt.

CONFLICT RESOLUTION

Ayse writes:

> Because conflict is viewed as harmful to both divine and communal harmony, Islam instructs Muslims to take action to resolve conflicts and restore harmony. This perspective is based on Qur'anic verses such as: "If two parties among the believers fall into a fight, make ye peace [*sulh*] between them. . . . Make peace between them with justice, and be fair; for Allah loves those who are fair (and just)" (Q49:9).
>
> *Sulh* or *sulha* refers to the Islamic peacemaking tradition and means conciliation. Based on various Qur'anic verses, Islamic law states, "The purpose of *sulh* is to end conflict and hostility among believers so that they may conduct their relationship in peace and amity."

Similarly to how *Just Peacemaking: Ten Practices*[8] distinguishes cooperative conflict resolution with its emphasis on justice from some versions of conflict resolution that neglect to emphasize justice, Kadayifci-Orellana stresses that Muslim practice emphasizes the importance of justice and the common good in the process of conflict resolution. And both similarly emphasize the helpfulness of respected "religious leaders, who know the parties, the history of the conflict," and who can "play the roles of arbitrators, mediators, facilitators, and educators of the parties towards the resolution of the conflict."

FIVE, SEVEN, OR TEN PRACTICES OF PEACEMAKING WITH JUSTICE

In conclusion, I have numbered five practices of just peacemaking that Ayse Kadayifci-Orellana has identified in the Qur'an, Hadith, and Muslim tradition. In the just-peacemaking ethics that a number of us Christians have been developing, two of these practices count double: economic justice and justice as human rights; international cooperation and the United Nations. This means that Ayse has actually identified practices that parallel seven of the ten practices in our just-peacemaking ethics. I can think of ways Islam would include the other three practices as well, but it is not my role to propose Muslim peacemaking practices. What is my role is to express my support and applause. I am excited because we are coming close to developing two parallel ethics of just-peacemaking theory, just as Ayse has rightly written that we have two parallel ethics of just-war theory.

If Muslims affirm what Ayse has written, then the result can be a Muslim just-peacemaking theory that Christian ethicists can point to: "Muslims do not just claim that Islam is a religion of peace; Muslims have just-peacemaking practices akin to ours." And Muslim just-peacemaking ethics can likewise strengthen the hand of those Christians who are working to help Christians become more concrete about what they mean when they say they are followers of Jesus, the Prince of Peace. We can strengthen each others' hands in dramatic ways. We can call attention to the peacemaking practices that we both are articulating and can embrace each other as brother and sister peacemakers.

And together we can point to the experience of history and the results of political science: these practices of peacemaking do in fact often work. Nations that support these practices get into war less often, suffer the hurt and horror of war less frequently, and experience freedom, justice, and peace more happily. These practices work. They make a difference for the common good.

JUST-WAR THEORY AND NONVIOLENCE

Ayse Kadayifci-Orellana makes clear that Islam has two or three varieties of just-war theory, and that some Muslims hold to nonviolence rather than just-war theory. The same is true of Christians.

One point needs to be very clear for all of us. A person can be committed to just-war theory, believing there are times when war is justified, and at the same time be committed to the practices of peacemaking with justice that we hope can prevent war and can achieve justice without going to war. A person can insist on the right to self-defense a thousand times, while hoping that preventive practices can make it unnecessary to engage in wars of self-defense. Most of those who developed the Christian just-peacemaking theory are themselves supporters of just-war theory. They would make a just war if it is in fact just. But they have a sense of the enormous destructiveness in lives, in property, and in moral corruption that comes from war, and therefore they are committed to pursuing the practices that history has shown do in fact work to make peace and avoid many wars. Many Generals and other military officers who know the pain and devastation of war are more supportive of responsible initiatives to solve problems without getting into war than are some politicians who have not seen war themselves and who choose war as a macho or ideologically motivated adventure.

This point needs to be clearly stated again and again because many people appear to act as if talk of peacemaking threatens to undermine their commitment to making war if war is just. So let us say clearly to our fellow citizens: if it makes you feel better, say a thousand times: "We have a right to self-defense." Then once you are clear about that, say a hundred times: "But I am realistically aware that war does devastating damage of many kinds." Therefore, "I support the practices of peacemaking, as well as the right of self-defense, because many times we can be better defended and so can our fellow human beings if we can solve problems with just-peacemaking practices before we ever go to war."

And let us also make respectful room for those among us who are committed to nonviolence, and who witness to the peacemaking that is "Islam" and to the peacemaking of Jesus, by committing themselves never to do violence and never to make war. Once we are clear about the effectiveness of the peacemaking practices that are taught in Islam and in Christianity, then we can see that a commitment to nonviolence is far from a commitment to inaction. It has many effective practices of peacemaking action in its way of life.

Deeply Grounded in the Qur'an and Hadith and in the Character of God

Ayse bases the peacemaking practices that she has identified in Islam not merely on some vague humanitarian argument but in the heart of the character of God and the central teachings of Islam.

"The central principle that the Islamic understanding of peace is derived from is the 'Principle of Unity of God and all being' (*Tawhid*)." This means that all humankind, irrespective of race, nationality, creed, or gender, has a fundamental unity. Similarly, Christian faith begins from the first chapter of Genesis with God as the Creator of the whole universe, with nothing left out. This is absolutely fundamental for Christian faith. All of us are God's creatures. Furthermore, Islam calls upon Muslims to pursue unity and harmony actively because, according to Islamic theology, when God created human beings, He made them His vicegerents or representatives on earth (Q2:30 and Q33:72). This also means we have a responsibility not to destroy the creation, as war with increasingly destructive weapons does so horribly, but to practice peacemaking, energy conservation, and respect for all of the created order. And it means that we all have a responsibility to work for unity and harmony with the creation and among ourselves.

Another key principle is *fitrah*—that every human being is worthy of respect because they are made "in the best of molds" (Q95:4). This is very much like the Christian teaching that all humankind is created in the image of God, is loved by God, and God wills justice and shalom for all people.

The concept of human rights emphasizes that these rights belong to all humans because they are humans created by God and not merely because they are members of a particular nation or race or gender or religion or ideology. This is why, for example, Christians both conservative and liberal and in between have risen up in criticism of the personally traumatizing and morally corrupting practice of the abuse and torture of prisoners in Iraq, Afghanistan, and Guantanamo.[9] As Sharify-Funk states, "*Fitrah* provides not only the foundational premise for a constructive politics of human potential and value maximization, but also a safeguard against dehumanizing 'the other' within the context of a conflict situation" (2001:279).

"*Al-Adl* (justice), like *As-Salam* (Peace) is one of the most beautiful names of God according to Islamic tradition. . . . Justice is an integral aspect of the Islamic discourse of peace, since the Qur'an clearly states the aim of religion is to bring justice." This, too, applies to all humankind irrespective of nationality, religious membership, race, ethnicity, social class, or gender. Similarly, the Bible teaches again and again of God's will for restorative justice—the kind of justice that delivers people from domination, oppression, exclusion, and violence into restoration to community and restoration of community.[10] In Jesus' day, the religious authorities were also the political and economic authorities. Jesus confronted them thirty-seven times for their injustice of greed, domination, exclusion, and violence. Jesus identified with the tradition of the prophets, who emphasized justice centrally. The four biblical words for justice (*tsedaqah, mishpat, dike,* and *dikaiosune*) are repeated 1,060 times in the Bible. "Then justice will dwell in the wilderness, and righteousness abide in the fruitful field, and the effect of righteousness will be peace, and the result of righteousness, quietness and trust forever. My people will abide in a peaceful habitation, in secure dwellings, and in quiet resting places" (Isaiah 32:15–18). In Hebrew, "righteousness" (*tsedaqah*) should be translated as "delivering justice" or "restorative justice"; it means the kind of justice that delivers the downtrodden from domination and brings the outcasts into the community. Peace, justice, and compassion come as a single package; they depend on each other because they are part and parcel of God's will and God's action of deliverance: "My covenant of peace shall not be cast away, says the Lord, who has compassion on you" (Isaiah 54:10).[11]

The fourth core value that Kadayifci-Orellana emphasizes is *afu* (forgiveness). That is also central for Christian faith, being the central meaning of the crucifixion. And it is a crucial practice of peacemaking, as she and I have both written in our essays.

Ayse also names numerous other key values in Islam that support peacemaking practices, from helping the poor to compassion, and universality and dignity of human life, in one list, to the common good, social responsibility, and accountability, in another list. And "there is a strong sense of community, solidarity of people and a collaborative understanding of freedom that is embedded in the notion of *Ummah,* the community of Muslims."

Truthfully, the Protestant and Evangelical traditions of Christian faith have a weaker sense of community, and many of us are working to correct that weakness with a recovery of the Biblical sense of community.

Biblical faith says that we are created very good, as does Islam; but it has an equally strong emphasis that we all sin and go astray, that we become entrapped in greed, idolatry, false trust in weapons of violence, and unfaith. Therefore Christian faith, when it is profound and not superficial, emphasizes that every one of us has propensities in us to sin as well as propensities to do good. Therefore we need humility, repentance, a respectful and listening ear to corrections coming from our brothers and sisters—and from our enemies as well. Wisdom is in learning from mistakes, not in stubborn and defensive insistence that we are not sinners.

And therefore also every concentration of power, whether political, economic, military, or religious, needs to be checked and balanced by laws and by others with power to correct for our mistakes. Arrogance, self-righteousness, and stubbornness are not helpful virtues for peacemakers. The truth of this wisdom is proven by the widely agreed awareness that some political leaders who claim to be Christians also combine their own errors with self-righteousness defensiveness. The axis of evil runs through the heart of every one of us. Christians *should* be more humble; often their actions persuade us that humility is a significant need. I have less experiential knowledge of Muslim political leaders than of Christian ones, but I am betting something similar is true there as well. Reinhold Niebuhr said the propensity to sin is one Christian doctrine that is easily proven by the facts. And it means that peacemaking practice needs the checks and balances of international law and international networks of cooperation.

Room for Self-Correction by All of Us

Abuse of Religion

Ayse writes, wisely: "There is also an urgent need to understand under what conditions (i.e. historical, cultural, socio-political experiences) religious traditions come to be used and abused to justify violence and conflict, in order to develop tools to prevent this from occurring."

Each of us can speak for our own religion. Speaking for Christianity, I need to acknowledge that my own religion has been misused to justify violence, as well as properly used to support peacemaking. I think we can all learn from Charles Kimball, *When Religion Becomes Evil,* which shows religion being abused to motivate to violence in Christianity, Islam, Buddhism, Hinduism, and Judaism.[12]

Some American demagogues in "Christian" clothing (Matthew 7 and Revelation 13) corrupt the churches and the gospel by entangling Jesus Christ with nationalism, militarism, and authoritarianism. My task is to call Christians to repent for such corruption. I know some Muslim leaders have a similar sense of responsibility among Muslims, analogous to the burden and the calling that I feel among my people. Having a specific just-peacemaking ethic with concrete and definite practices of peacemaking helps enormously in correcting errors of unknowing self-delusion and empty self-congratulation. God's thoughts are higher than our thoughts, and God's ways are better than our ways.

NOTES

1. Mohammed Abu-Nimer, *Nonviolence and Peace-building in Islam: Theory and Practice* (Gainesville: University Press of Florida: 2003), 78. Sohail H. Hashmi writes similarly in *Peace and Conflict Resolution in Islam*, ed. Abdul Azis Said, Nathan C. Funk, and Ayse S. Kadayifci-Orellana (Lanham, Md.: University Press of America, 2001), 108, yet says Islamic "states have formally committed themselves to the principles of international law, but there has yet to occur a theoretical incorporation of these principles into a coherent, modern elaboration of Islamic international law." Cf. Abudul Hamid A. Abu Sulayman in *Peace and Conflict Resolution in Islam*, 16.

2. Abu-Nimer, *Nonviolence and Peace-building in Islam*, 97.

3. Abu-Nimer, *Nonviolence and Peace-building in Islam*, 110. See Mohammed Muqtedar Khan's description of the increase of international networks in *Peace and Conflict Resolution in Islam*, 86f. His description almost exactly parallels that of Glen Stassen, ed., *Just Peacemaking: Ten Practices for Abolishing War* (Cleveland: Pilgrim, 1998/2004), chapters 7 and 8.

4. Stassen, *Just Peacemaking: Ten Practices*, chapters 6, 7, and 8.

5. Abu-Nimer, *Nonviolence and Peace-building in Islam*, 41, 48–57, 117, 119.

6. Stassen, *Just Peacemaking: Ten Practices*, chapters 5 and 6. See also extensive research by Bruce Russett and Rudy Rummel.

7. Abu-Nimer, *Nonviolence and Peace-building in Islam*.

8. Stassen, *Just Peacemaking: Ten Practices*, chapter 3.

9. See, e.g., www.nrcat.org; and David Gushee, "Why Torture Is Always Wrong," *Christianity Today* (February, 2006); Christopher Marshall, *Crowned with Glory & Honor: Human Rights in the Biblical Tradition* (Telford, Pa.: Pandora, 2001).

10. Christopher D. Marshall, *Beyond Retribution: A New Testament Vision for Justice, Crime, and Punishment* (Grad Rapids, Mich.: Eerdmans, 2001); Ronald Sider, *Just Generosity: A New Vision of Overcoming Poverty in America* (Grand Rapids, Mich.: Baker Books, 1999).

11. Glen Stassen and David Gushee, *Kingdom Ethics: Following Jesus in Contemporary Context* (Downers Grove: InterVarsity, 2003), chapters 7 and 17.

12. Charles Kimball, *When Religion Becomes Evil* (New York: HarperSanFrancisco, 2003).

5

Ten Just-Peacemaking Practices That Work

Glen Stassen

Muslims have a strong loyalty to scripture—the Qur'an. So did Martin Luther King Jr. have a strong loyalty to scripture—in his case, to the Bible, and especially the teaching of Jesus, as in the Sermon on the Mount. James Cone has written an intriguing book, *Martin & Malcolm in America,*[1] showing how Malcolm X and Martin Luther King Jr. were coming closer and closer in their thought before they were both tragically assassinated.

King came from a tradition of strong loyalty to Jesus' teaching in the Sermon on the Mount, but he did not see how Jesus' teaching about turning the other cheek and loving your enemies could be relevant to the deep sin of racism. He thought Jesus' teachings were only for individuals. But then he learned of Mahatma Gandhi's and Abdul Ghaffar Khan's concrete practice of Satyagraha (love-force) and nonviolent resistance, and how it successfully toppled British colonialist domination in India. It showed the power of love in action. And then he directly experienced the realistic power of the strategy of nonviolent direct action in the bus boycott in Montgomery, started by Rosa Parks. This showed its realistic effectiveness. In the final chapter of his book *Strength to Love,* "Pilgrimage to Nonviolence," King tells how this experience of the power of nonviolent direct action woke him up and gave him new direction in justice making that was a deeper kind of peacemaking. Scriptural teaching fused with the strategy of Satyagraha in India and the experience in Montgomery to produce a brilliant flash of insight. It is this fusion of scripture and the power of its implementation in effective practices that has produced our new ethic, "Just Peacemaking."

I will try to explain this new ethic in a short space. In addition, I am wondering if Muslim loyalty to the Qur'an can provide a similar basis for a just-peacemaking ethic as the one I find in the Bible. I think the answer is yes. But Muslim scholars can do that so much better than I can. Nevertheless, we share the experiential side: these practices do work to decrease injustice and make peace in the real world.

Neither Muslims nor Christians need to say that war is never ever justified in order to be able to say that much war is destructive and often wrong and that it is good if we can develop an ethic of just peacemaking that is effective in preventing much war. Affirming just-peacemaking ethics is not about saying all war is wrong; it is about articulating effective practices for reducing injustice by nonviolent means so we can avoid war that can be prevented. The just-peacemaking ethic does not try to answer the question of whether war is ever justified or not. Most of those who developed the just-peacemaking ethic think sometimes war is justified. But like presidents Eisenhower and Carter, and like my own father, who have known the devastation that war causes from their own service in the military, they believe we need to develop an ethic that can prevent war when it is preventable. And they want to make that belief specific, concrete, and practical—not just some vague ideal of being for peace without having much idea what to do about it.

Like Martin Luther King Jr., I too come from a strong loyalty to the way of Jesus and his teaching in the Sermon on the Mount (Matthew 5–7). Before the civil rights movement I was already sensing that Jesus' teachings are not merely about prohibitions of what we are not supposed to do but about initiatives that we are to take to participate in God's way of deliverance from vicious cycles like anger, injustice, and killing. So when the civil rights movement came to North Carolina, where I was studying, and to Kentucky, where I then went to teach, I immediately saw the connection between the way of Jesus and the methods of nonviolent direct action by which we overthrew the unjust laws of segregation. (I was very active in the civil rights movement in both those states, giving leadership to civil rights organizations there.)

Furthermore, I had begun my education and beginning career as a nuclear physicist, and I cared deeply about developing an ethic that could help prevent nuclear war. So I also saw connections between Jesus' way and the method of independent initiatives by which we got rid of a large number of nuclear weapons. (I will explain the strategy of independent initiatives below.) Thus, *nonviolent direct action* and *independent initiatives* became two of the key practices of just peacemaking.

The key, both for Martin Luther King Jr., the great leader, and for me, the ordinary person, was seeing the connection between the teachings of our scriptures and the practical strategies that have made a major difference for overcoming great evils in our world. As I tell the story of the just-peacemaking ethic that my fellow scholars and I have been involved in developing, I hope it can be suggestive for Muslims also. That will depend, of course, on their knowledge of the Qur'an and of practical strategies of peacemaking with justice in our world. I expect that Muslims' great loyalty to the teachings of the Qur'an connected with practical strategies that can make a major difference for overcoming great evils of injustice and war in our world can produce an impressive Islamic just-peacemaking ethic.

For me, frustration about ethics that avoided the practical questions came to a head at the time of the buildup for the first Gulf War against Iraq, when Iraq had occupied Kuwait. Christian ethicists debated the Gulf War at our annual meeting the first weekend of January, shortly before the war started. But they only concentrated on whether the war would be just and right. (Overwhelmingly they said it would not be; the other measures prior to making war had not been exhausted.) They voted and passed a resolution that the war would not be just. But what was enormously frustrating was that they failed to debate what measures should be taken instead of war, and the resolution said nothing about alternative ways to get Iraq out of Kuwait without all the killing of war. Iraq had accepted the first President Bush's invitation to negotiate, but George H. W. Bush rejected their acceptance of his invitation just as President George W. Bush rejected invitations to negotiate with Iran. Iraq even told France and Russia that they would get out of Kuwait just before the United States attacked, but this was ignored by President Bush. I wanted the Christian ethicists not only to say *no* to war, but also to say *yes* to negotiations and initiatives that could have avoided the war while getting Iraq out of Kuwait.

Merely opposing the war would have little effect on policy. But if the ethicists had pointed the way clearly to an alternative that should be tried before making war, it could have captured national attention. If they had said, "Ask Iraq if they will get out of Kuwait before you make war," that could have made a difference. If they had said, "Iraq has accepted Bush's invitation to talks, so engage in the promised talks before you make war," that could have made a difference. It could have saved untold lives in the war and also saved thousands of lives in the uprising in the south of Iraq after the war and in Saddam Hussein's massacres of those who rose in rebellion.

The problem was that the ethicists only had two widely understood ethics: pacifism, which says *no* to all wars, and just-war theory, which says *yes* or *no* depending on whether the war meets the rules of just war. There was no widely understood ethic spelling out the practices that make peace and solve injustices without war. So the debate and the resolution were inarticulate on the very points that could have made a very big difference.

I was deeply frustrated with Christians who say *we are for peace* but have no concrete and specific practices of peacemaking that commits us to positive action. Therefore they can say they are for peace while they support wars that come without trying the practices that make for peace. Jesus wept over Jerusalem because "they do not know the practices that make for peace," and God weeps over us now because we still do not know the practices that make for peace. I wanted Christians to "know the practices that make for peace." I was fed up with people saying they were in favor of peace or were followers of the Prince of Peace, but who had very little idea of what that meant they should be doing in their daily lives and what kind of policies they should be supporting in political leaders.

Furthermore, I knew that a specific set of practices, combined in a comprehensive set, like the Ten Commandments or the Five Pillars of Islam, would be far more effective than just an essay with a number of scattered points. Thus, just-war theory has an agreed set of eight rules (some have seven). Many know what those rules are; they can refer to them and use them as a test of policy. So I wanted a just-peacemaking theory with an agreed set of practices.

This set should consist of practices, not merely ideals. By practices I mean specific actions that should be taken to make peace, not merely wishes. A practice is not "be in favor of peace." My mother came home from church one Sunday and said that the pastor preached a sermon saying "we should be in favor of peace." She said, "Who didn't know that? The question is, what do you do about it? What do you do to make peace?" A practice is not "believe that every person is created by God." That is a belief, an ideal. A practice is "Acknowledge that we have some responsibility for conflict and injustice, and seek forgiveness and repentance." What you actually do to make peace is a concrete and specific practice, like nonviolent direct action, conflict resolution, work for sustainable economic justice.

So I wanted an ethic with a specific set of concrete practices that work to make peace. I wrote the book *Just Peacemaking: Transforming Initiatives for Justice and Peace* (Louisville: Westminster John Knox, 1992). First I looked for practices of peacemaking that are taught by Jesus in the New Testament (chapter 3). Then I looked for similar practices that are demonstrated by political science to be effective in peacemaking (chapter 4). The result was a just-peacemaking theory with seven key practices of just peacemaking.

The book sold well, and it was being studied in classes and in churches (and still is). Other ethicists said that is exactly what we need. So several ethicists who were influential in the ethics of peace and war formed a panel at the annual meeting of the Society of Christian Ethics in which they proposed what they would include in their ethic of just peacemaking. Six other panels were happening at the same time, but the just-peacemaking panel filled every seat in the room, and many were standing along the walls. There was huge interest. Many were saying, "This is just what we need."

So twenty-three ethicists and experts in international relations gathered at the Abbey of Gethsemani near Bardstown, Kentucky, in order to seek to develop a consensus just-peacemaking ethic. They worked by e-mail and by gatherings at the Society of Christian Ethics over the following four years to write consensus papers on the practices of just peacemaking, which had expanded to ten practices that work to prevent wars. Finally they gathered again at the Carter Center in Atlanta for a three-day working conference, and remarkably, miraculously, they achieved unanimous consensus on the ten practices of just-peacemaking theory, and on what had been written for each chapter of the new just-peacemaking book. It was a miracle, since the twenty-three scholars include Catholics and Protestants, mainline Protestants and evangelicals, pacifists and just-war theorists, peace-church denominations and non–peace-church denominations, ethicists, and international relations specialists. As a result, the book that emerged is a consensus new ethical paradigm, not merely a collection of chapters by different experts. This is the new just-peacemaking ethic. It was published as *Just Peacemaking: Ten Practices to Abolish War* (Cleveland: Pilgrim Press, 1998 and 2004). The new ethic has caught on: it is already in its second edition, and I am aware of fifty articles and chapters that have been published on it in various places. It is being widely discussed and commended. I list some of the articles on my website, www.fuller.edu/sot/faculty/stassen.

THE TEN PRACTICES OF JUST PEACEMAKING

We divide the practices into three groups: (A) peacemaking initiatives, (B) justice, and (C) cooperative forces. The first grouping, peacemaking initiatives, comes from the combination of scriptural teaching that we are to take initiatives of peacemaking that sometimes include nonviolent confrontation, as in the nonviolent action that has spread worldwide. Mahatma Gandhi and Abdul Ghaffar Khan pioneered some of these initiatives. Justice, the second grouping, is a central biblical theme. The four words for justice in Hebrew and Greek occur 1,060 times in the Bible. The third group, cooperative forces, may be seen as a dimension of love understood realistically rather than sentimentally: a key dimension of love in scriptural teaching is breaking down barriers to community and participation in cooperative community. All three are checks and balances against sin. So our groupings may be seen—for those who have eyes to see—as translations from specifically faith-based perspectives into practical and realistic practices that are working in the world to bring justice and prevent war.

Take Peacemaking Initiatives

1. Support nonviolent direct action.

Nonviolent direct action came to our attention primarily as the method used effectively by Gandhi and Ghaffar Khan in India and by Martin Luther King and the civil rights movement in the United States. Now it is spreading widely, ending dictatorship in the Philippines; ending rule by the Shah in Iran; bringing about nonviolent revolutions in Poland, East Germany, and Central Europe; transforming injustice into democratic change in human rights movements in Guatemala, Argentina, and elsewhere in Latin America, and in the nonviolent parts of the first people's intifadah campaign in Palestine and in the freedom campaign that ended apartheid in South Africa, and in many other countries.[2] Contrast the failures of violent campaigns in Bosnia, Somalia, and Northern Ireland. Governments and people have the obligation to make room for and support nonviolent direct action.

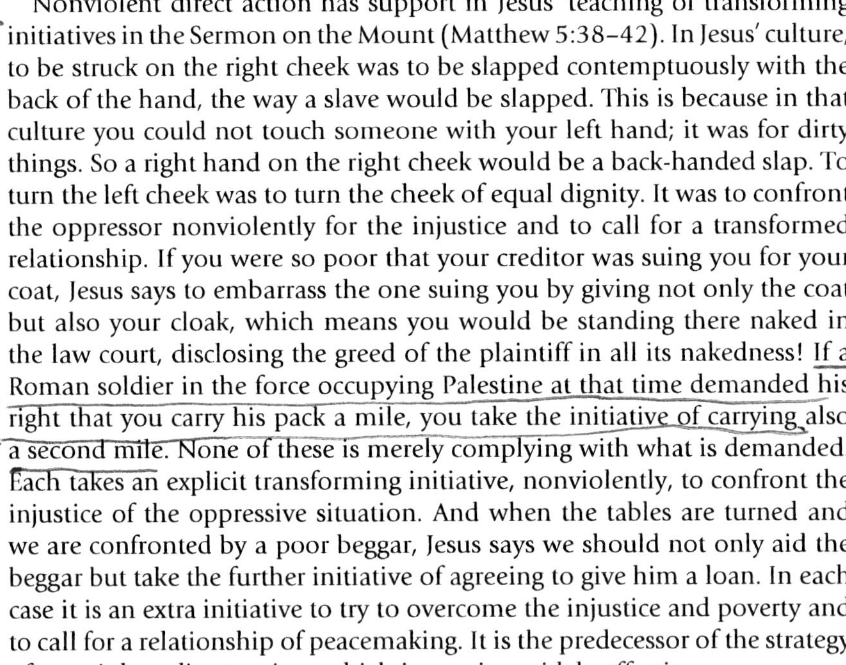

Nonviolent direct action has support in Jesus' teaching of transforming initiatives in the Sermon on the Mount (Matthew 5:38–42). In Jesus' culture, to be struck on the right cheek was to be slapped contemptuously with the back of the hand, the way a slave would be slapped. This is because in that culture you could not touch someone with your left hand; it was for dirty things. So a right hand on the right cheek would be a back-handed slap. To turn the left cheek was to turn the cheek of equal dignity. It was to confront the oppressor nonviolently for the injustice and to call for a transformed relationship. If you were so poor that your creditor was suing you for your coat, Jesus says to embarrass the one suing you by giving not only the coat but also your cloak, which means you would be standing there naked in the law court, disclosing the greed of the plaintiff in all its nakedness! If a Roman soldier in the force occupying Palestine at that time demanded his right that you carry his pack a mile, you take the initiative of carrying also a second mile. None of these is merely complying with what is demanded. Each takes an explicit transforming initiative, nonviolently, to confront the injustice of the oppressive situation. And when the tables are turned and we are confronted by a poor beggar, Jesus says we should not only aid the beggar but take the further initiative of agreeing to give him a loan. In each case it is an extra initiative to try to overcome the injustice and poverty and to call for a relationship of peacemaking. It is the predecessor of the strategy of nonviolent direct action, which is proving widely effective.

2. Take independent initiatives to reduce hostility.

The recently developed strategy of independent initiatives successfully achieved Austria's freeing itself from Soviet domination in the 1950s in exchange for Austrian neutrality and purely defensive military; the Atmospheric Test Ban Treaty of 1963 after Presidents Eisenhower and Kennedy halted atmospheric testing unilaterally; dramatic reductions in nuclear weapons via the series of initiatives by Gorbachev and the U.S. Congress and then president George Bush senior; breakthroughs in peacemaking by adversaries in Northern Ireland; and by Israel and Palestine at those unusual times when some little progress happened, such as a suspension of suicide bombing for a duration, recognition of Israel, Israel's withdrawal from Southern Lebanon and Gaza, and the return of some prisoners.

Independent initiatives (1) are independent of the slow process of negotiation; (2) are designed to decrease threat perception and distrust by the other side but not to leave the initiator weak; (3) are visible and verifiable actions; (4) have a timing announced in advance and carried out regardless of the other side's bluster; (5) have their purpose clearly announced—to shift toward deescalation and to invite reciprocation; (6) come in a series. If the other side refrains from reciprocating, small initiatives should continue in order to keep inviting reciprocation.

These, too, can be seen as implementation of Jesus' teaching on nonviolent initiatives. (I believe the Qur'an also teaches peacemaking initiatives, but it is not my role to pretend to be an expert in interpreting the Qur'an.) The strategies of independent initiatives and nonviolent direct action need to be understood more widely so they can be noticed when they cause breakthroughs, and so citizens can press for them and carry them out in a disciplined and effective way.

3. Use cooperative conflict resolution.

Conflict resolution is becoming a well-known practice, seen in the work of President Carter in the Camp David Accords between Egypt and Israel, and desperately needed between Israel and Palestine. A key test of the seriousness of governments' claims to be seeking peace is whether they develop imaginative solutions that show they understand their adversary's perspectives and needs. At the time of this writing, the world is urging the United States to talk with Iran and with North Korea, and urging Israel to talk with Palestine, and urging Hamas to help make that possible.

We prefer the term *cooperative* conflict resolution, which recognizes that in the real world of threat and potential destruction, our security depends on our adversary's sense of security, and theirs on ours. (1) We mean active partnership in developing solutions, not merely passive cooperation. (2) We seek to help adversaries listen to each other and experience each others' perspectives, including practicing cultural literacy to go beyond the surface positions and even the strategic interests of the adversaries in order to include aspects of culture, religion, spirituality, story, history, and emotion. (3) We seek long-term solutions that help prevent future conflict, even as we work to heal and resolve immediate conflict. (4) We seek justice as a core component for sustainable peace—echoing Dr. King, who said, "Peace is not the absence of tension, but the presence of justice." Mohammed Abu-Nimer criticizes Western practices of conflict resolution that overlook cultural diversity and faith, reducing all to "rational interests."[3] That is the distinction that we have in mind when we describe *cooperative* conflict resolution, including practices of cultural literacy and respect for faith and justice, rather than simply rational-interest conflict resolution.

We see Jesus advocating cooperative conflict resolution in the Sermon on the Mount. He is commenting on the first murder—Cain's murder of his brother Abel. Cain was offering his gift at the altar, and he was jealous of his brother's success as a farmer, apparently with God's favor, and was extremely angry. Jesus is teaching about murder when he says that if you are offering your gift at the altar and realize you are angry at your brother, drop your gift and go talk with your brother and make peace (Matthew 5:21–26). The Bible relates many cases of people practicing conflict resolution—for example, Jacob and Esau, and Joseph and his brothers.

4. *Acknowledge responsibility for conflict and injustice; seek repentance and forgiveness.*

Throughout most of history, leaders of nations have not acknowledged that they or their nations had made errors or were part of the cause of wars that should not have happened. But German Chancellor Willy Brandt and German president Richard von Weizsäcker initiated a new practice when they apologized specifically and concretely for German atrocities during the Third Reich of Adolf Hitler. And since then it has spread. The prime minister of Japan has apologized to South Korea for atrocities during World War II. President Bush senior signed reparation payments for Japanese Americans who were unjustly imprisoned during World War II. President Clinton has apologized for U.S. injustices in Guatemala and for not intervening to stop the massacre in Rwanda.

Donald Shriver has written two elegant and powerful books describing the process of repentance and forgiveness, both by political leaders and by education systems. The most honest countries are writing truth into history textbooks that enable youth to learn from injustices that their own country has committed in the past and to learn not to do it again. Shriver tells of Germany, South Africa, the United States, and Japan. The books are *An Ethic for Enemies: Forgiveness in Politics* and *Honest Patriots: Loving a Country Enough to Remember Its Misdeeds*, both from Oxford University Press (1995 and 2005).

Jesus calls us to practice forgiveness, to acknowledge "the log in our own eye" and to remove it rather than practicing judgment of others (Matthew 6:12–15 and 7:1–5). God is merciful and forgiving, and those who are faithful to God are commanded to acknowledge our own errors and to practice forgiveness of others. It can do so very much to pull out the thorn of resentment from past injustices, resentments, atrocities, and even massacres. Rwanda now seems to be doing a remarkable job of working at acknowledgment, repentance, and forgiveness. Enormous amounts of it are needed in the Middle East.

Advance Justice for All

Thirty-seven times Jesus confronted the ruling authorities in Jerusalem and their supporters for their injustices, including oppression of the poor, domination of the powerless, exclusion of outcasts, and violence against victims. Jesus turned over the tables in the temple area and freed the animals in protest against these four kinds of injustice.[4] Scriptures are full of warnings that injustice is a major cause of war. The prophet Isaiah says that when justice comes, then the effect will be peace (Isaiah 32:16).

5. Promote democracy, human rights, and religious liberty.

Extensive empirical evidence shows that spreading democracy and respect for human rights, including religious liberty, is widening the zones of peace.[5] Political scientists define a democracy as "a country in which nearly everyone can vote, elections are freely contested, . . . and civil rights and civil liberties are substantially guaranteed."[6] These criteria can be met in different ways in different cultures. "Since 1946 pairs of democratic states have been only one-eighth as likely as other kinds of states to threaten to use force against each other. . . . Established democracies fought no wars against one another during the entire twentieth century."[7] This does not mean that they make no wars against autocracies, or that they never use their resources to support clandestine coups or insurgencies or guerrilla wars carried out by others. Democracies are by no means perfect. But in disputes with each other, they are more likely to use practices of conflict resolution. Their own habits of democratic discussion and resolution seem to influence them to engage in discussion and resolution with other democracies more and seem to provide some checks and balances against rash decisions by autocrats or powerful rulers to engage in wars. Furthermore, their democratic habits tend to make them somewhat more respectful of international law and more likely to listen to wisdom and restraint from international organizations. On the average, they spend less for their militaries.

Seeing these empirical results from the research of many political scientists, and then observing the present U.S. administration greatly increase the military budget while cutting programs for human needs, withdraw from nine international treaties, declare international law concerning the treatments of prisoners inoperable, ignore the UN inspectors' reports that they could find no weapons of mass destruction in Iraq, bypass the United Nations in making war, and declare three wars during one presidential term (the permanent war on terrorism and the wars on Afghanistan and on Iraq), at first raises a question whether the United States is an exception to what has been called "the iron law of international relations" concerning the benign influence of democracy. But then we realize that money has become such a powerful influence on U.S. elections that politicians spend far more time raising money than engaging in discussion with the people. The Bush–Gore election cost half a billion dollars in campaign donations, much of it from people whose wealth comes from military–industrial corporations.[8] The United States is partly a plutocracy in which wealth rules, and it makes sense that under these conditions it only halfway resembles a democracy.

Just Peacemaking is clear that making war, as in the Iraq war, is the wrong way to try to spread democracy. "External military intervention, even against the most odious dictators, is a dangerous way to produce a democratic world order. . . . Any time an outside power supplants any existing government, the problem of legitimacy is paramount. The very democratic norms to be instilled may be compromised."[9] The resulting culture tends to be more violent, with opponents to the new government saying "this government was imposed by foreign intervention and patriots will fight against it," while the victors foster a culture that says "our freedom depends on making war, and patriots support war fought in the name of freedom"—as has often been said in Iraq and the United States since the Iraq War.

Influences that played significant parts in *producing* the recent extensive wave of transitions to democracy include changes in some religious institutions (including transnational ones) from primarily defending the status quo to opposing governmental authoritarianism; citizens' groups and nongovernmental organizations dedicated to human rights; and states and international organizations more actively promoting human rights and democracy.

> Under most circumstances, international bodies are better used as vehicles to promote democratic processes at times when the relevant domestic parties are ready. Peacekeeping operations to help provide the conditions for free elections, monitor those elections, and advise on the building of democratic institutions are usually far more promising and less costly for all concerned than is military intervention. . . . The United Nations has experienced highly publicized troubles in Somalia and the former Yugoslavia. . . . Nonetheless, its successes, though receiving less attention, outnumber the failures. It emerged as a major facilitator of peaceful transitions and democratic elections in such places as Cambodia, El Salvador, Eritrea, and Namibia. Its Electoral Assistance

Unit has provided election monitoring, technical assistance, or other aid to electoral processes in more than sixty states.[10]

Powerful threats to democracy sometimes undermine it or block it from spreading: grim economic conditions in numerous struggling democracies; ethnic, racial, nationalistic, and religious conflict; instabilities during the transition to democracy; external threats from nondemocratic neighbors. The possibility of a widespread and growing zone of peace thus requires a network of persons who are willing to work together to gain public attention for those they are trying to protect from human rights violations. And it requires financial and expert help to strengthen the just and sustainable economic development of struggling democracies.

6. Foster just and sustainable economic development.

Jim Wallis and his friends searched the Bible and found two thousand verses about justice for the poor. Economic justice runs throughout the Bible because God is a God of compassion for people in need and people who are outcasts, and a God who knows that greed and power combine to gather up special privilege for the powerful themselves and to deprive those who lack power. The Bible also says that greed and economic injustice are a major cause of war. Therefore, sustainable economic development is crucial for preventing war. *Sustainable* economic development occurs when the needs of today are met without threatening the needs of tomorrow—where those who lack adequate material and economic resources gain access and those who have learn to control resource use and prevent future exhaustion. Ecological destruction threatens the ability to meet needs.

As *Just Peacemaking* points out, people who turn to violence are usually those who have developed some expectations and then see their own or their fellows' conditions dropping well below those expectations. It is not the poorest of the poor, but those who experience economic and human rights deprivation *relative to what they had expected* who turn to violence.

Alan Krueger and Jitka Malecková study aggregate data carefully and conclude, rightly, that neither the poorest nor the least educated are likely to be terrorists. But they show that when Palestinian "college enrollment increased rapidly in the early 1980s, doubling between 1981 and 1985 . . . this remarkable rise in the education of the workforce coincided with a sharp increase in the unemployment rate for college graduates," and "the real daily wage of college graduates fell by around 30%, while the real wages of those with 12 years of schooling held steady and the real wages of those with 11 or fewer years of schooling increased slightly."[11] Then frustrated and angry Palestinians turned to the intifada of 1988. And when "the Israeli occupation of the territories and lack of an effective capital market or banking system . . . prevented the labor markets in the West Bank and Gaza Strip from equilibrating," the intifada of 2000 broke out.

This fits the relative deprivation hypothesis: dramatic increase in educational attainment plus the promise of the Oslo Accords caused rising expectations, but the economic expectations as well as expectations for political justice were dashed, and the intifadas broke out. The suicide bombers were disproportionately college graduates. Krueger and Malecková's data show similar disproportion of above-average education and less rewarding economies among Israeli, Hezbollah, and Palestinian terrorists. Krueger and Malecková do not consider the relative deprivation hypothesis, and hence they point out only the increased education without reaching the conclusion that I believe the data suggest: increased education correlates with increased expectations; when these expectations are dashed, it causes anger and frustration. They do point out that deprivation of civil liberties correlates significantly with increased terrorism.

Peter Hansen, Commissioner-General of UN Relief; Jean Ziegler, a Swiss sociologist and UN special envoy for the UN Human Rights Commission Agency; and The U.S. Agency for International Development, have each issued reports that in 2002, with the Israeli closures, unemployment increased to 80 percent in parts of the occupied territories of Palestine, and the level of absolute poverty rose disastrously, with some 70 percent of the population living on less than $2 per person per day. Levels of acute malnutrition reached 25 percent, hitting women and children the hardest. This drastic drop in basic economic sustenance against a background of higher expectations correlates with intense suicide bombings in that period.[12]

The chapter of *Just Peacemaking* on sustainable economic development argues that it is strategically crucial to focus on the poor and on providing them with opportunities. "Experience shows that not only are the majority of the poor extremely creative and entrepreneurial in eking a living out of the few resources to which they have access, but also that giving them access to resources, information, and opportunities produces impressive results."[13]

Strengthen Cooperative Forces

One of the most widely known teachings of Jesus is "Love your enemies." Jesus said God gives rain and sunshine to the just and the unjust alike, and therefore we must include even our enemies in the community of neighbors (Matthew 5:44–45). He was interpreting the well-known teaching in Leviticus 19:17–18 that we are to love our neighbors as ourselves. But the question being discussed was, "Who is included in the community of neighbors?" Jesus' answer says, all persons to whom God gives sunshine and rain. Similarly, the prophet Isaiah says we are to be a light to the nations—all people.

How can we implement this love and light in the world of nations? Surely it means that we must include the nations of the world in networks of relations—treaties, trade, communication, immigration, international study, dialogue and discussion. So also the prophet Amos said God expected justice in relations between Judah and the neighboring nations of Syria, Philistia, Tyre, Edom, Ammon, and Moab. And the Qur'an says all people are created by the same God. Mohammed made twenty-three treaties with other peoples. So Muslim scholars support international treaties, as do Muslim nations.

Furthermore, a realistic understanding of human nature teaches us that all persons, and all nations and all political leaders, have a proclivity to sin. The apostle Paul writes, "All have sinned and fall short of the glory of God" (Romans 3:23). Therefore realism argues that all nations need the check and balance of the wisdom of other nations, giving them correction when and where they are tempted to do wrong. To think that the U.S. government is the exception and does not sin, and therefore does not need the checks and balances that American tradition knows is necessary, is, Christianly speaking, pure heresy. It also keeps us from learning from our errors and making the right corrections so we cut down on errors next time. All sin and fall short. All.

7. Recognize emerging cooperative forces in the international system, and work with them.

Generations of leaders have worked to develop international networks of treaties, nongovernmental organizations, international cooperation, international travel and communication, international study, economic trade relations, emigration and immigration, international church organizations and missions, so that we are knitted together with networks that work to prevent war. Many returned from World War II determined to do what they could do to prevent World War III and nuclear war. They have built an impressive array of treaties and international networks of cooperation. And the empirical evidence in political science is clear: nations that are more engaged in international networks of cooperation make war less often.

Yet the present administration has withdrawn from nine international treaties. It has worked to tear apart the fabric of international treaties and international cooperation carefully woven by generations of responsible leaders. This has included lifting the protection of international law from defenseless prisoners in Guantanamo, Abu Ghraib, other prisons in Iraq and Afghanistan, and prisoners who have been "rendered" to other nations known for practicing torture. The result has been the deaths of dozens of prisoners, great trauma to many more prisoners, international shame for the United States, and intense anger by potential recruits for terrorism. It is not sufficient for us to disapprove of torture morally, which most all of us do, and rightly so; we need to make a course correction so that this great nation rejoins the networks of war-preventing international cooperation, international law, and international treaties.

8. Strengthen the United Nations and international efforts for cooperation and human rights.

International relations increasingly involve not only the traditional military–diplomatic arena but also the modern arena of economic interdependence, where governments are exposed to the forces of a global market they do not control. Additionally, there is the increasingly important third arena of demands for "people power" or for "citizens' say." The information revolution makes it harder for governments to control people's minds, and popular pressures can now set much of the agenda of foreign policies. States float in a sea of forces from outside their borders or from among their people. Acting alone, states cannot solve problems of trade, debt, interest rates; of pollution, ozone depletion, acid rain, depletion of fish stocks, global warming; of migrations and refugees seeking asylum; and of military security when weapons rapidly penetrate borders.

Therefore, collective action is increasingly necessary. U.S. citizens should press their government to act in small and large crises in ways that strengthen the effectiveness of the United Nations, of regional organizations, and of multilateral peacemaking, peacekeeping, and peacebuilding. Many multilateral practices are building effectiveness to resolve conflicts, to monitor, nurture, and even enforce truces and replace violent conflict with beginning cooperation. They are organizing to meet human needs for food, hygiene, medicine, education, and economic interaction. Furthermore, most wars now happen within states, not between states. Therefore, *Just Peacemaking* contends that collective action needs to include UN-approved humanitarian intervention in cases like the former Yugoslavia, Haiti, Somalia, and Rwanda "when a state's condition or behavior results in . . . grave and massive violations of human rights."

The United Nations is not perfect, but neither is the U.S. Congress or the Supreme Court or the president—which have been organized constitutionally to check and balance each other. American wisdom tested for over two centuries is clear that concentrations of power need checks and balances to correct them when they get stuck in erroneous and unjust courses. The powerful U.S. military under the control of the enormously powerful president needs checks and balances by listening to the wisdom and interests of other nations. Not only the U.S. government, the world needs checks and balances against rash responses and unwise actions by all nations. We do not want a world of pure anarchy, but a world that has some laws, some checks and balances from international wisdom.

Nations that cooperate more actively with various United Nations organizations and regional organizations make war less frequently. The present object lesson is that the current U.S. administration has worked consistently to undermine the United Nations, to ignore the evidence from the international inspectors in Iraq, to ignore the Geneva Convention and the warnings of the International Red Cross about abuse and torture of prisoners, to ignore their warnings that they should guard the 350 tons of high-intensity explosives that the inspectors were guarding at Al Qa Qa when they invaded, and to ignore president Bush's promise to get a vote in the UN Security Council as required by international law before invading Iraq. And this administration has declared three wars in one presidential term: a permanent war against terror, a war against Afghanistan, and a war against Iraq. Has any prior U.S. administration ever declared three wars during just one term?

9. Reduce offensive weapons and weapons trade.

Jesus teaches, "Put up your sword. Those who take up the sword, by the sword will die" (Matthew 26:52). In Jesus' day, there was great resentment against occupation of Israel's homeland by the Roman army. It has parallels now in the resentment of Palestinians against occupation of their homeland by the Israeli army. Every now and then a guerrilla leader would claim to be a Messiah and would lead a revolt against Rome. Jesus taught against taking up weapons; it would lead to the destruction of the temple and of Jerusalem. He wept over Jerusalem saying "you do not know the practices of peace." He taught constructive peacemaking initiatives to oppose and correct the injustice by *nonviolent* means, from which we are drawing the practices of just-peacemaking theory. His prophecy was validated when the resentment against Roman occupation boiled forth in a major rebellion against Rome in AD 66, and Rome retaliated and destroyed the temple, destroyed Jerusalem, and exiled Jews from their homeland in AD 70.

This is the context for the teachings of Jesus about constructive initiatives of peacemaking. His teachings of peacemaking practices are not merely scattered prooftexts; they are a consistent strategy supported by wisdom in the context of occupation. In our time, with almost infinitely more destructive weapons, the context cries out for all of us to teach constructive practices of peacemaking. This is realism in the face of such destructive power.

But there is another context as well. This is the context of the will of God for peace. God's will is not merely a distant ideal. It is specific and concrete. And one specific teaching is that reliance on military weapons while disdaining the practices of peace is idolatry and leads to destruction (Isaiah 30, 31; Jeremiah 2).

A key factor in the decrease of war between nations is the reality that weapons have become so destructive that war is not worth the price. The offense cannot destroy the defense before it does huge retaliatory damage. Reducing offensive weapons and shifting toward defensive force structures strengthens that equation. For example, Gorbachev removed half the Soviet Union's tanks from Central Europe and all its river-crossing equipment. This freed NATO to agree to get rid of all medium-range and shorter-range nuclear weapons on both sides from Eastern and Western Europe—the first dramatic step in ending the Cold War peacefully.

The war in Bosnia is the counterexample that proves the rule: Serbia controlled the former Yugoslavian army and its weapons. They had the offensive weapons to make war without expecting a destructive counterattack. This presented a temptation to make war, thinking there would not be much retaliation. Milosevic made three wars—against Bosnia-Herzegovina, against Croatia, and against Kosovo. The results were disastrous.

The United States now has a parallel temptation. The U.S. military budget is greater than all other nations combined. No other nation can match U.S. military power in a direct war. The present administration has succumbed to the temptation. It, too, has made three wars during one administration, again with disastrous consequences.

As nations turn toward democracy and human rights, their governments no longer need large militaries to keep them in power. As the ten practices of peacemaking reduce the threat in their environment, nations feel less need for weapons. As they struggle with their deep indebtedness, they have less ability to buy weapons. The International Monetary Fund requires big reductions in weapons expenditures before granting loans. For these reasons, arms imports by developing nations in 1995 dropped to one-quarter of their peak in 1988. Yet the United States continues to increase its military spending while its budget deficit has grown to an astounding half-trillion dollars each year, while children lack good schooling; 45 million people lack health insurance; and the resources for funding Medicaid and Social Security are undermined.

But the power of money invested by arms manufacturers in politicians' campaigns is a major obstacle to reductions. So is the ideology of the national security state, as well as real or perceived security needs. Support for reductions requires sharp curtailment of campaign spending and reductions in threats to security.

10. Encourage grassroots peacemaking groups and voluntary associations.

Just peacemaking requires associations of citizens organized independently of governments and linked together across boundaries of nation, class, and race, to learn peacemaking practices and press governments to employ these practices; governments should protect such associations in law and give citizens accurate information, not propaganda.

The existence of a growing worldwide people's movement constitutes one more historical force that makes just-peacemaking theory possible. A transnational network of groups, including faith groups, can partially transcend captivity by narrow national or ideological perspectives. Citizens' *groups* are not so committed to status-quo institutional maintenance as bureaucracies often are, nor are they as isolated and only temporarily engaged as lone individuals often are, and so they can provide long-term perseverance in peacemaking. They can serve as voices for the voiceless, as they did in churches in East Germany and in women's groups in Guatemala.[14] They can help to initiate, foster, or support transforming initiatives, where existing parties need support and courage to take risks to break out of the cycles that perpetuate violence and injustice. A citizens' network of NGOs and INGOs can often be a source of information and knowledge that persons in positions of governmental authority lack or resist acknowledging. They can criticize injustice and can initiate repentance and forgiveness. They can nurture a spirituality that sustains courage when just peacemaking is unpopular, hope when despair or cynicism is tempting, and grace and forgiveness when just peacemaking fails. The challenge is to encourage citizens to gather together in grassroots peacemaking groups, including groups of faith, to do the practices of peacemaking in their own churches (and mosques) and their own personal and community relations, and to prod governments to engage in the practices of peacemaking.

THE SHIFT TO PRACTICE NORMS

Those of us who developed the just-peacemaking theory were frustrated by Christian habits of talking about peace merely as a general ideal. It is like an alcoholic discussing sobriety as a general ideal. The real question is, "What are you doing about it in your daily practice, one day at a time?" So we were determined to develop a just-peacemaking ethic that identifies specific and concrete practices to carry out, one conflict at a time. We want Christians to learn to practice peace, not just talk about it.

We were focusing on our own learning and practice. We wanted to straighten out our own house. But we also hoped other faiths might find their own way to develop their own just-peacemaking ethic. We wrote, "We are addressing all persons of various faiths or no claimed faith who are concerned about peacemaking, or who could become concerned if they had a map that would make sense of events and of peacemaking trends for them and that would indicate directions their participation can take."[15] I know Islam has strength because Muslims know God's will is not only for one small part of our lives but for all of life; God is sovereign ruler over the whole of life. That means God has a will for what peacemaking practices we do. I know that Islam has strength because it does not simply have a scattered teaching here and there but has specific, systematic teachings like the Five Pillars of Islam. It must make sense that Muslims would develop a systematic set of just-peacemaking practices, analogous to what we have tried to develop to make Christians more faithful to God's will. If our work can in some way be useful to Muslims in developing an ethic of eight or ten or twelve practices of peacemaking that make sense in light of the Qur'an and Muslim practice, we would rejoice and give thanks to God.

Not all practices in our time are peacemaking practices by any means. There are powerful economic interests and natural drives for national security that can work good or evil. There are interests that do not want to make peace, and interests that think they want to make peace, but perceive things in such a way and with such loyalties that their actions work in cross purposes to peace. Some think the way to peace is to wipe out the enemy. There are enormous forces of evil: nuclear weapons and their delivery systems; chemical and biological weapons; devastating poverty and its offspring of population explosion; ecological devastation and nonrenewable energy consumption; and ethnic and religious wars within nations like Congo, Somalia, Iraq, Afghanistan, and Palestine-Israel. "Some 2 million children have died in dozens of wars during the past decade. . . . This is more than three times the number of battlefield deaths of American soldiers in all their wars since 1776. . . . Today, civilians account for more than 90 percent of war casualties."[16] Whatever peacemaking practices we may point to need to work their way into areas where they are still foreign. Each practice recognizes and seeks to resolve, lessen, discipline, or check and balance one or more of these negative forces.

Focusing on practices enabled us to unite in spite of our differing faiths, perspectives, and methodologies. We believe the practices are ethically normative because they bring peace, solve problems, and promote justice and cooperation. Each of us has additional reasons. Evangelicals among our group do our ethics with more biblical concreteness; mainline Protestants among us prefer more general theological grounding or middle axioms; peace-church members want arguments explicitly theological and faith-based; Roman Catholics work with general moral norms, natural law, and natural rights; and some who do not identify themselves as explicitly faith-based shy away from faith-based reasons. All of us appeal explicitly to persons and groups of various faiths who will join with us in seeking to make peace.

The process has dramatically deepened our engagement and commitment to what we are doing together. It has convinced us that in fact we are in touch with a historical learning that is happening in our time and from which we can find guidance, and has enabled us to reach unanimous consensus on the ten practices.

CONCLUSION

We argue that governments and citizens and gatherings of people of faith have an obligation to support these peacemaking practices both in long-term work to build conditions that make peace more likely and in crisis situations where peacemaking initiatives can make war less likely. They can guide people in prodding governments to engage in realistic peacemaking. In crisis situations, these initiatives should be tried before the last resort of war. We believe that whether a government employs these practices is a test of the sincerity of its claims that it is trying to make peace.

We recognize our work is incomplete. We hope to offer our best thinking and to ask, does it do real work? Does it make new sense of our historical context and point to faith-based, meaningful action and prayer in that context? Can these ten practices of just peacemaking help people participate in the peacemaking practices and forces that are in fact changing our world? Do they grapple with realistic evils that cause war and destroy peace? What can others add, and what improvements can they offer? How would others relate them to their faith or core beliefs and values? We are addressing all persons of various faiths or no claimed faith who are concerned about peacemaking or who could become concerned if they had a map that would make sense of events and of peacemaking trends and would indicate directions their participation could take.

NOTES

1. James Cone, *Martin & Malcolm in America* (Maryknoll, N.Y.: Orbis, 1991).
2. For more extensive examples and engaging narrative, see Daniel Buttry, *Christian Peacemaking* (Valley Forge, Pa.: Judson Press, 1994).
3. Mohammed Abu-Nimer, "Conflict Resolution in an Islamic Context: Some Conceptual Questions," *Peace and Change* 21, no. 1 (January 1996): 22.
4. Glen Stassen and David Gushee, *Kingdom Ethics: Following Jesus in Contemporary Context* (Downers Grove, Ill.: InterVarsity Press, 2003), chap. 17.
5. For some of the extensive empirical evidence, see Bruce Russett, *Grasping the Democratic Peace: Principles for a Post–Cold War World* (Princeton, N.J.: Princeton University Press, 1993); Spencer Weart, *Never at War: Why Democracies Will Never Fight Each Other* (New Haven, Conn.: Yale University Press, 1997); Bruce Russett, "Counterfactuals about War and Its Absence," in *Counterfactual Thought Experiments in World Politics: Logical, Methodological, and Psychological Perspectives*, ed. Philip Tetlock and Aaron Belkin (Princeton, N.J.: Princeton University Press, 1996).

6. Glen Stassen, ed., *Just Peacemaking: Ten Practices for Abolishing War* (Cleveland, Ohio: Pilgrim Press, 2004), 106.

7. Stassen, *Just Peacemaking: Ten Practices*, 107.

8. For congressional campaigns, see Stassen, *Just Peacemaking: Ten Practices*, 180.

9. Stassen, *Just Peacemaking: Ten Practices*, 114.

10. Stassen, *Just Peacemaking: Ten Practices*, 108–9, 115.

11. For this and the following references, see Alan Krueger and Jitka Malecková, "Education, Poverty and Terrorism: Is There a Causal Connection?" *Journal of Economic Perspectives* 17, no. 4 (Fall 2003): 132–33, 35, 37, 141.

12. Krueger and Malecková, "Education, Poverty and Terrorism," 128–29.

13. Stassen, *Just Peacemaking: Ten Practices*, 130–31, 140.

14. For the work of groups in churches to bring about the East German nonviolent revolution, see Jörg Swoboda, *Revolution of the Candles*, trans. Richard Pierard (Atlanta, Ga.: Mercer University Press, 1997); For Guatemala, see Michelle Tooley, *Voices of the Voiceless* (Scottdale, Pa.: Herald Press), 1997.

15. Stassen, *Just Peacemaking: Ten Practices*, 35.

16. Desmond Tutu, "Stop Killing the Children," *The Washington Post*, November 24, 1996, p. C7.

6

Response to Stassen's "Ten Just-Peacemaking Practices That Work"

Karim Douglas Crow

> La taghdab! / Do not be angered!
>
> —the Prophet Muhammad[1]

We thank Glen Stassen for his sincere and heartfelt restatement of a "new ethic"—a decalogue of "Ten Just-Peacemaking Practices"—and for the **call** he utters for Muslims to take up the challenge of "articulating effective practices for reducing injustices by nonviolent means so we can prevent war that can be prevented." The bloody events of our day echo the urgency for Muslims to adequately meet this challenge with creative wisdom and effectiveness by reaching beyond dogmas to the root of ideals that may have hardened to staleness and rising above the confusion of overwhelming forces, reinforcing their grieving sense of injustice and marginality. Professor Stassen is correct in saying that Muslims may uncover, refurbish, as well as innovate "concrete and specific practices of peacemaking" that realistically embody and incarnate the ideals people commonly acknowledge yet too frequently ignore in their actual conduct of life. This is why Stassen's insistence on an experiential **ethic** appears most apposite for the *terror of our situation:* the conflagration of violent bloodshed perpetrated by errant jihadists and the far-flung militarist adventures or regime changes pursued by the little Napoleons sweeping our globe moving all toward some dreaded apocalypse.[2] Perhaps one mark of the magnitude of the terror is that so many polities (including Western and Muslim ones) remain blind to its danger and ferocity by continuing to dwell in complacent calculations of self-interest, nationalist security agendas, or diversionary parochial pursuits.

Our response is necessarily limited and probably inadequate, given that contemporary Muslims appear to lag behind in pondering the nature and causes of violence, bloodshed, and war, while the religion of Islam is commonly perceived by many non-Muslims to possess an inherent disposition or bias facilitating violence. Yet recently it was a Muslim, Professor Muhammad Yunus, who was awarded the 2006 Nobel Prize for Peace in recognition of his prolonged efforts to help the poor through microcredits.[3] Furthermore, close study and intimacy with Islamic religious, intellectual, and spiritual traditions may convince one that peace and Islam are joined at the hip conceptually (Stassen mentions the example of the great Pathan nobleman Abdul Ghaffar Khan, d. 1984), despite historical and contemporary indications of Muslim amnesia. Peace studies as a genuine field of interest yielding practical efforts among Muslims remains in its infancy when compared to some other faith traditions. So we begin where we are, embracing hope and energy to move along a path that only now shows a way forward. To be defeated by the terror of our situation is not an option for thinking Muslims. As we are firmly convinced that Muslims should, we gladly accept and benefit from the wisdom of our fellow humans, whether Jewish, Christian, Hindu, or Buddhist (or even secular western political science and conflict studies), who generously offer the fruit of their own insights and experience.

Stassen emphasizes the two key practices of just peacemaking: nonviolent direct action and independent initiatives "that we are to take to participate in God's way of deliverance from vicious cycles like anger, injustice, and killing." He underlines the need to pursue *practical actions* that may alter political policy and effect positive change in human behavior in order to prevent preventable wars, solve injustice and make peace. Just war, as Stassen admits, is sometimes admissible, so (1) pacifism may not be viewed as a preferred position. Yet (2) "just-war" theory (admitted by most Reformed Protestants and Catholics) is distinguished from (3) "just peacemaking," while both differ from (4) "righteous war" (making peace by waging war). Recall that Islam very rarely admits of a pure pacifist position,[4] whereas the latter three alternatives all find some degree of adherence and justification within the normative spectrum of Muslim thought and practice. Thus in Stassen's view, praxis is valued more than mere lip service to ideals. We are confident he would agree that one informs the other, that worthy means in pursuit of noble ends requires us to connect the two within our own efforts. The crux lies in acknowledgement of responsibility manifested in our experiential response to this felt demand. To rephrase this more abstractly, cognizance of what is good and just must be blended with an effective act-of-will demonstrated in deeds, or cognition depends on connation in living a true ethic. In traditional Islamic terms, *'ilm* or knowledge requires *'amal* (practice) to achieve integral understanding and rectitude (*'aql*). A statement by the great eighth-century CE Muslim exponent Ja'far al-Sadiq may be cited, where the closely related notion of *ma'rifah* (experiential knowledge–cognition) occurs in conjunction with practice (*'amal*):[5]

> God accepts a person's practice only if performed with "cognizance"/*illa bi-ma'rifatin*, and God accepts a person's "cognition" only when accompanied by practice. Whoever knows/*'arafa*—the "cognition" directs them to the practice; and whoever does not practice—that person has no *ma'rifah*/cognition.

This insight is commonplace in the early Islamic literature on knowledge, yet like all truth it is quickly lost sight of and goes unheeded in human experience. Lacking the "realistic effectiveness" of practice informed and guided by deep understanding, our ideals evaporate into mere information floating in our heads. In order to touch and transform us and those around us, ideas must penetrate the heart (conscience) to impel the body; the best practical action embodies insight and understanding guiding will.[6] Stassen has indeed put his finger on the very nub of ethical concern, namely translating ideals into practice (*or* illuminating our practice with the light of ideals), thereby giving his attempt at a "new ethic" of praxis more weight.

Explaining this search for an ethically informed praxis of just-peacemaking, he candidly states: "First I looked for practices of peacemaking that are taught by Jesus in the New Testament. . . . Then I looked for similar practices that are demonstrated by political science to be effective in peacemaking." Both scripture and contemporary knowledge are to be exploited as sources for a new ethic, and received the blessings of a representative body of Christian ethicists and international relations experts, yielding "a consensus new ethical paradigm" (published in 1998 and again in 2004). Such consensus is indeed rare in the realm of religions, and one understands why Professor Stassen feels justifiable pride in this uncommon achievement. Yet it is important to note that political science and related or parallel disciplines such as conflict resolution may have supplied a certain number of the ten practices. While a number of these practices could be viewed as not specifically inspired by religious models or teachings (Nos. 5, 7, 8, and 10), and several might be questioned as reflecting pragmatic concerns of modernity colored by a definite political orientation (Nos. 3, 6, 9), we do not seriously question that underlying all ten breathes a spirit inspired by deeply ethical awareness linked to revealed guidance, however tenuous it may appear in certain cases. Ethical concerns often overlap and are congruent with religious teachings and ideals, but not necessarily. The divide between the sacred and the secular may at times be dissolved as an artificial barrier, for valid concerns of human needs.

It is more than possible that Muslims in search of a peacemaking ethic for this age may look beyond the boundaries of the Qur'an and Prophetic traditions (the two "canonical" sources of revealed authority in Islam)—and avail themselves of modern disciplines first developed and taught in Euro-American societies. Therefore I must ask: What stops Muslims from accomplishing what Stassen led his Christian colleagues in doing, and would this be seen as a legitimate endeavor? Creative efforts do not shrink from taking this path, while a significant mass of Muslims recoil from explicitly adopting principles or models taken from Western disciplines deemed unredeemingly secular, materialist, or simply profane. Naturally there exists a spectrum of responses, but almost everyone feels the need to provide a degree of religious authenticity by forging links to Scripture and tradition. In this way, the Tradition has always adapted and grown to encompass fresh challenges and new situations. Islam in its best modus operandi may be understood as being internally equipped with sufficient resources to accomplish such growth—even while Muslims generally insist that "Islam" in its essential mode is permanent and unchanging. What may change and adapt and grow, indeed must grow to survive, is the mentality and understanding Muslims possess regarding permanent timeless truths.

His formulation of the *ten* emphasizes just practices, a welcome emphasis to Muslims who invariably insist on framing issues of peace with an unyielding insistence on rectifying injustices and righting wrongs. We often hear this linkage when mention is made of "just peace" for the Israeli–Palestinian conflict. Muslim advocates who weigh in too heavily on the side of peace in ending conflicts or neutralizing violence open themselves to criticism from other Muslims that the cause of justice is integral to and a necessary condition for true peace.[7] Justice is one of the crucial components in the hierarchy of values embraced by Islam, and its first major historical theological school (the Mu'tazilah) was oriented primarily around it. Like all primary values, justice points to one of the facets of divinity and is embedded in the very nature of creation and order. So if there is to be peacemaking, let it be just peacemaking!

We respond to Stassen's *Ten Practices* by offering a complementary and more interior set of human attitudes conveying values. The human attitudes and ideals prompting actions and which are mediated by *values* also possess a theoretical or cognitive power shaping the collective worldview and the discourse of humans forming a community functioning for a definite purpose within God's created order. In Islam, these two related aspects of values are bound together through knowledge: the connative faith-induced dimension of knowledge yielding conviction and moral volition through the operation of human intelligence implanted in conscience, being intimately joined with the cognitive perceiving–knowing dimension. A closely related pair of Islamic concepts expressing these two dimensions is the joining of righteous action (*al-'amal al-salih*) with beneficial knowledge (*al-'ilm al-nafi'*). We stressed above that knowledge and practice must go hand in hand for values to become truly operative in human experience. The universal values to be upheld and taught should be clearly evident in the lived behavior of their practitioners, their exemplars or living examples. Otherwise, one is dealing with hypocrisy—with hollow words lacking any connative force that fails to touch and move us from within and thus fails to manifest outwardly in any genuine observable change of behavior.

One must be careful to distinguish between permanent universal values not conditioned by time or place, and those peripheral cultural norms and preferences (also often called by people today "values") that are really only expressive of culturally conditioned behaviors relative to specific times, places, and peoples. The proper understanding of values leads to the recognition of a cluster of universal values arranged in a particular hierarchy—in other words, values possess a definite priority within a hierarchical scale. Thus, from an Islamic perspective, justice is often seen as a primary core value within the hierarchical scale of values, since other values arrange themselves around Justice.

The most essential value at the heart of Islam may be characterized as "Security–Peace" (see Qur'anic *al-silm* and *al-salm*).[8] In classical Arabic usage, the term *salm* (peace) denotes the opposite of *harb* (war), whereas the contemporary widespread Arabic usage of *salaam* (salutations of safety and peaceful security) often takes it generally to connote "peace." The very name *al-Islam* signifies the safety and security experienced in acts of mutual harmony and concord between humans springing out of the inner peace between individual creatures and their Creator. This name *al-Islam* points to the real purpose and source of true security—to draw closer to the ultimate origin of Peace: Allah. *Peace may be achieved only through knowledge and understanding, never by force.* Suffering is the result of wrong thinking taking form in misdirected action. Therefore, Islam consciously names itself after the central experience of its practitioners, unlike other religions named after their founders or for a particular people.

The authentic Islamic application of beneficial knowledge (*al-'ilm al-nafi'*) with righteous action (*al-'amal al-salih*), when both are joined together in faith (*iman*), may be exemplified in the following ten essential Islamic values:

ISLAM: SECURITY, PEACE

Knowledge with Action yields Faith and Conviction

1. *Ikhlas*: True sincerity marked by genuine self-criticism (*muhasabat al-nafs*) and wariness of prideful self-conceit (*'ujb*).
2. *Niyyah*: Purity-of-intent arising from open-hearted resolve to act from the highest motives and goals, and to observe organic cleanliness (*taharah*) and humility or organic-shame (*haya'*) in one's physical and psychic states.
3. *Taqwa*: deep-rooted God-mindfulness (or reverential awe), manifested in inner contentment (*rida*), moderation in needs (*qana'ah*), and confident-hope (*tawakkul*).
4. *Rahmah*: Compassion (or loving kindness), objective concern for the ultimate welfare of all creatures and for our environment, marked by forbearance (*hilm*) and forgiveness (*'afw*).
5. *Tawhid*: Oneness or unity, recognition of our debt to the source and origin of all life, matched by an awareness of our collective creaturely identity in the human family and an active pursuit of our responsibilities in the providential plan of creation.
6. *Ijma'*: Consensus by mutual consultation and conciliation seeking harmonious common purpose through understanding and cooperation.
7. *'Aql and Fiqh*: Intelligence and understanding activating the full potential of our innate human constitution to fulfill obligations wisely, and to reflect critically on the manner and purpose of our existence (*tafakkur* and *tadabbur*).
8. *Sabr*: Patient perseverance marked by readiness to postpone immediate gratifications, and to consciously suffer injustice from others for exemplary communal purposes and for individual self-transformation.
9. *Jihad:* Selfless sacrifice and service when pursuing positive action through striving by proper means, including active suffering for a higher cause to realize worthy ends for ourselves and others.
10. *'Adl and Qist:* Justice and equity inspired by wisdom and understanding at all levels—from within the individual, to interpersonal and communal relations, to international relations, planetary equilibrium, and harmony with the created order.

Observe the movement in this suggested hierarchy of Islamic values from the more interior virtues to outward communal values, reflecting the harmony between individual and community, and private and public. (These values may be arranged differently and their precise components could vary within the understandings of Muslims, but all of them would find a place in any list of the most essential values mediated by *al-Islam*). Our reason for listing ten reflects teachings of the earliest generations of Muslims who advocated "Ten Traits" (*'ashr khisal*) as paradigmatic values inculcated by the practice of faith within the individual's personal and community life.[9] These Islamic listings normally depict the ten virtues as subsidiary branches of one chief or representative virtue: normally *iman* (faith) or *'aql* (conscience¬intelligence). The early *hadith* narratives of ten traits came to form the literary framework for the later genre of writings on virtues termed *makarim al-akhlaq* embodying normative Islamic ethics, or so-called hadith-based ethics.

Any sincere and serious effort to bring just peacemaking to life in our peculiar day and inverted age has to simultaneously strive to awaken and embody such primary values, in order for faith to join with knowledge in our lived experience. If the essence of the Islamic faith is peace and security in obedience to God's purpose for creation, then Muslims must creatively meet the challenges of the present and future with wisdom, energy, and intelligence. If human creatures together recognize and acknowledge their debt and dependence on their Creator, they must join hands to support one another's efforts to make an adequate response worthy of the name *human*.

NOTES

1. The Prophet made this utterance upon observing two men engaged in a contest of strength lifting heavy rocks, asking if they wished to know what true strength really was; see the narratives in al-Bukhari, *Adab;* al-Tirmidhi, *Birr*.

2. Premillennial dispensationalist evangelicals do not dread, but eagerly welcome, such an apocalypse.

3. Like many good ideas, Yunus's philanthropic scheme is now being exploited by commercial banks for profit seeking; see "Conflicts of Interest," *The Financial Times*, December 6, 2008, pp. 1–2, Life and Arts.

4. A notable exception is the body of work and example of ideas enunciated by the contemporary Syrian peace philosopher *Ustadh* Jawdat Said [Sa'īd]; see for example his classic work first published in 1966 and frequently reprinted: *Madhhab Ibn Adam al-Awwal: Mushkilat al-'Unf fi l-'Amal al-Islami* [The Doctrine of Adam's First Son: the Problem of Violence in 'Islamic Action'] (Damascus: 1966). Sa'īd insists that the prophetic paradigm from the very start was unmitigated pacific

nonviolence exemplified by readiness to consciously suffer unjust death, as with the Qur'anic model of Abel slain by Cain.

5. al-Kulayni, "On Employing Knowledge," in *Usul al-Kafi*, vol. I., *kitab fadl al-'ilm, bab isti'mal al-'ilm*, ed. al-Ghaffari, 3rd ed. (Tehran, 1388), 44§2.

6. We make this point about cognition and connation in more detail in "Nonviolence, Ethics, and Character Development in Islam," in *Peace and Conflict Resolution in Islam: Precept and Practice*, ed. Abdul Aziz Said et al. (Lanham, Md.: University Press of America, 2001), 213–26; and in our "Islam And Reason," *Al-Shajarah* vol. 8, no. 1 (2003): 109–37.

7. A notable example is the body of work by the contemporary Indian thinker Maulana Wahiduddin Khan (President, The Islamic Center, New Delhi), who has authored several books on Islam as nonviolent praxis.

8. In the chapter *al-Baqarah* 2:208, the Qur'an employs *silm* (peace and reconciliation) as an attribute of faith (*iman*) and/or as synonymous with *islam*, while in Q *al-Anfal* 8:61, *salm* (peacemaking) denotes the antonym of war/bloodshed.

9. Here, we have only provided a bare outline without proper documentation to the abundant literature nor accurate transliteration. In our unpublished study "Islamic Decalogues in Sapiential Perspective," the archaic Islamic literary genre of listings of Ten Traits is demonstrated to represent the true Islamic analogue to the Mosaic Ten Commandments, and we invoke the research of A. Alt, E. Gerstenberger, W. Richter, E. Nielsen, and J. Blenkinsopp establishing the common origin of tribal "apodictic" precepts and the exhortations and warnings of wisdom literature, expanding their insights by applying them to early Islamic narratives of ethical nature.

II

RELIGIOUS DIVERSITY AND IDENTITY

7

The Qur'anic Perspective on Religious Pluralism

Riffat Hassan

Prior to engaging in any discussion of specific issues pertaining to religious pluralism with reference to Islam, it is necessary to have a basic understanding of the framework of normative Muslim ethics. Given the widespread negative stereotyping of Islam in the West, particularly the United States, especially since September 11, 2001, I think that it is critically important to state the normative Islamic view on religious and ethical pluralism. My presentation, therefore, focuses on identifying major teachings of the Qur'an—which to Muslims is the primary source of the Islamic tradition—that are relevant in this context.

The cardinal principle of Islam is belief in the absolute oneness of God, or *Tawhid*. In the opening chapter of the Qur'an, *Al-Fatiha*, God is described as "Ar-Rahman" (The Most Merciful), "Ar-Rahim" (The Most Gracious), and as "Rabb al-'alamin" (The Lord of all the peoples and universes). As pointed out by Fathi Osman, in the Qur'an God is not related to any particular place or people but to all creation.[1] In this context it is interesting to note that while the Hebrew Bible or the Old Testament refers to God as the God of Abraham, Isaac, and Jacob, the Qur'an does not refer to God as the God of any particular prophet. God is the one and only creator of everything that exists and from the unity of God comes the unity of creation. The Qur'an points out that God not only creates and sustains all creatures but also gives moral guidance to humanity, which has been made "in the best of moulds" (Surah 95: *At-Tin*: 4).

The Qur'an affirms that God "cares for all creatures" (Surah 2: *Al-Baqarah*: 268) and testifies that the message it contains is universal, as may be seen from the following verses:

> Hallowed is He who from on high, step by step, has bestowed upon His servant the standard by which to discern the true from the false, so that to all the world it may be a warning. (Surah 25: *Al-Furqan*: 1)[2]

> (The Qur'an) is but a reminder and a divine discourse, clear in itself and clearly showing the truth, to the end that it may warn everyone who is alive (of heart). (Surah 36: *Yasin*: 69–70)[3]

> This (divine writ) behold, is no less than a reminder to all the worlds. (Surah 38: *Sad*: 87)[4]

> This (message) is no less than a reminder to all mankind—to every one of you who wills to walk a straight way. (Surah 81: *At-Takwir*: 27–28)[5]

The universal mission of the Prophet of Islam is also affirmed by the Qur'an as, for instance, in Surah 34: *Saba'*: 28, which states, "Now (as for thee Muhammad,) We have not sent thee otherwise than to mankind at large, to be a herald of glad tidings and a warner."[6]

The nonexclusive spirit of Islam also comes through the oft-repeated teaching of the Qur'an contained in verses such as the following:

> Verily, those who have attained to faith (in this divine writ), as well as those who follow the Jewish faith, and the Christians, and the Sabians—all who believe in God and the Last day and do righteous deeds—shall have their reward with their Sustainer; and no fear need they have, and neither shall they grieve. (Surah 2: *Al-Baqarah*: 62; this verse is repeated in almost identical form in Surah 5: *Al-Ma'idah*: 69)[7]

> And they claim, "None shall ever enter paradise unless he be a Jew"—or "a Christian." Such are their wishful beliefs! Say: "Produce an evidence for what you are claiming, if what you say is true!" Yea, indeed: everyone who surrenders his whole being unto God, and is a doer of good withal, shall have his reward with his Sustainer; and all such need have no fear, and neither shall they grieve. (Surah 2: *Al-Baqarah*:111–12)[8]

> And be conscious of the Day on which you shall be brought back unto God, whereupon every human being shall be repaid in full for what he has earned, and none shall be wronged. (Surah 2: *Al-Baqarah*: 281)[9]

Since God is the universal creator who sends guidance to all humanity, Muslims are commanded by the Qur'an to affirm the divine message given to all the previous Prophets. It is stated in Surah 40: *Ghafir*: 78,

"And, indeed, (O Muhammad,) We sent forth apostles before thy time; some of them We have mentioned to thee, and some of them We have not mentioned to thee."[10] While only twenty-five prophets are mentioned in the Qur'an, the above-cited verse indicates that there have also been other prophets. Indeed, Surah 16: *An-Nahl*: 84 tells us that God "shall raise up a witness out of every community"[11]

Muslims are required to affirm the continuity of Islam with previous revelations and Prophets and not to make a distinction among them, as can be seen from the following verses:

> Say: "We believe in God, and in that which has been bestowed from on high upon us, and that which has been bestowed upon Abraham and Ishmael and Isaac and Jacob and their descendants, and that which has been vouchsafed to Moses and Jesus, and that which has been vouchsafed to all the (other) prophets by their Sustainer: we make no distinction between any of them. And it is unto Him that we surrender ourselves" (Surah 2: *Al-Baqarah*: 136).[12]

> Step by step has He bestowed upon thee from on high this divine writ, setting forth the truth which confirms whatever there remains (of earlier revelations): for it is He who has bestowed from on high the Torah and the Gospel aforetime as a guidance to mankind, and it is He who has bestowed (upon man) the standard by which to discern the true from the false. (Surah 3: *Al*: *'Imran*: 3)[13]

> Say: "We believe in God, and in that which has been bestowed from on high upon us, and that which has been bestowed upon Abraham and Ishmael and Isaac and Jacob and their descendants, and that which has been vouchsafed by their Sustainer unto Moses and Jesus and all the (other) prophets: we make no distinction between any of them. And unto Him do we surrender ourselves." (Surah 3: *Al 'Imran*: 84)[14]

> Behold, We have inspired thee (O Prophet) just as We inspired Noah and all the Prophets after him—as We inspired Abraham, and Ishmael. And Isaac, and Jacob, and their descendants including Jesus and Job, and Jonah, and Aaron, and Solomon; and as We vouchsafed unto David a book of divine wisdom; and (We inspired other) apostles whom We have mentioned to thee ere this, as well as apostles whom We have not mentioned to thee; and as God spoke His Word unto Moses: (We sent all these) apostles as heralds of glad tidings and as warners, so that men might have no excuse before God after (the coming of) these apostles: and God is indeed almighty, wise. (Surah 4: *An-Nisa'*: 163)[15]

> In matters of faith, He has ordained for you that which He enjoined upon Noah—and into which We gave thee (O Muhammad) insight through revelation—as well as that which We had enjoined upon Abraham, and Moses, and Jesus: Steadfastly uphold the (true) faith, and do not break up your unity therein. (Surah 42: *Ash-Shura*: 13)[16]

One major reason why the Prophet Abraham is so important in the Islamic tradition is that he is seen as a symbol of the unity of all believers implicit in Qur'anic teaching. Not only is he the Prophet most often mentioned in the Qur'an after Muhammad, but he is also regarded in a significant way as the first "Muslim" because he surrendered his whole self to God. The Qur'an repeatedly describes Abraham as "hanif"—the true in faith—or one who turns away from all that is not-God to submit to God's law and order. It also emphasizes the point that Abraham was "neither a Jew nor a Christian." Abraham is regarded as a model monotheist whom the Qur'an refers to as "a friend of God" ("khalil Allah"):

> Who can be better
> In religion than one
> Who submits his whole self
> To God, does good,
> And follows the way
> Of Abraham the true in faith?
> For God did take
> Abraham for a friend. (Surah 4: *An-Nisa'*: 125)[17]

Surah 37: *Al-Saffat*: 83 and 84 point out that Abraham approached God with a heart and mind in total accord with the will of the creator and that God recognized and rewarded the faith of Abraham. In his poetry, Muhammad Iqbal—modern Islam's most outstanding poet-philosopher—frequently pictures Abraham as an iconoclast who is shown breaking his father's idols. To Iqbal it is necessary to negate all that is not-God (signified by the "la" in the "la ilaha illa Allah": "There is no god but God" in the Islamic Shahadah or confession of Faith) before God's existence can be affirmed. Iqbal's motif captures the spirit of the Qur'anic epithet "hanif," which refers not only to a belief in the one God but also a complete refusal to associate anything or anyone with God. Abraham is "hanif" precisely because he upheld the oneness and allness of God in the face of all opposition and obstacles.

According to the Qur'an, it is the spirit of Abraham that would enable Muslims (and other believers in God) to become "witnesses for humankind" as stated in Surah 22: *Al-Hajj*: 78:

> And strive hard in God's cause with all the striving that is due to Him: it is He who has elected you (to carry His message), and has laid no hardship on you in (anything that pertains to) religion, (and made you follow) the creed of your forefather Abraham. It is He who has named you—in bygone times as well as in this (divine writ)—"those who have surrendered themselves to God", so that the Apostle might bear witness to truth before you, and that you might bear witness to it before all mankind.[18]

Among the rights given by God to all human beings that are strongly affirmed by the Qur'an, the following may be regarded as particularly pertinent in the context of ethical pluralism:

Right to Life: The Qur'an upholds the sanctity and absolute value of human life and states in Surah 6: *Al-An'am*: 151: "Do not take any human being's life—(the life) which God has declared to be sacred—otherwise than in (the pursuit of) justice: this has He enjoined upon you so that you might use your reason."[19] In Surah 5: *Al-Ma'idah*: 32, the Qur'an points out that, in essence, the life of each individual is comparable to that of an entire community and, therefore, should be treated with the utmost care:

> We ordained
> For the Children of Israel
> That if any one slew
> A person—unless it be
> For murder or for spreading
> Mischief in the land—
> It would be as if
> He slew the whole people:
> And if any one saved a life,
> It would be as if he saved
> The life of the whole people.[20]

Right to Respect: In Surah 17: *Al-Isra'*: 70, the Qur'an says: "Now, indeed, worthy of esteem because of all creation they alone chose to accept the "trust" of freedom of the will (Surah 33: *Al-Ahzab*: 72). Human beings can exercise freedom of the will because they possess the rational faculty, which is what distinguishes them from all other creatures (Surah 2: *Al-Baqarah*: 30–34). Though human beings can become "the lowest of the low," the Qur'an declares that they have been made "in the best of moulds" (Surah 95: *At-Tin*: 4–6), having the ability to think, to have knowledge of right and wrong, to do the good and to avoid the evil. Thus, on account of the promise that is contained in being human, namely, the potential to be God's vicegerent on earth, the humanness of all human beings is to be respected and considered an end in itself.

Right to Freedom: A large part of the Qur'an's concern is to free human beings from the chains that bind them: traditionalism, authoritarianism (religious, political, economic), tribalism, racism, classism or caste system, sexism, and slavery.

The greatest guarantee of personal freedom for a Muslim lies in the Qur'anic decree that no one other than God can limit human freedom

(Surah 42: *Ash-Shura*: 21) and in the statement that "Judgment (as to what is right and what is wrong) rests with God alone" (Surah 12: *Yusuf*: 40).[21] As pointed out by Khalid M. Ishaque, an eminent Pakistani jurist:

> The Qur'an gives to responsible dissent the status of a fundamental right. In exercise of their powers, therefore, neither the legislature nor the executive can demand unquestioning obedience. . . . The Prophet, even though he was the recipient of Divine revelation, was required to consult the Muslims in public affairs. Allah addressing the Prophet says: "and consult with them upon the conduct of affairs. And . . . when thou art resolved, then put thy trust in Allah" (Surah 3: *Al-'Imran*: 159).[22]

The Qur'anic proclamation in Surah 2: *Al-Baqarah*: 256. "There shall be no coercion in matters of faith"[23] guarantees freedom of religion and worship. This means that, according to Qur'anic teaching, non-Muslims living in Muslim territories should have the freedom to follow their own faith-traditions without fear or harassment. A number of Qur'anic passages state clearly that the responsibility of the Prophet Muhammad is to communicate the message of God and not to compel anyone to believe. For instance:

> If it had been God's Plan
> They would not have taken
> False gods: but We
> Made thee not one
> To watch over their doings,
> Nor art thou set
> Over them to dispose
> Of their affairs. (Surah 6: *Al-An=am*: 107)[24]
>
> If it had been thy Lord's will
> They would have all believed,
> All who are on earth!
> Will thou then compel mankind,
> Against their will, to believe? (Surah 10: *Yunus*: 99)[25]
>
> But if they turn away,
> Thy duty is only to preach
> The clear message. (Surah 16: *An-Nahl*: 82)[26]
>
> If then they turn away,
> We have not sent thee
> As a guard over them.
> Their duty is but to convey
> (The Message). (Surah 42: *Ash-Shura*: 48)[27]

The right to exercise free choice in matters of belief is unambiguously endorsed by the Qur'an in Surah 18: *Al-Kahf*: 29, which states:

> The Truth is
> From your Lord:
> Let him who will
> Believe, and let him
> Who will, reject (it).[28]

The Qur'an also makes clear that God will judge human beings not on the basis of what they profess but on the basis of their belief and righteous conduct, as indicated by Surah 2: *Al-Baqarah*: 62 and Surah 5: *Al-Ma'idah*: 69, cited earlier.

The Qur'an recognizes the right to religious freedom not only in the case of other believers in God, but also in the case of nonbelievers in God (if they are not aggressing upon Muslims). For instance, Surah 6: *Al-An'am*: 108 states:

> Revile not ye
> Those whom they call upon
> Besides God, lest
> They out of spite
> Revile God
> In their ignorance.
> Thus have We made
> Alluring to each people
> Its own doings.
> In the end will they
> Return to their Lord,
> And We shall then
> Tell them the truth
> Of all that they did.[29]

In the context of the human right to exercise religious freedom, it is important to mention that the Qur'anic dictum "Let there be no compulsion in religion" applies not only to non-Muslims but also to Muslims. While those who renounced Islam after professing it and then engaged in "acts of war" against Muslims were to be treated as enemies and aggressors, the Qur'an does not prescribe any punishment for non-profession or renunciation of faith. The decision regarding a person's ultimate destiny in the hereafter rests with God.

The right to freedom includes the right to be free to tell the truth. The Qur'anic term for truth is *Haqq*, which is also one of God's most important attributes. Standing up for the truth is a right and a responsibility that a

Muslim may not disclaim even in the face of the greatest danger or difficulty (Surah 4: *An-Nisa'*: 135). While the Qur'an commands believers to testify to the truth, it also instructs society not to harm persons so testifying (Surah 2: *Al-Baqarah*: 282).[30]

The Qur'an regards diversity of peoples as well as religious and ethical perspectives as a part of God's design. In a remarkable passage in which reference is made both to the unity and diversity of humankind, the Qur'an states: "O men! Behold, We have created you all out of a male and a female, and have made you into nations and tribes, so that you might come to know one another. Verily, the noblest of you in the sight of God is the one who is most deeply conscious of Him. Behold, God is all-knowing, all-aware" (Surah 49: *Al-Hujurat*: 13).[31] From this verse it is clear that one of the basic purposes of diversity is to encourage dialogue among different peoples and also that a person's ultimate worth is determined not by what group he or she belongs to but how God-conscious he or she is.

That plurality of religions (and ethical viewpoints) is sanctioned by God is attested by the Qur'an in a number of verses. For example:

> To each is a goal
> To which God turns him;
> Then strive together (as in a race)
> Towards all that is good.
> Wheresoever ye are,
> God will bring you
> Together. For God
> Hath power over all things. (Surah 2: *Al-Baqarah*: 148)[32]

> To each among you
> Have We prescribed a Law
> And an Open Way.
> If God had so willed,
> He would have made you
> A single People, but (His
> Plan is) to test you in what
> He hath given you: so strive
> As in a race in all virtues.
> The goal of you all is to God;
> It is He that will show you
> The truth of the matters
> In which ye dispute. (Surah 5: *Al-Ma'idah*: 51)[33]

> And (know that) all mankind were once but one single community, and only later did they begin to hold divergent views. And had it not been for a decree that had already gone forth from thy Sustainer, all their differences would have been settled (from the outset). (Surah 10: *Yunus*: 19)[34]

The Qur'an advocates gracious conduct and tolerance toward persons who hold different religious and ethical views as a life-attitude. This can be seen clearly from verses such as the following:

> When a (courteous) greeting
> Is offered you, meet it
> With greeting still more
> Courteous, or (at least)
> Of equal courtesy,
> God takes careful account
> Of all things. (Surah 5: *Al-Ma'idah*: 86)[35]

> . . . If the enemy
> Incline towards peace,
> Do thou (also) incline
> Towards peace, and trust
> In God: for He is the One
> That heareth and knoweth
> (All things). (Surah 8: *Al-Anfal*: 61)[36]

> If one amongst the Pagans
> Ask thee for asylum,
> Grant it to him,
> So that he may hear the word
> Of God; and then extort him
> To where he can be secure. (Surah 9: *At-Taubah*: 6)[37]

> Call thou (all mankind) unto thy Sustainer's path with wisdom and goodly exhortation, and argue with them in the most kindly manner: for, behold, thy Sustainer knows best as to who strays from His path, and best knows He as to who are the right-guided. Hence, if you have to respond to an attack (in argument), respond only to the extent of the attack leveled against you; but to bear yourselves with patience is indeed far better for (you, since God is with) those who are patient in adversity. (Surah 16: *An-Nahl*: 125–26)[38]

> And do not argue with the followers of earlier revelation otherwise than in a most kindly manner—unless it be such as are bent on evildoing—and say: "We believe in that which has been bestowed from on high upon us, as well as that which has been bestowed upon you: for our God and your God is one and the same, and it is unto Him that we (all) surrender ourselves." (Surah 29: *Al-'Ankubat*: 46)[39]

The ethical imperative central to Qur'anic teaching and the normative Islamic worldview is to enjoin the good—"*al-mar'uf*"—and forbid the evil—"*al-munkar.*" Within the parameters of this categorical imperative,

Islam is open to accepting and cooperating with any ethical perspective. As pointed out by Fathi Osman in his encyclopedic work, *The Concepts of the Qur'an*, "God is not biased with or against any race, ethnicity, or gender, so His guidance secures absolute justice."[40]

NOTES

1. Fathi Osman, *Concepts of the Qur'an*, 2nd ed. (Los Angeles: MVI, 1999), 23.
2. Muhammad Asad, *The Message of the Qur'an* (Gibraltar: Dar Al-Andalus), 1980.
3. Asad, *Message of the Qur'an*.
4. Asad, *Message of the Qur'an*.
5. Asad, *Message of the Qur'an*.
6. Asad, *Message of the Qur'an*.
7. Asad, *Message of the Qur'an*.
8. Asad, *Message of the Qur'an*.
9. Asad, *Message of the Qur'an*.
10. Asad, *Message of the Qur'an*.
11. Asad, *Message of the Qur'an*.
12. Asad, *Message of the Qur'an*.
13. Asad, *Message of the Qur'an*.
14. Asad, *Message of the Qur'an*.
15. Asad, *Message of the Qur'an*.
16. Asad, *Message of the Qur'an*.
17. 'Abdullah Yusuf 'Ali, *The Holy Qur'an* (Brentwood, Md.: Amana), 1989.
18. Asad, *Message of the Qur'an*.
19. Asad, *Message of the Qur'an*.
20. 'Ali, *The Holy Qur'an*.
21. Asad, *Message of the Qur'an*.
22. Khalid M. Ishaque, "Islamic Law – Its Ideals and Principles," in *The Challenge of Islam*, ed. A. Gauher (London: Islamic Council of Europe, 1980), 157.
23. Asad, *Message of the Qur'an*.
24. 'Ali, *The Holy Qur'an*.
25. 'Ali, *The Holy Qur'an*.
26. 'Ali, *The Holy Qur'an*.
27. 'Ali, *The Holy Qur'an*.
28. 'Ali, *The Holy Qur'an*.
29. 'Ali, *The Holy Qur'an*.
30. G. A. Parwez, "Bunyadi Haquq-e-Insaniyat" [Fundamental Human Rights], *Tulu'-e-Islam* , Lahore, November 1981, pp. 34–35.
31. Asad, *Message of the Qur'an*.
32. 'Ali, *The Holy Qur'an*.
33. 'Ali, *The Holy Qur'an*.
34. Asad, *Message of the Qur'an*.
35. Asad, *Message of the Qur'an*.

36. 'Ali, *The Holy Qur'an*.
37. 'Ali, *The Holy Qur'an*.
38. Asad, *Message of the Qur'an*.
39. Asad, *Message of the Qur'an*.
40. Osman, *Concepts of the Qur'an*.

8

I Am As My Servant Thinks of Me

Theology and Identity in a Plural Society

Rabia Terri Harris

> *bismi Llah ir-rahman ir-rahim:* in the name of God all-compassionate, most merciful

> *As-salamu 'alaykum wa rahmatu Llahi wa barakatuhu:* peace be upon you, and the compassion and blessings of God.

I have taken the title of my chapter from a famous and provocative *hadith qudsi*, or non-Qur'anic, divine saying. I hope you will shortly see why.

I want to talk to you today about stories. So let me tell you one.

Once upon a time there was a little girl who was born into a middle-class East Coast American family, in which Mommy was a nondenominational Christian of the third generation after immigration from Germany and Holland (where people were reportedly originally Lutheran and Catholic), and in which Daddy was a secular agnostic Jew of the second generation after immigration from Latvia and Russia (where nobody had ever heard of different ways of being Jewish, you either were or you weren't, which led to a certain amount of angst by the time his generation arrived). What got Mommy and Daddy together was that they were the luckiest, the liveliest, and the most culturally oriented members of their respective families—and therefore the first members of their families to go to college. And their shared *sensibility* turned out to be far more important than their differences in religion. This homely fact is relevant to our present conversations.

Going to college, alone of all your fellows, changes your horizons. It changes your class. When someone undergoes a pioneering, border-crossing experience, the result is both a new social context and a new mentality. The old mentality simply ceases to fit. If you are the first in your circle to do something significantly new, something transforming, you become different from the people among whom you grew up. You become other than your origins. And the feelings that result from this "othering" may very well open your sympathies and curiosity toward all sorts of human beings who are other than your origins as well. Having crossed a boundary oneself can inspire a fondness for strangers.

That fondness may, however, inspire alarm and distrust, or envy, or defensiveness, or a sense of betrayal, among the old folks at home. *Where are you going? What are you doing? What about our traditions? Isn't your own kind good enough for you?* For people who have never willingly crossed a social boundary, who have never wanted to leave home, for whom home is all the protection there is in this cold, cold world, the notion of *permeability* of boundaries is disorienting and downright scary. For the stranger is intrinsically dangerous, and the fondness for strangers is intrinsically dangerous. Accepting strangers means accepting the unknown—but it is precisely the known that has enabled us to survive thus far. It is only our sense of certainty that grants us a sense of security. Compromise the perimeter of our reality, and you compromise the existence of our world.

There are many more phenomena than merely going to college that produce this sort of opportunity, along with this sort of threat and dislocation. I'll bet you can think of a few. What is important is not the content, but the process—it's the process that tells us what we really need to know. And speaking of processes, let's get back to our little girl.

So here is little Terri (as we call her), eight years old, who gets to celebrate two sets of holidays and gets two sets of presents and who has relatives who obviously come from two different universes—which nonetheless juxtapose matter-of-factly in her mind: she feels all that to be resoundingly normal. Yet she also feels somehow, in some obscure way, that something important is missing from her little life. There's something that ought to be at the center. Then she makes a schoolfriend, appropriately enough named Faith, who starts talking to her about faith—and who persuades Terri to come to her girls' group, at her church. Just don't tell your parents it's about . . . religion.

Cool. Terri's got a secret. And in only a week or two, Terri's a faithful evangelical Baptist. I kid you not. This is a true story.

Man, it felt so good! The fervor, the devotion, the personal relationship to God, the little kiddy fellowship. The sense of martyrdom, too, at appropriate scale: how very gratifying to be risking the displeasure of the world (i.e., Mom and Dad). We were practically meeting in the catacombs, how heroic. And I loved the Bible.

Only, two things stuck in my craw. I just couldn't manage to swallow them, no matter how I tried. One: the time I brought in a picture of a golden Buddha from Thailand, and was told what a shame it was that people should waste their money on something so dreadful. Except that I was the daughter of an artist, and the statue was very beautiful— and therefore, it seemed obvious, well worth having been made.

And Two: the fixed opinion of my teeny colleagues and our teacher that my father, being Jewish, was unfortunately going to Hell.

But why? But why? My father was a good man, he taught me to be honest. Why should God want to send him to Hell? What *kind* of God would send my father to Hell? *Only Christians get to Heaven: Jews and everybody else must go to Hell.* The whole notion was profoundly disturbing. So much so that when my parents finally figured out my little secret, pulled me out of Burlholm Baptist and dropped me promptly into the Girl Scouts, I felt a substantial eight-year-old sense of relief. No more daily moral struggle with the Word of God!

Nonetheless I missed the experience of faith, and of faith community. There was nothing else around that could take their place.

Okay, fast-forward twenty-two years. The drive toward faith being pretty strong, little Terri has been a Muslim for six years already, goes by the name of Rabia, and is still, unbelievably enough, in the honeymoon period. How wonderful Islam is, how perfect, how sublime! How beautifully it joins the ancient noble ethos of Judaism with the melting sweetness of Christian devotional spirituality! (If this sounds a little unfamiliar to some of you, you should know that I got my religion from the Turks.) How small the difficulties it imposes by way of discipline, and how large the vistas it affords! (They were Turkish Sufis, of course.) How all-embracing is this religion, how open-hearted, how universally generous!

So a friend of mine and I, driving to Manhattan, spot a New Jersey neighborhood mosque and pull over to make our ecstatic prayers. The door is open, but nobody's home. We want to greet somebody, so we start wandering around; we find our way into an empty classroom. And there I saw it, written at the top of the blackboard, so that all the eight-year-old kids would get it straight: *Only Muslims will go to Paradise: Christians and Jews will go to Hell.*

Welcome to the real world. It gives one pause. Did I come to Islam for *this?*

I am proposing this little tale as a story about *fitrah,* about the natural inclination toward God—which, in the famous hadith, is the primordial *islam,* the spiritual inheritance of every child: "It is their parents who make them into Jews or Christians or Zoroastrians." Or, as is illustrated here, into Muslims. If that's the way you want to use the word.

And I am making a hermeneutic proposal, which there isn't time here to argue, but which I would like us to think about. What if Muslims were not originally supposed to be another variety of "people of the Book?" What if the distinction the Qur'an makes between Muslims and "people of the Book" is an irreducible one, based on the difference between accepting the vastness of God's mercy in the present, and using our habits to set limits upon God's grace? What if *surrender*, as God uses the term in the Qur'an, is fundamentally a *sensibility*?

Then we might find Muslims anywhere, as well as in the community of Muhammad. And we could find them very simply, and very traditionally, since they would accept both the unity of God and the prophethood of Muhammad. There really need not be anything more to it than that. And it is not so difficult to find such people, if we don't start setting up all kinds of conditions. We aren't called upon to be identical to each other. We are merely called upon to recognize each other.

If we choose not to, we are doomed to live in fear.

"My group is going to Paradise, your group is going to Hell" is nothing but an echo. The original statement was Satan's: *You have created me of fire and him of clay: I am better.* We can seek refuge in God from the accursed Devil only when we stop confusing the two. *And the Devil promises only to deceive.*

I want to close with another true story, this one a hadith. Strangely, you don't hear this hadith quoted an awful lot, but it is in Sahih Muslim. I will tell it a little freely.

It seems that in Madinah, a Muslim got into a dispute in the marketplace with a Jew. "Yes, by Him who made Moses the best of humanity!" swore the Jew.

The Muslim was incensed. "How can you say that," he exclaimed, "when Muhammad is here among us?" And he hit him!

The Jew took his assailant before the Prophet. "Abul-Qasim," he said, "am I not protected here? And see what your follower has done!"

The Prophet became angry, which was as notable as it was rare. "How could you do such a thing?" he reproved the Muslim. "Don't you know that the prophets are all equal, and that none is less than any of the others? I would not make such a claim even about Jonah. As for Moses, when I rise on the Day of Judgment I will find him already awake, and I won't know whether he rose before me or whether he used up all his unconsciousness in his swoon on Sinai!" And he awarded damages to the Jew.

End of story. Several conclusions may be drawn. First, although the Muslim in his impulsiveness acted at least partly out of love, he was still wrong. Respect for the other has priority: that is the sunnah of the Prophet. Second, the justice of Madinah was such that a Jew did not hesitate to complain against a Muslim before the leader of the Muslims, and won his case: that is the social achievement of the Prophet. And third, the refusal to claim spiritual superiority demonstrated here: that is *in itself* the spiritual superiority of the Prophet.

One might also make a point about the usefulness of stories. All knowledge grows out of experience, and all experience is personal. What is knowable depends upon the knower: it is the knower himself, or herself, who must first be known, in order for that knowledge to be of use.

Theological thinking that removes the dimension of individuality thereby removes itself from reality, obscuring the forces that drive and inform it: it becomes a sort of hocus-pocus idol-worship. As in *The Wizard of Oz*, we are urged to look at the fearsome huge fiery head, but "Pay no attention to the man behind the curtain!" Yet the little guy behind the curtain is much more genuine than the big impressive special effect. And only he (or she) can really solve our problem.

We will meet each other only when we are ready to meet each other—which is when we ourselves are ready to be met. Then the concealing curtain, our protecting boundary, will not have to be defended anymore. And the appropriate theology will arise.

Stories are leveling, they are intimate, they are self-revealing, they teach us in a manner that is deeper than argumentation. Muslims have so many good ones to share. We should tell more of them.

A year has passed, and my colleagues tell me there is more to be said. "This story is too personal: open it up!" "Tell us other dimensions of this story!" "Tell us the *moral* of this story!" I suspect they are embarrassed for me because my piece is by far the shortest in this excellent book. That is the right length for bedtime stories; I was hoping it might also be an acceptable length for waking-up stories. But then again, perhaps not. So Reader, permit me to let you in on why I wrote what I have written here.

But first, let me suggest to you a series of thought experiments.

- Candidly tell yourself your own faith story. How did you come to believe what you believe? Was it all serene, or were there crises and struggles? If so, did they resolve? How is that resolution working for you now? If they did not resolve, how does your continuing struggle affect you?
- What is most precious to you about what you believe?
- What aspect of what you believe makes you feel most vulnerable?
- Suppose that part of what you believe turns out to be wrong. What happens?

- Imagine yourself belonging to another religion. Then imagine yourself belonging to another religion. Then imagine yourself belonging to another religion. What happens?
- Imagine yourself without any religion. What happens?
- Remember yourself as a little child. See all the people you are most afraid of as little children. See yourselves playing together. What happens? Now all of you are adults again.
- Imagine us all accepting each other *exactly the way we are*.

People have different reactions to these sorts of exercises. Some people find them entertaining, some interesting or enlightening, some frightening or offensive, and some merely stupid. Such reactions reflect differences in sensibility, defined as "awareness and responsiveness toward something." Our sensibility determines how we engage life, and how we retreat from it. It determines how smoothly we interact with other people as well as how comfortable we are in our own skins. It is conditioned by the basic assumptions we make about the nature of things, yet is potentially independent of them. I am suggesting in this chapter that sensibility is more fundamental than belief. And I am also suggesting that the deepest spiritual work before us does not concern belief but sensibility.

One of the great tools we have been given for extending and strengthening our sensibility is the power of empathic imagination: "Suppose" or "What if . . ." or "Once upon a time." What this tool does is to take away the heavy inevitability of our own experience, the ordinariness of it, by arraying before us not just one path but multitudes of branching paths. And once we realize the arbitrariness and singularity of our own way of being, two things happen—if all goes well. First, we realize that we have choices, where we thought we had none. And second, the path that we find ourselves following becomes strange and marvelous: the everyday empties into awe. Empathic imagination opens the gate of possibilities, which makes the world infinitely larger. At the right moment, the discovery of *normal infinity* constitutes a spiritual liberation. It is good to feel welcome in a universe that is its own natural size.

Some people, though, feel very uncomfortable in an infinite universe. They want a little secure one where they know what is going on. That feels like a survival issue, and sometimes it is—for if one does not feel welcomed, one feels threatened. People in such circumstances distrust the power of imagination, for it brings into the intimate space of the private mind the very threat that is most feared outside. Empathic imagination challenges our rightness. So threatened people want only one story, the "true" story, the story within which they feel justified and safe. Get your other lying stories out of here!

What we begin to recognize, though, is that there no longer exists any place where our stories will not encounter one another. There is no little secure universe to be found anymore. Only God knows what the future may bring—but my bet is that, no matter what the uproar, we will never again see a successful "Christian nation" or "Islamic state." There is only Planet Earth. And if Planet Earth is going to be livable for everyone, then we must learn how to hear each other's stories without feeling threatened by them. We must learn how to tell our own without posing a threat. We do not need to change our various beliefs. We need to raise the level of our sensibility.

What is important, it seems to me, is not whether there is only one way to God. What is important is how zealous we are about it.

Wars are not fought against persons: wars are fought against nonpersons. Suppose a great many of us refused to be other than persons, refused to see other than persons. These games we play are growing very tiresome, are they not? Couldn't we play something else?

Here, let me take the first step. I will just be myself, in your presence. And I am ready to listen. Will you tell me your story? No, I mean your *real* story?

The personal voice is a perilous voice. If I open myself up to you, who knows what might happen to me! Perhaps you might attack me or deride me. Perhaps I might lose my authority. Many of us *de*personalize our voices—speak abstractly, from outside ourselves, ex cathedra—in order to produce an impression of authority. But suppose we were to lose interest in that kind of authority. What happens?

Welcome. And Allah knows best.

9

Response to Hassan's "The Qur'anic Perspective on Religious Pluralism" and Harris's "I Am As My Servant Thinks of Me"

Wilbert R. Shenk

DR. RIFFAT HASSAN, "THE QUR'ANIC PERSPECTIVE ON RELIGIOUS PLURALISM"

Dr. Riffat Hassan's study of religious pluralism from the perspective of the Qur'an is most welcome. The presentation is clearly structured around the premise that the "cardinal principle of Islam" is that God is one. This fundamental monotheistic view, shared with Jews and Christians, affirms that God is God of all creation and all people. As Creator of all that is, God has compassion on all. This axiom is then developed and supported relative to religious pluralism through appeal to ten Qur'anic affirmations:

1. The message of the Qur'an about God and the world is universal.
2. The Qur'an makes clear that the mission of the Prophet of Islam is universal.
3. The Qur'an affirms that there are diverse ways to faith—Jews, Christians, and Sabians being mentioned specifically—but none can claim to be the exclusive way.
4. The Qur'an commands all Muslims to recognize the divine message of all previous prophets.
5. The Qur'an requires Muslims to recognize the continuity of Islam with previous prophets and revelations, making no distinction among them.

6. The Prophet Abraham holds special significance as the symbol of the unity of all believers. Abraham is the first Muslim inasmuch as he is a model of one who surrenders his entire self to God; he is a friend of God, the exemplary monotheist who cannot be claimed by one or the other varieties of monotheism.
7. God has bestowed certain rights on all humankind. These include the right to:
    - Life
    - Respect
    - Freedom, including the freedom to believe according to the dictates of conscience. This specifically disallows "compulsion in religion." Freedom means the right to tell the truth.
8. The Qur'an depicts religious and cultural diversity to be a part of God's design, that is, in regard to both religious and ethical aspects.
9. The Qur'an enjoins gracious treatment and tolerance toward those who hold different religioethical views.
10. The central ethical imperative of Qur'anic teaching is to uphold the good and reject the evil.

Although we can find parallel statements of most of these affirmations in the Hebrew and Christian scriptures, the Qur'an makes these statements with admirable forthrightness and clarity.

We immediately recognize that we are all subject to the tendency to read selectively. We see what we wish to see. Those wishing to demonstrate a particular point of view find the support needed to demonstrate that the scriptures do indeed support that view. Others preoccupied with another view can comb through the scriptures and find passages that support their contention.

In light of this observation, a threefold hermeneutical challenge is presented. First, as Dr. Hassan has demonstrated, the positive teaching of the Qur'an on the theme of religious pluralism deserves to be given full play. This view that contrasts with what appears generally in the media is hardly known. Second, in the Hebrew and Christian scriptures there is interplay between the universal and the particular so that one must work with both dimensions in arriving at a satisfactory interpretation. We need to pay close attention to the way the Islamic tradition works with this dialectic. Third, the message that God is the Creator of all, including religiocultural diversity, needs to be disseminated in the wider religious community, allowing it to leaven and temper the popular understanding.

Dr. Hassan has placed before us an urgent and promising agenda.

RABIA TERRI HARRIS, "I AM AS MY SERVANT THINKS OF ME"

In a spirit of openness and vulnerability, Rabia Terri Harris (a) uses her personal story to disclose who she is and (b) thereby challenges all of us to drop our camouflages and become honest with others. The implied criticism, and one that is irrefutable, is that we hold others at arm's length so that we are less than honest with them and ourselves.

As this presentation reminds us, story is powerful, disarming, life-giving, and life-threatening. We cannot know in advance the outcome of a story. Story unmasks our true humanity provided we are able to be vulnerable—that is, without pretense and defensiveness.

In today's world we seem to be losing our capacity to tell our own stories. We are being force-fed on many stories contrived for us by movies and television. The slick and powerful media intimidate us. Our own stories seem pallid and uninteresting by contrast. We become passive consumers of the stories fed to us in great quantity by others. This process can both diminish us and distort our judgment. Much of what is on offer reinforces negative and destructive values. The mission of the media is not to inculcate a vision of truth, beauty, compassion, justice, and respect. They answer to another demand and that is to show the investors a healthy profit.

Rabia Terri Harris is on to something. We each need to recover our story and the ability to tell it if we are to encounter the other in an attitude of expectant openness and empathetic respect.

10

Social Location and Christian Identity

Some Historical Perspectives

Wilbert R. Shenk and Alvin C. Dueck

Précis: Over a period of nearly two millennia, Christianity has been situated in diverse cultures. It is instructive to consider how Christians have renegotiated their identity in response to these diverse contexts. At times this has resulted in outcomes inconsistent with core Christian convictions. At other times this has moved Christian identity closer to its convictional core. What is to be appreciated is the dynamic interplay between core Christian convictions and social location. Of particular interest is the way Christian interaction with people of other faiths has been shaped by these dynamics.

This essay is a lament, an apology born of deep embarrassment and guilt. For more than a millennium Christianity has justified crusades against the Turk, the Muslim, and the Arab, all in the name of religion. Nations are aligned on an axis of evil. It appears our presence in Iraq is only one more example of spreading the "gospel," this time of Western democracy. This chapter traces the history of the collusion of religion and the sword that begins with Constantine and continues with modern religious empires. Augustine dealt with heretical Donatists in the fifth century CE using the power of the state. In so doing, Christianity was made into a religion to be universalized using the power of the sword when deemed necessary. No longer is it critical to listen to the religious stranger, to learn from the other in peaceful dialogue. A universal rationality would be the ligament that holds together disparate groups. The dark side of modernity is its failure to truly recognize difference, to celebrate otherness.

The thrust of modernity has been toward universality, sure foundations, and a common human nature. While the roots of this modern paradigm reach back to Platonic idealism, it has been articulated most clearly in the past five hundred years. The recovery of the significance of particularity is a fruit of the transition to postmodernity. This particularity derives from a sense of the "social location," that is, the historical, class, and economic influences that shape each individual's identity.

Social location determines a group's sense of power vis-à-vis other groups. The less powerful quickly learn that their survival depends on how they position themselves in relation to the more powerful. But power differentials do not have to be interpreted as a zero-sum game. Jesus the Messiah deliberately chose to operate from the margin of society but always in dialectical tension with the power structures of his day. The understanding that one's social location and vision of power influences construal of the world, the other, and one's own religious tradition opens the way to greater confessional dialogue between traditions.

This essay argues that as social location changes a group's sense of identity and the nature of peaceful dialogue between religious traditions are redefined. It explores the affirmation of social location in the early church as a contrast society, its demise beginning with Constantine, its reaffirmation in the sixteenth-century Radical Reformation, the confusion that resulted from association with modern religious expansionism and colonialism, and finally resurgent commitment in various forms of postmodern confessionalism. We recognize that western Christian sensibility has been largely uncritical of the coercive universalizing thrust of Christendom and now American imperialism.

IDENTITY AND THE CHRISTIAN COMMUNITY IN THE FIRST THREE CENTURIES AFTER JESUS CHRIST

The movement that formed around Jesus the Messiah some two thousand years ago initially was composed largely of people from the Galilee region, the political and social hinterland of Judaism. To be called a "Galilean" was no compliment, as Simon Peter was reminded at the time of the arrest of Jesus (Mark 14:70). The Jewish establishment viewed the Galileans with disdain while the Galileans did not conceal their mistrust of the Pharisees, Sadducees, scribes, and publicans. Added to this was the fact that the Romans controlled Palestine. As is characteristic of occupying powers, the Roman proconsuls were continually on their guard against insurgent elements that might threaten their power. Thus, this new religious movement that formed around Jesus faced a double jeopardy. From the Jewish viewpoint it was a renegade group that insisted on reinterpreting the tradition.

This new messianic movement mounted a strong critique of the religious status quo by appealing to the prophetic tradition of the Hebrew Prophets, thereby challenging the authority of the Jewish religious establishment. For the Romans this was a dissident element that potentially could foment an insurrection among an already restive people.

Yet the movement that grew out of the ministry of Jesus the Messiah refused to follow the model of a conventional revolution. Jesus and his followers rejected the usual political solution that involved seizing control by using military power. Jesus did not reject power per se. Rather he demonstrated that coercive power is not redemptive and cannot have the last word.[1] It is in this sense that Jesus maintained the stance of one who remained on the periphery of the system and carried out his mission as a Galilean. These were the sociopolitical conditions that defined the context and social location within which the New Testament scriptures were written and formed the patterns of worship and discipleship for Christians.

It is instructive to recall that the early Christians used the Sermon on the Mount (Gospel of Matthew 5–7) as the catechism to prepare prospective adherents for baptism. The Sermon on the Mount sets forth the essential teaching of Jesus and the ethic by which the disciple community is to live in the world. In a modern Christian classic, *The Cost of Discipleship*, Dietrich Bonhoeffer organized his exposition around the Sermon on the Mount. For Bonhoeffer, "The passion of Christ is the victory of divine love over the powers of evil, and therefore it is the only supportable basis for Christian obedience."[2] This ethic became problematic for Christians after the fourth century CE for reasons that will be set forth below.

The thrust of Matthew's Gospel is that the disciples of Jesus comprise a community that presents a contrast to the rest of society.[3] Their social location was then clear and circumscribed. The disciples were instructed to live fully in the world without being controlled by the worldview assumptions that governed the life of society. A key test was how the disciples of Jesus used power. Jesus rejected resort to lethal force to maim or to kill another. Instead Jesus set a new standard based on nonretaliation, love of enemy, transparency in relationships, and compassion. Discipleship was to be proactive. The disciple was instructed to be present in the culture as salt, light, and leaven. Disciples were mandated to be agents of transformation in a social order that did not measure up to God's ideal.[4] Their relationships with persons of other religious and political persuasions were to be characterized by peace as exemplified by Jesus' engagement with the Syrophonecian women, the Samaritans, and the Romans.

It is instructive to note how the first several generations of the Christian community regarded those who indicated interest in becoming disciples of Jesus. Scholars have remarked on the caution that these local groups exercised toward inquirers and those who expressed interest.[5] No effort was made to sweep as many people as possible into the Christian community. Instead they had to be on their guard against infiltrators with ulterior motives who possibly intended to do harm. Consequently, the church soon adopted rigorous and protracted procedures for preparing prospective members for initiation into the community. The individual seeking membership had to give evidence of having experienced a profound change from the old way of life that was now evident in terms of belief, behavior, and belonging.[6] The catechetical process could last as long as two years in order to test the sincerity and depth of understanding of the candidate for baptism. Sponsors who knew the candidate well had to attest that the person's behavior was exemplary. Christian identity involved giving up the social and economic distinctions used by the wider society to separate classes of people. The true test of being a disciple of Jesus was that conventional "dividing walls" had indeed been removed. The new community created in response to the Lordship of Jesus the Messiah constituted a new culture in which socially approved class distinctions were displaced. In the first three centuries, social location and Christian identity are synonymous.

THE RISE OF CHRISTENDOM IN THE FOURTH CENTURY

Historians are generally agreed that by the third century CE the Christian identity was evolving. The primitive focus and fervor were waning, preparing the way for a substantive redefinition of Christian self-understanding in the fourth century CE.[7] Symbolically, this decisive shift is linked to actions taken by Emperor Constantine early in the fourth century, starting with the issuing of the Edict of Milan in 313 CE in which he not only extended toleration to Christians but also baptized conquered peoples. A change in social location resulted in radical redefinition of identity. By the end of the century, under Emperor Theodosius I, Christianity had become the official religion of the Roman Empire. In a relatively short time the Christian movement went from being a marginal and persecuted people to the religious group that now participated in official power and privilege. Indeed, when the Roman Empire collapsed at the end of the fifth century the Church assumed critical governing functions. Inevitably, given this decisive shift in social location, Christian identity underwent profound change, the impact of which would be felt for the next 1,500 years. Christendom as the new empire presaged the modern drive for homogeneity, the vitiation of difference, and the refusal to affirm radical otherness.

Summarizing the way Christianity spread in the post-Constantinian period—for it was now in the interest of the state to extend the influence of Christianity—Ramsay MacMullen offers three observations: (1) since people did not convert willingly coercion was used; (2) conversion was less than complete; and (3) as a result, growth of the Church resulted in its reassimilation into the larger culture.[8] In other words, the Church was now fundamentally compromised. The elites of society were members of the Church, and Church leaders depended on members of this social class to bring the lower classes into the Church, authorizing them to use forceful means if necessary to compel their slaves, employees, and the peasants around them to become Christians. Although it is reported that the Church grew considerably between the fourth and eighth centuries, this *forced* growth came at a price, for the Church increasingly tolerated the pagan beliefs and practices of the masses. The Gospel is a message of God's grace freely extended to all; it is a contradiction of that grace whenever people are compelled to accept God's gift. Christendom was a system based on coercion. The new Church–state alliance required that every citizen be enrolled as a member of the Church, regardless of personal disposition, for the Church played a critical role in maintaining the sociopolitical order. All of this presents a striking contrast with the first three centuries as to who came into the Church and the requirements made of new adherents.

These fourth-century developments became the foundation of what emerged as Christendom. Church and state were linked together and exercised joint control over a whole territory. It also entailed other decisive changes. The way the Christian scriptures were read, the meaning of personal identity, and the development of theology all reflected the radically changed social location of the Church. For the next fifteen hundred years, the church of Christendom would struggle with the problem of the nominal faith of its members. Membership in the Church was now equivalent to citizenship in the nation. To be sure, there always was a select group deeply committed to Christian discipleship, but ordinary members were not expected to achieve this standard. The result was a compromised two-tiered membership: the religious (i.e., members of religious orders) and the masses.

The socio-politico-religious synthesis described above as Christendom was, in fact, not new. Rather it was the conventional model of government for human societies. The struggle between this conventional model and the prophetic alternative unfolds in the life of ancient Israel during the time of the prophet Samuel. The Book of Judges ends on this despairing note: "In those days there was no king in Israel; all the people did what was right in their own eyes" (Judges 21:25). Joshua, successor to Moses, instituted the system of judges; but over time the judges had become corrupt and order broke down. The prophet Samuel worked to restore Israel to their covenant relationship with God. Yet Samuel's sons, whom he had appointed to be judges, were as corrupt as all the others.

The council of elders confronted the aged Samuel and demanded that he appoint "a king to govern us, like other nations" (1 Samuel 8:5). Samuel was deeply grieved by their demand and poured out his disappointment before God. God told Samuel, "Listen to the voice of the people . . . they have not rejected you, but they have rejected me from being king over them" (1 Samuel 8:7). Samuel then reported to the people of Israel that their wish would be granted. But he also warned them about "the ways of the king who will reign over" them (1 Samuel 8:10c), for the king of Israel would be like other rulers, exploiting and oppressing the people by laying on heavy taxes, conscripting their young men for military service, and forcing the people to work for him in slave-like conditions.

This is the background out of which the prophetic tradition emerges in ancient Israel. The prophets of the Old Testament engage in sustained critique of both rulers and people, while continually reminding them of their covenant responsibility to God. The prophets kept alive the vision of God's righteousness/justice expressed through the jubilee laws, the divine promise of the peaceable kingdom, and the new order that would be inaugurated when God's messiah came. In his life and ministry, Jesus the Messiah identified with this prophetic tradition.

To repeat: Christendom is not unique; it may be compared with other historical examples of the synthesis of a religion and a culture: inter alia Hinduism, Buddhism, Judaism, and Islam. Marshall G. S. Hodgson argued that "to separate out religion from the rest of life is partly to falsify it."[9] Hodgson held that it is not correct to say that "Islamic culture" is fully Islamic in the sense of a culture that is wholly shaped by a religious vision. At best it represents an amalgam of religion and culture. The same historical observation can be made about "Christian culture."

Hodgson uses the term *Islamdom* in parallel with Christendom. "Islamdom, then, is the society in which the Muslims and their faith are recognized as prevalent and socially dominant, in one sense or another—a society in which, of course, non-Muslims have always formed an integral, if subordinate, element, as have Jews in Christendom."[10] The emphasis is not so much on a particular territory as the dominant socioreligious arrangement. The history of minority groups vis-à-vis established religions has varied greatly. In the modern period, with the emergence of constitutions that guarantee religious freedom, these relationships have taken on quite a new character.

What we must recall is that historical Christendom has always existed in tension with the prophetic tradition that reached its climax in the witness of Jesus the Messiah. The fundamental compromises made by the Christian church in order to enjoy official favor are not trifling for we continue to struggle with the persistent influence of these decisions.

CONSEQUENCES OF HISTORICAL CHRISTENDOM

Prior to the Constantinian era, the Roman Empire had been alive with religious diversity. An evidence of the presence of varieties of religion in the Roman Empire is reflected in the encounter of the Apostle Paul with the Athenian philosophers (Acts 17:16-23). But after the formation of Christendom, and the temporal extension of its sway, the hierarchy became increasingly concerned to eliminate the religious *others*. Whereas in the earliest centuries the Church Fathers had discussed the matter of the relationship between Christianity and other religions, over time theologians increasingly focused their energies on internal concerns and doctrinal matters but had little to say about relations with other faiths. This issue largely drops off the theological agenda.

A noteworthy exception to the above narrative is the fact that several Muslim scholars during the ninth to twelfth centuries wrote studies of other faiths. Tabarī (838–923) wrote a book about the Persian religion; Mas'udī (d. 956) studied Judaism, Christianity, and Indian religions, while Alberūnī (973–c. 1050) wrote on religion in India and Persia. Abū Muhammad ibn Hazim (994–1064), theologian and litterateur, wrote a five-volume study of religious beliefs of the Skeptics, Peripatetics, Brahmins, Zoroastrians, Christians, and Jews. Shahrastūnī (d. 1153) produced a study of religion in world literature. This book, *Religious Parties and Schools of Philosophy*, presents a systematic account of the religions of the known world, extending as far as China.[11]

But from the side of Christians between the eleventh and fourteenth centuries the atmosphere was poisoned by the Crusades, a logical extension of Christendom. The closest we come to a work by a Christian scholar devoted to the study of religions during this period is the typology of religions produced by the Franciscan, Roger Bacon, in the thirteenth century. Since his work was not published until 467 years later, it did not contribute to the development of a body of knowledge of religions. Only occasionally did a Christian advocate take a positive interest in other religions. In 1411 Peter the Venerable arranged for a translation of the Qur'an with a view toward developing a sympathetic understanding of Islam.

The year 1492 marks the point at which Christendom seemed to have achieved its goal of absolute control of European territory. That year Spain expelled the Moors and the Jews from its territory. But this also marks the beginning of the dissolution of Christendom, a process that would play itself out over several hundred years. The Protestant Reformation was an important contributor to this process for it led to the adoption of the principle *cuius regio, eius religio* (the religion of the prince is the religion of the people). While on the surface this seemed to be a way of perpetuating the

Christendom pattern, it was in fact the beginning of a gradual breakdown of Christendom.

Christendom's long-lasting legacy may be summarized in terms of three observations. First, in view of the way Christianity was redefined as a territorially based religion with exclusive rights to control the entire population in the post-Constantinian period, the vast majority of Europeans were increasingly cut off from contact with people of other religious faiths until the twentieth century. Only those who traveled abroad had opportunity to encounter other cultures, languages, and faiths. Second, in view of this ecclesiastical and political environment it is perhaps understandable that few Christian theologians paid attention to the other faiths in their writings. Finally, in the nineteenth century the comparative study of religion was established as an academic discipline and Christian theologians began to work with the questions of interreligious encounter within the modern Enlightenment framework. Modernity had no place for the nonempirical and consigned religion to the personal and subjective realm. It assumed that modern rationality, ultimately, would cause all religion to disappear. Modernity treated religions reductionistically by arguing that fundamentally all were of a single essence.

THE SIXTEENTH-CENTURY REFORMATION AND SECULARIZATION

The Protestant Reformation was ostensibly concerned with religious matters but its impact was equally great in terms of politics. The major Protestant reformers did not anticipate driving a wedge between Church and state. They assumed this relationship to be normative. But their challenge to the Roman Catholic Church inevitably undermined the structures of Christendom. The Reformation gave impetus to secularization by establishing the principle that German princes in their regional principalities could decide whether they would remain loyal to Rome or to Martin Luther. Luther was no match for the pope when it came to politics. The church was now effectively left out of this fundamental decision. The will of the prince determined which variety of Christianity his subjects would embrace. As political loyalty changes, so does one's sense of identity.

It was the Radical Reformation, however, that pressed the point further. This group idealized the pre-Constantinian Church and took this as the model for reform of the church. Against both the Protestant Reformers and the Roman Catholic Church, the Radical Reformers argued for the separation of church and state. They contended that the church should not be subject to state control. The church was answerable to Jesus Christ its head and not to a government. Infant baptism, which they rejected, had sealed the individual's relationship with Christendom. Seeking to follow the teachings of Jesus alone, including his prophetic critique of power, the radical pluralism of the Anabaptists created the possibility that identity could be shaped by a socially particular location, the church. Catholic and Protestant leaders alike opposed the Radical Reformers, leading to the death of thousands at the hands of Church and state in the sixteenth century.

The witness of the Radical Reformation proved to be prophetic.[12] First, the Radical Reformers insisted that authentic discipleship depends on a voluntary response. A coerced obedience is mere compliance and does not lead to transformation of the will. Second, discipleship calls forth personal responsibility. The priesthood of all believers means that every member has responsibility for the whole body.[13] Third, this alternative vision has given rise to a movement variously called free, nonconformist, or believers' church.[14] The free church vision became the model for Protestants in the United States so far as the relationship between Church and state was concerned. By the same token churches established outside the West as a result of the modern mission movement have all been free churches. By calling for the desacralization of the institutions of society, the way was opened for the secularization of structures and institutions and a pluralism that could create a context for a more genuine dialogue with other religious traditions.

During the seventeenth and eighteenth centuries Enlightenment thinkers developed new political theory based on the dignity of the person and the concept of individual "rights" conferred by God in the creation of humankind. In the American and French development of this political theory in the late eighteenth century, the power of the state derived from the will of the people and, as such, was limited, not absolute.

The Western experience can be described in terms of the transformation of culture in three main fields: (1) the economic, (2) the intellectual, and (3) the social.[15] The modern economy greatly increased productivity based on techniques. This enabled the Industrial and Agricultural Revolutions without which modernization could not have been sustained. Intellectual horizons were greatly altered through the development of experimental science that resulted in continually expanding our understanding of time and space. In the social realm old landed privileges were broken down and in their place bourgeois financial power emerged. This opened the way for a revolution in political theory embodied in the American and French Revolutions. These theoretical changes took place in the space of the seventeenth and eighteenth centuries, but over the past two centuries nations around the world have been confronted with the challenge democracy poses to other forms of government.

MODERN POLITICAL THEORY

One of the most important innovations in the modern period has been the separation of church and state. As a consequence, religious affiliation no longer confers social, economic, or professional advantage.[16] The individual's citizenship says nothing about religious affiliation. But it must be pointed out that implementation of this principle in many different societies has not followed a fixed pattern and it is useful to reflect on these developments.[17] The resulting models have been theorized in terms of two axes: (1) *the rigidity or flexibility of a situation* (i.e., from rigid to flexible) and (2) *the range of religious positions in a society* (i.e., from monopolistic to competitive). Four main patterns have emerged from the increasing political secularization over the past several centuries around the world.

1. **monopolistic, flexible**—Example: France: The Roman Catholic Church has been the dominant religion but minority religions are tolerated and the Catholic Church does not enjoy state patronage.
2. **competitive, flexible**—Example: United States: historically, three groups have been dominant: Protestants, Catholics, and Jews. But there has been no state control over any of these groups and as new groups have arisen in the United States they have been accorded the same rights as other religions.
3. **competitive, rigid**—Example: The Netherlands and Lebanon: these societies have been religiously columnized or compartmentalized along religious lines. They operate in the political realm as religious parties.
4. **monopolistic, rigid**—Example: Spain and Portugal.[18] The Roman Catholic Church is a dominant force and non-Catholics are put in categories that disadvantage them.

In addition, the attitude of government toward religion further determines how religious groups relate to the wider society. Three stances can be identified:

1. **Maintaining** (United States) means that the government takes a positive interest in religion. The relationship between Church and state is dynamic and evolving both in terms of laws and policies.
2. **Neutral** (Japan) denotes the situation where the government follows a "hands-off" policy.
3. **Constraining** (China), that is, the government actively regulates all religious groups.

Regardless of the particular political arrangements that have been adopted by modern states, all have been informed by Enlightenment ideals: universality, rationality, autonomy of the self, and empiricism. Beliefs based on Enlightenment ideals were a part of public discourse, but values, including religious convictions, were regarded as matters of private opinion and were disallowed in the public square. Proponents of Enlightenment concepts were committed to spreading their ideas. When the modern Christian missionary movement was launched, Enlightenment thought had already been widely embraced by Western society. Christian missions, influenced both by the Christendom tradition and Enlightenment ideals, played a role in the spread of Western influence and control during the period of imperialism and colonialism. Later it was recognized that this had been a mistake. The poet T. S. Eliot captured well the ambiguity of this venture:

> When your fathers fixed the place of GOD,
> And settled all the inconvenient saints,
> Apostles, martyrs, in a kind of Whipsnade,
> Then they could set about imperial expansion
> Accompanied by industrial development.
> Exporting iron, coal and cotton goods
> And intellectual enlightenment
> And everything, including capital
> And several versions of the Word of GOD:
> The British race assured of a mission
> Performed it, but left much at home unsure.[19]

In the twentieth century systems of government have been subjected to many tests due to increasing demands for democracy, intensified nationalism, the dignity of the individual, the impact of globalization, and threats that imperil the whole world community. Modern industrial societies have been characterized by great social mobility. The social embeddedness that characterized the individual in traditional society has been replaced by the demand for autonomy. From the standpoint of Christian faith one's identity should not be divided between public and private. Consequently, modernity has posed a major challenge to Christian identity.

SOCIAL LOCATION IN POSTMODERN CULTURE

For the past generation we have been preoccupied with a new set of questions. This is spoken of as the *postmodern* period. The Enlightenment vision and its foundational claims are being subjected to close interrogation. For example, the Enlightenment asserted the possibility of arriving at universal laws, or principles, applicable to all peoples everywhere. As a consequence, historical particularity and context were set aside. Postmodernity insists on retrieving the particular, the unique, and otherness.[20] There is growing awareness of the fact that we cannot understand other people without appreciating their social location and understanding historical, cultural, and religious differences. This opens up new space for conversation between people representing different traditions.

Postmodernity has brought other changes that are redefining the meaning of social location. Traditional and modern societies assumed that the values and character of a culture were shaped by "high" or "classical" culture that trickled down, permeating folk or popular culture. Today popular culture, driven to a large extent by its appeal to young people, has become the dominant cultural stream. Here cultural variety is valued and spirituality is affirmed. Popular culture has gained this defining role in part by the way the global economy has skillfully exploited the youth culture in terms of music, movies, and clothes that appeal to young people all over the world. Social location in postmodernity is increasingly determined by generational difference—Generation X, Millennials, and so on—rather than by social class. Blue jeans are the symbol par excellence of popular culture. Regardless of economic status, young people around the globe regard blue jeans as theirs.

The affirmation of pluralism, tradition, and particularity affords the postmodern person the possibility to speak out of his or her unique tradition in a confessional way. The assumption that there are no universal narratives, as purported by modernity, which supplant the particular narratives, means that Christians and Muslims can speak from their traditions with new freedom. A peaceable posture affirms difference, is open to the wisdom of the other, and refuses to violently demand the other must conform to my tradition.

NOTES

1. See John Howard Yoder, *The Politics of Jesus* (Grand Rapids, Mich.: Eerdmans, 1972; 2nd ed., 1994), for a redefinition of politics based on the messianic vision of Jesus.

2. Dietrich Bonhoeffer, *The Cost of Discipleship* (New York: Macmillan, 1949), 125.

3. Gerhard Lohfink, *Jesus and Community: The Social Dimension of Christian Faith*, trans. John P. Galvin (Philadelphia: Paulist, 1984).

4. Glen H. Stassen and David P. Gushee, *Kingdom Ethics: Following Jesus in Contemporary Context* (Downers Grove, Ill.: InterVarsity Press, 2003) develop an ethical vision based on this premise.

5. Alan Kreider, *Worship and Evangelism in Pre-Christendom* (Cambridge: Grove Books, 1995).

6. Alan Kreider, *The Change of Conversion and the Origin of Christendom* (Harrisburg, Penn.: Trinity, 1999), chap. 1.

7. Many historians have discussed this shift. See the judicious summary by Kenneth Scott Latourette, *A History of Christianity* (New York: Harper, 1953), 184–85. For a multifaceted study of the creation of Christendom and its effects on the faith and life of the church see Alan Kreider, ed., *The Origins of Christendom in the West* (Edinburgh: T. and T. Clark, 2001).

8. Ramsay MacMullen, "Christianity Shaped through Its Mission," in *Origins of Christendom*, ed. Alan Kreider (Edinburgh: T. and T. Clark, 2001), 97–117.

9. Marshall G. S. Hodgson, *The Venture of Islam*, vol. 1 (Chicago: University of Chicago Press, 1974), 57.

10. Hodgson, *The Venture of Islam*, 58.

11. Eric J. Sharpe, *Comparative Religion: A History*, 2nd ed. (LaSalle, Ill.: Open Court, 1986), 11.

12. Harold S. Bender, *The Anabaptists and Religious Liberty in the 16th Century* (Philadelphia: Fortress, 1970; reprint of essay first published in 1953).

13. Frequently, it has been pointed out that Martin Luther called for this emphasis early in the Reformation, but, ultimately, he concluded it set the bar too high and was unrealistic. The Radical Reformers insisted that it was integral to their ecclesiology.

14. Since the 1960s the term generally used is *believers' church*. See Donald F. Durnbaugh, *The Believers' Church: The History and Character of Radical Protestantism* (New York: Macmillan, 1968) for an interpretation of this ecclesial stream.

15. Hodgson, *The Venture of Islam*, vol. 3, 179.

16. Various studies have been made of the impact of the "democratization" of religion in post-Revolutionary America. For example, see Nathan O. Hatch, *The Democratization of American Christianity* (New Haven, Conn.: Yale University Press, 1989).

17. This follows Roland Robertson, *The Sociological Interpretation of Religion* (Oxford: Basil Blackwell, 1970), chap. 4.

18. It should be pointed out that Robertson's theory was formulated before the end of dictatorships in Spain and Portugal. Both countries have undergone extensive change since the early 1970s.

19. T. S. Eliot, "Choruses from 'The Rock,' in *T. S. Eliot, Collected Poems, 1909-1962* (New York: Harcourt, Brace and World, 1963), 153.

20. See Scott Lash, "Postmodernism as Humanism? Urban Space and Social Theory," in *Theories of Modernity and Postmodernity*, ed. Bryan S. Turner (London: Sage, 1990), 62–74, and Stephen Toulmin, *Cosmopolis: The Hidden Agenda of Modernity* (New York: Free Press, 1990), chap. 5.

11

Response to Shenk and Dueck's "Social Location and Christian Identity"

James (Jimmy) Jones

This ambitious, enlightening effort by Drs. Shenk and Dueck is to be commended for its reasoned attempt to make sense out of a very complex phenomenon—social location and Christian identity. As history, this chapter is clearly Christian history from one of several current Protestant perspectives. It is safe to say that this is not the way a believing Catholic would be likely to write Christian history. Additionally, what we lose in the authors' grand sweep of Christian development is the sense of Christianity's diversity at its beginnings and its pluralism today. In spite of these issues, the critically reflective, intellectually rigorous, forward-looking perspective of this piece reminds us that modern American Muslim academics and theologians have still not consistently produced this type of much-needed scholarship. Perhaps this will only be possible after Muslims establish their own seminaries and other institutions of higher learning in the United States.

As noted above, one concern that this chapter raises is the way in which it tends to portray Christianity as essentially monolithic. At its beginnings, Christianity was a sect of Judaism that developed its own variations (e.g., see Elaine Pagels' *Gnostic Gospels*). The authors seem to present pre-Constantine Christians as a somewhat monolithic band of "outsiders" who became "insiders" by the end of the fourth century. This probably was not their intention, but their approach presents a view of Christianity that belies the diversity of its beginnings. As Adolf Von Harnack makes clear in his classic work, *What Is Christianity*, a lot has happened within and outside of Christianity between Jesus Christ and modern times. This sense of the varieties of Christian expression is missing from the authors' depiction of

Christianity's beginnings and its current state of affairs. In some ways this criticism is unfair because the nature of their topic makes it difficult to look at such details without causing unwieldiness in and distraction from their main thesis.

A second concern is how easily the authors place the aims of Christendom and current U.S. foreign policy in the same philosophical boat. These ideas are clearly related. However, Pope Urban II's ambitions in launching the first Crusade and those of George W. Bush in launching the "war on terror" should not, as a matter of scholarship, be so easily conflated. In order to make such connections, the authors needed more evidence than they provide. One can disagree with them both without arguing that their motivations were essentially the same.

These two concerns aside, I think that Drs. Shenk and Dueck have contributed greatly to intra- and interfaith dialogue with this chapter. The chapter begins with a "lament and apology" that, given recent history, could be made (with obvious modifications) by Muslims toward Christians. They then present a discussion of modernity, postmodernity, and social location that provides a useful overall framework for their essay.

The sections "Identity and the Christian Community in the First Three Centuries after Jesus Christ" and "The Rise of Christendom in the Fourth Century" offer useful analyses on how "Christendom" came to be. It might have been overly ambitious to tackle such a massive topic in such a short chapter. However, what they do discuss provides both the Christian and non-Christian with critical historical background information. In particular, they argue that Jesus' ministry/movement was quite different from what Christendom and the church was to become (again, see Harnack; also, more recently, see Rosemary Radford Reuther in *Sexism and God-Talk*). For most Christians and non-Christians this idea is quite different from the way they tend to understand the development of Christianity.

In the three sections titled "Consequences of Historical Christendom," "The Sixteenth-Century Reformation and Secularism," and "Modern Political Theory," the authors argue that the entity that had become Christendom had, paradoxically, led to secularization and the separation of Church and state. Again, this is history with which most Christians and non-Christians are not familiar. However, the four models and two governmental attitudes toward church–state relations presented in "Modern Political Theory" were distractions that did not enhance the authors' arguments. On the other hand, the inclusion of T. S. Eliot's poem was a helpful amplification of the arguments they had made up until that point.

The concluding section, "Social location in Postmodern Culture," provides a useful starting place for both intra- and interfaith dialog. Unlike Fareed Zakaria in *The Future of Freedom*, they seem less wary of what Zakaria sees as the dangers of the democratization of culture brought about by our current "Democratic Age." It would have been valuable if the authors had explored this issue just a bit more. Nevertheless, Drs. Shenk and Dueck have done us a great service in writing this chapter. They educate us and give us much food for thought.

III

INTERFAITH AND INTRAFAITH DIALOGUE

12

Theological Foundation of Interfaith Dialogue and Peaceful Coexistence

The Qur'an's Universal Perspectives

Osman Bakar

INTRODUCTION

To Muslims the world over, who now number as many as 1.4 billion, the Qur'an and Hadiths[1] are the two most important sources of Islamic teachings on practically every subject that matters to human life. One subject that now matters a lot to human societies everywhere, especially to the more religiously and culturally pluralistic ones, is the subject of interfaith dialogue and, on a much broader as well as grander scale, the subject of dialogue of civilizations. Dialogue of civilizations, of which interfaith dialogue is the core element, is fast gaining popularity these days especially after Samuel Huntington "shocked" the world with his theory of clash of civilizations[2] and in the light of the September 11, 2001, tragedy.[3] Muslims have participated in interfaith and intercivilizational dialogues organized at various levels over the past one decade with admirable attitudes, some of which they themselves have initiated.

Many people in the West who generally know very little of the Qur'an may be surprised to know that this Muslim holy book actually has a lot of things to offer the contemporary world in the area of interfaith dialogues. There are indeed "pearls of wisdom" on the subject in the Qur'an that Muslims can share with the non-Muslim communities. In addition to this scriptural wisdom there are the exemplary views and moral conduct of Prophet Muhammad or those aspects of his *Sunnah* that have a direct bearing on the issue of dialogues of faiths and civilizations.

From the point of view of Islamic theology, however, it would have been surprising if the Qur'an and the Prophet had been completely silent on such an important issue. The Qur'an claims it is the last divine message to have been revealed to humankind to serve as their source of spiritual, moral, and intellectual guidance. As such, the Qur'an has to address itself to not only issues "peculiar" to the time of the Prophet but also "issues of the future" crucial to humankind of subsequent centuries and that would endure until the "end of the world." One "contemporary and future issue" the Qur'an has taken up in the seventh century in "anticipation" of its growing importance to the global human community in later centuries is the issue of ethnic and religious pluralism. This issue is hardly separable from the issue of dialogue of faiths, cultures, and civilizations, thus compelling the Qur'an to take it up as well. Common wisdom tells us dialogue is the best instrument of interfaith and interethnic understanding and peace in a plural society.

Ethnic and religious pluralism was a contemporary issue for the Prophet, because his mission was among others to create out of the "Arabian pluralism" a model of multifaith and multiethnic living founded on spiritual principles that future societies could look back upon for inspiration. However, as one can imagine, there is a vast difference between the kind of pluralism that the Prophet and his first generation of followers had experienced and the pluralism of our own times. Quite clearly various global forces and tendencies at work in the last two centuries have resulted in traditional culturally homogeneous societies becoming an almost extinct species as these societies were gradually transformed into pluralistic ones. So radical has been the transformation of the world's societal pattern of ethnic and religious pluralism that it now seems obvious that present and future world peace would be largely dependent on its successful management.

THE QUR'AN'S EXPLICIT REFERENCES TO INTERFAITH DIALOGUES

Some people may want to dispute the claim that the Qur'an is an important source of ideas on dialogue of faiths and civilizations by arguing that Arabic equivalents of the term *dialogue* as we understand it today are nowhere to be found in that book. The fact is that, contrary to this dissenting view, the Qur'an is very explicit about the idea of interfaith dialogue. It is enough to cite two verses from the Qur'an that prove this point. One verse reads:

> Say: "O People of the Book! Come here for a word which is in common between you and us: that we worship none but God; that we associate no partners with Him; that we erect not, from among ourselves, lords and patrons other than God." If they turn back, you say: "Bear witness that we are Muslims."[4]

In another verse, the Qur'an says:

> Invite (all) to the way of the Lord with wisdom and beautiful discourse; and argue with them in ways that are best and most gracious: for your Lord knows best who have strayed form His path and who receive guidance.[5]

A contemporary Muslim scholar, Khalid Duran, has accurately pointed out that in the first verse cited, the invitation statement "Come here for a word which is in common between you and us" offers "a literal translation of 'dialogue,' i.e. a 'word between' (*dia-logos*) conversation partners."[6] This means if in the verse we replace "word . . . between you and us" with "dialogue"—a literal rendering of the original Arabic—then we may rephrase the Muslim invitation to the "People of the Book" as follows: "Come to a dialogue with us on a common platform." The Qur'an's endorsement of dialogue, in this case clearly an interfaith dialogue appealing as it were to "People of the Book," is as explicit as any advocate of dialogue can make. Indeed, its clarity of purpose in the pursuit of interfaith dialogue and its well-focused dialogue partnership among religious communities with sacred scriptures has been unmatched by any other scripture.

The second verse previously cited from the Qur'an may be less explicit than the first verse in endorsing dialogue, but still in its spirit it seeks to affirm dialogue as the best way to present the Qur'an's positions and perspectives on numerous issues to people who are not its believers. The key phrase in the verse is "argue and plead with them (*jadilhum*) in ways that are best and gracious." The literal Arabic equivalent of the word *dialogue* does not appear here unlike in the first verse, but the idea of dialogue is clearly implied by the instruction "argue and plead with them," since dialogue demands arguing and pleading from its partners. However, the Qur'an has underscored its idea of an ideal dialogue when it insists on the presentation of arguments that are "good and gracious." Significantly, the verb *jadil* (argue) is closely related to the word *jadal* that was widely used in classical Islamic thought as a technical term for a certain type of intellectual discourse popular in the theological school of *kalam*.

Unlike in the first verse where the Qur'an calls on Muslims to specifically invite people of other faiths to interfaith dialogue, the invitation to dialogue in the second verse is extended to all humans, including those who do not consider themselves as belonging to any religion or faith-system. Appropriately, in conformity with the general nature of the dialogue invitation, the second verse has kept the purpose of the invitation as broad and as "vague" as possible, namely exploring the theme of "the way of the Lord." The two verses considered are by no means the only verses from the Qur'an supportive of interfaith and intercultural dialogues. But in themselves they are more than sufficient in providing a solid evidence of the Qur'an's pro-dialogue position.

THE QUR'AN AND THE IDEA OF CIVILIZATION

In the languages of the Muslim peoples, such as Arabic, Malay, Urdu, Turkish, and Persian, several terms have been used at various points of Islamic history to correspond to the English word *civilization*. Most of these terms are Arabic or some forms of their derivatives that are in conformity with the peculiarity of each of these Muslim languages.[7] One may try to look for the roots of these terms in the Qur'an and in the hadiths, but in this chapter we will be briefly introducing the fundamental elements that make up the Qur'an's idea of civilization.

The Qur'an complemented by the Sunnah of the Prophet Muhammad provides the core and permanent ideas that go into the formation of an integral and comprehensive concept of civilization. There are three central ideas underlying an Islamic theory of civilization: religion (*din*), religious community (*ummah*), and the city (*madinah*) as the center of urban civilization, of which the city of the Prophet (*madinat a-nabiy*) was the supreme model. As we pore through the pages of the Qur'an, it becomes very clear that religion, the religious community founded on its basis, and cities where its spiritual values and ethical and moral codes of conduct find societal expressions in an urban setting constitute the pillars of civilization throughout human history. In universal terms, the Qur'an is saying that every civilization is primarily the historical product of the dynamic interactions of those three elements.[8]

There are necessarily many civilizations in our world, since religions and religious communities are many and the moral characters of cities are also of many types. In the view of the Qur'an then, civilization must be God-centered since religion originates from God and the religious community to which it gave birth was originally founded by a prophet whom God had sent to teach that religion. As it had actually happened in history, the birth of the first Islamic community in Yathrib upon the Prophet's *hijrah* (emigration) to that city had been identified with the birth of the first Islamic city. This was the significance of the Prophet changing the name of Yathrib to *Madinat al-nabiy* (City of the Prophet).[9]

From the point of view of the science of civilization, at least as far as Islamic civilization is concerned, it is important to observe that Islam was primarily an urban phenomenon from its very beginning. It was in the Medinan urban setting that the seeds of Islamic civilization were first sown[10] and what Ibn Khaldun called *umran hadari* (urban civilization)[11] took firm roots. It is not the aim of this chapter to discuss in detail the nature and characteristics of Islamic civilization. The brief reference to this civilization's defining elements and to the beginning of its formative period is just meant to show that the Qur'an does have a distinctive concept of civilization and that the newly founded *ummah* under the Prophet's spiritual and temporal leadership had successfully struggled to turn that ideal concept into a practical reality in the form of the world's newest religious civilization.

In the light of its concept of civilization, the Qur'an affirms that humankind has been destined to live in a world split up into a multitude of religions, *ummahs*, and civilizations. Can these different and diverse faiths and civilizations live together on earth in peace? Peace is what the Qur'an wants. Toward that end it seeks to provide basic guidelines for peaceful coexistence among civilizations.

THE QUR'AN'S PERSPECTIVES ON INTERFAITH AND INTERCIVILIZATIONAL DIALOGUES

The primary aim of this chapter is to identify ideas in the Qur'an that are central to a global dialogue of faiths and civilizations and present them as interrelated concepts that are fundamental to the formulation of a comprehensive theory of interfaith dialogue. In particular, this chapter seeks to address four fundamental questions pertaining to interfaith and intercivilizational dialogues. The first question, why is there a paramount need for dialogues of faiths and civilizations, especially in our times? The second question, what are the goals sought to be achieved in such dialogues? The third question, what are the desirable methodological approaches to be adopted in the conduct of these dialogues? The fourth and last question, what are the core and outstanding issues to be deliberated and resolved in the pursuit of goals earlier identified?

In our view, the Qur'an in its unique way has addressed all of these questions. It is in its answers to these questions that we are furnished with precious ideas concerning dialogues of faiths and civilizations. What we propose to do here is to interpret and conceptualize these Qur'anic ideas in the light of the present global reality of the human community. This interpretation is strengthened with selected episodes in the Prophet's *Sunnah* that had a bearing on interfaith and intercivilizational dialogues.

WHY THE NEED FOR DIALOGUES OF FAITHS AND CIVILIZATIONS

Dialogues of faiths and civilizations are necessary, because different faiths and civilizations usually have different and quite often also contradictory philosophical standpoints on the various issues facing humankind. Faith-systems and civilizations also adopt different approaches to the solutions of many of these problems. There are certain basic facts about our world that we have to admit and confront with honesty and commitment if peaceful coexistence is to prevail among the different religions and civilizations. Our world is multiethnic and multireligious and therefore multicultural and multicivilizational in character. More often than not, we human beings have failed to live as good world citizens in conformity with this pluralistic character of the global community. We are basically ignorant of each other. We therefore need to cultivate greater mutual understanding and respect between cultures and civilizations. It is through dialogues of faiths and civilizations that people of different religions and civilizations can understand each other better, similarities between them be reaffirmed and strengthened,[12] and differences between them be respected. It is also through dialogues of faiths and civilizations that urgent solutions can be found to many of the contemporary problems of the world. Dialogue of faiths and civilizations is indeed the only sane alternative to the "Huntingtonian clash of civilizations."

More specific to the needs of our times, in the light of the precarious global conditions in which we humankind now live it is quite obvious that there is a paramount need for dialogues of faiths and civilizations. But the Qur'an's view is that dialogue is always necessary under all kinds of conditions. Dialogue is a virtue and an ideal to be pursued, thus elevated in the Qur'an to a matter of principle worthy of a divine command: ". . . and plead and argue with them in ways that are best and gracious." Let us try to understand why the Qur'an entertains such a view in sharp contrast to the negative perceptions of extreme right-wing Christian groups in the West who see Islam as a religion "violent to the core." In the Qur'an, Allah is God of all humankind, the Merciful and Compassionate who is concerned not only with the spiritual and material welfare of Muslims but of the whole human family. For this reason, the Qur'an directly addresses itself to humanity in numerous verses on common issues of global and even of cosmic dimensions.

From the Islamic point of view, there can be nothing more fundamental as common issues of humanity than spiritual and moral issues. The Qur'an calls on humankind to revere God who had created this beautiful planet earth for all of us to share and to develop and cultivate a God-consciousness. Says the Qur'an:

> O humankind! Adore your Lord, Who hath created you and those before you, so that you may attain God-consciousness; Who hath made the earth a resting-place for you and the sky a canopy; and causeth water to pour down from the sky, thereby producing fruits as food for you. And do not set up rivals to God when you know (better).[13]

In another verse, the Qur'an makes this invitation to humankind: "O humankind! Eat of what is on earth, lawful and good; and do not follow the footsteps of the Evil One, for he is to you an avowed enemy."[14] In modern times, we see plenty of wisdom in this injunction of the Qur'an. Issues of good and healthy food as natural food is increasingly threatened with contamination and artificial food products with implications for human health are on the increase and issues of food supply are no longer the concerns of individual nations but have become internationalized as can be seen from the works of the United Nations in this domain. In other words, food has emerged as an important issue for international dialogues and religious and cultural values will feature more prominently in these dialogues in years to come. In societies where many religions live side by side, the different dietary habits they have influenced will result in intercultural dialogues on food.

Yet another example:

> O humankind! Reverence your Guardian-Lord who created you from a single person, created, of like nature, his mate and from them twain scattered (like seeds) countless men and women; reverence God through whom you demand your mutual rights, and (reverence) the wombs (that bore you): for God ever watches over you.[15]

This verse is loaded with issues related to sexual relationships and human reproduction, gender relations, and the mistreatment of the female womb. Is this verse hinting at the growing practice in our times of showing disrespect to the wombs by turning them into "laboratories" for scientific experiments such as for cloning purposes? Apparently, it is so! Here by implication the Qur'an is calling on humankind to have dialogues on these issues on which it is so deeply divided but insisting that "our mutual rights" can only be secured through God. There are common threats to the sacred institution of marriage and traditional family values dear to all religions, and it is for the sake of the common good of all religions and civilizations that these traditional family institutions and values be preserved and protected. The Qur'an thus reaffirms this idea of the common good.

The Qur'an is also interested in dialogues among all peoples because it wants to impress upon them that the teachings Prophet Muhammad had brought from God are for the benefit of all humankind. "O humankind! The Apostle hath come to you in truth from God: believe in him, it is best for you. But if you reject faith, to God belong all things in the heavens and on earth; and God is All-knowing, All-wise."[16] Those who are taking up the position of the Qur'an in these dialogues have to be prepared for its rejection by the other parties, but they should find consolation in the knowledge that their efforts will not be in vain since their position has been made known to the world. Again we find that the Qur'an's interest in dialogues between Muslims and non-Muslims is primarily motivated by its concern for the general welfare of humankind. Although there are other verses that address the whole of humankind, the above verses we have cited are more than sufficient to illustrate Islam's universalism and its global vision of human problems.

Islam is also insistent on a global dialogue because it wants to share with the whole of humanity its understanding of the divine wisdom underlying human pluralism and diversity that characterizes our global community. Those who have this understanding are likely to celebrate pluralism and diversity. The Qur'an mentions among others as fruits of this wisdom "mutual acquaintance, recognition and understanding" among peoples of ethnic groups and nations, which is a necessary condition for international cooperation and world peace. Clearly, dialogue stands out as the best instrument to achieve this goal as envisioned by the Qur'an more than fourteen centuries ago. According to the Qur'an, God has divided humankind into many ethnic, racial, linguistic, and religious groups with a purpose. One verse states this purpose as follows:

> O humankind! We created you from a single (pair) of a male and a female, and made you into nations and tribes, that you may know each other (not that you may despise each other). Verily the most honored of you in the sight of God is (he who is) the most righteous of you. And God has full knowledge and is well acquainted (with all things).[17]

In another verse, God explains why there are many religious groups:

> To each among you have We prescribed a Law and an Open Way. If God had so willed, He would have made you a single people, but (His Plan is) to test you in what He had given you: so strive as in a race in all virtues. The goal of you all is to God; it is He that will show you the truth of the matters in which you dispute.[18]

According to the two verses just cited, it is part of God's plan to have pluralism and diversity in the human world in matters of ethnicity and religiosity. If He had wanted, He could have made all of us human beings members of one single ethnic group and one single religious community. But pluralism and diversity, as true also of the nonhuman domains of creation, is the preferred divine pattern of creation with its positive role in helping human beings to achieve the ultimate goals of their earthly existence even while it is always susceptible to destructive manipulation and exploitation such as by racist ideologies. Differences in ethnic identity can inspire the inquisitive human mind to look for underlying similarities and their common humanity and thus to know one another in various senses of the word. Dialogue appears as an important catalyst in the human endeavor to know one another, to cooperate despite differences, and to compete for excellence. What the Qur'an seeks to emphasize is that this excellence must be defined in universal moral terms alone. Nothing short of the moral criteria is acceptable. Blood, skin, and ancestry do not matter. Similarly, the idea of religious diversity is to serve a certain divine purpose, namely, to create a favorable condition for followers of the different religions "to strive in a race" for virtues and moral excellence.

As for the Muslim *ummah,* it is incumbent upon them to be passionately engaged in this global dialogue of faiths and civilizations because it is through such dialogues that they can best fulfill their divinely ordained global role as "the community of the middle path" (*ummatan wasatan*).[19] Says the Qur'an:

> Thus have We made of you an *ummat* (community) justly balanced, that you might be witnesses over the nations, and the Apostle (Muhammad) a witness over yourselves.[20]

To be "witnesses over the nations" is precisely to play a global role, and that role is to strive to be an exemplary community in the practice of moderation, justice, and equilibrium. Muslims today may be failing in the observance of this global duty, but the Qur'an has set the ideal for the global community. Certainly, this particular issue should be brought up as one of the main themes for deliberation in contemporary dialogues of faiths and civilizations.

THE GOALS OF DIALOGUES OF CIVILIZATIONS

What are the goals sought to be achieved in dialogues of faiths and civilizations? In response to this question, the Qur'an maintains that the primary goal of such dialogues is the promotion of the universal or common good of the entire humankind. As the Qur'an sees it, the domain of the universal good (*al-khayrat*) is so vast that it is almost limitless in nature, and it is the ideal basis for cooperation among peoples of different faiths, cultures, and political ideologies. Human beings by nature are drawn to all that is good and given the opportunity they will strive to achieve it. Dialogue is to remind ourselves of this basic truth and to create opportunities for all members of the global community to cooperate and collaborate in various kinds of activities for their common good. This quest for the common good of all has been clearly spelled out by the Qur'an:

> To each is a goal to which God turns him; then strive together (as in a race) toward all that is good (*al-khayrat*). Wherever you are, God will bring you together. For God has power over all things.[21]

The Qur'an also calls for a common spiritual understanding and commitment among the People of the Book, the immediate significance of which is directed at members of the three Abrahamic religions—Judaism, Christianity, and Islam:

> Say: "O People of the Book! Come to common terms as between us and you: that we worship none but God; that we associate no partners with Him; that we erect not, from among ourselves, lords and patrons other than God." If then they turn back, say ye: "Bear witness that we (at least) are Muslims (bowing to God's Will)."[22]

The Qur'anic pursuit of the common good is not limited to the production of positive good things that are generally recognized to be right, good, and useful in themselves, or what the Qur'an calls "enjoining what is right and good" (*amr bi'l-ma'ruf*). It also involves the rejection of things that are morally wrong, destructive, and harmful to a wholesome human life and societal peace and order, things that the Qur'an has categorized as *munkar*. Under the Qur'anic category of *ma'ruf*, we may refer to such universal goods commonly desired by all nations as universal education, kindness, tolerance, charity, global security, international peace and order, socioeconomic justice, protection of the environment, and adequate supplies of food and energy. Under the category of *munkar*, we have the common good in the form of collective prohibition of destructive acts and products like lying, corruption, oppression, prostitution, drugs, gambling, and weapons of mass destruction and elimination of common threats to human life and civilization such as environmental pollution, degradation of family values, violence, discriminations of all types, and all forms of extremism. The list of things that are right and good and that are wrong and evil is likely to change and grow with time. The global community should be pursuing dialogues of civilizations with the expressed aim of attempting to identify priorities in our collective good and realize them with determination. Mechanisms for achieving this objective, like the creation of international organizations and institutions, should be well placed.

Another important goal of interfaith and intercivilizational dialogues is the creation of better mutual understanding among nations, religions, and cultures. We have already referred to a number of verses in the Qur'an addressing humankind with that particular goal in view. In a sense, we may consider this goal as a subset of the earlier goal if we treat mutual understanding between nations as a common good of humanity. But here we consider the two goals as being distinct. The Qur'anic idea of "mutual acquaintance and understanding" as contained in the verse on ethnic pluralism and diversity[23] needs to be understood at various levels of knowledge.[24]We may conceive of this mutual understanding as ranging from knowledge of physical characteristics at its lowest level like skin color to knowledge of our common humanity which is spiritual in nature. In between, we have mutual understandings at the levels of knowledge of manners and customs and knowledge of the higher aspects of culture and civilization. This mutual acquaintance and understanding, if progressively pursued from the lowest to the highest levels, is to lead us to a better appreciation of our similarities and differences and the oneness of the human family. The higher purpose of ethnic diversity and pluralism is so that all ethnic and racial groups will come to recognize and acknowledge their common humanity. Without this recognition and acknowledgment, the pursuit of human solidarity and brotherhood on earth would only be a dream!

Dialogues should not end there. There is a new height of understanding to be reached. What a spiritual and intellectual achievement it would be for human beings if they were to realize that in their ethnic and civilizational diversity they are simply displaying one of the many signs of divine wisdom in creation. Only after having realized that consciousness can they celebrate diversity with honesty, joy, and satisfaction. Such a human consciousness would not allow any room for racism and sentiments of ethnic superiority. What the world really needs to cultivate is precisely that kind of collective consciousness. Human worth and human dignity is now viewed in a new light. As strongly emphasized in the Qur'an, the best person in the sight of God is the best person in moral conduct. In the final analysis, what matters most is the moral and spiritual worth of the human individual. The real worth of a person does not reside in his social status, his blood and color, his race or ethnicity, his wealth, and not his creed even. The divine criteria of judging the quality of human beings are spiritual in nature and also the most objective and the most universal, since these transcend subjective and sectarian considerations. This conception of human dignity means that in our world of ethnic and religious pluralism, the correct approach to dialogues of faiths and civilizations and the unity of humankind is based on spiritual principles.

METHODOLOGY OF DIALOGUE OF FAITHS AND CIVILIZATIONS

What are the desirable methodological approaches to be adopted in dialogues of faiths and civilizations? In response to this question, the Qur'an calls for a free and open dialogue in which Muslims as participants are expected to be guided by the ideals of a discourse conducted in the name of God. In general terms, the dialogue favored by the Qur'an is characterized by beautiful discourse, excellent and gracious argumentation and persuasion, lack of coercion, and a general respect for the beliefs and position of the other. Clearly the Qur'an expects intellectual decency from all participants of the dialogue. The Qur'an expresses the methodological characteristics of an ideal dialogue in the following terms:

> Invite (all) to the Way of thy Lord with wisdom and beautiful discourse; and argue with them in ways that are best and most gracious: for thy Lord knows best who have strayed from His path and who receive guidance.[25]

Commenting on this verse, Abdullah Yusuf Ali writes: "In this wonderful passage are laid down principles of religious teaching, which are good for all time. But where are the Teachers with such qualifications? We must invite all to the Way of God, and expound His Universal Will; we must do it with wisdom and discretion, meeting people on their own ground and convincing them with illustrations from their own knowledge and experience, which may be very narrow, or very wide. Our preaching must not be dogmatic, self-regarding, or offensive but gentle, considerate, and such as would attract their attention. Our manner and our arguments should not be acrimonious, but modeled on the most courteous and the most gracious example, so that the hearer may say to himself, "This man is not dealing merely with dialectics; he is not trying to get a rise out of me; he is sincerely expounding the faith that is in him, and his motive is the love of man and the love of God.""[26]

What Yusuf Ali writes here about the methodological characteristics of religious teaching generally is specifically true for interfaith and intercivilizational dialogue, since dialogue is seen in Islam as a particular form of *da'wah* (religious invitation). Thus the verse furnishes the Muslims with the following lasting principles of dialogue:

1. Dialogue is an invitation to everyone to the way of God. The way of God is the all-inclusive way of mercy and compassion, love, and justice and it represents all that is good for humankind. Given the divine command in the Qur'an to invite everyone to God's way, it is imperative for Muslims to be at the forefront of dialogues of civilizations.
2. Dialogue is an exposition of God's Will. Since God's Way and God's Will are interpreted and understood differently in different religions, it is the role of dialogues to allow for an exposition of these different interpretations and understandings in an intellectual environment of tolerance and respect. The Qur'an's teaching that "to each among you, We have prescribed a set of rules of practical conduct and a spiritual way"[27] would encourage Muslims to listen attentively to the experience of God and the meaning of religiosity in the other religious traditions as part of their attempt to study in depth the meaning of that Qur'anic teaching.
3. Dialogue needs to be conducted with wisdom and beautiful discourse. Wisdom here means a lot of things. Among other things, each party in

the dialogue has to take into account the other party's culture, values, history of their civilization, and mindset and to show understanding of its overall position. This consideration means that a lot of knowledge from various disciplines needs to go into the preparation of the dialogue, not to mention knowledge of the specific issues sought to be discussed in this dialogue. This is what a truly enlightened dialogue should be, which is what Islam has set as an ideal. Then the discourse itself should be beautiful in its manner of argumentation, gracious, and courteous, not acrimonious.

4. Dialogue should be constantly guided by the universal spirit of the love of man and the love of God. Admittedly, there are immediate objectives of dialogues like the finding of urgent solutions to contemporary problems affecting all civilizations. But even these short-term solutions need to be conceived and pursued in the light of the universal spiritual teachings shared by all humanity.

OUTSTANDING ISSUES IN DIALOGUES OF CIVILIZATIONS

What are the core and outstanding issues to be deliberated and resolved in dialogues of faiths and civilizations? In response to this fourth and last question, it ought to be said that in conformity with its nature as a book of general guidance the Qur'an only deals with principles that are meant to define the general context of dialogues and shape their basic contours. These general principles as already discussed include such ideas as the meaning of the common good and common interest of all communities and nations, the promotion of mutual understanding and global cooperation, and the necessary conditions for a peaceful and just world order. Still the Qur'an is not entirely devoid of ideas that are more specific in nature and absolutely relevant to the contemporary world and thus extremely appropriate for dialogues of faiths and civilizations. These specific issues of contemporary concern have been mostly mentioned earlier. These range from family values to environmental hazards and from human rights to global poverty and injustices. The Qur'an's unique contributions to dialogues of faiths and civilizations would be in the form of providing universal spiritual and moral perspectives for discourses on these global issues, perspectives that are very much lacking in contemporary discussions.

It is only fitting for a dialogue of faiths and civilizations in the true sense of the word to be concerned only with the most important of global issues and to be informed by the most universal of spiritual, intellectual, and moral principles, letting dialogues of a lesser cultural scale take care of the more minor issues. In addressing humankind in a number of verses, the

Qur'an precisely deals with global issues of the greatest importance to the future of humanity and reminds humankind of the spiritual roots of its problems and the spiritual context of their lasting solutions.

INTERFAITH DIALOGUES IN THE SUNNAH OF THE PROPHET

In Islamic tradition, the Prophet Muhammad is seen as the perfect embodiment of the teachings of the Qur'an. In the words of Aishah, one of his wives, his spiritual and moral portrait is the Qur'an. We may then state one important consequence of the Prophet's complete identification with the Qur'an. Insofar as the Qur'an contains teachings on dialogues between religions, cultures, and civilizations, the Prophet was the first person in Islam to have interpreted those teachings and put them into practice in the best possible forms and the most excellent way as dictated by the needs of the time. As a matter of fact, the Prophet had often been engaged in serious and intimate dialogues with Christian and Jewish leaders on issues that are now the concern of dialogues of faiths and civilizations. For example, the Prophet had received a Christian delegation from Najran in his Medina mosque and held discussion there with them on theological issues that were of a common concern to Christian and Muslim faiths.

During the time of the Prophet, there had been numerous conflicts and wars between the two contemporary superpowers, the Roman Empire and the Persian Empire. The Pagan Quraysh, who were enemies of the Prophet and the new message of Islam were pro-Persian. The Prophet and his companions were pro-Romans. That in these wars between the two rival empires the Muslims had supported the Romans was completely understandable. It was not only because the Prophet's Quraysh enemies were supporting the Persians but also because the Prophet clearly saw a greater "civilizational affinity" between Islam and Christianity, the religion of the Roman Empire and Civilization than between Islam and Zoroastrianism, the religion of the Persian Empire and Civilization. The position of the Muslims in this conflict of civilizations was thus adopted very much in the light of spiritual considerations. It was the same considerations that had influenced the Prophet's decision to send Islam's first emigrants to Abyssinia, a Christian nation, to escape the pagan Quraysh persecution.[28] The Prophet regarded its King Negus as a just ruler and spiritually enlightened. His judgment and appreciation of Negus was essentially spiritual and moral, and this was only to be confirmed by the treatment the King had accorded the Muslim emigrants.

Interestingly, King Negus's decision to grant a safe haven to the Muslim emigrants was made after he was convinced they had been persecuted in their own birthplace because of their religious beliefs, which he saw were in close affinity with Christianity. His decision followed a lively discourse or "dialogue" in the court between the leader of the Quraysh emissaries sent to persuade Negus to extradite the Muslims back to Arabia and the leader of the emigrants.[29] It was the latter's sincerity to the truth and eloquence that captivated the King and won him over to the side of the Muslims. The King's attitudes were nothing but admirable. He himself had asked for a discourse between the two sides because he wanted to know the real truth of the dispute. With the Quraysh envoy pleading for the Muslims' repatriation in the name of good diplomatic relations between Abyssinia and Arabia and attempting to overblow the theological differences between Christianity and the new religion on the divinity of Christ, the King could have complied with that request. But having heard both sides, what was ultimately decisive in the issue for the King was what he described as "the thin line that separates" the two religions.[30] In other words, spiritual and moral considerations prevailed. A moral lesson for everyone in the pursuit of dialogues of civilizations and more specifically interfaith dialogues is that commonalities far outweigh differences in importance in determining the spirit of cooperation and collaboration between cultures and civilizations. It is our belief that this historic encounter between the first Muslims and the Abyssinian Christians is of great relevance to contemporary dialogues of civilizations. Certainly, today those Christians who think Islam is a religion so alien to Christianity and who harbor so much animosity toward Islam should come to the same realization as King Negus did that the teachings of the two religions have more commonalities than differences.

Although in the conflicts between the Roman and Persian Civilizations the inclination of the Prophet was very clear as already alluded to, he extended the warring Emperors invitations to Islam. In this case, both the invitation and the responses to that invitation are instructive for proponents of dialogue. It is a sacred duty to invite everyone to dialogues concerned with universal truths and the collective good of humankind. High on the list of priorities are invitations to persons in positions of power, responsibility, and influence. Prophets of God never fail in discharging this duty. Prophet Muhammad saw it was his duty to invite the two Emperors to the new religion's teachings on universal truths and the collective good of humankind. In comparison to the discharge of this duty, how the invitees are going to respond is of secondary importance. Responses to the invitations, regardless of what they are, have to be faced and dealt with accordingly. As it turned out to be for the Prophet, Heraclius, the Roman Emperor reacted to his invitation with respect and a great interest in his personality and the teachings of the new religion even though he did not embrace it. At least, the Prophet's invitation and Heraclius' response to it had opened up spaces for discourses and dialogues between representatives of the two sides on the new religion and its implications for the contemporary world. From the time Heraclius received the Prophet's letter of invitation to Islam until his death, he was to hear more and more of the religion and had to confront its rapid spread as it gained several provinces around Arabia belonging to his Empire.

As for the Persian Emperor, he received the Prophet's envoy with contempt, including by tearing up the Prophet's letter. From the point of view of dialogue as a human virtue and a cultural necessity, the Emperor's behavior was utterly reprehensible. In question here was not his rejection of the Prophet's invitation to Islam, which was his complete right, but the manner in which he had done so. He could have turned down the invitation with grace and respect, just as the Prophet had extended his invitation with sincerity and grace. His whole response was all the more unacceptable to civilized behavior when he ordered his Governor in Yemen to arrest the Prophet, whom he accused of disrespect to "The King of Kings" for of all things daring to address him on equal terms! The Persian Emperor's response was consequential beyond his expectations. It did open up spaces for historic encounters between the Persians and the Prophet, leading to the Governor's acceptance of Islam. A moral lesson to be drawn from the contrasting responses of the two Emperors to the Prophet's invitation is that inviting others to dialogues on core human issues will open up spaces for meaningful encounters and discourses for which the inviters should be well prepared.

We have referred to the dialogues that the Prophet had conducted with various Christian delegations coming to see him. We can say that, in general, the scope of dialogues he had conducted with representatives of "People of the Book" had covered theological questions and other matters pertaining to the spiritual domain as well as political and cultural matters such as those pertaining to the rights and responsibilities of the various communities in the newly born Muslim state. In particular, the Pact the Prophet as leader of the Muslim *ummah* had concluded with Jews and Pagans in Medina soon after his emigration (*hijrah*) to that city is extremely important from the point of view of dialogues of cultures and civilizations. The Pact that the Prophet initiated and to which many non-Muslim groups were invited to be signatories was aimed at the collective good of cosmopolitan Medina. In the words of Abd al-Rahman Azzam, generally considered as the father of the Arab League, and whom the *New York Times* calls "one of the great statesmen of contemporary Islam":

> The Pact amounted to an agreement for peaceful coexistence, a defensive alliance for cooperation against aggression that sought to protect a group of small states, each enjoying under the provisions of the Pact control over its own people and freedom to preach its own religion. The signatories guaranteed to

> aid one another and to protect each other's beliefs against anyone who wished to bring harm upon their lands and peoples. Thus, they guaranteed freedom of belief and freedom of preaching to members of the Pact, despite the diversity of their beliefs.[31]

It is strongly believed that the document known as "The Medinan Constitution" consists of two parts that historians had put together.[32] One part is a documentation of this Pact between the Prophet's community and Jewish and Pagan tribes signed before the Muslims' victorious Battle of Badr against the Meccan Quraysh. The other part, written after that Battle, is a document the Prophet had intended exclusively for the Muslim community with the aim of realizing brotherhood and solidarity between the Emigrants (*Muhajirun*) and the local Helpers (*Ansar*). This document spells out the nature of the alliance between these two core groups of the community and the commitments, rights, and duties of all members of the community.

The significance of the Medinan Constitution has been interpreted by scholars in many different ways. Many rightly have referred to it as the first written state constitution in the world and one that has effectively dealt with the volatile and divisive issue of the collective good in a multiethnic and multireligious society. In this essay, we are primarily interested in the significance of the Constitution for dialogues of cultures and civilizations. In our view, this historic document is of great importance for those interested in interethnic, interreligious, intercultural, and intercivilizational dialogues in pluralistic societies. The document was not the result of the Prophet (*pbuh*) imposing his own views and will on both the Muslim community and non-Muslim communities in Medina. The peace treaty and alliance between the Muslims and the Jews and Pagans were based on mutual consultations and dialogues between them.[33] Similarly, the document on the rights and duties of the various groups constituting the *ummah* had been written following consultations among them. From the Muslim point of view then, there should be both dialogues with various non-Muslim groups and dialogues within the Muslim community itself with the view of preserving its social solidarity and cohesion. It is also clear that the spirit and content of the Medinan Constitution is very much in line with the goals of dialogues of civilizations that we have earlier expounded.

CONCLUSION

Our foregoing discussion clearly shows that the Qur'an and the *Sunnah* of the Prophet Muhamad are rich in ideas and experiences related to dialogues of faiths, cultures, and civilizations. The fundamental teachings of the Qur'an and the Prophet are spiritual and moral in nature, and these aim at the love of God and of humanity and at global peace and justice. These teachings may also provide useful guidance for humanity on how to promote and advance global cooperation in a world characterized by pluralism and diversity. Islam looks upon dialogue as a societal virtue, a cultural necessity, a symbol of human dignity, and the hallmark of civilization. In the light of all these assertions, Islam cannot but be opposed in its doctrines and practices to the idea of clash of civilizations.

Islam strongly believes in a multicivilizational world in which there is mutual borrowing and learning and mutual impact between the various civilizations. Throughout its history, Islamic civilization has lived and acted in accordance with that belief. It took pains to preserve the heritage of earlier civilizations only to create a new synthesis on their basis and the universal teachings of Islam. Similarly, in its encounters with contemporary ethnic cultures and civilizations, Islam's approach on the main was one of dialogue, peaceful coexistence, or synthesis, and not of confrontation, ethnic cleansing, or enforced assimilation. Islamic civilization was the first civilization to have encountered all of the world's major civilizations in a mutually beneficial way. Islam's most extensive encounter is with Western civilizations. Undeniably there had been conflicts between them arising mainly not from religious factors but those related to worldly power. However, during the greater part of this encounter, each faith-system and civilization has been enriched by the other, the details of which should be made available to both sides in further dialogues.

NOTES

1. Muslims traditionally distinguish between the Qur'an, which they believe is God's revelation verbatim to the Prophet Muhammad, and the hadiths, which are merely the documented sayings and actions attributed to the Prophet. In the Shi'ite branch of Islam, the hadiths are extended to include the sayings and actions of the Imams.

2. The theory first appeared in an article titled "The Clash of Civilizations?" *Foreign Affairs* 72, no. 3 (Summer 1993): 22–49. This article was subsequently expanded into a book bearing the title *The Clash of Civilizations and the Remaking of World Order* (New York: Simon & Schuster, 1996). Huntington's controversial thesis has provoked worldwide debates, which have helped to generate a global interest on its antithesis, the dialogue of civilizations.

3. The September 11 terrorist attack on America, described erroneously in certain circles in the West as "an attack on Western civilization," and the subsequent tensions between America and the Muslim world has tended to raise the profile of believers in an imminent clash of civilizations and dampen the spirit of advocates of dialogues of civilization, particularly among Muslims. But we are also reminded by the current dangerous situation confronting our global community that at no

other time in human history have we been in greater need of dialogues of cultures and civilizations than we are now.

4. *The Qur'an*, chap. 3 ("The Family of 'Imran"), verse 64.

5. *The Qur'an*, chap. 16 ("The Bee"), verse 125.

6. Khalid Duran, "The Drafting of a Global Ethic: A Muslim Perspective," *Envisioning a Global Ethic* (Global Dialogue Institute, 1998) (online publication).

7. The most well known of these terms are *tamaddun*, *hadarah*, *umran*, and *adab*, all of which were used by Ibn Khaldun (d. 808 A.H./1406 CE) in his celebrated work *The Muqaddimah*. These are key terms in the new science of civilization of which the modern world has come to regard him as the founder. In Malay-Indonesian language, e.g., *peradaban*, a derivative of *adab*, is used today to translate the English word *civilization*. The Malays under the impact of Arabization and Islamization have also used for centuries the word *tamaddun* as an equivalent term.

8. This Qur'anic view is accepted by many Western scholars of civilizations. Even Samuel Huntington, who is a political scientist dabbling into civilization issues rather than a scholar of civilizations, shares the same view on the place of religion in a civilization's making. Says he: "Of all the objective elements which define civilizations, the most important usually is religion." See Huntington, *Clash of Civilizations*, 42.

9. On the religious significance of the Prophet's inspired change of name from Yathrib to Al-Madinah, see Syed Muhammad Naquib al-Attas, *Islam: The Concept of Religion and the Foundation of Ethics and Morality* (Kuala Lumpur: ABIM, 1976). The relation between *din* and *madinah* which in the Arabic language are etymologically related must also been seen in its practical shape as realized in the new city under the Prophet's guidance.

10. On the characteristics of this new civilization, see e.g. Akram Diya' al 'Umari, *Medinan Society at the Time of the Prophet: Its Characteristics and Organization*, trans. Huda Khattab (Herndon, Va.: International Institute of Islamic Thought, 1981); and Abd al-Rahman Azzam, *The Eternal Message of Muhammad* (Cambridge: The Islamic Texts Society, 1993).

11. For a discussion of Ibn Khaldun's concept of civilization and his terminological usage in relation to the concept, see Rosenthal's preface to *The Muqaddimah*. See also Mohamed-Aziz Lahbabi, *Ibn Khaldun* (Paris: Editions Seghers, 1968).

12. It is these similarities that give birth to what we call "the common civilization" of humanity. On a discussion of the future of our common civilization, see *Towards A Common Civilization: Public Lectures by Hans Kueng and Mohd Kamal Hassan* (Kuala Lumpur: Institute of Islamic Understanding Malaysia, 1997).

13. *The Qur'an*, Chapter of the Cow (*surah al-baqarah*), verses 21–22.

14. *The Qur'an*, Chapter of the Cow, verse 168.

15. *The Qur'an*, Chapter of the Women (*surah al-nisa'*), verse 1.

16. *The Qur'an*, Chapter of the Women, verse 170.

17. *The Qur'an*, Chapter of the Inner Apartments (*surah al-hujurat*), verse 13.

18. *The Qur'an*, Chapter of the Table Spread (*surah al-maidah*), verse 51.

19. For a discussion of this idea in the context of dialogue of civilizations, see O. Bakar, *Islam and Inter-Civilizational Dialogues: The Quest for a Truly Universal Civilization* (Kuala Lumpur: University of Malaya Press, 1997), chap. 1.

20. *The Qur'an,* Chapter of the Cow, verse 143.

21. *The Qur'an,* Chapter of The Cow, verse 148.

22. *The Qur'an,* Chapter of the Family of 'Imran (*surah ali' imran*), verse 64. This verse may serve as a spiritual basis for interfaith dialogues among Jews, Christians, and Muslims.

23. *The Qur'an,* Chapter of the Inner Apartments, verse 13 (previously quoted).

24. For a discussion of the different levels of meaning of this idea, see O. Bakar, "Inter-civilizational Dialogue: Theory and Practice in Islam," in *Islam and Civil Society in Southeast Asia,* ed. Nakamura Mitsuo, Sharon Siddique, and Omar Farouk Bajunid (Singapore: Institute of Southeast Asian Studies, 2001), 169–171.

25. *The Qur'an,* Chapter of the Bee (*surah al-nahl*), verse 125.

26. Abdullah Yusuf Ali, *The Holy Quran: Text, Translation and Commentary* (Beirut: Dar Al Arabia, 1968), 689n2161.

27. *The Qur'an,* Chapter of the Table Spread, verse 51.

28. This decision of the Prophet "inaugurated the earliest international relations of the Muslims." See Abd al-Rahman Azzam, *The Eternal Message of Muhammad,* 127.

29. The Quraysh chief envoy was 'Amr ibn al-'As, who later converted to Islam, which he served with distinction as a conquering general, and the leader of the Muslim emigrants was Ja'far ibn Abu Talib, a cousin of the Prophet.

30. The "dialogue" in the King's court may be referred to in the hadiths of Imam al-Bukhari.

31. Abd al-Rahman Azzam, *The Eternal Message of Muhammad,* 128.

32. For a good discussion of the historical aspects of the Medinan Constitution as well the significance of its content, see Akram Diya' al-'Umari, *Madinan Society at the Time of the Prophet,* chap. X.

33. For traditional sources on the Prophet's dialogue with representatives of the Jews and Pagans on the content of the document, see Akram Diya' al-'Umari, *Madinan Society at the Time of the Prophet,* 104.

BIBLIOGRAPHY

Al-Attas, Syed Muhammad Naquib. *Islam: The Concept of Religion and the Foundation of Ethics and Morality.* Kuala Lumpur: Muslim Youth Movement of Malaysia, 1976.

Ali, Abdullah Yusuf. *The Holy Quran: Text, Translation and Commentary.* Beirut: Dar Al Arabia, 1986.

Al 'Umari, Akram Diya'. *Madinan Society at the Time of the Prophet: Its Characteristics and Organization.* Translated by Huda Khattab. Herndon, Va.: International Institute of Islamic Thought, 1981.

Azzam, Abd al-Rahman. *The Eternal Message of Muhammad.* Cambridge: Islamic Texts Society, 1993.

Bakar, Osman. *Islam and Inter-Civilizational Dialogues: The Quest for a Truly Universal Civilization.* Kuala Lumpur: University of Malaya Press, 1997.

Huntington, Samuel P. *The Clash of Civilizations and the Remaking of World Order.* New York: Simon & Schuster, 1996.

Ibn Khaldun. *The Muqaddimah*. Translated by Franz Rosenthal. 3 vols. New York: Pantheon Books, 1958; London and Henley: Routledge and Kegan Paul, 1986.

Institute of Islamic Understanding Malaysia. *Towards A Common Civilization: Public Lectures by Hans Kueng and Mohd Kamal Hassan*. Kuala Lumpur: Institute of Islamic Understanding Malaysia, 1997.

Lahbabi, Mohamed Aziz. *Ibn Khaldun*. Paris: Editions Seghers, 1968. *Sahih al-Bukhari*.

13

Fear and Muslim-Christian Conflict Transformation

Resources from Attachment Theory and Affect Regulation

Evelyne A. Reisacher

Not too long ago, I was sitting in the Los Angeles Airport on my way to Chicago, when a group of about twenty Muslims, going on pilgrimage, made their way to the plane I was about to board. At their view the crowd around me froze. The face of several passengers displayed a flushed pallor. To my utter surprise, I started to resonate with the fear of the crowd. My body got tense, my palms sweated, my mouth got dry, and my stomach churned. How could it be? I have hundreds of friends in the Muslim world whom I have known for years and enjoy being with. I suddenly realized what was happening within me. I was nonconsciously associating the view of Muslims to internal images of violence and danger that my mind had stored after watching threatening events on television in which some Muslims were involved. As I found my seat in the plane, one Muslim woman of the group walked by. We exchanged eye contact. She smiled at me. Her gaze radiated peace. After that exchange, I felt safe. She regulated my fears and reassured me. I leaned back, relaxed, and enjoyed the flight.

Experiencing fear in an airport is something that is understandable, especially after the recent events of planes crashing into buildings or being used for violent attacks against civilians. However, living in a constant state of dysregulated fear when encountering individuals who belong to the same religious group as a few perpetrators of violent acts may fuel more conflicts. In this chapter, I deal with the issue of fear, because it is an important emotion that conflict transformation theories say we must take into account. I draw resources from latest findings in attachment theory and affect regulation theory and see how these findings can help us Christians and Muslims form more secure bonds. I also list a number of fears expressed by Christians with the expectation that the Muslim community will resonate with and modulate them. I believe that Christians should also be aware and address the fears Muslims experience when interacting with Christians. Since this chapter is written from the perspective of a Christian talking to a Muslim, I leave it to Muslims to express their own fears from their own perspective, and I encourage Christians to be sensitive to these fears and resonate with them.

FEAR AND CONFLICT TRANSFORMATION

John Lederach (1997, 2003) from Eastern Mennonite University said that in conflict transformation we must look for a frame of reference that provides a focus on the restoration and rebuilding of relationships. The same author acknowledges the role that fear plays in conflict relationships and suggests that conflict transformation involves the recognition of this emotion and others, such as anger or grief.

How does one deal with emotions, feelings, or affect that play such a significant role in social interactions? In the case of fear, conflict theorists suggest it must be outwardly acknowledged and dealt with in order for effective conflict transformation to occur (Schrock-Shenk 2000). Today one does not need to be an expert in Muslim-Christian relations to see that fear plays a major role in their interactions. I propose that a better understanding of the nature of fear and fear regulation will help those already addressing this emotion as they do conflict-transformation workshops or assist communities wanting to live peacefully together.

ATTACHMENT THEORY AND THE SECURE BASE

As we reflect on how to build or maintain healthy relationships between Muslims and Christians in the midst of fear-triggering events, two disciplines that bring us useful resources are attachment theory and affect regulation. Since its inception by John Bowlby (1982) and Mary Ainsworth (1967), attachment research has looked into fear of strangers and anxiety in close relationships. Bowlby (1973) believed humans have a fear system activated by danger. He described fear behaviors such as avoidance, withdrawal, and attack (Kobak 1999). Mary Ainsworth first studied child–caregiver attachment patterns and developed a tool, the Strange Situation, to define whether a child was securely or insecurely attached to her caregiver (Ainsworth et al. 1978). Later other tools were created by various researchers to evaluate attachment between individuals throughout the lifespan and across cultures (Cassidy and Shaver 1999). Attachment researchers observed that securely attached children who faced a fearful stimulus reached out to their caregiver, who provided a secure base. This sense of security was then internalized in working models that children used to establish secure relationships from the cradle to the grave. Insecure attachment was observed when the caregiver could not provide this secure haven.

Drawing from attachment research, I posit that if as a Christian I cannot find a secure base in my relationship with a Muslim, I will not have a secure bond with him or her. For healthy attachments to develop, one needs first to feel that the other is safe to be with, so that one can reach out to him or her in case of danger. Bartholomew and Horowitz (1991) who conducted adult attachment research have defined in their four-category model of attachment derived from Bowlby, a fearful attachment style in which people say "I worry that I will be hurt if I allow myself to become too close to others." In my many interactions with Christians today, I have often heard this sentence almost word for word: "I worry that I will be hurt if I allow myself to become too close to a Muslim person."

In every people group, there are individuals who are dangerous and are not candidates for serving as a secure base. However, the rest of the individuals have the capacity to care and protect others and can therefore form secure attachments with people from their own community. Between cultures and religious groups, misconceptions and lack of familiarity may make it more difficult to see the other as caring and providing safety. One more spontaneously runs to the person of one's own cultural or religious group in case of danger. I argue that in cross-cultural or interreligious relations, people must practice being a secure base through repeated experiences of reaching out to others under stress for comfort and care. I encourage Christians to look for interactions that provide a sense of felt security with Muslims. This may take time but will eventually lead to the development of secure bonds. As Christians, the Bible calls us to reach out to others, to step out of the boundary of our own group and embrace people from other backgrounds. As we do that, we may not always experience joy but we will develop relationships that over time will prove to be secure. In the process we will also recognize those who are not providing safety and security in the relationship and avoid them.

I suggest that conflict transformation involves times where Christians and Muslims experience being a secure base for each other. If Christians try to find their secure base always outside the Muslim community and if Muslims always try to find their secure base outside the Christian community, the ties between the two will be weak or insecure. Whereas if the Muslim community can serve as a secure base in times of danger and threat for the

Christian community and vice versa the nature of the bond between the two will become more secure.

AFFECT REGULATION AND FEAR

Recent developments in attachment research have shed new light on the nature of what occurs during interpersonal relations. Today, many researchers see attachment not just as a spatial theory. In other words, the sense of security does not come only from drawing close to someone in case of fear. Allan N. Schore from the Department of Psychiatry and Biobehavioral Sciences at the University of California at Los Angeles argues that attachment theory is essentially a regulatory theory. He writes, "Attachment can thus be conceptualized as the interactive regulation of synchrony between psychobiologically attuned organisms. This attachment dynamic, which operates at levels beneath awareness, underlies the dyadic regulation of emotion" (Schore 2000, p. 34). In other words, if a Muslim feels how I as a Christian am scared, aligns to my own internal fear state, resonates with my fear, and attenuates it in a timely fashion, the bond between us will grow stronger. Therefore learning how to interactively regulate fear states becomes an important component of interpersonal relationships. Resonating with someone else's fear involves more than just listening. It is a meeting of internal emotional states where the fearful person can say, "I feel that you feel the kind of fear I have, with the same intensity and this comforts me and diminishes my fear."

One of the issues raised in this article is whether Christians and Muslims can currently interactively regulate their fears. The interactive regulation of fear involves empathy. It requires being sensitive to the affect state of the other. As Christians, the Bible encourages us to show empathy and compassion as, for example, in the following words: "be kind and compassionate to one another" (Ephesians 4:32).

Oftentimes, when individuals from communities are afraid of each other, they have the tendency of autoregulating their respective fears, which involves using their own internal resources to find a sense of felt security and only then reach out to individuals from the other community, once they have dealt with their own feelings. They do not allow for the individual from the other community to interactively regulate their fears. However, Schore (1994) contends that both autoregulation and interactive regulation are needed for the development of healthy attachments. Interactive affect regulation means drawing near to the other while being oneself in the state of dysregulation and using the other for one's regulation. To better understand this process of attachment, one has to look closely to the affect of fear and then discuss its regulation.

NOT ALL IS FEAR

Fear is vital for survival. Healthy people are all wired for fear. For Joseph LeDoux (2002), a professor and researcher at the Center for Neural Science at New York University, fear is related to survival because it helps people react instantaneously to a stimulus they perceive as dangerous. But fear can also be misleading. Fear can endanger social relations when individuals are not aware of their fear-reactions.

First, we must understand that emotions have both nonconscious and conscious processes. In conflict transformation, the danger lies in implicit dysregulated fear states that lead our actions and behaviors without our awareness. For example, researchers have found that the amygdala can be activated by threatening faces at levels below awareness (Morris et al. 1996). Repeated exposure to threatening faces of people from a specific culture may lead an entire community to stay nonconsciously in dysregulated fear and may explain stereotyping. To securely attach to another people group, we must be exposed to the whole spectrum of their facial expressions: happy faces, smiling faces, sad faces, and so on.

Second, fear regulation needs to be practiced in the context of a relation. Several brain structures are involved in the regulation of emotional states. One of them is the amygdala. It plays a central role in processing, expressing, and regulating fear (Cozolino 2002). However, the amygdala needs to be regulated by a higher brain structure. If not, individuals will be in constant fear-dysregulated states that would not allow them to function well socially. The orbitofrontal cortex, located in the prefrontal region of the brain, is a higher limbic structure that regulates the amygdala and other limbic structures so that individuals do not stay forever in fear states. It has an executive control function for the entire right brain dominant for nonconscious processes (Schore 2003). This structure allows for the development of nonconscious regulation of affective state. When I saw the group of Muslims, my amygdala was doing what it needs to do: preparing my body for action in the case of an imminent threat. Its response to the stimulus was fast, a split second, and out of awareness. The regulation by the orbitofrontal cortex allowed me to become peaceful again.

Third, fear can be an emotion that masks reality. LeDoux (2002) researched the function and structure of the amygdala and how it allows for an instantaneous, unthinking reaction in the face of a threat. He describes how when a person sees a snake, the amygdala prepares him or her for action. The person jumps back and only after this initial reaction reflects on what is reasonable to do. The initial reaction occurs at levels below awareness. This is why I say fear can mask reality. A first pathway from the visual cortex to the amygdala does not interpret details and allows for a quick reaction. A slower pathway exists in the brain that better defines the fearful event but takes longer to be processed and does not allow quick escape or fighting back. However, it is important for the regulation of our fears because it allows for a better interpretation of the cause of fear. In his article "How Our Brain Processes Terrorist Carnage," Robert Sylwester (2001), professor of education, writes:

> Our brain has two separate problem-solving systems. (1) Serious challenges with a sense of immediacy are rapidly and reflexively processed by our brain's innate stress-driven, conceptual problem-solving system. This system responds quickly on the basis of a small amount of emotionally intense information. It's not interested in details. It's thus quite vulnerable to making racist/sexist/elitist responses based on only a few highly visible emotion-charged elements—but it's also capable of making impulsive altruistic responses. (2) Challenges without a sense of immediacy are processed more slowly and reflectively by our brain's curiosity-driven, analytical problem-solving system (located principally in our frontal lobes).

Fourth, fears can be grounded or ungrounded. Louis Cozolino (2002, p. 237) says: "With the expansion of the cerebral cortex and the emergence of imagination, we have become capable of feeling anxious about potential outcomes and situations that can never exist." To share in the fears of one another in conflict transformation, it is important to take into account both types of fear and recognize their source.

Fifth, fear can be acquired. Harmless individuals, objects, or events can become fearful through fear conditioning. I had never connected fear to Muslims before my event in the airport. Because of my long exposure to the Muslim world, I have developed many friendships with Muslims and usually enjoy meeting them. It brings back positive emotional memories of drinking coffee with Muslim friends at the Bosporus or celebrating the wedding of good friends in Tunis. My usual reaction when seeing Muslims is to have pleasant feelings. Since this was not my first reaction in the airport, I realize that I associated a fearful element to the people I saw, which in this case was the airport—a potentially dangerous place since the recent hijackings. Associations occur all the time in our brain. By touching a hot stove, a child learns not to try again. The hot stove becomes associated to its fears. Once burnt, the child remembers the heat by seeing the stove. Studies have been made of pairing tone and shock. After several experiences of feeling the shock and hearing the tone, people reacted to tone as fearfully as to shock. In my experience in the airport, I had nonconsciously paired the Muslims waiting in the boarding area with hijackers. The message to my emotional brain was: Muslims equal danger. My amygdala prepared me for action in case of danger. If I had met these same Muslims in another location, I may have reacted differently. Since I had previous positive experiences of encounters, the smile of the Muslim woman quickly calmed my fears, but I can imagine that someone without previous positive encounters with Muslims might have reacted differently and taken longer to calm down.

If fear is not autoregulated or interactively regulated, secure relations will never develop. I could have stayed in a high-alert-amygdala state long after this event. I could have also given in to phobia. Fortunately the brain, and more specifically the orbitofrontal cortex, has the capacity to regulate fear and stress either by autoregulation or interactive regulation. Attachment research shows how in childhood, the child uses the caregiver's smiling face to return to joy and keeps the memory of this joyful face that he or she recalls later to regulate negative emotional states during safe social interactions (Schore 1994). Some adults use important comforting figures in their religious beliefs, such as God for example, as a secure base that calms their fears and brings them joy. Others need an individual or an entire community to regulate their fears.

Individuals attach securely to those who regulate their fears. If Christians want to develop secure bonds with Muslims, they need to either autoregulate their fears with positive internal images of smiling faces of Muslims, and that means proactively engage in social exchange with them to be able to experience joy in their presence, or interactively regulate as they engage in increasing small episodes of fear regulation with them. Attachment grows over a long period of time, and one learns to recognize the joyful smile of another person after much cross-cultural practice and interactions. One also learns in this process to recognize the threatening face that needs to be avoided for survival.

TERROR: ANOTHER KIND OF FEAR

The fear of many Americans, whether Muslims or Christians, of a direct attack to their country is a genuine fear. However, the fear can vary in its intensity. The more intense state of fear is terror. Two categories of people may experience terror states. First, those present on site during the attacks on the World Trade Center experienced trauma through strong stimuli such as extremely loud noise, suffocating fumes and smoke inhalation, physical injuries, etc. For them, terror was bodily felt and will be bodily remembered in future social interactions. Others have not been present in the attack but the images they have seen on television have resonated with memories of past traumas they have experienced. They will also experience very intense fears, difficult to regulate in the presence of a fearful individual or event.

One cannot attach securely after terror states and trauma. In childhood, traumatic events lead to disorganized attachment patterns (Schore 2002). In adulthood, trauma can also deeply affect the regulation structures in the brain. Wars and conflicts trigger high amygdala alert states in individuals. I remember sitting at the same table with a Lebanese man who had gone through the war in his country in the 1980s. We had lunch in a very quiet restaurant in Switzerland. Someone dropped a glass. Most people just turned their heads toward the person who dropped the glass and stopped eating for a second. But the reaction of my friend was very different. He tipped over from the chair, because the noise had sent signals to his amygdala that there was imminent danger. His mind was associating the noise of the glass dropping to the floor with the noise of bombs falling in his neighborhood for seventeen years. The bodily reaction was intense, a result of trauma. It took him longer to regulate his fear.

How can one regulate a strong affect like terror felt in the body after direct exposure to violent events? Affect regulation suggests that the intensity of the emotion has to be taken into account in the process of healing. Trying to help a terrorized individual by saying "Don't worry, you are OK" will not be very useful. Regulating his or her fear is different from regulating the fears of someone who has not been directly attacked. Restoration of secure relations will take longer. There is often a need for greater care by health specialists trained to assist people with posttraumatic stress disorder.

In conflict transformation, the intensity of the fear must be taken into account. Not all fears are the same. And when one interactively regulates with the affective fear state of a person, one needs to regulate not just with the emotion but with its intensity. In this chapter, as I said earlier, I am not addressing the type of fear directly connected to terror states. However, the current discourse on terror may lead some people to experience more intense fears; they will be different from terror states but their intensity needs to be addressed in affect regulation. In interactive regulation, this means that the person who feels this intense fear will expect the other to resonate not just with the fear but with its intensity.

WHAT DO CHRISTIANS FEAR?

It would have been good for this section to conduct research in churches and Christian communities to find out what kind of fears Christians harbor when they interact with Muslims. The fear that comes immediately to mind is the one related to the current discourse on terrorism. But are there other fears that Christians have? In this section, I only mention a few that I observed in my interactions with Christians. Further research should document these fears more precisely. In this chapter they serve as a platform for discussion between Muslims and Christians in an attempt to underline the need for affect regulation between the two communities.

Historical Fear

Earlier I wrote that our brain and mind keeps memories of our fears. These fears are then passed down from generation to generation in stories and narratives. They may also sometimes be passed down as affect dysregulation when, for example, a parent experienced trauma followed with no repair and is therefore not able to regulate the affective states of his or her children. Furthermore, according to Louise Higgins (2004), who conducted research on the cultural effects of the expression of some fears by Chinese and British female students, "Some human fears are thought to be learned either vicariously by observing other's behaviors or by association with aversive consequences."

Fearful episodes in history, such as wars and violent conflicts, can become integral parts of religious narratives. When there has been no repair of the bond between communities, no experience of positive and joyful encounters, this fear can divide communities forever. It would be helpful to trace the history of the "fear of the Turks" that comes up regularly in the European discourse and goes back many centuries to the time of the Ottoman Empire. Instead of being a fear regulator, the word "Turk" becomes a strong affect dysregulator, especially in times of tensions between the two communities.

I suggest Christian communities look for stories of positive emotional interactions within Muslim–Christian relationships that can be used as fear regulators. There is a need for stories where Muslims and Christians acted as a secure base for each other. These stories are especially necessary when the initial dyadic encounter has not been happy but fearful. Attachment researchers emphasize the importance of the emotion of joy for making connections and the formation of a bond where there was no relationship (Schore 1994). Many Christians in the United States never had a personal Muslim friend when the recent conflict broke out. The encounter between the two groups started on a negative tone. What are the happy and joyful memories that people can recall between the two communities that will help them reconnect? For many Christians, there was no memory of happy interaction because the bond was simply nonexistent. Furthermore, the stories they hear from history are accounts of wars, conflicts, disagreements, and misunderstandings. There are many other examples of affect-dysregulating images that are included in the collective unconscious of people and amplify rather than decrease the fear in times of danger and terror. As we engage in conflict transformation, let us address these areas of dysregulation in history. Left unrepaired, the bond will continue to be insecure.

Fear of Losing Land

The fear of losing one's personal space or territory is another kind of fear expressed in the Christian community. I said at the beginning of this chapter that attachment theory was first considered a spatial theory. This is still true even if affect regulation now has been added as a central theoretical framework.

Everyone needs a space where he or she feels secure. Christians often express a concern about Muslims invading their space. Statements such as "Will Europe (or America) become Muslim?" are often uttered. This reaction by Christians is not new. In the past, Christian minorities under the *dhimmi* system in Muslim-majority countries often feared losing their space although this system was originally set up to protect religious minorities, according to Muslims. Countries with a majority of Christians feel often threatened by the expansion of Muslim neighboring states. The demographic rate among Muslims is also seen as a threat. To establish secure bonds, Muslims will need to listen to the fears of Christians and modulate them. Anglican Bishop Michael Nazir-Ali (2002) recently wrote, "After the renaissance of Nationalism in different parts of the world the religious minorities, whoever they may be, are not willing to be dhimmis, they want to be citizens and while the history of dhimma may provide some inspiration it cannot be the model for the future." To address these fears, well-documented facts need to be provided and if it turns out that these facts are correct and the fears are grounded, the two communities will have to negotiate how they will share space so that everyone can feel secure.

Sharing the same neighborhood can also trigger fears and affect dysregulation. A recent controversy in Hamtramck, Michigan, between the Muslim and non-Muslim community concerning the call to prayer from mosque loudspeakers is just one example of tensions that can occur in neighborhoods over space. In this instance, it was more the sound than the space that was a problem. Sound, in this case the call to prayer—which is an unfamiliar sound to many non-Muslims—is processed implicitly by the right brain, which also processes symbols, rhythms, and other important elements of worship. This can lead to out-of-awareness dysregulation and disruption of bonds between communities. One way to solve this problem is for Muslims to address the anxiety and stress created by the nonconscious processing of a sound that was considered foreign, unfamiliar, and threatening to the Christian community in the neighborhood. This was done in reducing the volume of the call to prayer.

Fear of Beliefs

Since the early days of Christian–Muslim encounters, an elaborate mechanism of defense in the form of polemics, apologetics or debate, has been established to defend each other's beliefs. One of the early Christian apologists, John of Damascus, was more concerned about protecting the beliefs of the Christian community than to enter in a conversation with Islam (Sahas 1972).

The mode of theological interaction was defensive or offensive and served as a shield against beliefs that were not in accord with Christian thinking.

The Christian community faces the challenge to conduct healthy theological interactions while acting Christ-like in their social interactions with Muslims. Dialogue is one approach that fosters positively felt interactions in the defense of each other's faith. It emphasizes empathy and acceptance of one another without necessarily agreeing on every point of the discussion.

Some Christians struggle with the concept of dialogue because they are afraid this means compromising their beliefs. Attachment theory and affect regulation may become a useful resource for them. Developing secure relationships does not mean thinking the same. When Fuller started to enter in dialogue with Muslims on the issue of conflict transformation, some Christians were afraid that we had made concessions to Muslims in regards to our Christology. The Christian self seemed to them threatened by this project. I argue that attachment does not mean symbiosis. One does not need to be like the other to relate securely to him or her. Attachment allows two different selves to enter in a dyadic secure relation. In human attachment there is room for detachment when the integrity of the self is threatened.

Fear of Death and Persecution

There are reports from Christians in some parts of the Muslim world that trigger strong affect dysregulation. One of them concerns the issue of apostasy. Some Christians who have shared their faith with Muslims have reported being ostracized by society and put to jail and some have been reported to have died as a result of persecution. Other Christians talk about social pressures and restrictions on churches that cannot thrive as if they would be in a non-Muslim context. These stories create deep anxiety and fear. Muslims must resonate with this fear. Again, a good understanding of fear may be helpful. Are these fears grounded or not? The serious documentation of each individual case, with all parties invited to express their views, will be helpful in dealing with such issues.

Sharî'ah law is another fear-triggering concept for Christians. As we engage in a conversation between Evangelicals and Muslims, these are some areas that must be seriously addressed, with specific attention given to the "fear factor" of legal systems that are unfamiliar to the Christian community and feel sometimes threatening to churches and individuals.

CONCLUSION

In this chapter I have argued that affect regulation is an important component of conflict transformation. I have underlined the importance of looking at concepts such as attachment, the secure base, and fear regulation when dealing with conflict. I have focused on the emotion of fear and its modulation and offered new avenues for transforming conflict through self-regulation and interactive regulation of fear for the formation of secure bonds between individuals. Of course, conflict transformation includes much more than fear regulation, but nevertheless affect regulation is an important element of it.

I explained briefly the mechanism and effect of fear. Those who want to better understand the neurobiology of fear can consult the scores of articles published as a result of rapid advances in brain research. Keeping up with the current research on fear circuitry in the brain is important. It will further explain the nonconscious effect of fear on our behaviors and relations.

I have explained that there are different kinds of fears. Some fears are grounded and need to be addressed by Muslims. Others are ungrounded and also need to be addressed in order for Christians to become aware of how harmless they are.

Awareness and consciousness are important elements in the process of fear regulation. I mentioned that actions may precede reasoning in case of fear. But once the danger fades away, there can be a tendency to stay in an amygdala high-alert state. Actions should be based not only on emotional cues but also on rational assessments. Julie Polter (2004) wrote that "the power of fear to skew a person's choices has been shown to diminish when fears are acknowledged and confronted consciously and directly."

I have defined some of the fears that Christians express when they encounter Muslims and suggested some ways to regulate fears. There are many more to discover. The list of fears I quoted in this chapter is limited. Further research must be more specific and describe the fears and their implications in greater detail, looking for each fear and its specific nature. As Muslims and Christians both experience fear, if they want to form secure bonds, they must be able to become a regulator for the other.

I sometimes hear from the Christian community: "Can we really trust Muslims? They paint a picture of a peaceful, benevolent, and tolerant religion, but are they telling us everything?" This fear can only be found grounded or ungrounded as one enters into a relationship where both parties can experience the other as a secure base. Earned attachment is an important concept in attachment theory (Schore 2003). It means that whereas the relationship was insecure and may be even disorganized, the relationship now has become secure. This however takes place after numerous interpersonal experiences of affect dysregulations followed by the repair of the bond. This type of relationship is not built overnight. It should not be built with individuals that are dangerous and harmful unless they change their ways. However, it can happen with those who are safe to be with and provide affect regulation.

This chapter was written by a Christian addressing both Christians and Muslims. I am aware of the limitations of this discussion because it does not include a list of the fears that Muslims have of Christians. I did not provide a platform for discussing the fears of Muslims because I did not want to speak on their behalf. But I would like to discuss the fears of Muslims in another context.

The Bible provides numerous examples of God regulating the fears of humans. On numerous examples in the Bible, God addresses people with "Don't be afraid." He said to Abraham, "Do not be afraid, Abram. I am your shield, your very great reward" (Genesis 15:1). He said to Hagar, "Do not be afraid, I have heard the boy crying as he lies there" (Genesis 21:17). On numerous occasions he addressed people with the same expression in the Gospel to calm their fears, such as for example when he said to the disciples, "Indeed, the very hairs of your head are all numbered. Don't be afraid; you are worth more than many sparrows" (Luke 12:7). When people were afraid, God was able to bring comfort and security.

In the Bible, Christians are encouraged to show similar concerns for their neighbors and those among whom they live. They are encouraged to serve as a secure base for others. They are called to love their neighbors and do good and be ready to defend those who are wrongly accused and stereotyped. Many themes in the Bible refer to the care that believers should provide for those whom the society does fear such as the aliens in the Old Testament (Exodus 22 and 23) or the Samaritans in the Gospel and the Greeks, also called Barbarians during that time, in the Epistles. God's message points believers toward the embrace and reconciliation with fellow humans rather than fear, mistrust, or prejudice.

Eventually, God calls Christians to see people as they truly are, with their strength and weakness. Sometimes our fears can be like a screen hiding the true identity of the other person. We look at our fears, rather than at who the person really is. God says in Exodus 23:1, "Do not spread false reports." Fear can make us blind, so that we do not witness the reality anymore. According to Proverb 12:17, "A truthful witness gives honest testimony." These passages, like many more in the Bible call us to see others as they truly are and care for each other as we all participate in the same humanity.

REFERENCES

Ainsworth, Mary. 1967. *Infancy in Uganda*. Baltimore: Johns Hopkins University Press.

Ainsworth, M., M. Blehar, E. Waters, and S. Wall. 1978. *Patterns of Attachment*. Hillsdale, N.J.: Erlbaum.

Bartholomew, K., and L. M. Horowitz. 1991. Attachment styles among young adults: A test of a four-category model. *Journal of Personality and Social Psychology* 61: 226–44.

Bowlby, John. 1973. *Attachment and loss*. Vol. 2, *Separation anxiety and anger*. London: Hogarth Press and Institute of Psycho-Analysis.

———. 1982. *Attachment and Loss*. Vol. 1, *Attachment*. 2nd ed. New York: Basic Books.

Cassidy, Jude, and Phillip R. Shaver, eds. *Handbook of attachment: Theory, research, and clinical applications*. New York: Guilford, 1999.

Cozolino, Louis. 2002. *The neuroscience of psychotherapy: Building and rebuilding the human brain*. New York: Norton.

Higgins, Louise T. 2004. Cultural effects on the expression of some fears by Chinese and British female students. *The Journal of Genetic Psychology* 165 (1): 37–49.

Kobak, Roger. 1999. The emotional dynamics of disruptions in attachment relationships: Implications for theory, research and clinical intervention. In *Handbook of attachment: Theory, research, and clinical applications*, ed. Jude Cassidy and Phillip R. Shaver, 21–43. New York: Guilford.

Lederach, John Paul. 1997. *Building peace: Sustainable reconciliation in divided societies*. Washington, DC: Institute of Peace Press.

———. 2003. *The little book of conflict transformation*. Intercourse, PA: Good Books.

LeDoux, Joseph. 2002. *Synaptic self: How our brains become who we are*. New York: Viking.

Morris, J. S., C. D. Frith, D. I. Perrett, D. Rowland, A. W. Young, A. J. Calder, and R. J. Dolan. 1996. A differential neural response in the human amygdala to fearful and happy facial expressions. *Nature* 383: 812–15.

Nazir-Ali, Michael. 2002. The Primates Meeting 2002. NIFCON. www.anglicannifcon .org/NazirAli-PF.htm.

Polter, Julie. 2004. The politics of fear. *Sojourners* 33 (10): 16–17.

Sahas, Daniel J. 1972. *John of Damascus on Islam: The "Heresy of the Ishmaelites*. Leiden, Brill.

Schore, Allan N. 1994. *Affect regulation and the origin of the self: The neurobiology of emotional development*. Hillsdale, NJ: Lawrence Erlbaum.

———. 2000. Attachment and the regulation of the right brain. *Attachment and Human Development* 2 (1): 23–47.

———. 2002. Dysregulation of the right brain: A fundamental mechanism of traumatic attachment and the psychopathogenesis of posttraumatic stress disorder. *Australian and New Zealand Journal of Psychiatry* 36: 9–30.

———. 2003. *Affect regulation and the repair of the self*. New York: Norton.

Schrock-Shenk, Carolyn. 2000. *Mediation and facilitation training manual: Foundations and skills for constructive conflict transformation*. 4th ed. Akron, Pa.: Mennonite Conciliation Service.

Sylwester, Robert. 2001. How our brain processes terrorist carnage. www.brain connection.com/content/169_1.

14

Toward Mutual Respectful Witness

J. Dudley Woodberry

Our Muslim partners listed "the ethics of mission and proselytization" as the first item that they wished to discuss with partners from the Fuller Theological Seminary. To facilitate this let me suggest some general definitions of terms, leaving more detailed analysis until later in this chapter:

Witness—the expression of our faith in God by worship, service, and proclamation. The Qur'an uses various forms of *shahada*, "to bear witness," among people (2:143; 3:64) as Jesus told his disciples to be his "witnesses" (*martures*) to the end of the earth (Acts 1:8).

Mission—being "sent" to share the "good news" of the gospel by word (*kerygma*) and deed (*diakonia*) and worship.

Da'wah—the "call" to share the message by word (Qur'an 16:125) and deed and worship.

Evangelism—as part of holistic missions, the focus on proclaiming and demonstrating the "good news" of the gospel toward the end that people will become disciples of Jesus and be transformed by God's Spirit.

Proselytism—though a neutral or positive term in the Bible (e.g., Acts 2:10) and in international law, it has come to be used negatively of unworthy witness because of coercion or inducements external to the gospel or scriptural message. It will be used here in the latter, negative sense.

We shall demonstrate that witness through *da'wah* and mission are enjoined in the Qur'an and Bible, respectively. Then we shall comment on the understanding and practice of the witness of each faith community worldwide. After indicating tensions and criticism that have arisen between them, we shall suggest guidelines for mutually responsible and respectful witness.

SCRIPTURAL GROUNDS FOR MUTUAL WITNESS

Both Islam and Christianity are missionary religions as we shall see and are called on to engage in witness in a kind manner. To do this meaningfully, we shall note both where our understandings of our scriptures agree and where they differ.

Common Ground

Helpfully, we start with considerable common ground:

- We both worship the One God but understand some significant things about him differently (e.g., the type of unity [Qur'an 4:17; Galatians 3:20; Matthew 28:19] and whether God loves sinners [Qur'an 3:31–32; 1 John 1:14]).
- We honor Jesus and use some of the same descriptors of him even though we may mean different things by some of them—for example, the word from God (Qur'an 3:45; John 1:14).
- We agree on humans as stewards of God on earth (*khalifa*) under God and over creation (Qur'an 2:30; Genesis 1:26–28).
- We have similar understandings of God's law,[1] but differ on its ability to transform society (Qur'an 46:12; Romans 7:18–8:4).
- We have similar views of the importance of faith and works but differ on their respective roles in salvation (Qur'an 19:60; Ephesians 2:8–10).
- We are both enjoined to invite to what is good and forbid what is wrong (Qur'an 3:104; Galatians 5:16–23).

Common but, at Times, Competing Claims

What challenges our relationship is that some of the statements of our respective scriptures sometimes compete with each other:

- Both are missionary religions with a message for all people:
  - Qur'an 25: 1 — "Blessed is he who has sent down the criterion (*furqan*) [for judging right and wrong] upon his servant so that he may be the warner to all beings."

- Qur'an 38: 87 — "This is no less than a reminder to [all] the worlds."

- The intended recipients include Jews and Christians:
  - Qur'an 3:20 — "Say to the People of the Book and to those who are unlearned, 'Do you also submit yourselves (*aslamtum*)?' If they do, they are in right guidance, but if they turn back, your duty is to convey the message."
  - John 3:16 — "For God so loved the world that He gave His only Son that whosoever believes in Him should not perish but have everlasting life."

- Both claim the final messenger:
  - Qur'an 33:40 — "Muhammad . . . is the seal of the Prophets."
  - Hebrews 1: 1–2 — "In many and various ways God spoke of old to our fathers by the prophets, but in these last days He has spoken to us by *His* Son, whom He appointed the heir of all things."

- Both groups of followers are to be witnesses:
  - Qur'an 2:143 — "Thus have we made of you community justly balanced that you might be witnesses."
  - Acts 1:8 — "You shall be my witnesses in Jerusalem and in all Judea and Samaria and to the end of the earth."

- Both make apparently exclusive claims for their message, although some Muslims and Christians interpret the passages in less exclusive ways:
  - Qur'an 3:85 — "If anyone desires a religion other than Islam (or submission), never will it be accepted of him, and in the Hereafter he will be in the ranks of those who have lost" (cf. vs 19).

    Note that the exclusiveness is determined by whether the Arabic word *islam* in this context describes a distinct religion or a general response of submission to God as when it is used of Jesus' disciples (Qur'an 3:52; 5:111–112).
  - John 14:6 — "I am the Way, the Truth, and the Life. No one comes unto the Father but by Me."
  - Acts 4:12 — "And there is salvation in no one else for there is no other name under heaven given among mortals by which we must be saved."

Some Christians would say that it is possible to affirm these verses and still trust, or hope, that God might save others through the life, death, and resurrection of Jesus even though they do not clearly understand him, even as various Old Testament personages through their faith are included in heaven (Hebrews 11:16–40).

- Both are to witness in a gracious way:
    - Qur'an 16:125 "Invite to the Way of your Lord with wisdom and good exhortation and dispute with them with what is better (or in a better way)."
    - Qur'an 29:46 "Dispute not with the People of the Book except with what is better (or in a better way)."
    - I Peter 3:15 "Always be prepared to give an answer to anyone who calls you to account for the hope that is in you with gentleness and respect."

UNDERSTANDINGS AND EXTENT OF WITNESS WORLDWIDE

The late Isma'il al-Faruqi presented a paper "On the Nature of Islamic Da'wah" at the conference on "Christian Mission and Islamic Da'wah" in Chambésy, Switzerland, in 1976.[2] His description of it shows considerable parallels with Christian Mission. He says it is a call (Qur'an 16:125) and therefore not coercive—a theme also stressed by Christian participants in the joint statement of the Conference as well as by John Stott, whom many would consider one of the two major spokespersons for Evangelical thought.[3] Faruqi adds that *da'wah* is directed at Muslims as well as non-Muslims, which our subsequent overview of mission practice will also show to be true of Christians.

Faruqi's characterization of *da'wah* as not only proclamation but also serving culture and civilization is similar to a Christian view of mission,[4] though he does not recognize the fact. As Jesus healed a leper and then said "tell no one" (Matt. 8:4), Christians recognize that there are times where only the deed is appropriate, as frequently practiced by Christian relief and development agencies like World Vision.[5]

A preliminary quantitative assessment of the extent of Christian mission and Islamic *da'wah* includes the major church groupings (Anglican, Independent, Marginal, Orthodox, Protestant, and Roman Catholic) and Muslim groups with international ministries from the political Jama'at-i Islami to the largely nonpolitical Tabligh-i Jama'at. In their published article comparing Christian mission and *da'wah,* the authors Todd M. Johnson and David R. Scoggins calculated that about 57,300 Christian missionaries worked in Muslim contexts and 141,630 Muslim *da'is* worked outside their home country.[6] They have reduced the latter figure to 113,380 in a subsequent expanded but unpublished paper.

The comparison indicates that the vast majority of missionaries from both faith communities minister among their own adherents to revive and equip them. Also the majority of Christians now are already in the Southern rather than the Northern hemisphere and in the East rather than the West, so the previous power differential between missionaries and recipients has shifted.[7]

RESPECTIVE CRITIQUES OF FORMS OF WITNESS

Since both Islam and Christianity are seen to be missionary faiths with a world mission, they can be and often are rivals, but there are other problems that exacerbate the situation.[8] One is the disparity of power and wealth. During the colonial period this often helped the Christian missionary but not always. For example, Islam in Northern Nigeria prospered from the British support of the Muslim rulers. And Western interests such as the East India Company often opposed missionary activity. The Arabic press in the Middle East, however, ascribed a close linkage between Christian mission and Western imperialism. In the 1980s and 1990s the antimissionary tone broadened to an anti-Christian one and thus was also directed against ancient churches like the Coptic Orthodox Church.[9] Different types of power have hindered free witness. In Indonesia and Malaysia the Chinese Christians have economic power, but the Muslim Malays have political power. Then there is the power of religious tradition and the street. Even after police had released Christian converts when charges of apostasy or "blasphemy" have been dismissed, they were killed by common citizens in Iran and Pakistan. It is in the area of religious freedom that many Christians have concerns.[10]

GUIDELINES FOR RESPECTFUL MUTUAL WITNESS

There have been two consultations in particular that have been helpful in drawing up guidelines for mutual witness. The first, already mentioned, was the conference on "Christian Mission and Islamic Da'wah" in Chambésy, Switzerland, June 26–30, 1976, organized by the Commission on World Mission and Evangelism of the World Council of Churches, Geneva, in consultation with the Islamic Foundation, Leicester, and the Centre for the Study of Islam and Christian-Muslim Relations, Selly Oak Colleges, Birmingham, England. The other in which I was privileged to take part was the "Christian-Muslim Consultation on Religious Freedom" sponsored by the World Council of Churches and held at Hartford Seminary, October 15, 1999. I have felt free to adopt and adapt materials from these consultation reports when they are relevant to our context with the hope that Muslim and Christian colleagues will feel free to make modifications if they do not agree.

- We recognize that *da'wah* and mission are essential privileges and responsibilities of Muslims and Christians.
- The respective communities, wherever they are a minority of the population, should enjoy the legal right to exist and should be permitted to conduct their religious life freely and have liberty to convince and be convinced.
- We as Christians and Muslims are grieved that our respective communities have caused each other suffering by sometimes denying the above freedoms or exercising our power in harmful ways.
- In making any comparisons of beliefs and practices we shall endeavor to compare similar issues—religious ideals with ideals and realities with realities.
- In joint activities we shall try to the extent possible to keep an equitable balance between Muslims and Christians and men and women.
- We shall strive to foster the peace and welfare of our life together.

If we Christians and Muslims abide by these guidelines, we shall be faithful dictates of our respective scriptures and, in doing so, facilitate contexts where people can live in harmony while following their conscience.

NOTES

1. See Robert Roberts, *The Social Laws of the Qoran* (London: Williams and Norgate, 1925).
2. Reprinted in the *International Review of Mission* 5, no. 260 (October 1976) and in *Evangelical Review of Theology* 20, no. 2 (April 1996): 126–35.
3. www.christianitytoday.com/ct/2003/009/2.50.html.
4. See, e.g., articles 5 on "Christian Social Responsibility" and 10 on "Evangelism and Culture" of the Lausanne Covenant of the Lausanne Committee for World Evangelization, the most representative movement of Evangelicals worldwide. See www.feb.org/lausanne_covenant:htm (accessed July 27, 2006). Also see "Mission and Evangelism in Unity Today," adapted by the World Council of Churches' Commission on World Mission and Evangelism in Morges, Switzerland, 2000, p. 2 in *Ecumenical Letter on Evangelism*, no. 3 (Geneva: Mission and Evangelism, World Council of Churches, November 2005): 2–9.
5. See *Christianity Today*, March 2005, 50–56.

6. Todd M. Johnson and David R. Scoggins, "Christian Missions and Islamic *Da'wah*: A Preliminary Quantitative Assessment," *International Bulletin of Missionary Research* 29, no. 1 (January 2005): 8–11.

7. Mark Laing, "The Changing Face of Mission: Implications for the Southern Shift in Christianity," *Missiology: An International Review* 34, no. 2 (April 2006): 165–77.

8. For Muslim concerns see Seyyed Hossein Nasr, *Islamic-Christian Dialogue—Problems and Obstacles to be Pondered and Overcome* (Washington, DC: Center for Muslim-Christian Understanding, 1998), 17–19.

9. Heather J. Sharkey, "Arabic Antimissionary Treatises: Muslim Responses to Christian Evangelism in the Modern Middle East," "Arabic Antimissionary Treatises: A Select Annotated Bibliography," *International Bulletin* 28, no. 3 (July 2004), 98–106.

10. See Paul Marshall, "Persecution of Christians in the Contemporary World," *International Bulletin* 22, no. 1 (January 1998), 2–8; Annual Reports of the United States Commission on International Religious Freedom, Washington, DC.

15

The Right to Religious Conversion

Between Apostasy and Proselytization[1]

Abdul Rashied Omar

In the Spring of 2006 an Afghan citizen, Abdul Rahman, who had converted from Islam to Christianity was arrested under local shari'ah law, which mandates the death penalty for apostasy. As a result of international pressure, Abdul Rahman was released and given asylum in Italy.[2] This widely publicized incident highlighted the urgent need for Muslims to seriously reexamine the restrictive shari'ah laws on apostasy. It is unfortunate, however, that this case took place in the war-ravaged context of Afghanistan, where relief aid for the victims of war is dispensed by Christian agencies, some with a primarily evangelistic agenda. A similar program of aid evangelism has been undertaken in war-torn Iraq. The activities of such groups have reinvigorated the debate over whether it is ethical for philanthropical activities and humanitarian service to be undertaken with the primary intent to proselytize. The legitimacy of religious conversion and the ethics of mission are challenging issues. But they are also pertinent issues that should form part of an honest dialogical encounter between Christians and Muslims, since they have important implications for conflict transformation and interreligious peace-building.

Taking this conflict as its point of departure, this chapter argues that both the prevailing Muslim positions on apostasy and Christian engagement in aid with the primary intent of evangelism generate a harmful environment for Christian-Muslim relations and interreligious peace-building. The chapter concludes by challenging Christians and Muslims committed to interreligious dialogue to go beyond mere *declarations* of the right of any individual to change his or her religion and decrying the use of inappropriate means to entice the person to switch his or her faith. The deeper challenge is to find creative ways of making such affirmations a key part of the *modus vivendi* of convivial relations between the two communities. It might be useful to commence by revisiting the question of religious conversion in the context of Christian-Muslim dialogue.

RELIGIOUS CONVERSION AS A SOURCE OF CONFLICT

The problem of the right to religious conversion and the ethics of Christian mission and Islamic *da'wah*[3] has been a longstanding topic of debate in interreligious dialogue. The subject was considered at length during a meeting between Christian and Muslim scholars and leaders in Chambesy, Switzerland, in 1976.[4] Since then, the issue has been raised intermittently, most notably at a Christian-Muslim Consultation on "Religious Freedom, Community Rights and Individual Rights" sponsored by the Interreligious Office of the World Council of Churches (WCC) at the Duncan MacDonald Center for the Study of Islam and Christian-Muslim Relations in Hartford, Connecticut, in 1999.[5] More recently, the question has resurfaced at a number of interreligious forums. For example, at the "Critical Moment in Interreligious Dialogue Conference" convened by the WCC in Geneva from 7 to 9 June 2005, the problem of religious conversion and the ethics of mission was raised as one of the most divisive issues between religious communities.[6]

Both Christian and Muslim scholars of interreligious relations share concerns over the right to conversion and the ethics of mission. Elizabeth Scantlebury, for example, has argued that the matter of Christian mission and Islamic *da'wah* is central to the negative model of interaction between the followers of the two religions.[7] Similarly, the Muslim thinker and scholar Seyyed Hossein Nasr observed that "one of the most contentious issues in the dialogue between Islam and Christianity is missionary activity." He goes on to describe it as one of the obstacles and outstanding problems in Islamic–Christian dialogue.[8] While for many Muslims, Christian mission is the obstacle, for Christians according to the Evangelical scholar J. Dudley Woodberry, the concern is in the area of religious freedom, and in particular the right of Muslims to convert from Islam.

The question of changing or disseminating one's religion is not only a source of tension and distrust between Christians and Muslims it is also a bone of contention between Christians, Muslims, and other religious communities in diverse parts of the world. In India, for example, religious conversion and Christian evangelism are viewed as sources of deadly conflict. The widespread violence directed against Christians in India, a direct result of Hindu protests against religious conversion, is documented in the Human Rights Watch Report (1999), *Politics by Other Means: Attacks against Christians in India.*[9]

Explicating the conflict over the right to religious conversion, the Montreal-based philosopher of religion Arvind Sharma states that "most modern Hindus are opposed to the idea of conversion, from one religion to another per se." He further argues that "the Hindu view of religious freedom is not based on the freedom to proselytize, but the right to retain one's religion and not be subject to proselytization."[10] A similar viewpoint is expressed by Swami Agnivesh, a renowned interreligious activist and the president of Arya Samaj, an international Hindu revivalist movement. Agnivesh confirms Sharma's position, arguing, "It is the prevalent view of most Hindu thinkers, including Mahatma Gandhi, who was known for his religious tolerance, that a true pluralist person seeking dialogue would demand that Christianity and Islam liquidate their missionary apparatus."[11] As a direct consequence of such views, legislation in several Indian states against conversion has been debated and in some cases implemented. The most recent case is that of the so-called Freedom of Religion Bill adopted by the Rajasthan Cabinet of Chief Minister Vasundhra Raje Scindia and is currently before the Legislative Assembly for approval. A number of nongovernmental organizations have challenged the legal validity of such legislation all over India and pointed out that it violates the fundamental right of freedom of conscience.[12]

The topic of changing and disseminating one's religion as it relates to the Indian context is also a raging debate within scholarly circles. A multidisciplinary symposium on the subject formed part of the 19th World Congress of the International History of Religions, in Tokyo, Japan, in March 2005.[13] Arvind Sharma is one of the leading advocates for changing the existing formulation of the freedom of religion clause in the Universal Declaration of Human Rights, for he believes that the existing formulation favors those religions which proselytize.[14]

Yet other scholars, like the Dutch anthropologist of religion Peter van der Veer, have questioned the validity of the central assumption on which the Hindu case against the legitimacy of religious conversion is based, stating, "I find it quite important to point out that the 'naturalness' or 'givenness' of Hinduism is a myth."[15] Van der Veer's suggestion that Indians have not been primordially Hindu, and that they converted to what came to be known as Hinduism at some point in history is a challenging proposition that needs to be further explored. Moreover, there are some Hindu strands such as the Hare Krishna who do engage in mission activities. Notwithstanding the outreach activities of these Hindu groups, it needs to be unequivocally acknowledged that Hindu missions pale into insignificance in the face of the global proselytization efforts sponsored by Christians. Not surprisingly, therefore, the question of religious conversion and the ethics of mission pose a different challenge for Muslims. Unlike mainstream modern Hinduism as depicted by Sharma and Swami Agnivesh, Islam also encourages its adherents to share the teachings and faith with others. But how similar or disparate is Christian mission to that of Islamic *da'wah*?

CHRISTIAN MISSION AND ISLAMIC DA'WAH: A COMPARATIVE PERSPECTIVE

Notwithstanding the fact that Christian mission and Islamic *da'wah* was the exclusive concern of a meeting between Christian and Muslim scholars and leaders in Chambesy (1976), the renowned scholar of Christian-Muslim relations David Kerr correctly argues that "little scholarly attention has yet been given to the comparative study of Islamic da'wa and Christian mission."[16] A noticeable trend in the paucity of comparative studies that do exist is that while non-Muslim scholars such as William Wagner,[17] J. Dudley Woodberry,[18] and to a lesser extent Antoine Wessels[19] have highlighted the parallels between Muslim *da'wah* and Christian mission, Muslim scholars have been eager to point out significant differences. Three renowned Muslim scholars who have emphasized the differences are the Pakistani economist and thinker Khurshid Ahmad, the late Syed Zainul Abedin, founder of the Institute for Muslim Minority Affairs, and the late Palestinian-American scholar Ismai'l Raji al-Faruqi.[20]

In his editorial to the published proceedings of the 1976 Chambesy Consultation Ahmad, for example, called attention to the differences in the way Muslims and Christians "offer their message to others and at a deeper level, in the way they concern themselves with the world."[21] In particular, he drew a sharp distinction between the methods of doing *da'wah* from what he called "the widespread abuse of Christian *diakonia*."[22] Ahmad's position was reflected in the final declaration of the Chambesy Consultation, which condemned in clear terms the misuse of *diakonia* (caritative service and support) and strongly urged Christian churches and organizations to suspend their misused *diakonia* activities in the world of Islam.[23] Notwithstanding the fact that representatives of two of the leading Christian bodies, the Pontifical Council for Interreligious Dialogue and the Interreligious Office of the WCC, were part of the Chambesy declaration, not all Christians agreed with the strong stance adopted by it. Some Christian scholars have since made similar charges of Muslim organizations offering monetary enticements to Christians in exchange for their conversion to Islam.

Abidin takes Ahmad's critique even further and proposes that *da'wah* is witnessing the truth solely by means of the exemplary lives of individuals and communities. He contends that making religious conversion the explicit and measurable objective of *da'wah* violates both the prerogative of God, who changes the hearts of human beings, and God-given freedom of choice, without which the call of Islam to faithful submission would be meaningless.[24] Abedin also draws a sharp distinction between *da'wah* and dialogue. He defines interfaith dialogue as different from evangelism and mission, and sees its primary function as that of social solidarity, joining hands in equality and respect to fashion a better world.[25] Abedin's definition of *da'wah* and its methodology is idiosyncratic but may provide us with a useful clue for the development of an ethic of mission and *da'wah*.

Of the three scholarly perspectives on *da'wah*, Faruqi in particular has accentuated its divergences from Christian mission. During his presentation at Chambesy he defined *da'wah* as "ecumenical *par excellence*. All religious traditions," he proposed, are "*de jure*," by which he means that "they have all issued from and are based upon a common source, the religion of God which he planted equally in all men . . . *din al-fitrah*." While committed to religious pluralism in principle, al-Faruqi opposes relativism and what he describes as "kitchen cooperation," a kind of lazy ecumenism. Based on this novel outlook on religious mission, al-Faruqi views Islamic *da'wah* as "an ecumenical cooperative critique of the other religion rather than its invasion by a new truth."[26]

The tension between Christian and Muslim perspectives on their common commitment to mission is usefully illustrated by J. Dudley Woodberry when he claims that Faruqi's conception of the nature and ethics of *da'wah* "shows considerable parallels with Christian mission, though he does not recognize it."[27] Woodberry's assertion suggests that there is a significant gap in understanding between many Christians and Muslims on the way in which they perceive of their respective missions. David Kerr is one of the few scholars who have been attentive to this tension. Kerr develops a conceptual distinction between what he calls the "sending" notion of Christian mission and the "calling notion" of Islamic *da'wah*. "The former," Kerr suggests, "entails a centrifugal process while the second is centripetal."[28] He is acutely aware that these theological concepts are shaped by historical experience and actual practice. He furthermore proposes that Christian-Muslim reflections on mutual understandings of mission and *da'wah* may find renewed consensus in the Eastern Orthodox Church concept of "witness" (Greek *martyria*). The concept resonates with the Qur'anic concept of *shahada* and may provide a way of clarifying intentions and avoiding the malpractices of proselytism.[29] The ongoing challenge for Muslims and Christians is to find an ethical consensus on what Woodberry usefully describes as "mutual respectful witness."[30]

Recently, partly in recognition of the pressing nature of this challenge to interreligious dialogue, Dr. Hans Ucko, program secretary of the WCC's Office on Interreligious Relations and Dialogue called on the Pontifical

Council for Interreligious Dialogue to join the WCC in assuming responsibility to address what he described as "one of the most controversial issues in interreligious relations: conversion."[31] But why have the questions of religious conversion and the ethics of mission and *da'wah* reemerged as critical issues for interreligious dialogue at this time?

THE CONTEXT FOR THE REEMERGENCE OF THE DEBATE

A number of reasons account for the reemergence of the themes of religious conversion and the ethics of mission as critical issues for interreligious dialogue. Chiefly, the questions of religious conversion and the ethics of mission and *da'wah*, while extensively debated at Chambesy and elsewhere, have never been adequately resolved. Second, there is a gaping chasm between well-intentioned and benevolent statements of interreligious consultations and living realities on the ground. Third is the negative impact on Christian-Muslim relations resulting from the current belligerent environment generated by the terrorist attacks on the United States of America on September 11, 2001, and the Bush administration's subsequent decision to wage an "enduring war on terrorism" in Afghanistan and Iraq.

I argue that geopolitics are the key source of the renewed interest in the debate about the right to religious conversion and the ethics of mission and *da'wah*. In support of my contention I draw on the theoretical insights offered by Elizabeth Scantlebury. In a seminal article published exactly two decades after the Chambesy dialogue on *da'wah* and mission, Scantlebury argued that the contestation of the two faiths to gain converts at the other's expense always takes place within specific social and historical contexts, which in turn significantly affects the way those involved interpret the situation.[32] The sociopolitical context may account for why many Christians and Muslims see the relationship between mission and *da'wah* differently. The negative experience of Christian mission due to its symbiotic relationship with colonialism may be propelling Muslims to distance their understanding of *da'wah* from the historical practice of Christian mission in Muslim contexts. Following Scantlebury, I contend that the challenge of religious conversion and the ethics of mission and *da'wah* have taken on even greater urgency precisely because of the heightened religious tensions resulting from the contentiousness of certain Christian aid agencies accompanying the U.S.-led wars in Afghanistan and Iraq.

In this regard it may be expedient to note, for example, the views of the American evangelical scholar Charles Marsh. Marsh has brought the problem of war as a context for proselytization into sharp relief in an editorial in the *New York Times* of January 21, 2006.[33] He contends that not only did "an astonishing 87% of all white evangelical Christians in the United

States" provide overt religious legitimation for the American invasions of Afghanistan and Iraq but some of their most prominent leaders, like Franklin Graham[34] and Marvin Olasky,[35] drummed up support for the wars through Sunday congregational sermons touting such conflicts as creating "exciting new prospects for proselytizing Muslims."[36]

Given that the religious legitimation for the U.S. war in Afghanistan was even stronger than that for the war in Iraq, since that country's Taliban regime was more directly linked to the September 11 attacks, it is not surprising that these same members of the Evangelical community coveted the Afghanistan war's evangelizing prospects more zealously. In fact the question of proselytization was already a contentious issue prior to the toppling of the Taliban regime. In August 2001, the Taliban charged eight members of a German aid agency, Shelter Now, of promoting Christianity under the cover of relief efforts. The workers were all later rescued by a U.S. helicopter. This incident, however, was greeted with great antipathy by some Christian organizations, who denounced the Taliban regime, and was touted as yet another example of the lack of religious freedom in Muslim countries.[37] The freeing of the aid workers was greeted with great fanfare by these groups. Not unexpectedly, almost four years after the U.S. invasion of Afghanistan the question of the right to religious conversion found its most publicized case in Afghanistan. There have been many other similar cases, frequently charged under the Taliban's harsh "blasphemy laws." Yet another of these cases of religious persecution would dominate the international headlines another four years on.

THE CONFLICT BETWEEN RELIGIOUS FREEDOM AND THE ISLAMIC LAW OF APOSTASY

In February 2006, an Afghan national, Abdul Rahman, who had converted to Christianity in 1990 while working as a medical assistant for a Christian nongovernmental aid group in Peshawar, Pakistan, was arrested and charged with apostasy under what was interpreted to be traditional shari'ah laws. The case received worldwide publicity, with an Afghan court threatening to execute Abdul Rahman if he did not repent. As a direct consequence of the vociferous international outcry over the persecution of Abdul Rahman, he was released after the judge dismissed the case on grounds of insanity. Despite his acquittal, the defendant was forced to leave Afghanistan and given asylum in Italy for fear of social recriminations from Afghan civil society.[38]

The case of Abdul Rahman's conversion to Christianity has once again highlighted the urgent need for Muslims to seriously reexamine the restrictive traditional shari'ah laws on religious conversion from Islam. It is not good enough for Muslims engaged in interreligious dialogue to skirt this issue by hiding behind their support for the Chambesy statement affirming "the right to convince or to be convinced."[39] A close reading of the Chambesy discussions discloses that despite their support for the declaration, the Muslim interlocutors were equivocating. At one point in the discussions, Bishop Kenneth Cragg felt compelled to spell out unambiguously the Christian concern about the Muslim position on religious freedom in the following manner: "We are not talking about freedom of belief, or of religious practice, but the freedom of movement of belief; and there is a radical difference between these two. A faith which you are not free to leave becomes a prison, and no self-respecting faith should be a prison for those within it."[40]

Yet more serious is the fact that the right to be convinced and to convert from Islam to another religion is held by only a minority of Muslim scholars. This view of religious freedom is however not shared by the vast majority of Muslim scholars both past as well as present. Most classical and modern Muslim jurists regard apostasy (*riddah*), defined by them as an act of rejection of faith committed by a Muslim whose Islam had been affirmed without coercion, as a crime deserving the death penalty. Almost all traditional books of Islamic jurisprudence (*fiqh*) deal extensively with the penalties to be imposed on apostates such as the disposition of the apostate's property and inheritance and the dissolution of their marriages.[41] Indeed the preponderance of classical Islamic positions proscribing apostasy makes understandable the harsh contemporary Muslim responses to Abdul Rahman's conversion to Christianity. Contemporary Muslim jurists are uncritically transporting medieval juristic positions that were negotiated in radically different historical circumstances to present-day realities.[42] How else is one to explain the widespread attachment to the death penalty verdict among traditional Muslim scholars and the social ostracization meted to so-called apostates in many Muslim societies?

At the same time a number of modern Muslim scholars have argued for more lenient and humane positions on apostasy, marshalling strong support for their views.[43] In this regard, the viewpoint issued by Louay Safi of the Islamic Society of North America (ISNA) in the context of the Abdul Rahman furor in Afghanistan was noteworthy. Safi declares unequivocally that a "Muslim who converts to Christianity is no more a Muslim, but a Christian and must be respected as such."[44] Notwithstanding these and other tolerant Islamic positions on religious conversion, Muslims engaged in interreligious dialogue need to be more honest and forthcoming about the enormous challenge they face in reforming the hegemonic traditional Muslim position on apostasy. To use the same words of the Muslim scholar, Ataullah Siddiqui, in the context of Christian efforts to curtail aid evangelism, "There is a big gap between our pious hopes and our practical realities, something which we do not perhaps wish to face."[45] Strengthening the Muslim reformist case to reform traditional laws on apostasy will require some Christian help. Their Christian interlocutors might need to labor hard to calm inappropriate Christian proselytization efforts. Without such a moratorium on inappropriate proselytization, as recommended by the Chambesy declaration, it will be hard to convince Muslim hardliners that the reform of apostasy laws are opportunistic Christian demands to make conversion possible.

A number of Muslim scholars, such as Mahmoud Ayoub, have pointed out that apostasy has been a political problem in both early and later Muslim societies, and has increased with the advent of colonialism and the expansion of Christian missionary activity.[46] While it would be incorrect to suggest that the harsh shari'ah views on apostasy were first formulated in the colonial era, there can be no doubt that colonial-era Christian missions generated a harsher interpretation of the shari'ah law. Similarly, the recent debate triggered by the legal persecution of Abdul Rahman emerged from a war-ravaged context where relief aid for the victims of the war was dispensed by agencies linked to the perceived aggressors. I contend that the Abdul Rahman furor did not occur in a social vacuum but in a concrete political context and was not surprisingly enhanced by it. Here again the challenging question of religious conversion and the ethics of aid evangelism arise in a war context. There are of course many other instances of religious conversion that do not take place in the context of aid evangelism, which still incur religious persecution in Muslim societies. However, these cases are regrettably overshadowed by the former.

MISSION AND *DA'WAH* IN A WAR CONTEXT

Both Christians and Muslims have historically been implicated in spreading their faiths through war and conquests, though this is not the complete story of the growth and expansion of these world traditions. In fact more peaceful and humane methods predominate as ways in which Christianity and Islam have historically been transmitted. The problem, however, is the romanticization of our historical legacies and the consequent denial that such abuses ever occurred, a tendency that is compounded by polemical scholarship that attempts to show that one religion has been more culpable than the other. Such dispositions stand in the way of serious efforts at seeking interreligious coexistence and sustainable peace-building in the contemporary era. Our times demand instead sincere acts of contrition through apologies and forgiveness to heal the memories of our trespasses. Yet even more critical is the interreligious challenge of together finding ways to prevent such atrocities from ever occurring again. It is against this background that the proselytization efforts of some Christian aid organizations in war-torn Iraq can become contentious and inflammatory.

In April 2003, almost exactly one month after the United States of America launched a preemptive war against Iraq, *Time Magazine* reported that two Christian aid organizations, the International Missions Board of the Southern Baptist Convention and the Samaritan's Purse, were waiting on the border between Jordan and Iraq for a green light from the U.S. military command to enter Iraq in order to engage in what they called "aid evangelism."[47] Rev. Franklin Graham, son of the influential evangelist Billy Graham and head of the Samaritan's Purse, justified their actions by claiming that the goal of the aid ministry in Iraq was "to heal people, and hopefully they will see God." The controversial context and insensitive timing of Samaritan's Purse's proselytization program was not accidental. It was a deliberate and well-orchestrated strategy. Samaritan's Purse and its leader Rev. Franklin Graham are some of the most ardent religious supporters of the U.S. war in Iraq. Moreover, this was not the first time in recent history that Christian evangelists had used a war context as a means for spreading the Christian gospel. It is well known that during the 1991 Gulf war, Rev. Franklin Graham's organization gave U.S. soldiers deployed in Iraq 30,000 Bibles in Arabic for distribution in Iraq and the neighboring Muslim majority countries.

As has already been noted, the proselytization actions by these Christian evangelists are further compounded by the fact that many of their most influential leaders and institutions at home have made belligerent pronouncements against Islam. For example, prominent evangelical leaders such as Franklin Graham,[48] Jerry Falwell, Pat Robertson, and Jerry Vines have all made derogatory statements against Islam. Graham, for example, has called Islam "a very evil and wicked religion."[49] In a recent book, *Secrets of the Koran*, evangelical missionary Don Richardson claims, "The Koran's good verses are like the food an assassin adds to poison to disguise a deadly taste."[50] And prominent evangelical Churches such as the Southern Baptist Convention regularly convene seminars and lectures on Islam that criticize the religion as regressive and violent.[51] It is therefore not surprising that the vice president for governmental affairs of the National Association of Evangelicals, Rev. Richard Cizik, is on record saying, "Evangelicals have substituted Islam for the Soviet Union" and that "the Muslims have become the modern-day equivalent of the Evil Empire."[52] The belligerent positions of these prominent Evangelical leaders drown out the more balanced perspective on Islam advocated by the National Association of Evangelicals in conjunction with the Washington, DC, based Institute of Religion and Democracy. The latter have formulated positive guidelines for Christian-Muslim dialogue that emphasized the necessity to "affirm some points of theology and morality that Islam and Christianity have in common" and furthermore called on Christians to "work together with some Muslims on certain public issues in which they have similar concerns."[53]

All of this raises two pertinent and interrelated questions. First, can the evangelical outreach to Muslims be seen as a new crusade against Islam, however unintentionally? Or even as a recurring colonial theme of Christian mission and military dominance, seen often, but not always, as going hand in hand. Second, is it ethical for philanthropical activities and humanitarian service to be undertaken among victims of war with the ulterior motives of proselytism? These are challenging but pertinent issues that should form part of an honest dialogical encounter between Christians and Muslims, since they have important implications for conflict transformation and interreligious peace-building.

THE ETHICS OF AID EVANGELISM

As has already been noted, aid evangelism was one of the key questions addressed by the Chambesy Dialogue, and the conference took a firm position. It strongly condemned any *diakonia* (service) undertaken for any ulterior motive and not as an expression of *agape* (love).[54] The conference urged Christian churches and religious organizations to immediately suspend such efforts in the Muslim world. It was indeed a courageous and ambitious resolution. But did the Chambesy participants really believe that they or even the institutions they represented had the power to implement the resolutions with immediate effect? Subsequent events have suggested otherwise.

Perhaps Muslim participants naively believed that their Christian interlocutors had such an authority. Five years later, the Islamic Foundation based in the United Kingdom decided to republish the proceedings of the Chambesy Dialogue in protest, saying; "The misused *diakonia* ties in the world of Islam not only have not been discontinued, but in fact expanded since 1976, on a vast scale and with the knowledge and participation of the very same institutions whose members were participants at Chambesy."[55] In support of its claim, the Islamic Foundation cited the research findings of one of its members, Ahmad von Denffer. Von Denffer had uncovered a multimillion-dollar campaign launched by the Lutheran Churches in Germany, an affiliate of the WCC, to evangelize Fulani Muslims all over West Africa using *diakonia* as a cover.[56] It is against this backdrop that the interreligious movement needs to once again address the question of the ethics of the aid evangelism undertaken by some prominent evangelical institutions in war-torn Iraq. There clearly does not seem to be a consensus with regard to the ethical efficacy of aid evangelism on the part of all Christians. The one-time consensus expressed at Chambesy has clearly unraveled.

To its credit, both the WCC and the Pontifical Council on Interreligious Affairs have since Chambesy consistently reaffirmed their commitment to eschewing unethical forms of mission, including that of aid evangelism. In fact, during a 1999 WCC-sponsored "Christian-Muslim Consultation on Religious Freedom" held at Hartford Seminary, Connecticut, the participants recommitted themselves to "the relevance and value of the 1976 Chambesy statement" and affirmed the importance of distinguishing between proselytism and witness as the WCC has done within the Christian context, and emphasize the necessity to express an ethics of mission and *da'wah* to which both Christians and Muslims can agree.[57] Even more recently, the recent President of the Pontifical Council for Interreligious Relations, Archbishop Michael Fitzgerald, proposed that "Christians do not engage in works of mercy as a pretext for preaching about Jesus Christ but, like the Good Samaritan, out of compassion for those who are suffering. So it can be said that interreligious dialogue is not aimed at bringing the partner in dialogue into the Catholic Church."[58]

Unfortunately, this Catholic understanding of the Christian narrative of the Good Samaritan is not shared by the evangelical relief organization bearing the same name. The Samaritan Purse's international director of projects, Ken Isaacs, interprets his divine calling as not merely to address the physical needs of the Iraqi Muslims but also to tend to their spiritual penury. In response to concerns raised about the ethics and strategic wisdom of their relief efforts in Iraq he responded by saying, "We do not deny the name of Christ. We believe in sharing him in deed and word."

CONCLUSION

In conclusion it seems clear that while various Christian denominations disagree about the ethics of aid evangelism in the context of war, Muslims are far more united in condemning it. The reverse is the case on the question of the right to religious conversion. While Muslims are ambivalent about the right of their coreligionists to change their religion, Christians affirm this right. Of course the different theological postures adopted by Christian and Muslim scholars are profoundly influenced by historical reality and power relations, as was so impressively illustrated by Elizabeth Scantlebury. Honest dialogue can only begin with a clear recognition of this reality. A joint Christian-Muslim assessment of power imbalances should include not only misuses of mission and *da'wah* but also a strong rejection of all forms of violence and terrorism, including state terror. The belligerent environment resulting from these acts of barbarism threatens the relations of Christians and Muslims around the world.

As a way forward, I advise Muslims to heed the late Professor Isma'il al-Faruqi's call to engage in an "ecumenical cooperative critique of the other religion." For Christians I recommend the invitation of Father Henri Sanson, SJ, of Algiers to reflect on their vocation toward Muslims "in the mirror of Islam," that is, taking into account at every step the missionary vocation that their Muslim partners, in faith, know themselves to be charged with.[59] And for both communities, I commend J. Dudley Woodberry's recognition that there are times when only the deed is appropriate, as was the case when Jesus healed a leper and then instructed him to tell no one. The deeper challenge for both Christians and Muslims committed to interreligious dialogue and peace-building is to go beyond mere *declarations* of the right of any individual to change his or her religion and decry the use of inappropriate means to entice the person to switch his or her faith. Instead, Christian and Muslim interreligious leaders and activists need to urgently find creative ways of making such positive affirmations a key part of the *modus vivendi* of convivial relations between the two communities.

NOTES

1. I use the term *proselytization* here in its negative sense of describing unfair methods of missionary work.
2. For a detailed account of the Abdul Rahman conversion and trial in Afghanistan see en.wikipedia.org/wiki/Abdul_Rahman_(convert).
3. *Da'wah* is an Arabic word meaning "call" or "invitation," and the noun form *da'i* (plural *du'at*) refers to "one who calls or invites to Islam." I will discuss its nature more extensively later in this paper.
4. For the full proceedings of the Chambesy meeting see *Christian Mission and Islamic Da'wah: Proceedings of the Chambesy Dialogue Consultation* (Leicester, UK: Islamic Foundation, 1977).
5. I was privileged to cochair this meeting together with Tarek Mitri of the WCC's interreligious office. For the final report on this conference see *Current Dialogue* 34 (Geneva: World Council of Churches, February 2000), www.wcc coe.org/wcc/what/interreligious/cd34-19.html (accessed March 2006).
6. For a brief report see World Council of Churches, *From Harare to Porto Alegre 1998-2006: An Illustrated Account of the Life of the World Council of Churches* (Geneva: 2005), 89. For more details on the "Critical Moment in Interreligious Dialogue Conference" see www.oikoumene.org/interreligious.html (accessed March 2006).
7. Elizabeth Scantlebury, "Islamic Da'wah and Christian Mission: Positive and Negative Models of Interaction between Muslims and Christians," *Islam and Christian-Muslim Relations* 7, no. 3 (1996): 253–69.
8. Seyyed Hossein Nasr, "Islamic-Christian Dialogue: Problems and Obstacles to be Pondered and Overcome," *Islam and Christian-Muslim Relations* 11, no. 2 (July 2000): 213–27.

9. For the full report online, see www.hrw.org/reports/1999/indiachr/.

10. www.hrw.org/reports/1999/indiachr/.

11. Swami Agnivesh, *Religion, Spirituality and Social Action: New Agenda for Humanity*, 2nd ed. (Delhi: Hope India, 2003), 30.

12. For details on this controversial bill see "Hindutva Conspiracy Clear in Rajasthan 'Freedom of Religion Bill,'" *Milli Gazette Online*, April 6, 2006, www.milligazette.com/dailyupdate/2006/20060406_hindutva_rajasthan.htm

13. See "Proselytization Revisited: Rights, Free Markets, and Culture Wars" (symposium of the 19th World Congress of the International History of Religions, Tokyo, Japan, March 25–30, 2005), www.1.u-tokyo.ac.jp/iahr2005/

14. "Proselytization Revisited: Rights, Free Markets."

15. Peter van der Veer, "Tradition and Violence in South Asia" (unpublished paper delivered at the "Women and the Contested State: Religion and Agency and South Asia" conference convened on April 11–12, 2003, Kroc Institute, University of Notre Dame).

16. David A. Kerr, "Islamic Da'wa and Christian Mission: Towards a Comparative Analysis," *International Review of Mission* 89.353 (2000): 150–71. For the full proceedings of the Chambesy meeting see *Christian Mission and Islamic Da'wah* (Leicester, UK: Islamic Foundation, 1977).

17. William Wagner, "A Comparison of Christian Mission and Islamic Da'wah," *Missiology* 31, no. 3 (2003): 339–47.

18. J. Dudley Woodberry, "Toward Mutual Respectful Witness" (unpublished paper delivered at the Conflict Transformation Project: Interfaith Dialogue, Fuller Theological Seminary and Salam Institute for Peace & Justice, Rockville, Md., April 22–23, 2005).

19. Antoine Wessels, "Mission and Da'wah: From Exclusion to Mutual Witness," *Church and Society* 84, no. 1 (1994): 101–12.

20. For a discussion of these differences see Ataullah Siddiqui, *Christian-Muslim Dialogue in the Twentieth Century* (London: Macmillan, 1997).

21. Khurshid Ahmad, "Editorial," *Christian Mission and Islamic Da'wah* (Leicester, UK: Islamic Foundation, 1977).

22. Ahmad, "Editorial."

23. Ahmad, *Christian Mission and Islamic Da'wah*, 101.

24. Sayed Zainul Abedin, "Da'wa and Dialogue: Believers and Promotion of Mutual Trust," in *Beyond Frontiers: Islam and Contemporary Needs* (London: Mansell, 1989).

25. Abedin, "Da'wa and Dialogue: Believers and Promotion," 54.

26. Isma'il Raji al-Faruqi, "On the Nature of Islamic Da'wah," *International Review of Mission* LXV, no. 260 (1976): 391–400. See also Isma'il Raji al-Faruqi, *Islam and Other Faiths*, ed. Ataullah Siddiqui (Leicester, UK: Islamic Foundation, 1989), 312.

27. Woodberry, "Toward Mutual Respectful Witness."

28. Woodberry, "Toward Mutual Respectful Witness," 153.

29. Woodberry, "Toward Mutual Respectful Witness," 163.

30. Woodberry, "Toward Mutual Respectful Witness."

31. Hans Ucko, "Pontifical Council for Interreligious Dialogue 40 years," *Current Dialogue* 45 (Geneva: World Council of Churches, July 2005), wcc-coe.org/wcc/what/interreligious/cd45-03.html (accessed March 2006).

32. Scantlebury, "Islamic Da'wah and Christian Mission," 253.

33. Charles Marsh, "Wayward Christian Soldiers," *New York Times*, January 21, 2006.

34. Rev. Franklin Graham delivered the invocation prayers at the inauguration of President George W. Bush.

35. Marvin Olasky is the editor of the conservative *World* magazine and a former advisor to President Bush on faith-based policy.

36. Charles Marsh, "Wayward Christian Soldiers" in *New York Times*, January 21, 2006. Marsh is professor of religion at the University of Virginia and is author of *The Beloved Community: How Faith Shapes Social Justice, from the Civil Rights Movement to Today*.

37. For a report about this incident, see www.pbs.org/wnet/religionandethics/week505/news.html

38. For a detailed account of the Abdul Rahman conversion and trial in Afghanistan, see en.wikipedia.org/wiki/Abdul_Rahman_(convert)

39. *Christian Mission and Islamic Da'wah* (Leicester, UK: Islamic Foundation, 1977).

40. *Christian Mission and Islamic Da'wah* (Leicester, UK: Islamic Foundation, 1977), 92.

41. For a useful summary of the classical Muslim position on apostasy see Yohanan Friedmann, *Tolerance and Coercion in Islam* (New York: Cambridge University Press, 2003), 121–59.

42. This point is well argued by Louay Safi, "Apostasy and Religious Freedom," 1insight.org/articles/Print/Apostasy.htm.

43. For a survey of some modern discussions of the topic see Abdullah Saeed and Hassan Saeed, *Freedom of Religion, Apostasy and Islam* (Aldershot, UK: Ashgate, 2004). See also Mohammad Hashim Kamali, *Freedom of Expression in Islam* (Cambridge: Islamic Texts Society, 1997); Abdullahi Ahmed An-Na'im, "Islamic Law and Apostasy and Its Modern Applicability," *Religion* 16 (1986): 197–224; and Mahmoud Ayoub, "Religious Freedom and the Law of Apostasy in Islam," *Islamochristiana* 20 (1994): 73–91.

44. Safi, "Apostasy and Religious Freedom."

45. Ataullah Siddiqui, "Fifty Years of Christian-Muslim Relations: Exploring and Engaging in a New Relationship" (paper delivered on the occasion of the Pontificio Instituto Di Studi Arabi E D 'Islamistica's [PISIA's] 50th Anniversary, May 12, 2000). For text see www.islamic-foundation.org.uk/Fifty%20Years%20of%20Christian-Rev.05.pdf.

46. Ayoub, "Religious Freedom and the Law of Apostasy," 75–91.

47. Johanna McGeary, "A Faith-Based Initiative," *Time Magazine*, April 21, 2003.

48. Franklin Graham's statement was carried very widely in the media. See Nicholas Kristof, "Bigotry in Islam—And Here," *New York Times*, July 2, 2002.

49. Laurie Goodstein, "Seeing Islam as 'Evil,' Evangelicals Seek Converts," *New York Times*, May 27, 2003, A3.

50. Goodstein, "Seeing Islam as 'Evil.'".

51. Goodstein, "Seeing Islam as 'Evil.'"

52. Goodstein, "Seeing Islam as 'Evil.'"

53. Mark Stricherz, "Evangelicals Advise on Muslim Dialogue," *Christianity Today*, July 2003, 21, www.ird-renew.org/muslimdialogue (accessed June 2006).

54. Siddiqui, *Christian-Muslim Dialogue* (London: Macmillan, 1997), 101.

55. Ahmad von Denffer, "Preface," in Siddiqui, *Christian-Muslim Dialogue* (London: Macmillan, 1997).

56. Ahmad von Denffer, *The Fulani Evangelism Project in West Africa* (Leicester, UK: Islamic Foundation, 1980).

57. "Report from the Consultation on 'Religious Freedom, Community Rights and Individual Rights': A Christian Muslim Perspective," *Current Dialogue* 34 (Geneva: World Council of Churches, February 2000), www.wcccoe.org/wcc/what/interreligious/cd34-19.html (accessed March 2006).

58. Unpublished keynote address delivered by Archbishop Michael Fitzgerald at a conference titled "In Our Time: Interreligious Relations in a Divided World," sponsored by Brandeis and Boston College, March 16–17, 2006. Just before addressing the conference Archbishop Fitzgerald was appointed by the Vatican as its Nuncio to the Arab League in Egypt.

59. For a useful discussion of this challenge see Christian W. Troll, "Witness Meets Witness: The Church's Mission in the Context of the Worldwide Encounter of Christians and Muslim Believers Today," *Encounters* 4, no. 1 (1998): 15–34.

16

Response to Chapters

Asma Afsaruddin

I want to begin by thanking the organizers of these historic meetings and dialogue between Christians and Muslims in very fractious times indeed. I want to particularly laud our Christian friends for embarking on this bold initiative and welcoming us to their institute. I think I speak for all the Muslim participants here when I say that we greatly appreciate your courage in reaching out to us and for the abundant goodwill you have shown toward us.

I enjoyed reading all the chapters and reflecting on their content. The issues are very timely and highly relevant to our project of fostering inter-religious encounters and dialogue in a respectful and informed manner. Below are my comments on each individual chapter.

COMMENTS ON EVELYNE A. REISACHER'S CHAPTER

The issue of fear is a most important one. I liked the highly evocative way in which Evelyne demonstrated how fear overcame her rational faculties and overpowered her otherwise normal positive feelings toward Muslims based on her acquaintance and interactions with Muslim friends in different parts of the world.

She brings in attachment theory and affect regulation to explain how fear mediates the quality of our relationships with others, especially when those "others" are perceived as a source, or even as the source of danger, as

Muslims generally are perceived today in post-9/11 America. Therefore, the question she poses is a central one in contemporary Christian-Muslim relations. She asks, "As we engage in conflict transformation can Christians and Muslims provide a secure base for each other?" The answer she provides is illuminating and prods us into further reflecting on its implications. Evelyne suggests that "if the Muslim community can serve as a secure base in times of danger and threat for the Christian community and vice versa the nature of the bond between the two will become more secure" (pp. 159–160).

Fear is related to survival and in certain contexts is necessary and perhaps even rational. In other contexts, fear can be visceral and triggered by irrational associations. Thus seeing a group of Muslim pilgrims at an airport in particular might generate a reflexive association with hijackers. Seeing the same pilgrims or other Muslims in the mall or in a neighborhood school would not necessarily elicit the same reaction. Thus, negative associations can be consciously replaced with positive ones. And the best way—and possibly the only way to do so—is to, as Evelyne puts it, proactively engage in social exchange with the object of our fears. This is the main ingredient in interactive fear regulation, with the other individual perceived as representing the feared community. Although this suggestion sounds eminently commonsensical, it is not an option we willingly choose. We tend to instinctively avoid the feared person or object.

Yet Evelyn shows through her own experiences with Muslim friends and interlocutors that it is necessary to overcome our built-in barriers to reaching out to those we instinctively fear and to get to know them as real human beings and individuals. Only positive images can replace the negative ones—we cannot will negative perceptions away, hence the importance of interpersonal and intersocietal exchanges.

I would think that her discussion of vicarious fears will resonate strongly with many of us. We learn and internalize fear not only through our own experiences but also through the experiences of our loved ones and members of our community, however we may define that community—on a religious, ethnic, or national basis. Historical memories of a constructed negative past involving the feared "other" also play a role in shaping these negative images. Therefore, the checkered Muslim-Christian encounters through time color our perceptions of one another. But, as Evelyne rightly emphasizes, replacement of these negative images or counterbalancing them with examples of positive interaction goes a very long way in changing attitudes.

For example, accounts of the Crusades and images of Muslim warriors besieging European borders often constitute the dominant discourse about Muslim-Christian encounters in our media and history textbooks. Such accounts can be replaced or supplemented with accounts of positive interchange and learning from one another through time. I know it is often an eye opener for my students to learn of how Christian-Muslim interactions through the ages seminally shaped each civilization. Syriac- and Arabic-speaking Christians translated the learning of classical antiquity for their Muslim patrons in ninth-century Abbasid Baghdad, creating a revolution in learning and the flowering of the arts and sciences in the Islamic world. Colleges (*madrasas*) sprang up in most corners of the medieval Islamic world, an institution that would be transplanted to Europe by the twelfth century. The transmission of the philosophical and natural sciences to Europe from the world of Islam would eventually usher in the European Renaissance. Even the Crusades, for all its bloodshed, played a role in this intellectual-cultural exchange. Returning Crusaders from the Holy Land often came back with better knowledge about medicine, educational practices, and so on that found fertile ground in Christian lands. In this regard, I highly recommend Richard Bulliet's learned book titled *The Case for Islamo-Christian Civilization*, which draws our attention to these shared cultural and historical episodes, the recounting of which has the power to dispel many of our deeply divisive stereotypes of one another.

Today many Muslims travel to the West to learn the latest developments in science and medicine, engineering, and computer technology. Such a transfer of knowledge from the West to the East is profoundly changing the nature of traditional societies (not necessarily to everyone's satisfaction) and often creating new opportunities for self-realization in Muslim-majority countries.

As Evelyne's experience shows, there is no substitute for education and personal interaction to effect important changes in public perceptions of religious and ethnic minorities. Recent nationwide surveys show that the percentage of Americans who have an overall negative perception of Islam and Muslims now, five years after 9/11, has actually grown. We, therefore, have to redouble our efforts to educate the public and keep the lines of communication among us open, especially to counteract the often deleterious effects of skewed media coverage of Muslims.

COMMENTS ON J. DUDLEY WOODBERRY'S CHAPTER

Dudley's insightful chapter starts out with an articulation of the rich common ground between Islam and Christianity, starting with how we worship the same God, although we may conceptualize Him somewhat differently. We also revere Christ equally although some of his religious functions are conceived of differently. We both agree on the notion of stewardship of the Earth, the importance of a divinely revealed law, and the importance of faith and deeds. We also each claim a universal message and the obligation to proclaim that message among diverse peoples. The overlap in the meanings of *da'wa* and mission is nicely shown by Dudley.

Some of our common claims thus also appear to be competing and this is how Dudley presents them; particularly in regard to notions of the finality of each religion's message and supersession of previous revelations.

Here I do wish to interject an important qualification. From the Muslim point of view or, I should say more accurately and more precisely, from the Qur'anic point of view, the Abrahamic communities were not meant to compete with one another but to be complementary to one another. In the Qur'an, the verb *aslama*, "to submit to God," and the noun Islam, "submission to God," is generally used nonconfessionally in reference to true believers, that is, those who truly and sincerely submit to God, regardless of the denominational labels they wear. To read the later confessional understanding back into the Qur'an is anachronistic. The Qur'an usually addresses its audience as "O those who believe," signifying a capacious understanding of "believers," in which the People of the Book, understood to constitute salvific communities along with Muslims, are naturally included. This is something that Muslims in particular need to be reminded of today, because in our confessional understanding of ourselves in relation to the People of the Book, we have significantly departed from the spirit of the Qur'an. To forge better relations with Jews and Christians, we need to emphasize this Qur'anic inclusive understanding of believers and their relationship to God. The Qur'an always refers to itself as confirming the prior Biblical revelations, never as superseding them or abrogating them. However, some Muslim theologians did go on to develop a theory of supersession and abrogation, and this is where the notion of competition and rivalry starts to arise.

Muslims would be well advised to resurrect the Qur'anically mandated way of relating to diverse communities, which is to be accomplished in a spirit of cooperation and with an awareness of our commonalities in terms of values and worship of the one God. The last part of Qur'an 5:48 exhorts us:

> Hasten to do good works! To God you all must return; and then He will make you truly understand all that on which you were inclined to differ.

We are indeed much better off emphasizing common ethical ground between us and leaving the theological differences to be sorted out by the Almighty in the hereafter.

COMMENTS ON OSMAN BAKAR'S CHAPTER

Dudley's chapter allows for a neat segue to Osman Bakar's chapter, who emphasizes this pluralistic spirit of the Qur'an that, in the course of time, Muslims have progressively compromised out of worldly ambition and the competitive quest for worldly gain. Qur'an 3:64 states: "Say, O People of the Book! Come here for a word which is in common between you and us: that we worship none but God; that we associate no partners with Him; that we erect not, from among ourselves, lords and patrons other than God." If they turn back, you say: "Bear witness that we are Muslims." This verse very nicely illustrates the earlier point I made in connection with Dudley's chapter—that, according to the Qur'an, we should be stressing our commonalities, particularly on the basis of our shared, monotheistic faith. I think Osman is absolutely right when he says we are justified in understanding the Arabic word *kalima* in the context of this verse as dialogue, than simply "a word." A word or more exchanged in goodwill and to stress common ground is dialogue in its basic sense. The Qur'an's favorable attitude toward interfaith dialogue may also be discerned in Qur'an 16:125, which states, "Invite (all) to the way of the Lord with wisdom and beautiful discourse; and argue with them in ways that are best and most gracious: for your Lord knows best who have strayed from His path and who receive guidance." As Osman comments, Qur'an 3:64 is a specific invitation to the people of the Book while Qur'an 16:125 concerns all of humankind.

The two most important verses cited from the Qur'an in support of a divinely mandated diversity and pluralism are Qur'an 49:13 and 5:48. Qur'an 49:13 states,

> O humankind! We created you from a single (pair) of a male and a female, and made you into nations and tribes, that you may know each other (not that you may despise each other). Verily the most honored of you in the sight of God is (he who is) the most righteous of you. And God has full knowledge and is well acquainted (with all things).

And Qur'an 5:48 in full states,

> To each among you have We prescribed a Law and an Open Way. If God had so willed, He would have made you a single people, but (His Plan is) to test you in what He had given you: so strive as in a race in all virtues. The goal of you all is to God; it is He that will show you the truth of the matters in which you dispute.

Due to these divine directives, Osman reminds us, it is incumbent upon the Muslim *umma* to be, as he puts it, "passionately engaged in the global dialogue of faiths and civilizations because it is through such dialogues that they can best fulfill their divinely ordained global role as 'the community of the middle path'" (Ar. *ummatan wasatan*, Q 2:143). This community of the middle path has also been entrusted with a global mission as inferred from Q 2:143. Furthermore, the only competition that is in fact allowed between righteous people is competition in the sphere of good deeds. It is precisely this pluralistic ethos that resonates with today's Muslims so strongly, especially since the worlds we inhabit now are increasingly bound with one another, and the matter of peaceful coexistence takes on a special urgency in the aftermath of the 9/11 attacks. At the risk of sounding like a broken record, I would like to reiterate that the way to do that is to seek commonalities on the basis of shared values and moral principles. And this is very nicely articulated by Osman when he says, "This conception of human dignity means that in our world of ethnic and religious pluralism, the correct approach to dialogues of faiths and civilizations and the unity of humankind is based on spiritual principles" (p. 145). He also points to the *sunna* and early historical praxis to show that the Prophet and the early Muslims acted in this pluralistic spirit toward other faith communities, for example, the Prophet's historic meeting with the Christians from Najran and the special status that was granted to the Ethiopian or Abyssinian Christians on account of the exceptional hospitality they had showed toward a group of persecuted Muslims who took refuge with them out of desperation.

The Pact or Constitution of Medina concluded between Medinan Muslims and Jews is a critical document from the first century of Islam that points to the early pluralist character of the *umma*. In fact, to lend even greater weight to Osman's position, I would point out that the Qur'an uses the word *umma* in a very complimentary way in relation to believing Jews and Christians as well; for example in Q 5:66 and Q 3:113, where the people of the book are respectively referred to as constituting a "balanced nation" (*umma muqtasida*) and "a righteous nation" (*umma qa'ima*). Righteousness and moderation are therefore not attributes of Muslims alone but of all pious people. As Osman shows, it is precisely by going back to the Qur'an itself and by pointing to the praxis of the early community of Muslims that we can persuasively undermine the perspective of those exclusivist and triumphalist Muslims who insist, contrary to the Qur'an, that the truth was vouchsafed only to them and that they alone have a monopoly on it.

COMMENTS ON RASHIED OMAR'S CHAPTER

In his reflections and comments, Rashied brings up some thorny issues that cast a shadow over Christian-Muslim relations: namely, what is deemed to be conventional legal Muslim views of apostasy and Christian practices of aid evangelism. Religious conversion remains a highly controversial issue among Muslims and Christians and Rashied gives us a useful review of some perspectives on this topic as well as an insightful comparison between mission and *da'wa*. David Kerr, whom Rashied cites, rightly emphasizes the influence of historical experience and actual practice (p. 183) in the shaping of Christian and Muslim attitudes toward mission and *da'wa*.

One of the reasons these issues are centerstage now is, first of all, that due to the recent invasions of Iraq and Afghanistan, new opportunities have been created for zealous evangelicals from the United States to proselytize in these countries, as Rashied points out. Another recent reason has been the case of Abdul Rahman, an Afghan national, who converted to Christianity while in Afghanistan, as a consequence of which he was threatened with execution. This has led a number of people to publicly lament that there is no freedom of religion, meaning in this case the right to renounce one's religion and adopt another, within the Islamic tradition.

This is where things start getting murky. The primary reason things start getting murky is because of an innate and critical problem of translation. *Ridda* is translated by Rashied, as many others have, as "apostasy." Apostasy, in English, however refers to a simple change in faith and implies nothing more. The Arabic term *ridda* (or the other commonly used term *irtidad*), however, is not and has never been plain and simple apostasy. The earliest usage of *ridda* was in the context of the political revolts that occurred during the reign of Abu Bakr, the first caliph, right after the death of the Prophet. The punishable offense in this case was the political rebellion and the act of disloyalty and causing disorder in the land (Ar. *hiraba*), not renunciation of faith. In fact, most of the tribes implicated in the *ridda* did not in fact apostasize (in the English sense of the word) but were deemed guilty of treason, which is a punishable offense, even to the extent of death. Therefore, to say that the majority of jurists supported execution for apostasy is highly misleading. In the legal understanding of the term, *ridda* or *irtidad* implied treasonous behavior against the state, which may or may not involve conversion to a different faith. As is well known, or should be well known, the Qur'an has no prescribed penalty for mere apostasy in the English sense of the word. For example, Qur'an 2:217 says: "And whoever turns away from their religion and dies disbelieving, their works have failed in this world and the next; these are the inhabitants of the Fire; therein they shall dwell forever." Even as a political offense, *irtidad* or *ridda* did not always merit the death penalty; the verdict was left to the discretion of the presiding judge. It is telling that there is no single, legal term in Arabic that is the exact equivalent of "apostasy" in English.

It is problematic that Rashied seems to be relying a great deal on Yohann Friedman's book for his information concerning apostasy, a book that cherry picks its sources and is tendentious in its scholarship. A depressingly large percentage of Muslims these days have lost touch with their own intellectual and religious heritage and are mostly unable to read the primary sources. Relying mainly on secondary sources written in Western languages allows for the kind of grievous semantic and interpretive mistakes that our discussion of the history of the term *ridda* reveals. In the climate of political and economic subservience that most Muslims worldwide live in today, they have sometimes regrettably internalized discourses about themselves generated from the outside, which frequently lead to ahistorical perceptions about their own past and present.

With a thorough historical grounding and equipped with the ability to consult primary sources, Muslim scholars can today critically reevaluate premodern perspectives on apostasy and *ridda*. Muslims have ample theological and legal grounds, as sound scholarship proves, to revisit and rethink this highly emotive issue. As my brief discussion shows above, the concept of religious freedom that implies one can adopt any religion he or she wishes to is not, therefore, fundamentally at odds with the historical understanding of *ridda*. Muslims have always accepted on the basis of Qur'an 2:256, which states, "There can be no compulsion in religion"—that no one can be forced to embrace a religion. Similarly we need to add in our time, no one can be forced to remain in it if he or she no longer wants to.

The problem remains that many not so well informed Muslims, including religious leaders of all stripe, do believe that it is mere apostasy that is deserving of death. In this case, Muslims need to invoke scriptural authority and point to Qur'anic verses and the praxis of the Prophet Muhammad in defense of freedom of conscience and of religion. We need to forefront the views of early Muslims, like Sufyan al-Thawri and Ibrahim al-Nakha'i, for example, who did not believe that renunciation of Islam merited punishment by death. As many theologians and jurists have historically maintained, mere apostasy represented an infringement against the rights of God (*huquq Allah*), and only God may judge such acts. Who are we, as mere humans, to claim such a prerogative?

Such an educational enterprise in the contemporary period is by no means guaranteed success. If anything, present political circumstances militate against the possibility that most Muslims would be receptive to this kind of historical and hermeneutic exercise. Feeling besieged by a perceived hegemonic West and threatened by cultural globalization, a considerable number of Muslims today would consider revisiting the "apostasy" issue as a form of capitulation to secularists and to those Westerners who only seek, as may appear to them, the emasculation of Islam. Rashied is thus right to point out the significance of sociopolitical factors, which inordinately complicate Christian-Muslim encounters today. Constructive, respectful dialogue that takes into account these myriad, complex issues may, however, by God's grace, lead us to a better way forward.

Asma Afsaruddin
Associate Professor
Arabic and Islamic Studies
University of Notre Dame
Indiana

17

A Christian Response to Chapters on Interfaith Dialogue

J. Dudley Woodberry

First, I would like to thank the Muslim participants for their contribution to our understanding so that we might more intelligently love our neighbors.

OSMAN BAKAR'S CHAPTER

In Osman Bakar's chapter on a "Theological Foundation of Interfaith Dialogue and Peaceful Coexistence: The Qur'an's Universal Perspectives," he reaches back to the previous section on "Diversity and Pluralism" to argue that the Qur'an supports a diversity of ethnic and religious groups.

He points to two classic verses:

> We have . . . made you confederations and tribes, that you may know each other. Truly the most noble of you in God's eyes is the most pious. (49:13)[1]

> To each of you we have prescribed a way (*shir'ah*) and a road. If God had willed he could have made you a single community (*ummah*), but [he has not done so] so that he may try you in what has come to you; so strive in what is good (*khayrat*). (5:48)

This charge to "strive in what is good" provides rich resources for dialogue because there are so many common values and good actions that are enjoined in our Scriptures. We might compare passages like the following:

> For men and women who submit [to God] . . . are believing . . . devout . . . truthful . . . patient . . . humble . . . give alms . . . fast . . . are chaste . . . praise God. . . . God prepared forgiveness and a great reward. (Qur'an 33:35)

> Whatever is true . . . honorable . . . pure . . . lovely . . . gracious . . . any excellence . . . anything worthy of praise, think on these things. (Philippians 4:8)

> Love is patient . . . kind . . . not jealous or boastful . . . arrogant or rude. (I Corinthians 13:4)

On the other hand the reference in Qur'an 5:48 that God has provided for every community a way (*shir'ah*)—a word later used for Law (*shari'ah*)—raises another need for dialogue between Muslims and Christians, for Islamic Law as it developed in the Medieval Period made Christians second class, even though it protected them better than some of the practices of so-called Christian rulers of that time protected Muslims. To the extent that Islamists are calling for the adoption of *shari'ah,* this obviously raises fears among Christian minorities that will need to be dealt with to develop the mutual sense of security that Evelyne Reisacher calls for in her chapter.

To support his case for the Qur'anic advocacy of dialogue, Dr. Bakar refers to the qur'anic injunction to "argue (*jadil*) with others" (16:25). Even in the context of inviting "to the way of the Lord with wisdom and good exhortation," it is a more confrontational word than we might today use for "dialogue." However, the Greek word *dialogismos* can mean "argue" as in Luke 9:46.

In his section on "Why the Need for Dialogues of Faiths and Civilizations," Dr. Bakar asserts that "the Koran's view is that dialogue is always necessary under all kinds of conditions." He has certainly made his case that there is Qur'anic support for dialogue but to make this a broad generalization about the Qur'an, one needs to discuss how moderate Muslims like himself deal with verses advocating "holy war." How do such explanations as "occasions of revelation," abrogation, and so forth fit into the total picture? In like manner, moderate Christians will need to show how they deal with militant Zionist verses in the Old Testament by such means as Jesus' words, "You have heard it said, an eye for an eye. . . , but I say to you, 'Do not resist one who is evil . . . love your enemies'" (Matthew 5:38–39, 44).

Although all scholars may not agree on the authenticity of certain of the stories attributed to Muhammad,[2] enough are provided to demonstrate some cordial relations between the early Muslims and Christians to serve as helpful resources for healthy relationships between the two communities today.

RASHIED OMAR'S CHAPTER

Dr. Omar's thoughtful chapter raises a number of issues that warrant comment. The first is his discussion of conversion as a source of conflict. As I have pointed out in my chapter entitled, "Toward Mutual Respectful Witness," the scriptures of both faiths make truth and allegiance claims that although overlapping are not identical. The Qur'an calls Muslims to debate or argue (*jadil*) with People of the Book (29:46), a designation that includes Christians. The New Testament in turn makes the crucifixion, resurrection, and Lordship of Jesus central in the proclamation of the message (Acts 2:21–36), while Muslims reject the possibility of his Lordship (Qur'an 3:64, 80) and the fact of his crucifixion (Qur'an 4:157–158)—or at least its necessity, though major Qur'anic commentators have allowed for it as a possible interpretation of the Qur'an.[3] Thus, conversions either way may be expected, and the thrust of my chapter as well as Dr. Omar's is that witness should be respectful and should not use inappropriate means.

Comparing Christian Mission and Islamic Da'wah

In his section comparing Christian mission and Islamic *da'wah*, Dr. Omar cites Muslim scholars who claim that there are significant differences between the two. He quotes Khurshid Ahmad as referring to the widespread abuse of Christian *diakonia* (service)—a charge that he notes has also been made against certain Muslim organizations. Omar calls attention to the final declaration of the Chambésy Consultation, which "strongly urges Christian churches and religious organizations to suspend their misused *diakonia* activities in the world of Islam."[4] The Chambésy text is not clear as to whether all *diakonia* activities should be suspended since they are misused or whether just the misused ones should be. The suspension of service ministries is a complex issue since neither Christian nor Muslims should "misuse" ministries of mercy, yet our scriptural injunctions to bear witness include both proclamation (Qur'an 16:125; I Peter 3:15) and service (Qur'an 3:104; Matthew 25:31–46; 28:19–20). Furthermore, Christian relief and development organizations increasingly see a seamless connection between word and deed, between evangelism and service.[5] The challenge is not to misuse the difference of power between those who minister and those to whom ministered and not to have ulterior motives in ministry. Rather, if ministry is done in the spirit of Christ, it raises questions to which Christians believe the gospel is the answer.

As an illustration of the differences Muslims have claimed to exist between Christian mission and Islamic *da'wah*, Omar cites Syed Zainul Abedin: "*da'wah* is witnessing the truth solely by means of exemplary lives." This, as we have seen, is more restrictive than the Qur'anic and biblical views, which also include proclamation (e.g., Qur'an 16:125; Matthew 28:19–20), but it does have a parallel in Jesus' command, "Let your light so shine before people that they may see your good works and glorify your Father who is in heaven" (Matthew 5:16). Here is an area where we should work together to demonstrate some of our common values.

Omar then cites the late Isma'il al-Faruqi who contrasts Muslim *da'wah* and Christian mission, by arguing that the former is "ecumenical *par excellence.*" Faruqi asserts that "all religious traditions are based on a common source, the religion of God which he planted in all . . . *din al-fitrah.*" Consequently, he claims that *da'wah* is "an ecumenical cooperative critique of the other religion rather than an invasion by a new truth."[6] There is a biblical parallel to this *fitrah* concept of an inner knowledge of God (Qur'an 30:30) in Paul's assertion that what God requires is written on human hearts (Romans 2:14–15). Faruqi's ecumenical view can find some support in the Qur'anic declaration that "those who have faith, and those who are Jews, Christians, and Sabeans—whoever has faith in God and the last day and performs good deeds—these will have their reward with their Lord. No fear shall come upon them, nor will they grieve" (2:62; 5:69). This position certainly creates a better climate and resource for dialogue than some alternate Muslim positions that posit that differences in Christian faith have been abrogated (*tansikh*) by later revelation or that Christian faith became corrupted.[7]

Al-Faruqi describes *da'wah* as "an ecumenical cooperative critique of the other religion rather than an invasion by a new truth." Nevertheless, however one defines *da'wah,* it should deal with such contrasts as Jesus being called only a messenger in the Qur'an (5:75) and being the message in the New Testament (1 Corinthians 2:2).

Omar notes David Kerr's observation concerning the centrifugal "sending" notion of Christian mission and the centripetal "calling" notion of the Islamic *da'wah*[8]—which is also a characteristic of Israelite attraction of proselytes in biblical times. What actually transpired in the history of the Muslim–Christian encounter, however, had many similarities. Preachers and *da'is* followed Muslim conquerors or merchants, even as Christian missionaries followed Western colonizing or trading ventures.[9] Despite Muslim protest concerning the latter phenomenon,[10] it is noteworthy that significant church growth did not take place until after the colonial period.[11]

In the twentieth century, Muslim *da'wah* as expressed by Rashid Rida (1865–1935) called for the revival of Muslims before the attempt to convert non-Muslims, and this has been a theme of subsequent revivalist movements like the Muslims Brethren in the Middle East, *Tablighi Jama'at* in South Asia and worldwide, and *Jama'at-i Islami* in Pakistan.[12] Likewise, Christian mission to Muslims have resulted from revivals in England and

North America in the 1790s and 1850s and subsequent revivals among Christians in the Middle East, South Asia, and Southeast Asia.[13]

As training centers for Christian missionaries arose in places like Selly Oak Colleges in Birmingham, England, the Kennedy School of Missions in Hartford, CT, and Fuller Theological Seminary, so *da'wah* colleges or departments were established at institutions like al-Azhar University in Cairo and the Islamic University in Islamabad to equip *da'is* for ministries around the world.[14]

In 1910 the World Missionary Conference was held in Edinburgh to plan and coordinate Protestant Christian missions, the same year that Rashid Rida worked to create a *da'wah* college in Istanbul, the capital of the Ottoman Empire. In 1974, the first Lausanne Congress for World Evangelization was held in Switzerland to coordinate Evangelical missions, the same year that the Muslim World League Conference was held in Mecca to counteract Christian missions and plan for Muslim expansion around the world and especially in Africa.

As the United Bible Societies print Bibles in languages around the world so Saudi Arabia's Kind Fahd bin Abdul Aziz Koran Printing Complex prints translations of the Qur'an for distribution throughout the world. The Organization of the Islamic Conference from fifty-seven nations funds Islamic Institutions worldwide. And organizations like the Islamic Society of North America and the Islamic Society of Europe include among their goals and those of their member organizations propagating the faith. And as there are Christian missionary radio stations such as Trans World Radio so there are stations such as the Voice of Islam, which has had the world's most powerful radio transmitter. Obviously both Christians and Muslims are carrying out their missionary mandate and often in similar ways. In my chapter "Toward Mutual Respectful Witness," I have drawn attention to the research of Todd M. Johnson and David R. Scoggins who calculate that there are actually more Muslim *da'is* working outside their own countries than Christian missionaries working in Muslim areas, and that the vast majority of both groups are working among their own adherents to facilitate their revival and equipping.

"Aid Evangelism"

Omar in particular raises the problem of what he calls Christian "aid evangelism," which he portrays as aid with an ulterior motive. He sees the problem as compounded in contexts of war such as those in Afghanistan and Iraq, where he sees a convergence of U.S. policy and Christian missions suggestive of former colonial times. Both concerns have also been expressed in published articles by Evangelicals.[15] Conferences were also held in Washington, DC, and Seattle on evangelism and persecution, sponsored by the Council of Faith and International Affairs at the Institute for Global Engagement in Washington, DC. The papers explored persecution that was a result of foolish and unworthy proselytism as well as worthy witness.[16]

Christians certainly need to repent for inappropriate proselytism and learn from Jesus, who indicated that there are times when the deed alone is appropriate, as when he healed a leper and then said, "Tell no one" (Matthew 8:1–4). Yet as has been noted, the example and commission of Jesus includes word and deed as part of witness. Jesus saw his calling as "to preach good news to the poor . . . to proclaim freedom for the prisoners, the recovery of sight to the blind, to release the oppressed, to proclaim the year of the Lord's favor" (Luke 4:18–19). He subsequently said, "As the father has sent me, so send I you" (John 20:21).

The major Christian relief and development agencies are acutely aware of the need to avoid exploiting the difference in power between the dispensers of aid and the recipients. At the same time a biblical understanding of the answer to poverty and injustice is *shalom* (or *salam*)—peace that expresses human well-being and health, including their spiritual and material aspects, and reconciles created beings with God and each other. This involves lifelong "transformational development" toward the recovery of our identity as created in the image of God and a calling to be stewards who care for the world and our neighbors. Although such aid must involve our lives and deeds from the beginning, it will also involve word—normally as a result of questions our lives and deeds elicit.[17]

Although in contexts of war even greater sensitivity is called for—especially if the witnesses are perceived as aggressors or their accomplices—a biblical understanding of the solution involves justice, forgiveness, love, and reconciliation (Micah 6:8; Ephesians 4:32; Matthew 5:44; 2 Corinthians 5:18). For the Christian, the example and means are found in Jesus and the transforming power of God's Spirit (Ephesians 4:32; Colossians 3:13; 2 Corinthians 5:18; Galations 5:22). And all are communicated by life, deed, and word. Fortunately, now that a majority of Christians live in the Southern Hemisphere or the East, they carry on much of the work of holistic witness in areas of conflict without having to carry the baggage of Western sins.[18] Unfortunately, however, some emerging churches and missions have also not always been sufficiently sensitive to their context in their witness.[19]

Contextualization

Although Dr. Omar did not include the topic of contextualization in the final draft of his chapter, it was mentioned in the first draft as an example of deceptive proselytism by some Christians in which they called themselves "Muslims" or "Muslim followers of Jesus." This engendered considerable discussion at the joint Muslim–Christian consultation concerning these chapters. The discussion indicated there is a lot of interest in and misunderstanding of the practice among both Muslims and Christians. Therefore, I shall comment on it.

Some Christians may use it as deceptive proselytism, but that should not be its purpose. As the New Testament teaches that God's Word was incarnated in Jesus Christ in a first-century Palestinian context, "contextualization" has as its goal that God's Word, Jesus Christ, will be authentically experienced in each new context that it enters.[20] Islam like Judaism is based on relating to God by faith and following a specific Law, which designates forms to be used in worship and life. Therefore, when these faiths cross cultural or religious boundaries they bring these forms, and even their sacred language with them. Conversely, Christian faith, based on relating to God by means of commitment to God's Word, Jesus Christ, is more easily translated into different cultural forms, since a system of forms is not central to its nature. The New Testament itself translates Jesus' Aramaic into popular Greek so that there is not even a sacred language.

The New Testament says, "God sent forth his Son . . . born under the Law to redeem those who were under the Law" (Galatians 4:4–5). Jesus observed the Mosaic Law, though he rejected additional traditions that nullified the Law (Matthew 15:1–9). He internalized and deepened its meaning in the Sermon on the Mount. Therefore, his incarnation included following and internalizing the Mosaic Law. Islamic Law in turn is quite similar to large parts of Judaic Law.[21] The early Jewish followers of Jesus continued to go to the Temple and synagogue even though other Jews did not consider Jesus to be more than a prophet (Acts 3:1; Matthew 16:14). From these examples it is argued that individuals may follow Christ while retaining all of their religious practice that is compatible with that allegiance. Thus, as Messianic Jews follow Jesus while retaining all that is compatible with that allegiance in Judaism, so some Muslims have followed Jesus while retaining all that is compatible from Islam.

Paul, a Jew with Roman citizenship, wrote to the church in Corinth:

> To the Jews I became a Jew, that I might win the Jews; to those who are under the Law, as under the Law . . . that I might win those who are under the Law . . . I have become all things to all people that I might by all means save some. (1 Corinthians 9:20–21)

He then said, "Be imitators of me as I am of Christ" (11:1). In the early church, some Jewish followers of Christ who continued to follow the Law argued that Gentile converts should do so as well. Thus, the leaders of the Church met in Jerusalem and decided, after prayer and discussion, that followers of Jesus were free to follow Judaic Law or not to do so. The restrictions that applied to all, however, were that they should abstain from immorality (Acts 15:20, 29), from what might cause others to stumble by going against their consciences (vss. 20, 29; cf. 1 Corinthians 8:1–13), and that which would hinder fellowship when Jews and Gentiles ate together (Acts 15:21).

There is a spectrum of ways that people try to follow Christ. Some use vocabulary and forms of worship used by traditional Muslims. They note that the Qur'anic religious vocabulary and the five "Pillars of Islam," except references to Muhammad and Mecca, were previously used by Jews and/or Christians.[22] Some call themselves "Muslim followers of Jesus" since the word *islam* means "to submit to God" (2:112) and in the Qur'an Jesus' disciples bear witness that "we are Muslims" (lit., "those who submit"). Likewise, the Qur'an speaks of certain individuals who received the book before who said, "We were Muslims before" (28:52–53), and Muslim commentators say some were Christians.[23] Since, however, the word *Muslim* has developed a more restrictive meaning, most would qualify this designation by affirming that "I submit to God (*aslamtu*) through Jesus the Messiah." Obviously, this has aroused debate among Christians as well as Muslims.

In the end we must return to the Guidelines for Witness that I have suggested at the end of my chapter "Toward Mutual Respectful Witness." We need to repent for our insensitivity and those of members of the communities we represent. And we need to witness by life, deed, and word with the respect our commissions enjoin.

NOTES

1. Here and elsewhere I have altered the translation slightly to bring it closer to the Arabic.
2. E.g., W. Montgomery Watt, *Muhammad at Medina* (Oxford: Clarendon Press, 1956), 345–47.
3. Al-Tabari, al-Razi, al-Qurtabi, al-Baydawi, and Sayyid Qutb on Qur'an 3:55 and 5:117 in Joseph Cumming, "Did Jesus Die on the Cross? Reflections in Muslim Commentaries" in *Muslim and Christian Reflections on Peace: Divine and Human Dimensions*, ed. J. Dudley Woodberry, Osman Zümrüt, and Mustafa Köylü (Lanham, Md.: University Press of America, 2005), 32–50.
4. *Christian Mission and Islamic Da'wah: Proceedings of the Chambésy Dialogue Consultation* (Leicester, UK: The Islamic Foundation, 1982), 101.
5. Bryant L. Myers, *Walking with the Poor: Principles and Practices of Transformational Development* (Maryknoll, N.Y.: Orbis Books, 1999), 17–19; Bruce Bradshaw, *Bridging the Gap: Evangelism, Development and Shalom* (Monrovia, Calif.: MARC, 1993), 5–20.
6. *Christian Mission and Islamic Da'wah*, 38–39.
7. Elaborated in David Kerr, "Islamic *Da'wah* and Christian Mission: Towards a Comparative Analysis," *International Review of Missions* 89 (January–October 2000): 160–62.

8. Kerr, "Islamic *Da'wah* and Christian Mission," 163.

9. T. W. Arnold, *The Preaching of Islam: A History of the Propagation of the Muslim Faith* (London: Constable, 1913); Richard W. Bulliet, *Conversion to Islam in the Medieval Period* (Cambridge, Mass.: Harvard University Press, 1979); Nehemiah Levtzion, *Conversion to Islam* (New York: Holmes & Meier, 1979).

10. Heather Sharkey, "Arabic Antimissionary Treatises: Muslim Responses to Christian Evangelism in the Modern Middle East," *International Bulletin of Missionary Research* 28, no. 3 (July 2004): 98–104.

11. See, e.g., Lamin Sanneh, *Whose Religion Is Christianity? The Gospel beyond the West* (Grand Rapids, Mich.: Eerdmans, 2003).

12. Kerr, "Islamic *Da'wah* and Christian Mission," 155–60.

13. J. Edwin Orr, "The Call to Spiritual Renewal," *The Gospel and Islam*, ed. Don M. McCurry (Monrovia, Calif.: MARC, 1979), 419–25.

14. Kerr, "Islamic *Da'wah* and Christian Mission," 155–58.

15. Josh Anderson, "Praise the Lord and Pass the Ammunition: Is the Advance of God's Kingdom Through Missions Being Confused with the Advance of American Hegemony Through the Military?" *Sojourners Magazine* (February 2005): www.sojo.net/index.cfm?action=magazine.article&mode=printer_friendly&issue=so (accessed February 18, 2005); Colin Chapman, "Time to Give Up the Idea of Christian Mission to Muslims? Some Reflections from the Middle East," *International Bulletin of Missionary Research* 28, no. 3 (July 2004): 113–14.

16. The papers are being edited by Robert A. Seiple and Dennis R. Hoover with anticipated publication by University Press of America.

17. See, e.g., Myers, *Walking with the Poor*, 3–4, 225; Bradshaw, *Bridging the Gap*, 17–19; Tim Stafford, "The Colossus of Care," *Christianity Today* (March 2005): 51–56.

18. Mark Laing, "The Changing Face of Mission: Implications for the Southern Shift in Christianity," *Missiology* 34, no. 2 (April 2006): 165–77; Deann Alford, "Gospel Work in Time of War," Christianity Today.com (posted July 23, 2006, 10:30 a.m.).

19. E.g., hundreds of Korean Christians from the Institute of Asian Culture and Development who went to Afghanistan for a peace march to be held August 5–7, 2005. The Afghan government canceled it after there were local protests (asia.news.yahoo.com/060801/3/2nvfx.html).

20. See Stephen B. Bevans, *Models of Contextual Theology* (Maryknoll, N.Y.: Orbis, 1992); Dean Gilliland, *The Word Among Us* (Waco, Tex.: Word Publishers, 1989); Dean Flemming, *Contextualization in the New Testament: Patterns for Theology and Mission* (Downers Grove, Ill.: InterVarsity Press, 2005); Scott Moreau, "Contextualization That Is Comprehensive," *Missiology* 34, no. 3 (July 2006): 325–35.

21. Robert Roberts, *The Social Laws of the Qoran* (London: William and Norgate, 1925); Jacob Neusner and Tamara Sonn, *Comparing Religions Through Law: Judaism and Islam* (New York: Routledge, 1999).

22. J. Dudley Woodberry, "Contextualization among Muslims: Reusing Common Pillars," in Gilliland, *The Word Among Us* (Waco, Tex.: Word Publishers, 1989), 282–312, revised with additional notes in *International Journal of Frontier Missions* 13, no. 4 (October–December 1996): 171–86.

23. Jane Dammen McAuliffe, *Qur'anic Christians* (Cambridge, UK: Cambridge University Press, 1991), 240–46.

IV

CONTEMPORARY ISSUES, CASE STUDIES

18

Rethinking Human Rights

A Common Challenge for Muslims and Christians

David L. Johnston

Human rights—the notion that people, simply because they are human beings, are the bearers of certain inalienable rights—is a contested issue today. This chapter attempts to get at the bottom of that discussion, both the philosophical/theological issues and the practical questions behind the reality of a fundamentally unjust international order. Building on that, it seeks to highlight how Muslims and Christians in partnership can make significant contributions toward making the world more peaceful and just.

In a book on Muslim–Christian dialogue, the spiritual father of Lebanon's Hizbullah, Sayyid Hasan Nasrallah, sets out a number of relevant themes to our discussion of human rights.[1] Here are two facets of his thinking that is picked up subsequently in this chapter:

1. The world is currently divided into two groups: *al-mustad'afun* (the downtrodden or oppressed) are the impoverished countries, the ethnic groups or socioeconomic strata in all places; and the "worldly arrogance" (*al-istikbar al-'alami*) is represented by the Western powers, the forces of "colonialism and imperialism."[2] Fadlallah writes that Muslims and Christians must draw on the spiritual resources of their revealed texts and enable the "oppressed" (whatever their religion) to confront the evil designs of the "arrogant."[3]
2. Muslims are commanded in the Qur'an itself to enter into dialogue with Christians on the basis of their common faith in the unity of God. "Say: People of the Book! Come now to a word common between us

and you, that we serve none but God, and that we associate not aught with Him, and do not some of us take others as Lords, apart from God" (Q 3:64, Arberry). Both sides must study the other faith in depth, learning from the others on their own terms. He is optimistic that in so doing many of the most sensitive issues, including the pent-up anger and bitterness from centuries of fighting, will largely melt away.[4]

With this exhortation in mind, I turn to some current disputes over the meaning and function of human rights.

THE CONTESTED NATURE OF HUMAN RIGHTS

Any discussion of human rights eventually refers to the historical document promulgated by the newly founded United Nations after the Second World War in 1948, the Universal Declaration of Human Rights (UDHR). This document, as well as the several covenants and conventions signed since then, forms the basis of a growing corpus of international law. Yet they all look back to the UDHR as the founding document, which begins under the shadow of the greatest massacres in human history:

> *Whereas* recognition of the inherent dignity and of the equal and inalienable rights of all members of the human family is the foundation of freedom, justice and peace in the world,
>
> *Whereas* disregard and contempt for human rights have resulted in barbarous acts which have outraged the conscience of mankind, and the advent of a world in which human beings shall enjoy freedom of speech and belief and freedom from fear and want has been proclaimed as the highest aspiration of the common people.[5]

The attractive phrase, "the inherent dignity and the equal and inalienable rights of all members of the human family," is nevertheless questioned from several quarters in human society today. It raises not only difficult philosophical questions but moral, political, and cultural ones as well.

Philosophical Questions

To understand the issues at stake here, we must comment briefly on the origins of the idea in the West. Katarina Dalacoura, in a study of the political cultures of Egypt and Tunisia, argues that the human rights concept resulted from the convergence of two currents:

a. Natural law, which goes back to the Greeks but was framed by the medieval theologian Thomas Aquinas as "the rational individual's participation in the divine law, and consequently the guide to morality and ethics," and[6]

b. Enlightenment secular rationalism.

Indeed, with the seventeenth-century writers Thomas Hobbes (d. 1679) and John Locke (d. 1704), the idea that human rational ability guaranteed natural rights for all human beings became widespread. This at least is the official account of the origin of the human rights concept. However, Glen Stassen has supplied us with a missing, yet crucial, ingredient: the Puritans, and Richard Overton in particular, developed a philosophy of human rights half a century before the Enlightenment that was grounded in reason, biblical faith, and in their experience of religious persecution.[7] And what is striking in light of today's Muslim–Christian dialogue is that Overton, in a series of pamphlets that helped to stir up the English Revolution of the 1640s, pleaded for "the general and equal rights and liberties of the common people," whether they be Christian, Jewish, Muslim, or pagan.[8] What is more, he advocated not only the legal enactment of civil and political rights, but also economic rights for the poor and marginalized.

This philosophy—both in its Christian and more secular versions—was picked up by political activists in a variety of settings and it led to the Declaration of Independence of the United States of America (1776), the French Declaration of the Rights of Man and of the Citizen (1789), and the Bill of Rights of the United States of America (1791). It is true that England had proclaimed the universal right to overthrow tyranny the century before (English Bill of Rights, 1689), but the concept was still narrow, admitting only of the "indubitable rights and liberties of the people of this kingdom."[9] Furthermore, while the French revolutionaries named the rights of "liberty, property, security, and resistance to oppression," the American Declaration of Independence cited "Life, Liberty and the pursuit of Happiness" as foundational human rights.

In my view, three sets of philosophical problems have emerged around this human rights discourse. The first can be seen already by contrasting the French and American versions above: whereas freedom is common to both versions, only the French formulation includes "property" and "security." Though maybe not intentional at this stage, I believe that the contrast between *rights as moral claims to social goods* (including health, education, and income) and *rights as individual rights to self-fulfillment* still stands as a choice before us today. For instance, the United States fully supports the International Covenant on Civil and Political Rights (ICCPR), but plainly struggles with the International Covenant on Economic, Social and Cultural Rights (ICESCR).[10]

German philosopher Jürgen Habermas traces this back to Hobbes's theory of rights, which envisioned liberty as a social good on the basis of people's enlightened self-interest. Leaning on this *consequentialist* version of the good (an act is good if it leads to good consequences), Hobbes advocated "a bourgeois rule of law without democracy"—a strategy of institutionalized selfishness that is neither sustainable nor universalizable, contends Habermas.[11] Missing here is a moral norm that would confer legitimacy to a system of international law. Emmanuel Kant in the nineteenth century therefore devised a *deontological* theory of the good: human beings are inherently worthy of dignity and respect. Hence, they must be treated as ends and not means (to an end). This has profound implications for the idea of social justice.

The second objection is related, yet distinct from the first: *the concept of human rights is based on a Western individualistic view of the human person.* Most other cultures—unlike the modern secular view adopted since the Enlightenment—see people as primarily part of a network of community relations, from family and clan to village, ethnic, religious, and national groupings. This sentiment has fueled the promulgation of human rights documents by Africans, Arabs, Muslims, and other regional groupings.[12] So the human rights concept, as a product of the Enlightenment, is both individualistic and secular.

A third objection comes from Western scholars in the social sciences who argue from a position of *cultural relativism*. Dalacoura rightly contends that, left to follow its natural course, modernism (child of the Enlightenment) led to postmodernism, which separates fact from value and leads in the end to the negation of all truth that might be universally grasped. To those who deny the global validity of any ethical argument, she (and many others) avers that the concept of human rights has a metaphysical dimension—only some kind of faith could guarantee the dignity of the human person.[13] Whether this foundation is laid in a secular or religious context, for her it cannot be attributed solely to reason. Yet because of this, she continues, it is naturally more hospitable to religious faith.

The Moral Issues Raised by the Current World Order

If like *New York Times* columnist Thomas Friedman you see the current phenomenon of globalization as a positive force,[14] you will find it difficult to follow me in this section. With few exceptions, Muslim scholars writing on globalization in the post–Cold War era agree with Columbia University's Joseph Stiglitz, also former chief economist at the World Bank and a Nobel laureate in economics (2001). According to Stiglitz, the "Structural Assistance Plans" of the International Monetary Fund (IMF) and the World Bank (WB) and the World Trade Organization (WTO) did in general more harm than good for the countries they sought to save from bankruptcy in the 1980s and 1990s. Due to the mostly devastating results, the earlier neoliberal ideology (the reigning paradigm since the early 1980s) was somewhat watered down and the more recent interventions in failing economies are now called "poverty reduction strategies."[15]

For Stiglitz, the steady stream of protesters at virtually every international gathering of the IMF, WB, and WTO does to some extent overlook some obvious benefits of globalization: countless people worldwide have gained employment and in Asia especially it has meant a vast swath of prosperity for millions; international connectedness through the Internet allowed global civil society to pressure 121 states to sign the international landmines treaty and faith-based groups like Jubilee 2000 have been able to advocate debt relief for the most impoverished countries. Yet "the proponents of globalization have been, if anything, even more unbalanced."[16] In the last quarter of century the gap between the haves and the have-nots has widened dramatically. Africa has seen its growing life expectancy diminish of late, along with plunging rates of income and standards of living.

Finally, these American-directed global institutions,[17] far from being able to alleviate the suffering of the three billion souls living under two dollars a day, actually contribute to world instability. Take the East Asia crisis of 1997–1998, writes Stiglitz. There was no mystery to the so-called East Asia Miracle—these countries had saved heavily for decades, and through wise government control had invested in education and state-led industrialization in order to reduce poverty and narrow inequalities. Meanwhile, the IMF and WB are run by finance ministers and top bank executives. Their main concern is to recoup their loans and losses, not the general welfare of the populations affected by their policies.

This "Washington Consensus," in Stiglitz's words, was "only interested in rapid financial and capital market liberalization." Hence, following its persistent pressure during the 1990s, deregulation of the capital markets meant a colossal influx of "hot money" from the outside—speculating on currency fluctuations in the local stock markets. But as investors pulled out their money from Asia with the first signs of difficulties, the crisis only worsened due to the policies of the IMF and its largest stakeholder, the U.S. Treasury. Instead of letting these countries deal with what was at that point simply an economic downturn according to their well-proven policies, the IMF imposed harsh austerity measures (cutting down government expenses and/or raising taxes, raising interest rates, lowering further tariffs on imported goods, etc.) and injected huge sums to keep their exchange rates at about their present level. As a result, the recession turned into a crisis of huge proportions—economically, but even worse, socially: "the unemployment rate was up fourfold in Korea, threefold in Thailand, tenfold in Indonesia. . . . Three years after the crisis, Thailand's GDP was still 7.5 percent below that before the crisis, Indonesia's 2.3 percent lower."[18] Hence, riots developed, raising the specter of political instability.

I have no space to detail this ugly side of globalization any further, except to allow some Muslim scholars to speak for themselves. Unlike Indonesia, another Muslim country fared much better in the 1997 crisis. As Stiglitz puts it, "only Malaysia was brave enough to risk the wrath of the IMF." This Muslim nation had always maintained a critical eye toward the new American-led world order: "Though Prime Minister Mahathir's policies—trying to keep interest rates low, trying to put brakes on the rapid flow of speculative money out of the country—were attacked from all quarters, Malaysia's downturn was shorter and shallower than any of the other countries."[19]

To be sure, Malaysia is better off than many Muslim countries. In a chapter presented to a conference of Muslim economists in Malaysia at this time, one expert laments the fact that the Muslims' main representative body, the Organization of the Islamic Conference (OIC) counts a majority of the world's poorest countries. In fact, most of its fifty-four members are considered "developing economies," and most of those "are located in the no-growth or very slow-growth regions of the world, with a high degree of trade dependence on extra-regional sources."[20] The chairman of the Institute of Islamic Understanding Malaysia (IKIM) expresses the frustration of most Muslim leaders when he writes that the West's exploitation of poorer countries is carried out through its control of international trade ("many poor commodity producers have to sell cheap but are forced to buy dearer industrial products, including technology") and its "control over raw materials, sources of capital, markets, and competitive advantages in the production of highly valued goods."[21]

In December 1994, another conference was convened in the capital city of Malaysia, Kuala Lumpur, on the theme of "Rethinking Human Rights."[22] Delegates from more than sixty countries gathered in Kuala Lumpur for this conference sponsored by Just World Trust (JUST, founded by Chandra Muzaffar). These were human rights theoreticians and activists, many of them Muslim, but many of them also secular or from other faith traditions. In the "Introductory Remarks" of the published version of the conference, Muzaffar explains that 90 percent of human rights activism has focused on the "power of oppressive, authoritarian ruling elites within nation-states" and the egregious impact of the following internal factors: "caste and colour domination, ethnic and religious domination, class and gender domination."[23] But what of "Western dominance as a major cause of the suppression of human dignity?" Muzaffar's bold rhetoric is worth quoting here. Notice that Israel/Palestine is in "West Asia":

> It is because of the arrogant desire of a superpower and its intimate ally to ensure their dominance that five million men, women and children in a certain part of West Asia continue to bear so much pain and agony as they struggle to

> regain just a small portion of the land they lost in 1948. It is partly because the powerful want to perpetuate, even enhance their suffocating grip over a crucial region of the world that the entire population of another West Asian country is being starved into submission and surrender. It is because of the economic power of the dominant West that 650,000 die every year in Asia and Latin America—as a result of harsh debt servicing requirements imposed by the strong upon the weak.[24]

Plainly, this conference took place with the full support of the Malaysian government. The "Keynote Address" was presented by Prime Minister Mahathir Mohamad and a "Special Address" by Finance Minister Anwar Ibrahim.[25] But as main convener of the event, Muzaffar in his chapter seeks to solve some of the philosophical difficulties I have highlighted above. On the positive side, the human rights concept born of the Enlightenment has

1. empowered the individual by proclaiming rights "that inhere in the individual as a human being";[26]
2. curbed the reach of authoritarian regimes and created social space for the growth of civil society;
3. effectively lobbied for a separation and balancing of powers; and
4. developed the norm of political rule as accountable to the people.[27]

Sadly, because of the irresistible power of the Security Council, the effective functioning of what should be a community of nations is at a distant horizon. What is worse, the West determines the policies of developing countries through the IMF, World Bank, and WTO and continues to use these levers to pry open new markets in these countries for its multinational corporations, to the expense of their already extremely vulnerable economies. Finally, the West effectively controls global information through its news outlets and dominates global culture in the area of music, clothing, food, and films, leaving little room for local expression.

As the West seems incapable of guaranteeing basic human rights at home,[28] it would seem appropriate to question the individualism and obsession with freedom that has fueled the Western understanding of human rights. At what point does individualism start eroding the vital fabric of community, asks Muzaffar? Are we not evacuating any ethical notion of human dignity and solidarity? For Muzaffar the greatest danger facing a world in which extreme poverty is on the rise comes from separating civil and political rights from social and economic ones. What is most needed, he urges, is "a vision of human dignity which is more just, more holistic and more universal."[29] We should tap into the world's religious traditions in order to find a more secure and diverse grounding for the notion of human rights.

Here is Muzaffar's conviction as a Muslim and as a world citizen, eager to build bridges with other spiritualities:

> The idea that the human being is vicegerent or trustee of God whose primary role is to fulfil God's trust is lucidly articulated in various religions. As God's trustee the human being lives his life according to clearly established spiritual and moral values and principles. The rights he possesses, like the responsibilities he undertakes, must be guided by these values and principles. What this means is that human rights and human freedoms are part of a larger spiritual and moral worldview.

I could not agree more, and this ethical and theological grounding of the concept of human dignity is the topic of the next section.

COMMON THEOLOGICAL RESOURCES

Starting with the doctrine of creation, I find more common ground for Muslims and Christians in their scriptures on the themes of justice and forgiveness. Finally, I argue that Jesus' priority concern for the poor and oppressed finds many parallels in the Qur'an.[30]

Creation and Humanity's Trusteeship

The Qur'an indicates that God, upon creating Adam and placing him on earth, entrusted him with the function of "caliph," or deputy, trustee, or vicegerent (*khalīfa*, Q 2:30). Another single instance of this term is applied to David in Q 38:26, who is called to follow God's path and judge with justice. A number of verses also use the term in the plural, implying that humankind in general has been honored with this calling. As we saw in the above quote from Muzaffar, the idea of humankind as God's trustee involves an affirmation of dignity and accountability. In fact, in my own readings, from the more traditionalist and conservative writers who impugn human rights on the basis of its Western origins to the more liberal and progressive ones who want to make tradition fit contemporary democratic norms come what may, the issue of human trusteeship remains central. According to German scholar Stefan Reichmuth, "The concept of Man as God's Vicegerent on Earth has become one of the cornerstones of contemporary Islamic political and economic theory."[31]

It is not difficult to see how this meshes well with the Genesis account of humanity, both created in God's image and empowered to fill the earth and manage it: "Be fruitful and multiply, and fill the earth and subdue it; and have dominion over the fish of the sea and over the birds of the air and over every living thing that moves upon the earth" (Gen. 1:28 RSV).[32]

In the second creation account, "The Lord God took the man and put him in the garden of Eden to till it and keep it" (2:15 RSV). This kind of call to care and safeguard the Garden, received as a trust, should guide humanity's role in the earth as a whole, particularly as interpreted in the light of the Mosaic laws.

Above all, it is the implied dignity of the human person in both cases that acts as the foundation for inalienable rights, along with a sense of moral accountability to the Creator for the way their stewardship is carried out both in the physical world and human society.

An Ethical Vision of Justice and Reconciliation

The Qur'an repeatedly exhorts its hearers and readers to be just. Perhaps the two most quoted verses are the following:

> O you who believe! Stand out firmly for justice, as witnesses to God, even against yourselves, or your parents, or your kin, and whether it be against rich or poor. (Q 4:135)

> O you who believe! Stand out firmly for God, as witnesses to fair dealing, and let not the hatred of others to you make you swerve to wrong and depart from justice. (Q 5:8)

Along with justice, the Qur'an consistently reminds its readers that humankind was originally one couple, implying an equality of rights and an ethical vision of solidarity: "O mankind, We created you from a single pair of a male and female, and made you into nations and tribes, so that you would get to know one another. Truly, the most honored in God's sight is the one who is most righteous" (Q 49:13).

The ethical vision of Christians takes its inspiration from the teaching of Jesus, whose proclamation of the coming of God's kingdom in his person finds its roots in the five books of Moses, the Bible's wisdom literature (including the Psalms), and the prophets of Israel. Yet it soon became clear to his hearers that his parables (his favorite way of teaching) portrayed a reinterpretation of "God's kingdom" as understood by first-century Jews.[33] For example, his parable of the evil vineyard tenants (Mat. 21:33–44//Mark 12:1–12//Luke 20:9–19) was an obvious retelling of Israel's story, in which all of the previous prophets were mistreated, killed, and rejected by the Jewish leaders and now, as God sends his own Son, they plan to kill him too. In the parable of the banquet feast (Mat. 22:1–14), also told during his last week in Jerusalem, the king's servants sent out to invite the guests are either ignored or beaten and even killed by them. Again, the invitation to the Jews is now open to all, in parallel with Jesus' last words to his disciples to "make disciples of all nations" (Mat. 28:19). Jesus comes to fulfill the prophecy made to Abraham (his descendants would be a blessing to all nations, Genesis 12) and Isaiah's prophecy that Israel was to be "light to all nations" (Is. 49:13).

This widening of Israel's calling goes back both to the creation account and to the law revealed to Moses. Jesus summarizes the law in two commandments: loving God (Deut. 6:5) and loving neighbor as oneself (Lev. 19:18). To the Jewish legal expert who asked him who his neighbor might be, Jesus answered by telling the Parable of the Good Samaritan. While a Jewish priest and a Levite passed by the wounded man on the road, it was a Samaritan (an ethnic group the Jews held in particular contempt), who fulfills the ethical ideal of loving one's neighbor—rescuing the dying man, carrying him to an inn where he would recover, and paying for all his expenses. Clearly, Jesus intends "neighbor" to be any other human being in need. It would be difficult to escape the implications of this teaching in the kind of shrunk, Internet-wired and polluted world we now inhabit. In our present context, human solidarity cries out in any serious reading of the Qur'an and Bible.

At the same time, while both stress righteousness and justice,[34] the virtue of forgiveness and reconciliation are stressed even more. The Afghan scholar of Islamic law (teaching in Malaysia for over two decades) Mohammad Hashim Kamali writes,

> Thus, while justice must be served and oppressed persons granted the opportunity to express their grievances, there may be instances, as the Qur'an reminds us, when maintaining peaceful communal relations merits greater attention. To this end, it is forgiveness and tolerance that often take priority over a persistent demand for retributive justice. As indicated in the following text, the Qur'an repeatedly stresses the value of forgiveness: ". . . and those who swallow their anger and forgive others" are elevated to the rank of the virtuous (*muhsinin*). And yet in another text we read ". . . and he who exercises patience and forgiveness—verily that is a matter to be resolved upon" (3:134, 42:43).[35]

Jesus told Peter to forgive his brother seven times seventy times, and practiced it during his execution, "Forgive them Father, for they know not what they do" (Luke 23:34). Initiating reconciliation with estranged people, turning the other cheek, walking a second mile with a soldier of the occupying army and love of enemies are just some of the "transforming initiatives" Jesus enjoins his disciples to practice as a way to overcome evil, spread God's light and concretely participate in God's reconciling mission with humanity.[36] Further, Jesus' answer to the question about taxes paid to the Romans has been often misunderstood, both by Christians and by Muslims: "Render to Caesar what is Caesar's and to God what is God's." Jesus was not thereby relegating godly ethics to the realm of the private, thus paving the way for the modern secular state. In this loaded question that put Jesus on the razor's edge between the priestly collaborators with Rome and the zealots who took up arms against the occupiers, he answered in the form of a Hebraic antithetical parallel: "Render to Caesar what is Caesar's" was uttered while he held up a coin he borrowed from the audience—a strategy of silent confrontation and protest of the idolatrous effigy of the Roman emperor who would be worshiped as "god." Then the second item of the parallelism, "and to God what is God's," became a bold prophetic declaration of monotheistic faith, with an underlying sarcastic tone. In essence, Jesus was saying, "render to Caesar only what is consistent with God's will."[37]

THE PREFERENTIAL OPTION FOR THE POOR

In the launching of his public ministry (in his hometown of Nazareth), Jesus chooses the following prophecy of Isaiah to flesh out the content of his mission—expand the borders of God's kingdom: "The Spirit of the Lord is upon me, because he has anointed me to preach good news to the poor. He has sent me to proclaim freedom for the prisoners, and recovery of sight to the blind, to release the oppressed, to proclaim the year of the Lord's favor" (Luke 4:18–19, NIV, quoting from Is. 61:1–2). Indeed, Jesus spent most of those three years with the poor and oppressed populations in the Galilee and healing the sick and disheartened wherever he encountered them.

The Qur'an is replete with admonitions to remember the poor and disenfranchised. Perhaps the most powerful one is also very personal. In the early Meccan sura al-Duha, we read,

> And soon will thy Guardian-Lord give thee (that wherewith) thou shalt be pleased. Did He not find thee an orphan and give thee shelter (and care)? And found thee wandering, and He gave thee guidance; and He found thee in need, and made thee independent. Therefore, treat not the orphan with harshness, nor repulse the petitioner (unheard) (Q 93:5–10, Yusuf Ali).

This essay began with the most respected spiritual leader of Lebanon's traditionally marginalized Shi'ite community, Shaykh Fadlallah. It was precisely this Qur'anic theme of the "oppressed of the earth" that he and the Hizbullah movement seized and used as inspiration. Consider this verse, "Remember when you were few and despised on the earth (*mustad'afun fi-l-ard*), afraid that people would carry you away. But He sheltered you and strengthened you with His power and provided you with good things. May you be grateful!" (Q 8:26). This is consistent with the "great reversal" theme in the Hebrew Bible—and also Mary's Song:

> My soul glorifies the Lord and my spirit rejoices in God my Savior, for he has been mindful of the humble state of his servant. . .

> He has performed mighty deeds with his arm; he has scattered those who are proud in their innermost thoughts. He has brought down rulers from their thrones but has lifted up the humble. He has filled the hungry with good things but has sent the rich away empty (Luke 1:46, 51–3, NIV).

Hence I conclude this section with the confident assertion that Muslims and Christians have more than enough common spiritual and theological resources to embark on joint ventures to defend human dignity and actively promote a more just and peaceful world. I end with a few obstacles, however, in order to stimulate discussion and, hopefully, more fruitful collaboration.

CHALLENGES ON THE ROAD TO HOLISTIC HUMAN RIGHTS

The challenges are on both sides, but I begin with Christians.

On the Christian Side

1. Western Christians, and Americans in particular, will need to become more aware of the structural impediments to a more just global system of governance.[38] We must work with others to make international institutions more effective in reaching extreme poverty reduction schemes, like the Millennium Goals, while pressing for measurable standards of environmental protection.
2. Evangelicals will have to curb their tendency to compartmentalize Jesus' ethic to the personal sphere of human experience while ignoring the myriad calls throughout the Bible to establish a just society and care for the earth as a whole. Muslims have rightly pointed this out repeatedly. The fault comes not from the Bible, but rather from a tradition of interpretation that began in the fourth century, when the ethics of the Sermon on the Mount (Mat. 5–7) were confined to the personal level.[39]
3. A corollary to the preceding is that human rights must be holistic, that is, they must uphold the dignity of the human person at all levels—hence the necessity of marrying civil and political rights to social, cultural, and economic rights. This of course challenges the prevailing neoliberal capitalist paradigm to the core. The central role played by the market today should be denounced as inhuman and oppressive for the weakest elements of society, as well as idolatrous. You cannot serve both Mammon and God, said Jesus.
4. This realization should press Christians to rethink the present capitalist system, including the role of powerful multinational corporations that yield greater power than dozens of poor countries combined, as

well as their role in virtually dictating U.S. politics. More reflection is needed in this area.

5. Evangelicals should advocate for human rights in a holistic way, beyond simply "religious freedom," to include economic and cultural rights alongside civil and political ones.[40]

On the Muslim Side

In my view, the first challenge is for Muslim thinkers to overcome a predominantly defensive posture in this area. Historically, the voluminous Muslim literature on human rights has been *mostly apologetic*, that is, a discourse reacting to a perceived Western phenomenon (and on the whole threatening). The South Asian scholar and activist Abul A'la Mawdudi (d. 1979) is representative of the tone, if not the content, of much of this literature. For him the human person as God's representative on earth is "required to exercise Divine authority in this world within the limits prescribed by God."[41] But this representation is also collective. All citizens equally participate in this divine charge of representation by democratically electing those who will lead them according to these principles. Elsewhere, Mawdudi calls this system a theo-democracy. For him the notion of human rights was a Western invention of the Enlightenment. Yet in a form clearly reminiscent of the UDHR, Mawdudi lists "Islamic" human rights: right to life and safety, right to a basic standard of life, right to individual freedom, right to justice, equality of human beings, security of life and property, right to protest tyranny, and so on. Other points come from a more traditional Muslim cultural framework: respect for women's chastity, protection of honor, and right to avoid sin. The whole exercise aims to demonstrate the superiority of the Islamic worldview and jurisprudence, without any hint or admission that (1) he is actually advancing new interpretations and (2) that whereas the West wreaks havoc in the world, there might also be difficulties in applying these ideals in Muslim contexts.

The human rights discourse found in Muzaffar's work, by contrast, is open to dialogue and mutual enrichment, however critical it is of Western hegemony. This is also the case with Swiss thinker Tariq Ramadan.[42] Grandson of Hasan al-Banna and popular religious leader with the Muslim youth of Europe, he nevertheless is fully conversant with Western philosophy and politics. While careful to observe time-honored principles of Islamic jurisprudence and theology, he advocates that European Muslims develop their own theology, one that engages with current European political and legal norms and that seeks to contribute its own distinctive approach to solving challenges common to all.

As I see it, the greatest challenge for Muslims is at the intersection of theology and law. It involves rethinking both epistemology (what we can know and how we come to know it) and hermeneutics (how we interpret the sacred text). I have argued elsewhere that a progression in Islamic legal theory is observable in the twentieth century.[43] The emphasis on the "purposes of shari'a," developed in the late classical period, has gradually become central in current legal theory, even in conservative circles. For many it has not produced any changes in actual rulings, but it does represent nevertheless a growing emphasis on the "spirit of the law," as opposed to the "letter of the law." Kamali has recently argued that depending on the circumstances, even clear rulings in the texts (Qur'an and Sunna) should be laid aside if they contradict the ethical imperatives of shari'a.[44] This is less radical than it sounds, for most Muslim legal scholars admit that the traditional division of the world between the abode of Islam and the abode of war (and later the abode of covenant) no longer applies. The same goes for many of the traditional penalties, like the amputation of the hand for thieves or the death penalty for apostasy. Yet the debates continue, both in these areas and in the rulings that are considered "discriminatory" according to current international law: the status of non-Muslims in an "Islamic" state and the rights of women.[45]

Finally, in a similar way for Christians in many parts of the world, Muslims face the challenge of denouncing oppression, abuse of power, and corruption in their own Muslim-majority states.

Moving from Talk to Action

As Muslims and Christians engage in dialogue about these issues, they will need to get beyond words and proceed to action. As this book illustrates, mosques are already coming together with churches and synagogues in the United States and elsewhere to tackle social and economic issues of concern to both sides. In developing countries, there will need to be greater coordination and dialogue between Muslim and Christian NGOs in the fields of relief and development work.

Also with regard to thorny areas of conflict such as Israel/Palestine, American evangelicals will need to listen more carefully to their Arab Muslim and Christian counterparts. A recent conference in Wheaton, Illinois, entitled "Sounds of Hope in the Middle East," cosponsored by the Billy Graham Center and Venture International, took some significant steps in this direction. Still, American evangelical leaders were only listening to Arab Christian leaders.[46]

I end with a recent conference held in Malaysia that graphically illustrates interfaith cooperation in a peacebuilding effort. In March 2005 a conference was held in Putraya, Malaysia, on the theme of "Peace in Palestine." The five hundred activists who participated came from thirty-four different countries. Though it was not a specifically Muslim–Christian gathering, there were indeed many Christians working together with Muslims in that setting. The outcome of the conference was a document called the "Putraya Action Plan," based on the idea of justice (a viable two-state solution, return of refugees or compensation for those who elect not to return, dismantling of the "apartheid wall," etc.) and reconciliation (Israeli peace groups were represented along with Palestinian ones). The only solution now can come from the uniting of global civil society in order to provide the kind of pressure that will bring about a true peace based on justice.

One of the outcomes of the conference, then, was the establishment of the International Centre on Palestine for Civil Society in the South (ICPCSS), to be headquartered in Malaysia. The stated purpose of the Action Plan is to "struggle relentlessly for the emergence of a multi-polar world," one in which interfaith dialogue would lead to joint action:

> 9) Promote active and continuous dialogue leading to effective action amongst Jews, Christians and Muslims not only in Israel and Palestine but also in various other parts of the world. This dialogue should aim to eradicate prejudices and misconceptions; to strengthen mutual respect and trust and to build joint solidarity actions in the cause of justice and our common humanity. To this end, academic centres for inter-faith and inter-civilisational dialogue should be established in both Israel and Palestine and in other countries of the South.[47]

This kind of common action represents on ongoing "rethinking of human rights," in a way that will promote peace in a more just world. Part of the problem with human rights as they have been trumpeted and applied by international institutions in a unipolar world is that they lack a clear ethical vision—something that common Muslim–Christian theologizing can help remedy. Perhaps the biggest challenge will be for Muslims and Christians to compete in how best to contribute their holistic vision of human dignity—people as God's trustees of creation—in a way that will truly make a difference to the status quo and bring understanding and reconciliation between estranged states and ethnic and religious groups.

NOTES

1. Sayyid Hasan Nasrallah has been the leader of Hizbullah right after its inception in the early 1980s. For a recent study of this movement, see Ahmad Nizar Hamzeh, *In the Path of Hizbullah* (Syracuse, NY: Syracuse University Press, 2004).
2. M. H. Fadlallah, *Fi afaq al-hiwar al-Islami al-masihi* (*On the Horizons of Muslim-Christian Dialogue*), 2nd ed. (Beirut: Dar al-Malak), 48.
3. Fadlallah explains this in liberation theology terminology: "The oppressed (*al-mustad'afun*) are to rise up from their positions of strength in order to confront the arrogant (*al mustakbirin*), something that may lead the oppressed peoples (*al-shu'ub*

al-mustad'afa) to discover in a dynamic religion (*al-din al-haraki*) the meaning of freedom and justice" (Fadlallah, *Fi afaq al-hiwar al-Islami al-masihi*, v).

4. Fadlallah, *Fi afaq al-hiwar al-Islami al-masihi*, e.g., vi–vii, 454.

5. UDHR (1948), quoted in Patrick Hayden, ed., *The Philosophy of Human Rights*, Paragon Issues in Philosophy (St. Paul, MN: Paragon House, 2001), 353–58.

6. Katarina Dalacoura, *Islam, Liberalism and Human Rights: Implications for International Relations* (London: Tauris, 1998), 6. In fact, the Dutch legal philosopher Hugo Grotius (d. 1645) was the first to claim natural rights for all human persons by virtue of their reason, independently of God—a distinctly secular turn from natural law theory to natural rights, which Hobbes and Locke would continue to build on.

7. Glen H. Stassen, *Just Peacemaking: Transforming Initiatives for Justice and Peace* (Louisville, KY: Westminster/John Knox, 1992), 141–55.

8. Stassen, *Just Peacemaking: Transforming Initiatives*, 146, 148.

9. Available in Hayden, *The Philosophy of Human Rights*, 339–42.

10. Both date to 1966 and came into force in 1976.

11. Jürgen Habermas, *Between Facts and Norms: Contributions to a Discourse Theory of Law and Democracy* (Cambridge, Mass.: MIT Press, 1996), 90.

12. At least two significant Islamic contributions have been made: the 1981 Universal Islamic Declaration of Human Rights (affiliated to the Muslim World League, with headquarters in Saudi Arabia), and the 1993 Cairo Declaration on Human Rights in Islam presented by the Saudi foreign minister to the 1993 World Conference on Human Rights in Vienna. He declared that it represented a consensus of the member states of the Organization of the Islamic Conference—a dubious statement with hindsight (see Ann Elizabeth Mayer, *Islam and Human Rights: Tradition and Politics*, 3rd ed. [Boulder, Colo.: Westview, 1999], 22).

13. See the following contributions to Hayden's *The Philosophy of Human Rights*: Joel Feinberg, "The Nature and Value of Human Rights," 174–86; Thomas W. Pogge, "How Should Human Rights Be Conceived?" 187–211; and Martha C. Nussbaum, "Capabilities and Human Rights," 212–40. For contrasting views, see Richard Rorty, "Human Rights, Rationality, and Sentimentality" (in Hayden, *The Philosophy of Human Rights*, 241–57); Michael Freeman, *Human Rights: An Interdisciplinary Approach* (Cambridge, UK: Polity, 2002), especially his chapter 6, "Universality, Diversity and Difference: Culture and Human Rights"; Michael Ignatieff, *Human Rights as Politics and Idolatry*, edited and introduced by Amy Gutmann (Princeton, N.J.: Princeton University Press, 2001).

14. See his *The Lexus and the Olive Tree* (New York: Farrar, Straus & Giroux, 1999), which makes the classic liberal argument that free trade will benefit everyone in the end.

15. For a succinct statement on these issues, see Greg Palast, *The Best Democracy Money Can Buy: An Investigative Reporter Exposes the Truth about Globalization* (London: Pluto, 2002), 50–53.

16. Joseph E. Stiglitz, *Globalization and Its Discontents* (London: Norton, 2002), 5.

17. Stiglitz reveals that the IMF, financed by taxpayers worldwide, nevertheless only "reports to the ministries of finance and the central banks of the world . . . the major developed countries run the show, with only one country, the United States, having effective veto" (Stiglitz, *Globalization and Its Discontents*, 12). This is even

more unbalanced than the UN, where the United States shares veto power with four other countries.

18. Stiglitz, *Globalization and Its Discontents*, 97.

19. Stiglitz, *Globalization and Its Discontents*, 93.

20. Syed Nawab Haider Naqvi, "Exogenous Shocks and Islamic Economic Response," in *The Economic and Financial Imperatives of Globalization: An Islamic Response*, ed. Nik Mustapha Nik Hassan and Mazilan Musa (Kuala Lumpur: Institute of Islamic Understanding Malaysia, 2000).

21. Tan Sri Dato Seri (Dr) Ahmad Sarij bin Abdul Hamid, "Preface," in *The Economic and Financial Imperatives of Globalization* (Kuala Lumpur: Institute of Islamic Understanding Malaysia, 2000), xi, xii.

22. I read about this conference after I had already given my title to the present paper. It is all the more fitting, I believe, in view of the contributions of those who participated in this "Rethinking Human Rights" conference.

23. "Introductory Remarks," in *Human Wrongs: Reflection on Western Global Dominance and Its Impact upon Human Rights*, ed. Chandra Muzaffar (Penang, Malaysia: Just World Trust, 1996), p. 2.

24. Muzaffar, "Introductory Remarks."

25. In a more recent collection of articles and essays, Muzaffar reproduces two letters by Asian activist friends, who express dismay at his inviting these two political figures. How could he, Muzaffar, the ceaseless campaigner against Malaysia's Internal Security Act (ISA), invite the architects of this repressive system to his conference on human rights? His answer is simple: though he still openly disagrees with the regime's clampdown on civil rights, he can nevertheless support its positive record on social and economic rights. Also, they were invited because of the theme—a special emphasis on Western hegemony and its impact on human rights ("Rethinking Human Rights: A Philosophical Debate," in *Rights, Religion and Reform: Enhancing Human Dignity through Spiritual and Moral Transformation* [London: Routledge Curzon, 2002], 59–102).

26. Muzaffar, "Towards Human Dignity," in *Rethinking Human Rights*, 268–75, at p. 268.

27. Muzaffar, "Towards Human Dignity," 269.

28. He list four problem areas: (1) racism on the rise in the west, (2) rising unemployment, (3) mounting violence, and (4) a dramatic erosion of family cohesion.

29. Muzaffar, "Towards Human Dignity," 273.

30. I have written on these topics elsewhere: "The Human *Khiläfa*: A Growing Overlap between Islamists and Reformists on Human Rights Discourse?" *Islamochristiana* 28 (2002): 35–53; "*Maqäæid al-Sharïæa*: Epistemology and Hermeneutics of Muslim Theologies of Human Rights," *Die Welt des Islams* (forthcoming); and *Toward Muslims and Christians as Joint Trustees of Creation in a Postmodern World* (forthcoming).

31. Stefan Reichmuth, "Murtada az-Zabidi (d. 1791) in Biographical and Autobiographical Accounts: Glimpses of Islamic Scholarship in the 18th Century," *Die Welt des Islams* 39, no. 1 (1999), 64–102, at 86–87.

32. "God created Adam in His image" is also a phrase occurring in several well-attested hadiths of the prophet Muhammad.

33. In my opinion, the best study available on the Jewish setting of Jesus' proclamation of the kingdom of God is British theologian N. T. Wright's *Christian Origins and the Question of God* (3 vols.), and particularly the second volume, *Jesus and the Victory of God* (Minneapolis, Minn.: Fortress, 1996).

34. The most famous of Jesus' comments on justice comes from the Beatitudes: "Blessed are those who hunger and thirst for justice, for they shall be satisfied" (Mat. 5:6).

35. *Freedom of Expression in Islam*, rev. ed. (Cambridge, UK: Islamic Texts Society, 1997), 168–69.

36. Glen H. Stassen and David P. Gushee, *Kingdom Ethics: Following Jesus in the Contemporary Context* (Downers Grove, Ill.: InterVarsity Press, 2004), 125–45.

37. Stassen and Gushee, *Kingdom Ethics: Following Jesus*, 359.

38. For an encouraging step forward see the April 2005 Declaration of the National Association of Evangelicals, "For the Health of the Nation: An Evangelical Call to Civic Responsibility," available on their website: www.nae.net.

39. Stassen and Gushee, *Kingdom Ethics: Following Jesus*, 128–32.

40. It was largely due to evangelical lobbying that the U.S. Commission for International Religious Freedom came into being in the late nineties under President Clinton. Though they have widened their initial agenda, they are still vulnerable, in my view, to the Muslim criticism of being more concerned for the freedom of Christians in Muslim-majority nations than for the well-being of Muslim and other minorities who also suffer discrimination and violence in other parts of the world. Ethnic profiling—predominantly of Muslims—in the United States since the passing of the Patriot Act may well be something the Commission should take up.

41. Abul A'la Mawdudi, *Human Rights in Islam* (Lahore, Pakistan: Islamic Publication Ltd., 1976), 6. This book was based on public lectures he had given the year before.

42. Tariq Ramadan, *Western Muslims and the Future of Islam* (Oxford, UK: Oxford University Press, 2004).

43. David Johnston, "An Epistemological and Hermeneutical Turn in Twentieth-Century *Uæül al-Fiqh*," in *Islamic Law and Society* 11, no. 2 (2004), 233–82.

44. Mohammad Hashim Kamali, "Issues in the Understanding of *Jihäd* and *Ijtihäd*," in *Islamic Studies* 41, no. 4 (2002), 617–34.

45. Hashmi, "Islamic Ethics," 164. See also Mayer, *Islam and Human Rights*, pp. 83–130.

46. This was held on April 22–23, 2006.

47. This is the ninth of ten points. The entire text of the Putraya Action Plan can be found online: www.worldcivilsociety.com/re.asp.

19

Let Peace Flourish

Descriptive and Applied Research from the Conflict Transformation Study

Alvin C. Dueck, Kevin S. Reimer, Joshua P. Morgan, and Steve Brown

> Oh you who believe!
> Stand out firmly for justice, as witnesses to God,
> even against yourselves, or your parents, or your kin,
> and whether it be against rich or poor,
> for God can best protect both.
>
> —Qur'an 4:135

> You have heard that it was said,
> "You shall love your neighbor and hate your enemy."
> But I say unto you, love your enemies and pray for those who persecute you.
>
> —Matthew 5:43–44

In the aftermath of 9/11, are there Muslim and Christian peacemakers who will contribute to lasting peace between these two ancient traditions? Since the thirty years' war (1611–1648) it has been assumed that religion and violence are inextricably linked. While we believe this totalizing perspective to be false, we also recognize that disproving the link is a tall order. Part of the difficulty is related to the uneven landscape of the contemporary American context. Auspiciously "Christian" peacemakers such as Bono, Jimmy Carter, Martin Luther King Jr., and Desmond Tutu are widely recognized in the West. Comparatively, Muslim peacemakers are much less well known or celebrated. Edward Said comments:

> There is a consensus on "Islam" as a kind of scapegoat for everything we do not happen to like about the world's new political, social, and economic patterns. For the right, Islam represents barbarism; for the left, medieval theocracy; for the center, a kind of distasteful exoticism. In all camps, however, there is agreement that even though little enough is known about the Islamic world, there is not much to be approved of there.[1]

If Said is correct, much work is required to demonstrate the commensurability of religion and peace, particularly with regard to the excellent work of Muslim peacemakers around the globe. We frame this calling with the Muslim *hadith*: "Whenever violence enters into something, it disgraces it, and whenever 'gentle-civility' enters into something it graces it. Truly, God bestows on account of gentle conduct what he does not bestow on account of violent conduct."[2]

How will peace flourish between Muslims and Christians? Our preoccupation with this question differs somewhat from other chapters in the present volume. We are social scientists commissioned to study peacemaking for the Conflict Transformation Grant. As a consequence, our principal contribution to Muslim-Christian dialogue is peacemaking as a topic of *descriptive* and *applied* research. That is, we wish to understand how a "bottom-up" description of peacemaking practice might inform (or be informed by) a "top-down" religious peace model yet untested in the real world. It is our hope that in the intersection of descriptive and applied processes, we might discern useful insights for the present conversation along with future directions for research in peace psychology. As we are Christians, we present findings with the assumption that this work is incomplete, awaiting the contributions of Muslim scientific colleagues.

The study of Muslim and Christian peacemakers is relatively unknown in the psychological literature. In the absence of other studies to direct our work, we felt it necessary to begin with a descriptive investigation of peacemaking practices. One descriptive option is to engage actual peacemakers in open-ended conversation about their perceptions, attitudes, and strategies.[3] Muslim and Christian peacemakers are a rare breed, meaning that such an approach is idiosyncratic. While findings from this kind of study are limited in terms of generalizability, the approach offers a distinct advantage in providing "bottom-up" accounts of how religious particularity (e.g., Muslim or Christian faith) is woven into peacemaking practice. A descriptive account, however, is not the end of the story. Peace psychology also anticipates applied research. We note that excellent work was recently completed on Muslim and Christian models for peacemaking. These models were constructed by academicians sensitive to the religious, social, and cultural contours of peace. As a complement to descriptive research, we attempted to boil down one of these models into a self-report instrument that could be used in a top–down manner to identify educational interventions for religious populations. Because of our spiritual orientation, we felt best qualified to do this for the Christian peacemaking model. Thus, we present two studies that approach the peacemaking question from somewhat different vantages. It is our hope that the confluence of these findings will eventually lead to a fuller, more comprehensive understanding of peacemaking in two great world religions.

DESCRIPTIVE FINDINGS: A QUALITATIVE INVESTIGATION OF MUSLIM AND CHRISTIAN PEACEMAKERS

The descriptive aspect of the research project involved telephone interviews with Muslim and Christian peacemakers from around the globe. Our descriptive goals were focused on the perceptions, attitudes, and strategies of peace in this unique population. We solicited Muslim and Christian peacemakers with nomination criteria in active (current) peacemaking practice and open identification with either Muslim or Christian religious faith. Interviews were conducted by phone using a semistructured protocol. Questions were open-ended, taken from the Life Narrative Interview.[4] Thirteen Muslim and thirteen Christian peacemakers were interviewed. Interviews were transcribed and analyzed using grounded theory methodology with ATLAS.ti qualitative software. Open coding was designed to identify peacemaking perceptions, attitudes, and practices along with religious commitments; 163 codes resulted from this process. Codes were subsequently

Table 19.1. Peacemaking Interview Protocol

1. **Peacemaking.** Please describe a situation where you faced a difficult conflict that required peacemaking. What was the conflict in that situation? What was it about this conflict that made it so important to you? What was at stake for you in this conflict? What were the various points of view in the conflict? What was your strategy to resolve the conflict? How was the conflict resolved?
2. **Personal ideology.** What motivates you to engage in peacemaking activities? What sustains you in these activities? Is God significant to your peacemaking activities? If so, how?
3. **Critical Life Events.** Please describe a *peak experience, a low-point experience,* and *turning point.*
4. **Life Challenge.** Please describe the single greatest challenge that you have faced in your life. How have you faced, handled, or dealt with this challenge? Have other people assisted you in dealing with this challenge? How has this challenge had an impact on your life story?
5. **Significant people.** Are there past relationships that have been important to your development as a peacemaker? Do you recall any changes in relationships that have had a significant impact on your way of thinking about peace and peacemaking?

distilled into five core themes that characterized both peacemaker cohorts. In this manner, the study attempted to identify principles amenable for use in peacemaking both within and between religious traditions. We briefly define each theme, providing Muslim and Christian narrative examples as illustrations.[5]

Theme 1: Faith Commitment

Faith commitment implies perspectives, opinions, worldviews, and beliefs that are generally informed by the religious faith of peacemakers. Beyond specific political or philosophical commitments, this theme refers to the resoluteness of the individual to particular aspects of his or her faith tradition. Commitment to a faith tradition is thick, essentially describing what people believe about their perceived reality, why they believe it, how sure they are of that belief and what they believe about that belief's meaning (e.g., their meta-belief). For one Muslim peacemaker, faith commitment results in a meta-belief of spiritual maturity foundational to a peacemaking ethos:

> Being mature in your faith is not worrying about what other people think or say about you. You're sort of at peace with yourself. It's that you're at peace with yourself and your relationship with God. And then you can move from that place of peace into bringing that to other people. And then your life is in service of God, seeking the pleasure of God. And the way I look at it, too, God describes faith as light, which, that is a theme that exists in all the texts of religion and spirituality. You bring that light to the world so that when you've achieved that peace and sense of maturity, you're a source of light in other people's lives. Until you get to that point, you're struggling. I mean, you're always struggling. We never get to that point of completion because human beings are not perfect. But you're emerging all the time and moving towards that. When you say mature, it almost sounds like you're finished, but no one is ever finished.

This quotation includes a tradition-sensitive perspective of personal meaning (being in the service of God and seeking God's pleasure), a description of faith (as light), and theological wisdom. Faith commitment is viewed with some flexibility as it allows for growth and change but ultimately remains secure in terms of foundational beliefs. Similar convictions are evident in a Christian peacemaker narrative:

> When people have a conflict about a moral issue that means there is at least two or three different perspectives. Often people are on one side that does not have a good understanding of the other perspective. But they are morally obligated to try to understand the other perspective. In this environment, it is not going to be an easy thing. It is a lot of work, and it's going to be constant

> work. But I think we have something that others do not have. As a Christian, I see peacemaking as the core of New Testament teaching with the politics of Jesus as the core of peacemaking.

Faith commitment in this instance is presented through peacemaker fidelity to the New Testament and Jesus' politics. The Jesus of the New Testament is viewed by the peacemaker as a core identity that allows one to live life in a manner consistent with a tradition that prioritizes peace. This is not an exclusive claim insofar as the peacemaker still asserts that other religious bodies can and must contribute to a dialogue for the purpose of peace. Indeed, the peacemaker's comments suggest that one can only come to appreciate the viewpoint of others when grounded in a particular tradition. The Christian peacemaker appeals for organic peace dialogue where everyone's religious commitment is welcome for the sake of mutual understanding. Both Muslim and Christian peacemakers hint at the need, or even the inevitability of a peacemaking practice in part premised upon thick traditions rather than thin universals.[6]

Theme 2: Peacemaking Methodology

Peacemaking methodology is understood in terms of strategies and practices of peace. Briefly, peacemaking methodology emphasizes strategies inherent to what peacemakers do. The peacemaking methodology theme is immediately visible in the current peace literature. Training manuals foundational to the Conflict Transformation Grant focus on specific peacemaking actions or strategies.[7] We found that for peacemakers in our study, peacemaking methodology is often forced to evolve, changing on the fly to accommodate impasse situations or moments where ambiguity threatens to derail dialogue. In one Muslim peacemaker's words:

> We hung in there for about a year. The whole idea was to come open-minded, to represent our points of view, to listen to theirs, and to find the areas where we disagreed and could not come to agreement, and the areas where we had flexibility. And like I said, we were able to do that up to a certain point, when we got to redline issues for both sides. We haven't really had conflict with the individuals, since we decided it wasn't working. But in the end, we were on good terms, just as far as basic interaction. And so it's a group I could approach if it was for some other basic issue. It left it clear where each other stood. But we couldn't resolve the redline issues. So we felt that instead of trying to force each other to change each other's views, we would instead just continue in the spirit of friendship and dialogue without trying to resolve these major issues beforehand.

The peacemaker demonstrates marked willingness to take on the perspective of others, discovering points of agreement and disagreement that clarify the discussion without attempting to change the other. The Muslim peacemaker upholds a peacemaking methodology that emphasizes a "spirit of friendship and dialogue," entering peacemaking with a flexible set of objectives and a willingness to end dialogue without clear resolutions. The methodology is deeply pragmatic, alluding to the peacemaker's recognition of "redline issues" that are appropriately addressed within the context of a relationship characterized by trust. Peacemaking is highly attuned to the transformation of individual participants in dialogue. The peacemaker undertakes peace work with this expectation but recognizes that change is bigger than the peacemaker or even the dialogue itself.

The peacemaker's account reminds us that effective peacemaking methodology lives within the ambiguities of particular relationships, requiring virtue as much as technique. This is similarly evident in the methodology of a Christian peacemaker:

> I will not say the conflict was resolved, it was just we were able to make one positive step and so in that way it was a success. But it was a journey that is still continuing and has made positive steps and some backward steps. But in that particular case our strategy was twofold—one was that we wanted to listen to them and have face-to-face exchange. In many Asian relationships this is very important and so we wanted to establish face-to-face relationship and in that setting to listen to them and try to break down some of the stereotypes and accusations which can be made at a distance but which take on a different form when you are face-to-face. The second strategy was that in our earlier talks we had called for a ceasefire among all the indigenous groups. Since the splits among the indigenous factions, as many had died in violence as died in the conflict with the army.

As with the Muslim example, the ambiguity of the situation implies the lack of ideal resolution, acknowledging that progress requires great patience. As such, the Christian peacemaker describes peacemaking methodology as a journey of both forward and backward motion, listening to the other in the interest of establishing a relationship capable of breaking down stereotypes. This involves an intentional effort to humanize the other toward the goal of a ceasefire. Rather than a fixed template or prescription, the peacemaking methodologies used by both Muslim and Christian peacemakers suggest a slow process of listening and reengagement through periods of misunderstanding.

Theme 3: Pragmatism

For the present study, *pragmatism* includes two related conceptual levels: practicality and concreteness. *Practicality* refers to realism in understanding the effectiveness of peacemaking activity. It is the peacemaker's internal check on whether one's theology and outward behavior are consistent. *Concreteness* describes the level of abstraction specific to peacemaking practice. Together, these constituents affirm a theme of pragmatism that is essentially ideology at work in everyday conversations and circumstances. Rather than emphasizing abstract peacemaking theory, this theme is focused on practical applications in real-world situations. Such application often translates into methodology but additionally includes the manner by which peace serves as an interface between one's commitment to tradition and outside community. In the words of a Muslim peacemaker:

> We're building interfaith homes. We're planning on building homes next year. President Carter is going to come work on it. We just had an interfaith prayer service, kicked off a new home, a blitz; we have a blitz every year, where a bunch of homes are built in a week. It was all kicked off with interfaith prayer. I was there. It was three weeks ago. It was pretty well publicized in the media, in the newspapers and television. We had people, Muslims, Christians, and Jews, who worked on it. See, that's where my effort has switched now. Before, it was prayer service and dialogue. Now the effort and focus is doing things together, building homes, doing a play with the kids, doing blood drives, practical things. When we do things, we build confidence; get to know each other better. Prayer service is a symbolic thing that we need, but building relationships, you got to do things together.

This narrative emphasizes the importance of addressing practical needs for physical and psychological survival (e.g., shelter, recreation, blood, and relationships) rather than more esoteric aspects of interpersonal reconciliation. Simple practices accomplished together become a foundation for identifying and attending to needs. Resulting relationships help to form a community context within which peacemaking can occur. For a Christian peacemaker:

> Basically, they try to be a nonviolent presence in the middle of the conflict. They take risks themselves. They make sacrifices for the purpose of trying to reduce the level of violence between the two communities. If they have to physically stand between the two groups they will do that. If they need to accompany a child from one place to another, say from home to school or if they need to accompany a farmer going to his fields, they will do that. They will be a presence to reduce the violence to reduce the conflict. They, obviously in doing that, are not finding a permanent solution to the violence; but they're just reducing the level of violence on a particular day in a particular place.

As with the Muslim peacemaker, interventions focus on practical needs. Needs are detailed with great specificity, along with concrete steps for implementation. For both Muslim and Christian peacemakers, pragmatic interventions are as varied as the creative programs and cooperative projects envisioned by local participants in a given conflict. The critical issue remains the identification of concrete objectives for joint activity, imbued with culturally and religiously sensitive boundaries for implementation.

Theme 4: Community Support

Community refers to supportive relationships available to the peacemaker. While community describes the interpersonal environment in which the peacemaker lives, it most importantly refers to the peacemaker's support system. The community theme encompasses many groups in the social network, including faith community, mentor figures, family and peer associations, or friendships. Community serves as a motivational impetus for peacemaking work that helps to sustain peacemakers over time and through failure. The primacy of community context as an ethical influence is well known in the psychological literature on moral exemplars similar to the individuals interviewed for the present study.[8] For one Muslim peacemaker, community took on a civic flavor consonant with newly acquired citizenship:

> I remember the day I was sworn in to be a U.S. citizen. It was just life turning for me. I was so happy. I had my wife, my child, and my in-laws all around me as I raised my hand for the first time in my life ever to be a citizen of, or to be recognized. I was never a citizen of any country. I was a refugee, and now to be a citizen to pledge to protect the country in non-combatant ways and to be someone, it was something I don't think I can find words to describe, a simple act of extending a citizenship to someone as you are restoring the human faith and telling that person you are someone not just as a number or known as this, you are somebody, you count, and you are one of us. Not to say the challenges ended, but it's just from being stateless into a citizen of the world. That was, I would say, back in July of 1999. It just was overwhelming to me.

Social support in this instance provides a stabilizing, nurturing effect on the peacemaker's motivation to work toward peace. Community for this peacemaker becomes exchangeable with a larger civic identity on the basis of American citizenship. The effect of community support can be profound, particularly amid personal difficulties, as in the narrative of this Christian peacemaker:

> About a year and a half before I graduated I was very depressed, and I needed to go see a counselor mostly because I had no direction. I did not know where I was going. I had pretty much completed one master's degree, and I was working on another. But I did not know what I was going to do with that master's degree, and I did not know what I was called to in the world. I realized that God had not called me to church ministry as I had thought. At that time also, I was in between relationships. I had hoped to be dating someone and I was not.

> Since then I have got married, and that helped a lot. Yeah, I even had some thoughts of suicide at that time. I do not know if there were really a lot of specifics. I guess you could say I have lived somewhat of a boring life that did not have anything major positive or negative. I had a couple of close friends at the time that talked me into seeing a counselor. The counseling experience was not extraordinarily good or bad. I guess I was looking for a purpose in my life. And even though I was a Christian and everything, I was looking for a purpose.

Elements of community in this quotation suggest a slightly different emphasis on support relative to the Muslim peacemaker. Whereas the Muslim's narrative is given to collective (e.g., civic) definitions of community, the Christian's is widely varied and more interpersonally autonomous, including counselors, God, romantic relationships, close friends, and parents. This support system allows the Christian peacemaker to survive difficult times. In both instances, personal experiences of community have changed the peacemaker's outlook on self and peacemaking interventions. The community theme is implicated as a means by which religious faith is reciprocally modeled in relationships supportive of the peacemaker and his or her efforts. Both Muslim and Christian peacemakers indicated that their faith communities conferred this kind of support, although some also noted that faith communities at times did not fully understand their efforts or interest in peace.

Theme 5: Personal Responsibility

This theme includes the manner by which individuals understand peacemaking events relative to the self. It is the way the individual construes personal involvement in peacemaking activities, taking responsibility for the event along with potential impacts on others. On the basis of the personalization theme, peace becomes a dimension of social responsibility. This theme is perhaps best captured by the idea of ownership. A critical value of peacemakers is that they own their commitment to peace along with related consequences. For a Muslim peacemaker:

> Well, as the person who runs the mosque and promotes it, I felt particularly responsible for this guy being allowed in. And I try to advertise so that only people who we know and trust know about the mosque. I felt kind of responsible. But mostly, what was important was the safety of other members and keeping the space safe.

In this example, the peacemaker takes responsibility for a particular conflict but also the larger Muslim community he serves. Beyond this, the peacemaker personalizes the conflict in its extended form, including perceptions of his mosque in the wider community. The public forum of peacemaking forces peacemakers to take responsibility for aspects of their work that extends far beyond participants seated at a roundtable. A Christian peacemaker noted this tension in the context of peace conducted in a university setting:

> I genuinely wanted to be able to have a more open dialogue with the Messianic Jewish people on campus. I do not want them to think I am anti-Semitic. They have told me before that they think I am anti-Semitic and I want to explain that I do not dislike them, that I have nothing against them. I just have a different view on this conflict.

This peacemaker feels deep personal responsibility for peacemaking activity and its perception within a particular Jewish community on campus. At times, personalization in peacemakers appears to cross a fine line from responsibility to outright anxiety. The peacemaker's hopes and desires are woven into peacemaking activities in a personal manner, making external misunderstandings potentially painful. Across the board, we found that peacemakers favor direct involvement as participants in conflict rather than deferring responsibility to third parties. This pattern of serving as primary participant hints at the tremendous personalization of peacemaking activity upheld by peacemakers. Peacemakers come to identify the self in terms of peacemaking, ratifying personal meaning on the basis of experiences undertaken in the interest of conflict transformation. In summary, the descriptive process suggested more similarities than differences between Muslim and Christian peacemakers. This snapshot of peace in the trenches confirms a level of uniformity where peacemakers from both traditions emphasize like perceptions, attitudes, and strategies resourced through the insights of their respective faith tradition.

APPLIED FINDINGS: THE JUST-PEACEMAKING INVENTORY

In contrast to the organic, bottom–up approach in the first study we wanted to consider how religious models of peacemaking might be applied toward the goal of specifying educational interventions. Such a top–down approach must grapple with the tumultuous milieu of contemporary Muslim-Christian relations. Given the cultural stereotypes that abound, the research team began by reading some of the current peace literature, with focus given to Mohammed Abu-Nimer[9] and Glen Stassen.[10] Each has written extensively on the nuances of peacemaking in religious perspective. From this study it was quickly obvious that neither Muslim nor Christian traditions are monolithic with regard to peacemaking approaches. Both models reflect pragmatic and flexible principles not unlike the peacemakers interviewed in the first study. In his book *Nonviolence and Peace Building in*

Islam, Abu-Nimer constructs a model on the foundation of the Qu'ran and the tradition of the Prophets (*hadith*).

1. The pursuit of justice (*'adl*) is a divine command and one can resist injustice through activism, third-party intervention and divine intervention.
2. Social empowerment by doing good (*khayr* and *ihsan*), that is, maintain good and honorable interpersonal relationships, meeting the needs of the underprivileged whether Muslim or not.
3. The universality and dignity of humanity, equality of origins and rights, and the essential solidarity of all people is affirmed since God is the creator of all people and since all people are the children of Adam and Eve.
4. Islam aspires to unite the human family based on the equality of all members, rather than based on privilege, race, or ethnicity.
5. Human life is sacred and must be protected, so human resources should not be destroyed.
6. Peacemaking and reconciliation of differences and conflict are preferred over avoidance, as highlighted by the Prophet's tradition.
7. Rationality, wisdom (*hikma*), and cost–benefit calculations are presumed to be more effective in successful dialogue and most conflict resolution processes.
8. Creativity and innovation require new options that do not compromise justice.
9. Forgiveness is part of conflict transformation since God has mercy upon those who are merciful to others (Qur'an 7:151).
10. Deeds and actions are part of making peace since in Islam the real test is in action.
11. Involvement is through individual responsibility and choice since persuasion is a major strategy.
12. To be patient (*sabr*) and to suspend judgment of others is important whether with Muslim or non-Muslim.
13. Collaborative actions to resolve a problem are more productive and solidarity with others is wider than the Muslim community.
14. The Ummah is the universal community under God which creates future bonds, relationships, and agreements, and which makes for peace.
15. Inclusivity and participatory processes encourage forums and inclusive procedures that are more productive and effective than authoritarian decision-making approaches.
16. Pluralism is recognized by the Qur'an as including diversity and tolerance of differences based on gender (49:13; 53:45), skin color, language (30:23), belief, and rank (64:2, 6:165).

From a Christian standpoint, Glen Stassen's book *Just Peacemaking* integrates justice with particular virtues from Protestant Christianity.[11] *Just Peacemaking* is the work of twenty-three scholars, including ethicists, theologians, international relations experts, peace activists, and conflict mediators. *Just Peacemaking* advocates specific practices utilized by groups of concerned citizens to address the causes of war before they fully materialize. These practices aim for the transformation of violent or unjust situations into greater opportunities for peace. *Just Peacemaking* contributors unabashedly affirm "deeply held faith perspectives" as central to their theory.[12] These initiatives are constructed on theological convictions such as being disciples of Jesus (Matthew 5–7), initiating peace, seeking the peace of the city (Jeremiah 29:7), and advocating for justice, love, and community (Luke 4:18–19). The ten *Just Peacemaking* practices are characterized as follows:

1. Support for nonviolent direct action (boycotts, strikes, marches, civil disobedience, or public disclosure) as practiced by Gandhi and King.
2. Taking independent, verifiable initiatives to reduce threats and encourage deescalation, negotiation, and reconciliation.
3. Using cooperative conflict resolution that seeks to understand the other and to create lasting change.
4. Acknowledging responsibility for conflict and injustice through apology while seeking repentance and forgiveness.
5. Advancing democracy, human rights, and religious liberty through political involvement and representation.
6. Fostering just and sustainable economic development through the development of civic society of local communities (education, health services, etc.).
7. Working with emerging cooperative forces in the international community.
8. Strengthening the United Nations and international efforts for cooperation, human rights, and conflict resolution.
9. Reducing offensive weapons and weapons trade.
10. Encouraging grassroots peacemaking in churches, college groups, local communities, and clans.

Both Abu-Nimer and Stassen draw deeply from the wells of their respective religious traditions to justify peacemaking in scriptures (Qur'an/Bible), key leaders (Mohammed/Jesus), and commentators (Sunnah/patristic church leaders). Both build on values for peacemaking. Core Muslim values for nonviolence include *'adl* (justice), *ihsan* (benevolence), *rahmah* (compassion), and *hikmah* (wisdom). Core Christian values include forgiveness, cooperation, and personal responsibility. Each model suggests a set of critical principles for peacemaking demonstrating considerable overlap including belief in unity, supreme love of the Creator, mercy, subjection of passion, and accountability for actions. Both models use the language of human rights and justice. Both affirm basic pluralism, diversity, respect, human rights, and human dignity. Each model is practical, designed to facilitate peacemaking practice across a variety of situations. Beyond the immediate value of promoting peacemaking practices, the models provide a basis for understanding how peacemaking is conceptualized in target populations. Put another way, the conceptual ideas embedded in the models may be useful for determining where religious populations may require specific interventions given to peace awareness and educational praxis.

Social scientists are able to apply conceptual content to a given population in the form of a self-report questionnaire or survey instrument. The advantage of such an approach is the ability to gauge the efficacy of concepts with real people, to find out whether concepts are understood in the manner by which they were intended. Moreover, survey instruments represent a way of testing how a group might change or grow. Instruments administered in a "pre/post" (e.g., before educational intervention/after educational intervention) manner are powerful indicators of program effectiveness. We perceived that the models reviewed above might be applied to real-world situations in the form of a survey instrument. From our Christian perspective, Stassen's *Just Peacemaking* practices could be developed into a survey for use with Christian university students. The application of a preexisting theoretical model as survey instrument represents a top–down approach to research. In this application, a *Just Peacemaking* instrument offers twin advantages in (a) gauging the relevance and comprehensiveness of Stassen's principles with a religious population that might one day be targeted for peacemaking education and (b) finding those aspects of *Just Peacemaking* that are not central to their worldview. Thus, the second study comprised our effort to boil down the principles of just peacemaking for applied research with a religious population.

Just-Peacemaking Inventory

Earlier attempts at peace measurement considered attitudes toward war, nuclear activism, and the role of moral disengagement in collective violence.[13] Examples include Elliott's *Pacifism Scale,* which measured four dimensions, including physical violence, psychological violence, active value orientation, and locus of control. [14] The *Nonviolence Test* measured predispositions that differentiated violent and nonviolent participant attitudes.[15] Our application research differed somewhat from these instruments in that our starting point was an explicitly religious model. Because of this, we began by brainstorming survey items based on *Just Peacemaking* principles. The resulting survey instrument had seventy-seven items and was voluntarily completed by a sample of 289 undergraduate and graduate students from evangelical Protestant universities in California. Seventy-one percent of student participants identified themselves as European, 17 percent as Asian, 7 percent as Hispanic, and 3 percent as African American. Participants ranged from eighteen to sixty-six years of age with an average of twenty-seven. The participants included 147 women and 142 men. They reported levels of education as 34 percent completed high school, 2 percent completed trade school or associate's degree, 54 percent completed college or bachelor's degree, 8 percent completed master's degree, and 2 percent completed doctoral degree.

In order to get a sense of response patterns, we used a statistical technique called exploratory factor analysis.[16] Based on these results we identified five themes that best characterized the responses of participants. The first theme was labeled "Concern for Just and Sustainable Development" and reflected practices designed to increase the welfare of the poor. The second theme, "Activism," included items reflecting practices such as protests, advocacy, and civil disobedience. The third theme, "American Unilateral Action," highlighted participant attitudes on American military activities. The fourth theme was labeled "Empathy" since it clearly emphasized compassionate concern for victims and perpetrators. The fifth theme of "Religious Exclusivism" reflected peacemaking concerns for tolerance and openness to other religious traditions. With these themes in mind, we titled the instrument the "Just-Peacemaking Inventory" (JPI). In table 19.2 we present JPI themes with survey items.

The analysis indicated loose affiliation between Concern for Just and Sustainable Development, Activism, and Empathy. Interestingly, these three themes were negatively correlated with American Unilateral Action and Religious Exclusivism. That is, participants understood the conceptual underpinnings of American Unilateral Action and Religious Exclusivism but did not agree with them. Instead, participants stressed American innocence in the state of affairs that led to the terrorist attacks of September 11, 2001, along with hegemonic justification for use of military force in the world. These attitudes collide with just-peacemaking practices calling for independent initiatives to reduce distrust or threat perception in other groups. The prominence of these attitudes in the applied study sample may reflect notions of just-war theory or neoconservative political mandates that have widespread support among the conservative wing of American Protestantism. The polarization between these two different theme clusters suggests considerable moral ambivalence associated with peacemaking attitudes in the Protestant sample. We believe that this demonstrates the efficacy of just-peacemaking principles in the real world while simultaneously underscoring the fact that work is urgently required in the business of peace education with evangelical Christians.

Table 19.2. **Just-Peacemaking Inventory Statistical Themes**

Theme 1: Concern for Sustainable Development

I support the use of tax dollars as relief funds for Iraqi and Afghani civilians.

It is better to spend money assisting our potential enemies in time of need so that money need not be spent later in war with them.

Spending money on education and industry in foreign countries is the moral duty of countries with financial power.

I would be willing to engage in an exchange project with those from Arab or Muslim society (Westerner) or a Western society (Arab or Muslim).

I believe my side should take initiatives to reduce the threat of the other side and build trust even though the other side is not taking initiatives and might misunderstand them as weakness.

Theme 2: Activism

I have been involved in actions designed to isolate an individual, group, or nation to express disapproval for its injustice.

I have been involved in actions designed to isolate an individual, group, or nation to cause change for the sake of justice.

I have been involved in mass public demonstrations to dramatize an injustice.

I have joined with others to break a law because I perceived it to be unjust.

I have acted to bring secret information to public attention for the sake of justice.

I am involved in spreading information about my cause to people who see things differently.

I engage in protest and collaborative actions against practices relied on by groups that violate human rights.

I spend considerable time, energy, or money to gain public attention for my protests and the people I am trying to protect.

I am part of a small group of people who meet regularly to advocate for those not in our immediate community.

Theme 3: American Unilateral Action

I think that major military intervention should not happen unless it can get the approval of the United Nations or an international organization.

America has antagonized others in a manner leading to terrorist attacks.

An effective response to the 9/11 terrorist attacks would have been to go to the leaders of Muslim countries and apologize for American antagonism.

Swift and hard military retaliation was a necessary response to the 9/11 terrorist attacks.

Some violence may be used against those who are opposing me only to enable negotiations to safely take place.

Theme 4: Empathy

I believe it is important to offer a place of sanctuary in order to secure safety for victims.

I believe it is important to make partnerships or coalitions with other groups in order to solve our disputes.

I try to understand the perspectives of those who oppose me.

I share some of the responsibility for conflict between myself and others who oppose me.

(continued)

Table 19.2. (*continued*)

My efforts are aimed at long-term peace in addition to resolving current conflicts.
I am prepared to abide by third-party solutions.

Theme 5: Religious Exclusivism
I believe that transforming the spiritual and ideological framework of the Iraqis and Afghanis is more important than helping them to build an infrastructure.
I think that the only valid way to experience human potential is through the path laid out by my religion.
I think that other religious paths may be equally valid for finding God and fulfilling human potential.
I am unwilling to engage in prayer services and peace vigils with those of other faiths.

DESCRIPTION MEETS APPLICATION

How might the descriptive research effort in the first study intersect with the applied aspect of the second study? Presumably, the confluence of these two studies would suggest paragon themes worthy of inclusion in peacemaking curricula. JPI principles might be shared among Muslim and Christian peacemakers, implicating knowledge domains that promote peacemaking behaviors, at least within the *Just Peacemaking* framework.[17] Consequently, the JPI was given to Muslim and Christian peacemakers from the first study. A total of thirty-four peacemakers completed the questionnaire, with an equal number coming from each tradition. The average age of the Muslim peacemakers was forty-four. Christian peacemakers averaged forty-eight years of age. In the Muslim sample 38.5 percent were female and 61.5 percent were male while in the Christian sample, 7.7 percent were female and 92.3 percent were male. Education varied from high school through earned doctorate in each group. Peacemakers were compared to a control group of thirty-four individuals matched to peacemakers on age, gender, and ethnicity. We used an independent samples *t*-test to consider differences in means between (a) Muslim peacemakers, (b) Christian peacemakers, (c) total group of peacemakers, and (d) controls. Results are provided in table 19.3.

Two findings are of immediate interest. First, Muslim and Christian peacemakers did not differ significantly on any of the five JPI themes. This is a remarkable and unexpected finding. JPI themes are evidently meaningful for peacemakers from both religious traditions. We note two different interpretive directions for this convergent finding. Consonant with the many similarities noted between peacemakers in the descriptive study, the JPI application suggests that Muslim and Christian peacemakers share similar perceptions and attitudes toward peace. In effect, the administration of the JPI to this unique group validates earlier qualitative conclusions that

Table 19.3. JPI Comparison of Peacemakers and Controls

	Group	*N*	*Mean*	*t*	*Sig.*
Sustained development	Muslim peacemakers	17	22.1		.24
	Christian peacemakers	17	23.6		
	Peacemakers	34	22.8	5.39	.00
	Control	34	19.3		
Activism	Muslim peacemakers	17	32.4		.49
	Christian peacemakers	17	34.9		
	Peacemakers	34	33.7	11.13	.00
	Control	34	17.0		
American unilateralism	Muslim peacemakers	17	9.7		.94
	Christian peacemakers	17	9.8		
	Peacemakers	34	10.2	−5.37	.00
	Control	34	14.2		
Empathy	Muslim peacemakers	17	6.4		.78
	Christian peacemakers	17	6.4		
	Peacemakers	35	27.7	4.41	.00
	Control	35	25.1		
Religious exclusivism	Muslim peacemakers	17	6.4		.99
	Christian peacemakers	17	6.4		
	Peacemakers	35	6.3	−6.13	.00
	Control	35	9.6		

peacemakers are on the same page in spite of religious differences. An alternative interpretation points to the relevance of JPI themes to peacemaking practice, with the caveat that the same protocol must also be considered with the use of Abu-Nimer's peacemaking model. Clearly, JPI themes resonate with actual Muslim and Christian peacemakers. As different as these two traditions may be, the peacemakers that emerge from the respective communities share similar convictions about the role of empathy, empowerment, exclusivism, development, and activism. Educational interventions that uphold peacemakers as worthy of emulation must take seriously the convergence noted in this aspect of the study.

Second, peacemakers were found to differ significantly from controls on all five JPI themes. This finding suggests that peacemakers have perceptions and attitudes worth emulating as conceptualized through the JPI. Qualitative themes characterizing peacemakers in the descriptive study are sufficiently distinct from everyday folk to merit consideration as educational touchstones in applied curricula. We offer these conclusions as tentative and exploratory given the preliminary nature of these studies. Much work remains to validate the descriptive findings from study 1 and the applied findings from study 2 with different populations. With these limitations in mind, we note that descriptive themes in the first study effectively complement the applied (statistical) JPI themes in the second study. Together, these themes offer traction on the question of how to configure interventions within and between religious traditions toward the greater goal of peace.

CONCLUSION

It was our objective to construct an exploratory study of peacemaking that considered descriptive and applied issues with a view toward peace educational interventions. The confluence of descriptive and applied research suggests that Muslim and Christian peacemakers share many commonalities. Themes that characterize their outlook (description) and their attitudes (application) are worthy of consideration in curricula. We are cautious, however, with regard to oversimplification of study findings as identical between religious traditions. In particular, we recognize difficulties associated with peacemaker understanding of their own work. In a prescient reflection on human experience as understood through different cultural or religious lenses, the cultural psychologist Richard Shweder notes:

> Experience is often so complex that its facticity is sometimes better described by one discourse and sometimes by another. . . . It is often advantageous to have more than one discourse for interpreting a situation or solving a problem. Not only alternative solutions but multidimensional ones addressing several "orders of reality" or "orders of experience" may be more practical for solving complex human problems. An antidogmatic casuistry with multiple (but rationally limited) discursive resources may be the most effective method to meet the vicissitudes of human ethical experience. It is useful to keep in mind the tenet that cognized reality is incomplete if described from any one point of view and incoherent if described from all points of view at once.[18]

There can be little doubt that peacemaking directly engages the most complex of all human moral problems. Anticipating these difficulties, we implemented descriptive and applied techniques in order to better apprehend different discourses in peacemaking. We offer two practical observations from this exercise.

First, Muslim and Christian peacemaking builds on a trajectory that begins with religious foundations and ends with morally autonomous, interpersonally oriented practices. To our thinking, this means that effective peacemakers are deeply committed to their own religious beliefs. This is consonant with recent arguments in moral psychology and philosophy suggesting that coherent and transformative moral functioning is in part found through thicker religious particularity.[19] Educational interventions on behalf of peace should make use of theologies and religious observances that directly support the reconciliation and healing of persons. In the aftermath of the study we observe that in addition to being remarkable human beings, peacemakers were simply good Muslims and Christians. Peacemaking praxis should take care to foster deep and meaningful spirituality as a precursor to the instruction of those techniques that enable dialogue between disenfranchised groups.

Second, Muslim and Christian peacemaking requires fluency in the public square. The language of deontological and utilitarian ethics is prominent in the practical efforts of peacemakers from both traditions. Peacemakers demonstrate great sensitivity to the traditions of others in public peacemaking venues but doggedly work to find language that is equitable for involved parties. For some, this may include democratic priorities of personal rights and moral autonomy. For others, this may require local knowledge of the traditions and practices of particular groups. Peacemakers are appropriately multilingual in their practice, demonstrating a persistent interest to understand the perspectives of others with a genuinely open-minded posture. In this regard, we observe that praxis should capitalize on open-mindedness as both virtue and personality trait. From a social scientific vantage, virtues are learned and personality traits believed to be hard-wired, meaning that not everyone may share the unique suite of peacemaking gifts evident in the peacemakers interviewed for the study. Nevertheless, those who serve on the frontlines of peacemaking do so with support from their communities, meaning that everyone holds a virtuous and personality-specific stake in the peacemaking enterprise. Multilingual peacemakers are able to effectively cast a vision for peace that is comprehensible to people from widely divergent backgrounds. Praxis should emphasize this ability to speak across fences in an open-minded embrace of radical otherness.[20]

We are struck by the fact that peacemaker skills, strategies, and attitudes are powerfully reminiscent of experienced clinical psychologists. For both peacemaker and clinician, relationship is a critical element. Without an authentic commitment to relationship with others, peace is unlikely to become a lasting fixture between tribal leaders or spouses in the family system. Peacemakers seem to have arrived at this knowledge on their own, through processes we can only indirectly ascertain. Given their narratives, we believe that one way of undertaking the educational task in a peacemaking curriculum is to consider interventions that foster a process of self-reflection such that pragmatic strategies become coherent, personalized schemas resilient to failure. Social support networks are an important complement to the growing wisdom of the peacemaking exemplar, suggesting that interventions should be intentionally situated within communities capable of understanding the purpose and practice of peace. Based on the common wisdom revealed through exemplars, peacemaking arises from within tradition-contexts, finding its deepest expression in relationship structures that respect, honor, and validate the perspective of the other.

We conclude this brief discussion with an invitation. Through the course of the chapter we have attempted to provide a sketch of peacemaking attitudes and practices amenable for praxis between Muslim and Christian traditions. As social scientists, we have made every effort to present the findings of this study in an equitable manner. Yet we acknowledge that our observations are inevitably biased by our own Christian faith commitments. Consequently, we observe that the effort to frame a scientific understanding of peacemaking in this chapter is only partial and incomplete. We perceive that without the complementary work of Muslim social scientists on these and questions yet unanswered, peace psychology will remain a fragmented and unfinished business. It is our hope that Muslim colleagues will in the future provide us with their own observations such that everyone will benefit from a richer understanding of peacemaking practice and its psychological constituents.

NOTES

1. Edward Said, *Covering Islam* (New York: Pantheon, 1981), 15.
2. Mohammed Abu-Nimer, *Nonviolence and Peace Building in Islam: Theory and Practice* (Gainesville, Fla.: University Press of Florida, 2003), 42.
3. We follow a well-known example of qualitative research on moral functioning in Anne Colby and William Damon, *Some Do Care: Contemporary Lives of Moral Commitment* (New York: Free Press, 1992).
4. The Life Narrative Interview attempts to unearth aspects of identity across the human life span. See Dan P. McAdams, *The Stories We Live By: Personal Myths and the Making of the Self* (New York: Guilford, 1997).
5. In order to protect peacemaker anonymity, identifying information in transcripts was altered or removed.
6. See Al Dueck and Kevin Reimer, "Retrieving the Virtues in Psychotherapy: Thick and Thin Discourse," *American Behavioral Scientist* 47 (2003): 427–41; Kevin Reimer and Al Dueck, "Inviting Soheil: Narrative and Embrace in Christian Caregiving," *Christian Scholars' Review* 48 (2006): 205–19.
7. See Mohammed Abu-Nimer, *Interfaith Peace-building Guide* (United Religions Initiative, 2004); Duane Ruth-Heffelbower, *Conflict and Peacemaking Across Cultures: Training for Trainers* (Fresno, Calif.: Fresno Pacific University, 1999); Ken Sehested and Rabia Harris, *Peace Primer: Quotes From Christian and Islamic Scripture and Tradition* (Charlotte, N.C.: Baptist Peace Fellowship of North America, 2002); J. Denny Weaver and Gerald Biesecker-Mast, *Teaching Peace: Nonviolence and the Liberal Arts* (Lanham, Md.: Rowman & Littlefield, 2003); and Daniel J. Christie, Richard V. Wagner, and Deborah Du Nann Winter, *Peace, Conflict, and Violence: Peace Psychology for the 21st Century* (Upper Saddle River, N.J.: Prentice Hall, 2001).

8. See Kevin Reimer, "Natural Character: Psychological Realism for the Downwardly Mobile," *Theology & Science* 2 (2004): 35–54; Kevin Reimer and David Wade-Stein, "Moral Identity in Adolescence: Self and Other in Semantic Space," *Identity: An International Journal of Theory and Research* 4 (2004): 229–49.

9. Abu Nimer, *Nonviolence.*

10. Glen Stassen, *Just Peacemaking: Ten Practices for Abolishing War* (Cleveland, Ohio: Pilgrim, 1998).

11. Stassen, *Just Peacemaking.*

12. Stassen, *Just Peacemaking,* 7.

13. See S. Ericksen, "A Skeptical Note on the Use of Attitude Scales toward War: III," *The Journal of Social Psychology,* 27 (1948): 79–90. Also, P. Werner and P. Roy, "Measuring Activism Regarding the Nuclear Arms Race," *Journal of Personality Assessment* 49 (1985): 181–86. Finally, J. Grussendorf et al., "Resisting Moral Disengagement in Support for War: Use of the 'Peace Test' Scale Among Student Groups in 21 nations," *Peace and Conflict: Journal of Peace Psychology* 8 (2002): 73–83.

14. G. Elliott, "Components of Pacifism," *Journal of Conflict Resolution* 24 (1980): 27–54.

15. V. Kool and M. Sen, "The Nonviolence Test," in *Second Handbook of Psychological and Social Instruments,* ed. D. Pestonjee (Ahmedabad, India: Indian Institute of Management, 1984): 48–55.

16. For technical report on these findings see Steve Brown, Kevin Reimer, Al Dueck, Richard Gorsuch, and Tracy Sidesinger, "A Particular Peace: Psychometric Properties of the Just-Peacemaking Inventory," submitted for publication.

17. We note that this is an incomplete consideration of descriptive-applied convergence given that we did not transpose Abu-Nimer's peacemaking model into a survey instrument. Future studies in Muslim–Christian peacemaking must take this additional step.

18. Richard Shweder, N. Much, M. Mahapatra, and L. Park, "The 'Big Three' of Morality (Autonomy, Community, Divinity) and the 'Big Three' Explanations of Suffering," In *Morality and Health,* ed. A. Brandt and P. Rozin (Florence, Ky.: Taylor & Francis/Routledge, 1997), 140–41.

19. See Lawrence J. Walker and Kevin Reimer, "The Relationship between Moral and Spiritual Development," in *The Handbook of Spiritual Development in Childhood and Adolescence,* ed. Peter Benson, Pamela King, Linda Wagener, and Eugene Roehlkepartain (Newbury Park, Calif.: Sage, 2005): 265–301. Also, Alasdair MacIntyre, *Three Rival Versions of Moral Enquiry: Encyclopedia, Geneology, and Tradition* (Notre Dame, Ind.: University of Notre Dame Press, 1991).

20. Reimer and Dueck, *Soheil.*

20

Abrahamic Faiths

Models of Interfaith Dialogue in the United States (A Case Study of Rochester, New York, Experience)

Muhammad Shafiq

The New World order makes cross-religious and cross-cultural contacts practically unavoidable, as television, radio, film, books, and the Internet all work to narrow the gulfs that once separated religions and cultures. The world is fast changing. The globalization of the modern world has made it impossible for the believers of one religion to be indifferent to another. Cross-cultural and interreligious contacts are unavoidable. It is becoming more and more difficult for any religious groups, ethnic group, or race to remain unaware of the teachings and practices of other religions and cultures.

The religious landscape of America is changing too. It is becoming the land of many religions where people of different ethnic groups and races live together. As this change makes America religiously and culturally rich and diverse, we need to be more aware of religious diversity so that we will be able to better understand and appreciate humanity's evolving religious heritage.

It is this need that has led all religions and especially the Abrahamic faiths to dialogue for better understanding of the other's faith and bridge building. Rochester, New York, has been a model in this outreach interfaith dialogue and a case study of the interfaith work that is taking place in the Greater Rochester Area is presented here. This chapter will look into the following areas:

1. Levels of interfaith dialogue in Rochester
2. Creating an interfaith dialogue group

3. Contemporary models of interfaith documents and mission statements; and
4. Models of interfaith programs between Jews, Christians, and Muslims

INTERFAITH DIALOGUE IN ROCHESTER: DIFFERENT LEVELS OF DIALOGUE

When we talk about interfaith dialogue, we mean interreligious dialogue between religious communities aimed at better understanding one another's faith and building better relations. This type of dialogue is a bridge-building movement to ease tension and hatred between followers of different religions. How can religions live together in peace in our contemporary world? It can happen through organized efforts of understanding, appreciating, and building relation. This effort is called today as interfaith dialogue.

Interfaith dialogue is not creating a civil religion. It is to hold one's faith and at the same time to understand the other's faith. This type of dialogue demands honesty from participants to present their faith in most sincere and accurate ways and not hypocritically. Uniformity and agreement are not the goals of interfaith dialogue. The goal is to collaborate and to combine our different strengths for the welfare of humanity.

Interfaith dialogue is not ecumenism. Ecumenism was intrafaith dialogue that started between Christian denominations to bridge the gap and build better understanding and cooperation. Interfaith dialogue is between the followers of world religions and especially between people of Abrahamic faiths in the West.

This type of dialogue is different from the medieval and premodern period dialogue, which was like a debate to defeat the other, to put down the other's argument, and even to shame him or her and his or her faith. The Qur'an referred to such dialogue as *Mujadila* (a debate/polemic) asking the Muslims to be respectful if they were to meet in a debate with people of the Book. The Qur'an uses the word *Ahsan* (to excel, to be the best in respecting and in dealing with the other).[1] The contemporary interfaith dialogue is to explore commonalties, appreciate differences, and learn to respectfully tolerate. It is an effort to live together in peace with freedom to worship in a diverse and pluralistic society in the modern age. It can be called as *Majalis lita'arafu* (dialogue for better understanding) or *Al Hiwar bayn al Adyan* (dialogue or conversations between religions) from the Qur'anic perspective.[2] Some other Qur'anic words that could be used are *Al Sulh* (dialogue for peace making and reconciliation) and *Ta'awun bayn al Adyan* (dialogue for seeking cooperation between religions) for humanitarian causes.[3]

This type of dialogue can be divided into two major categories:

a. Interfaith dialogue of faith communities
b. Interfaith dialogue in academic institutions

Some examples of these two kinds of interfaith dialogue that is taking place in Rochester, New York, are presented below:

Interfaith Dialogue of Faith Communities

The Spiritual Journey

This is the most common one, which is taking place in many cities in American communities. People of one faith are visiting another church, a *masjid*, or a synagogue in an attempt to understand the other's faith. In Rochester, New York, this is the most common, especially between Abrahamic faiths. In most cases, it is called "the *spiritual journey*." People from different faiths visit places of worship, observe worship, and listen to a talk. Islamic Center of Rochester has hosted such groups with food and refreshments whenever they had come on a visit to learn about the Muslim faith. When such groups come to visit, the hosting institution should make sure that a clergy or an expert leader of the community with adequate knowledge of the faith and with understanding of interfaith work is present to lead the discussion. Once, in a dialogue like this one, a member of the congregation pointed to the clergy and asked him how many of these people he had converted. Remember that the effort here is not to convert people, but to make them understand the faith and dispel some of the stereotypes. Any efforts of conversion or of a missionary activity would be detrimental to interfaith work.

Interfaith Dialogue of Religious Leaders

This type of dialogue has different names. In Washington, D.C., it is called the "Interfaith Conference" and in Rochester, New York, it is called the "Interfaith Forum." Religious leaders representing their respective faiths are its active members. There are about twenty-two or more faith communities participating in the Rochester Forum. The imams in the Forum represent Muslim Community in Rochester. It is to be noted that many clergies and ministers who participate in this type of dialogue are ordained ministers and highly educated. Faiths, not represented by their clergies, do not hold a respectful impact in such dialogue.

Interfaith Alliance

This is a national organization that has an active branch in Rochester. The Rochester dialogue group is known as The Interfaith Alliance of Rochester (TIAR). The Alliance believes that people running for or serving in public office should express their views in a way that encourages civil discussion of issues. The Alliance educates its members about public policy issues. They strive to promote the Golden Rule as the core value to bring about economic justice. TIAR provides an enlightened faith-based voice in an evolving community that understands the relevance and value of religious diversity. They strive to encourage all people to stand for justice, love, and mercy for all. The Muslim community of Rochester work along with other communities in the Interfaith Alliance. For more details see the website www.tia-roch.org.

Interfaith Dialogue of Women

Women's groups belonging to various faiths also participate in interfaith dialogue. Like many cities there is a women's interfaith group in Rochester too. The group members meet in their homes and strive to build good relations. The group is also very active on women's issues and social justice programs. Muslim, Jewish, and Christian women mostly participate in this dialogue.

Faith to Faith

This is a new group comparatively. Some Jewish, Christian, and Muslim members got together to dialogue with more focus on the issue of Israel and Palestine as a peace initiative group and to increase understanding. The group has successfully done a few programs in Rochester.

Rochester Area Interfaith Hospitality Network (RAIHN)

It officially opened its doors to guest families in April 2004. The goal of RAIHN is to provide temporary accommodations, food, and compassionate friendship to those families in the Rochester area who have been temporarily displaced from their homes. It is a network of host and support organizations (interdenominational faith communities) who are led by a Rochester-based nonprofit corporation and board of directors.

The Interfaith Hospitality Network provides benefits to *both* the guests in the program as well as benefits to the faith community congregations and volunteers. To the guests in the program, RAIHN actually provides shelter from the storm. To the organizations and their volunteers, RAIHN is truly an uplifting and worthwhile experience. The Rochester Interfaith Hospitality Network is one of many such organizations in the country that provides this much-needed service. For more information, look at their website www.coatclip.com/raihn.

Interfaith Partnership

This dialogue happens between families of Abrahamic faith communities. Former Rochester Mayor Bill Johnson initiated the partnership. He established a commission on ethnic and interfaith leaders for faith and racial harmony in the city. The Commission came up with the idea of ethnic and religious partnership pairing individuals and families to build relations. They invite one another to their homes for building bridges and understanding. Strangers become friends through the partnership program.

Interfaith Picnic

Interfaith picnic is another form of interfaith activity for getting to know people, socializing, and encouraging relationships of mutual understanding. In Rochester, Temple Sinai, a Jewish Reform Synagogue, an Islamic center, and a Christian Barbour Church have been conducting these types of picnics for the last three years.

Interfaith Dialogue at Rochester Academic Institutions

Nazareth College, Center for Interfaith Studies and Dialogue (CISD)

The Center was formally created on November 28, 2001, shortly after the September 11 tragedies, to prepare people to live peacefully in a religiously diverse world. The Center's first public act was to hold a September 11, 2002 memorial service. CISD includes individuals who are diverse in religion, faith, ethnicity, race, gender and education. The common denominator is a desire to develop skills to clarify and improve individual and community-wide communications on matters of religion, faith, and spirituality; to understand individual and communal faiths; and to develop the capacity for living in a pluralistic world. CISD seeks to understand and develop research tools, knowledge, and skills to benefit our common humanity. CISD found a permanent home in 2005 on the campus of Nazareth College. The Center's goals are:

- To establish an environment conducive to understanding the diversity of faiths in our world and community.
- To communicate the skills necessary for people of diverse faiths to live together in peace and justice.

- To provide educational resources to aid in establishing an environment of understanding and equality.
- To teach individuals, communities and institutions how to live and communicate more effectively with those from other religions and faith backgrounds.

CISD offers a wide range of Community Education and Outreach programs such as: specialized seminars and workshops for people in the workplace like yearly seminars for school teachers, nurses, hospice care workers, and prison chaplains. Some of these seminars are conducted in different places, as they are found suitable. Through these programs, CISD has garnered broad community support. CISD also offers seminars that are open to the public, college faculty, students, and staff. Most of these seminars deal with topics around issues related to religion and interfaith dialogue. For example, CISD conducted very informative seminars on Islam and the challenge of modernity; religion and religious extremism; religion in public life and where America is heading; development of Abrahamic religions in US: challenges and prospects. CISD offers two certificate programs in the summer each year with concentration on world religions and interfaith studies. One is Training of the Trainers, and the second is The Next Generation Living Together in a Pluralistic World.

CISD recently started a quarterly book review. Dr. Nathan Kollar, CISD Chair, is the coordinator of the program. We had three very successful book reviews last year. The books selected for reviews are related to interfaith studies. The Center hopes to add interfaith dialogue of theology to its programs as well as to create a research devoted to interfaith dialogue. CISD is also planning for national interfaith dialogue in April 2010 with a hope that all interfaith organizations, community as well as academic institutions, will participate. For more information on CISD programs, see its website, www.naz.edu/dept/cisd.

Nazareth College, Center for Spirituality (CFS)

The Center was previously known as Campus ministry. The new name was adopted to broaden the work of the Center and include a new emphasis on spirituality and diversity. Today, CFS encourages reflection on personal beliefs; it assists students to discover and develop their spiritual identity within an enthusiastic and supportive community.

CFS staff and student leaders collaborate with the Nazareth community to provide ministry and educational opportunities for individuals from various faiths, traditions, and beliefs. Interfaith programs such as the religious diversity dinner and ecumenical/interfaith programs build relationships and encourage communication and solidarity among community members. Responding to the needs of our local, regional, national, and global communities, CFS empowers students to integrate their quest for personal development with the broader community through advocacy and service. To strengthen the sense of family within our campus community, CFS sponsors campuswide celebrations, memorials, and gatherings in response to current events and holidays, including Veterans' Day, Thanksgiving, Martin Luther King Jr. Day, and Interfaith memorial. For more details on CFS, look at the website www.naz/dept/cfs.

University of Rochester, Interfaith Chapel

The chapel was built in 1970 as a bold signal of University commitment to diversity. It was built to be "a house of prayer for all people" to celebrate their religious traditions and spiritual practices. Today the chapel has grown up as a place of diversity in the University: a place that supports the particular expression and celebration of different faith traditions while promoting discovery and learning about the common threads that bind people. The chapel offers the University and Rochester community a home for exploring and celebrating the familiar, and the not so familiar, in an environment characterized by respect and dialogue. For more details, see www.rochester.edu/interfaithchapel.

RIT, Center for Religious Life

The Center was previously known as Interfaith Chapel. The new name was adopted to expand diversity and endorse interfaith dialogue. Today, it is a place of personal and community exploration within the diverse and rich religious, cultural, and spiritual traditions of our campus community. All individuals, communities, and congregations are welcome together in this place to study or talk, worship and pray, visit and share. Students come in to the chapel to pray, or stop in the chaplains' offices to visit, or just find a quiet place to think and reflect. For more details, see www.rit.edu/studentaffair/religion.

Youth Interfaith Dialogue

There are many such efforts taking place, especially among Abrahamic faiths, and youth interfaith dialogues are very common. The Center for Interfaith Studies and Dialogue (CISD) has an annual summer program for youth training in interfaith work. The program is open to all faiths. For more information on the program, see its website www.naz.edu/dept/cisd.

Interfaith Dialogue of Student Communities

This type of dialogue happens on many campuses. Many colleges have interfaith/campus ministries. They bring different student groups together and facilitate their activities. Many faith communities have chaplains representing their faiths on the campuses. In Rochester, the Muslim community has appointed imams as Muslim chaplains at the educational institutions to guide students in interfaith dialogue, religious affairs, and counseling.

Rochester is a unique place for interfaith dialogue. It has not only created academic institutions for teaching, researching, and promoting interfaith dialogue, but its community-level dialogue has become more formal as compared to other cities. Today, Rochester dialogue groups have mission statements and organizational networks with support from major religious organizations to make sure the mission statement is implemented. It has also signed agreements and organized bodies oversee those agreements. It is this type of dialogue that we discuss later in detail in this chapter.

CREATING AN INTERFAITH DIALOGUE GROUP

Creating a formal and an organized interfaith group on the community level with community institutional support is a real issue. Many interfaith dialogues are informal. There could be many reasons why a formal dialogue with institutional support between faith communities is difficult to create.

People, especially those from the minority faiths, are fearful and reluctant when they meet with leaders of the majority community in interreligious conversation. They are hesitant to speak fairly about their faith. They are fearful of persecution. They are afraid of being influenced and even afraid of missionary activities of losing members of the group. This fear is not limited to immigrant people, but even African Americans fear too. Some are even afraid that they would lose their jobs if their bosses come to know about their original faith. Recently an African American Muslim denied being in a group photo with other Muslims fearing that he might face bias at his workplace if people know that he was a Muslim.

Another major obstacle in interfaith dialogue is the teaching of exclusive ideas and especially about salvation. Almost every religion preaches of having a sort of monopoly over salvation, such as "no body goes to the Father but through me." Many believe that the other shall be converted to their faiths to save him or her from the hell fire. Once a large group of people was in interfaith dialogue when someone shouted asking the people to covert to his faith otherwise they would go to hell. Such voices are not alone; many support them. Participating in interfaith dialogue for the first time, a community leader said that he was fearful of "losing his job" or even "harm" if he would enter into a formal dialogue with followers of another religion.

Having these fears and reservations in mind, interfaith dialogue goes through many stages. First is a personal relation; second would be creating an informal dialogue group; and third a formal dialogue group with institutional support. Rabbi Miller of the Jewish Temple B'rith Kodesh, Rochester, New York, was active in the interfaith forum. He was very interested in building bridges and better relations between the Jewish and Muslim communities. The leadership of the Islamic Center responded positively to the Rabbi's efforts. The friendship of the two led the Reform Jewish Community of Temple B'rith Kodesh and the Islamic Center to join hands together in many activities and especially during the Bosnia crisis. Once we had a fund-raising dinner for Bosnia victims of war at the Temple in 1993. A large number of people along with state and federal government representatives attended. It was on that occasion for the first time that Adhan (a Muslim call for worship) was given in the synagogue and Muslims prayed in congregation their sunset prayers. To many people, it was a historic occasion.

Rabbi Miller was a recognized leader of the reform Jewish community and took initiatives in building bridges. He would come to the Islamic Center, sometimes without a prior notice, if he had a new idea to share. One day Rabbi Miller called this writer early in the morning. He was calling from the airport and telling him about the sad incident that happened at the Hebron mosque, in which a Jewish man fired on Muslims during their congregational worship. He asked the imam to call a joint press conference for the next morning to condemn the incident.

The Center was packed with media, and community leaders from both sides were present. During the press conference, Rabbi Miller called the attacker on the Hebron Masjid an impostor, a betrayer to the Jewish faith, and asked the Jewish government of Israel and the Jewish people to repair the relationship.

This informal dialogue took a few years. We then created a Jewish-Muslim contact group. Finally, we were able to create a formal "Commission on Jewish-Muslim understanding" in 2002. See the Commission mission statement and its bylaws in appendix A.

The same is true about Christian–Muslim dialogue. Rev. James Rice, a Presbyterian pastor, was very active in the interfaith dialogue. He did his best to build good relations with Muslims and Jews. When he retired, Rev. Gordon Webster was appointed in his place. Rev. Webster had lived in the Middle East and is married to a Palestinian Christian woman. The leadership of the two communities had dinners together and sponsored educational programs. Soon the word of goodwill spread all over and Rev. Webster and some other Christian and Muslim leaders agreed to establish a

"Commission on Christian Muslim Relation" in 1993. See the commission mission statement and its bylaws in appendix B.

Some members of the Commission were Catholics. They were very pleased with the work that the Commission on Christian Muslim Relations was doing. The good news spread and that encouraged the Muslims and Catholics of the Greater Rochester Area to sign an agreement, the "Muslim Catholic Alliance," in 2003. See appendix C for the mission statement and the bylaws of the alliance.

There is a rising opposition among some Christians to dialogue with Muslims. The evangelical rightwing is very opposed to dialogue with other faiths and especially with Muslims. According to some evangelists, Christians who dialogue with Muslims are acting like infidels. Dialogue with infidels is committing of infidelity and Muslims are infidels to these people.

Once there was interfaith dialogue between Christians and Muslims and the announcement was posted in a local newspaper. About 250 people were participating in the dialogue. Some people reacted to that angrily, asking why such dialogue was taking place; some others were protesting on the roadside. Such people exist in every faith. If the world were left in the hands of these people, life on earth would become very difficult.

There are some angry Catholics too. Whenever there is a dialogue between Muslims and Catholics, you would find one or two bitterly opposed to dialogue. Such people know one language: become a Catholic, the only way of God for humanity. This does not mean that there are no such Muslims. It was very hard to make the announcement of interfaith dialogue in a mosque between Muslims and Christians or Muslims and Jews before 9/11. There were some worshippers who were very opposed to interfaith dialogue. Some such Muslims and Christians would call interfaith dialogue a heresy. This shows how interfaith dialogue is difficult and what the obstacles in its way are.

CONTEMPORARY MODELS OF INTERFAITH DOCUMENTS AND MISSION STATEMENTS

To create a formal dialogue group with a mission statement requires a lot of work and having dedicated partners willing to devote their time. A formal dialogue has a mission statement with rules of engagement that helps to bring new members to the interfaith group. It is hard to expect volunteers to stay engaged for a long period. The pastors' assignments change from time to time. Similarly, many mosques do not have imams and those that have are either not fluent in English or hesitant to participate in the dialogue.

Formal dialogue derives its strength from institutions and builds on public support. Any organization that is supported by the institutional structure and gets public support through its work becomes successful. But many faiths are reluctant to give institutional support to interfaith dialogue. Interfaith dialogue being new in existence is still debated about, that is, whether it is a right step or not. Many congregations have serious observations. Once a Catholic member of the community protested loudly during a dialogue between Catholics and Muslims that it was wrong to dialogue with Muslims because Muslims believed that people of other faiths would go to hell, ignoring that his own faith demands the same.

On another occasion, a Catholic priest was asked in interfaith dialogue on heaven and hell in Abrahamic faith of what his faith believed about people of other faiths. The priest narrated a story and said that Catholics were in heaven when the others arrived at the gate.

Though Christians and Muslims have a lot in common in faith and history still there are many obstacles to a successful dialogue. The same is true about Muslims and Jewish dialogue. The two communities have experienced a remarkable cultural renaissance in Spain from the tenth to the twelfth centuries. Hasdai ibn Shaprut served in the court of Caliph Abd al Rahman III of Cordova. With Hasdai's encouragement, Jewish poets and scholars flocked to Andalusia from all over the world, launching a new era that was to become known in Jewish history as the Golden Age of Spain.

Today, Muslim and Jewish communities are locked up in misunderstanding. The Israel and Palestine conflict has created distrust and hard feelings, which makes the dialogue difficult in America and elsewhere. However, there are some Reform and Conservative rabbis and some imams who are willing to dialogue. Many Jews and Muslims realize the significance of the dialogue between the two communities and understand its relevance in modern society. September 11 and its aftereffect makes interfaith dialogue between the two communities imperative. Muslims and Jewish bridge building is not only in the interest of the two communities but also in the interest of a peaceful world. A successful dialogue between the two communities in America may lead also to a peaceful resolution of the Israel and Palestine conflict.

However, it is still difficult to discuss openly the issue of Israel and Palestine. The Jews and Muslims in Rochester have formed a Commission for a formal dialogue with institutional support but have not yet gone beyond Muslim-Jewish relations in America to discuss the issue of Israel and Palestine openly.

The Jewish-Muslim dialogue becomes more difficult when there is a renewed conflict in the Middle East. Rochester is unique in the sense that it has made great progress in relations between the two communities.

The Commission leadership has a better understanding of mutual respect and even to stand together in worst conditions. There was a time when a Muslim would hesitate to enter a synagogue or a rabbi to enter a mosque. Rochester dialogue has overcome that hesitation.

Once there was a Jewish-Muslim dialogue at the Islamic Center. A large crowd showed up and the main worship area was opened to provide people more space. It was a historic occasion to see the imam and a rabbi standing together in the *minbar* (a place where the imam gives a worship sermon) speaking on Jewish-Muslim dialogue.

As I said before, the interfaith dialogue is still in its formative years. Whenever there is a dialogue, there are fears of mistreatment, use of disrespectful language, or fears of intimidation. The Rochester dialogue has many successes but fears still loom. The interfaith leadership must stay together and face these challenges. If the leadership becomes divided or uses disrespectful language, the dialogue collapses. In anticipation of these challenges, the Rochester interfaith leadership came up with a pledge to be signed with commitment by all leaders participating in the dialogue.

The pledge acknowledged that Rochester is a remarkable community for interfaith cooperation. Rochester is a community of people of faith fervently praying for peace in the world and in their community in this time of increasing crisis. While some may feel helpless about being able to change the course of global events, they do not believe they are spiritually or politically powerless. All of our traditions call us to value each human life and to stand up for injustice and human rights. They believe there is an important role each of them can play in peacemaking in this community—their community—with potential ripples in the world beyond Rochester. (For more details of the Pledge text, see appendix D.)

Rochester interfaith community has been very concerned that its leadership remains committed to dialogue and respectful to each other. But another hard issue was organizing interfaith programs and seminars. The fear of proselytizing and mismanaging was always there whenever any activity was planned.

SOME MODELS OF INTERFAITH PROGRAMS BETWEEN JEWS, CHRISTIANS, AND MUSLIMS

Forming an interfaith group and agreeing on a mission statement or even signing an agreement may be a difficult but an exciting event. But the most difficult task is planning a program, its execution, and making sure that the interfaith group is behind the efforts. To conduct a successful interfaith seminar or a workshop or any other program, the following must be taken into consideration:

Subcommittees

Interfaith dialogue groups should create subcommittees to cover and pay adequate attention to each and every article of their mission statement. There could be subcommittees for media outreach, education, and seminar, a committee for social justice and dealing with natural disasters, and a committee for the protection of civil rights. These committees should meet periodically and present their recommendations to the joint commission or interfaith dialogue group.

Planning Committees

On the recommendation of the subcommittees, when interfaith partners decide on a joint program, they must come up with a planning committee. The planning committee then meets several times to decide about the date, time, and a place where the program will take place. The planning committee should prepare a flyer, publicity, and reach out to other interested groups in the program. The planning committee has to decide who will be the coordinator, prepare an evaluation paper, and take care of security, reception, and other essential items.

The interfaith leadership needs to ensure the following:

1. *Avoid proselytizing:* Make sure that speakers and others follow the golden rule: "Listen to others as you would like them to listen to you."
2. *Equal distribution of responsibilities*: Share the responsibilities equally with all participating faith communities. Do not seek to dominate, but consult one another.
3. *Respect for each organizer's voice*: The level of participation of a faith community, be it large or small, once it is participating in organizing a program should be equally respected. More involvement of one individual should not translate into more weight to his or her opinion.
4. *Fair time management*: First, programs should begin on time. Second, everyone should be given equal time; and third, there must be Q&A time. Mostly one-third of the time is given to Q&A.
5. *In case of tension or complaints*: No complaints either from a large group or a small faith community or from an individual should be brushed aside, but rather proper attention should be paid to it. Evaluations collected after the program should be critically analyzed and implemented in the next program.
6. *Do not conduct all programs in one place*: Programs and meetings of interfaith partners should rotate among the participating partners. This would create a sense of ownership and would strengthen the bond of partnership.

7. *No faith community should be allowed to chair interfaith group* or subcommittees or planning committees consecutively. The rules should be of rotation among different participating members of faith.

As it was said before, the Commission on Christian Muslim Relations, the Muslim Catholic Alliance (MCA), and the Commission on Jewish-Muslim Understanding (CJMU) sponsored many education programs, seminars, and picnics, for understanding Islam, Judaism, and Christianity and for bridge building in Jewish, Christian, and Muslim relations.

Islam is the most misunderstood religion in America. Many when they hear the name of Islam think of terrorism. Others think of Arab Bedouins and a dark-color religion of uncivilized people. Some think the God of Islam is the Satan of Christianity. Media carry frightening themes almost daily, reinforcing the fear of American people.

The Commission on Christian Muslim Relation offered many Islam 101 series such as Islam: The Message and the Messenger; Muslim Life Around the Clock; Faith and Worship; Women in Islam; Jihad: Personal and Public; and other many topics. These seminars were received very favorably and were attended by more than two hundred people each time. (For more details of these series, see appendix E.)

After attending many of these programs, the Christian leadership received some complaints that the Muslim leadership is preaching and unknowingly criticizing Christianity. It was a serious thing and some of us were afraid that it would damage the dialogue.

The problem with Muslims is that they look at Christianity from the Qur'anic worldview and explain it accordingly, for example, the story of creation, original sin, Mary and Jesus, heaven and hell, and many other things. By contrast, each Christian denomination has its own explanation for it. So, many times when a Muslim says that this is what Christians believe and this is what Islam says, the Christian audience is caught up in surprise to hear something that they have never heard before as a Christian belief.

Rochester Interfaith dialogue did two things to overcome this issue. One, Muslim speakers were asked to stay limited to Islam and avoid speaking comparatively; and second, Muslim speakers were trained in Christian sensitivity.

One evening about twenty-five Muslim leaders got together and invited to dinner some Christian leaders of different denominations to train Muslims in Christian sensitivity. There were representatives of Catholics, Baptists, Presbyterians, Episcopalians, and others among them. They spoke to Muslims on the following topics: (1) creation; (2) original sin; (3) the trinity; (4) Jesus Christ—who is he? and (5) What unites Christians? (for more details of the program, see appendix F). It was a great evening and very appreciated.

Muslim Catholic Alliance offered series of seminars in spring and autumn on comparative theology of Islam and Catholicism such as the cycles of life, belief, and worship, including heaven and hell. These seminars helped both communities not only to be educated about one another's faith, but also reduced the gap of misunderstanding. Thus, people from both communities who were fearful before became friends.

In the Jewish-Muslim series, the "Our Journey to America: Obstacles and Challenges" seminar was most appreciated. It was a learning experience of listening to speakers from both faiths. How the Jews lived in fear in America in their early years was felt as very much like what Muslims are passing through. The Muslims felt they had plenty of good lessons to learn from how the Jewish community was able to overcome their fears and earn respect in the community. Many Muslims had very good comments to make about their experience in the program.

Most of the seminars offered by the Muslim Catholic Alliance or the Commission on Jewish-Muslim Understanding were comparatives, having two speakers, one from each faith community. The goal was to pass information about one's own faith and avoid talking about the other. Some objections of one undermining the other were received. To meet with those challenges, the Rochester interfaith leadership decided to make the speakers from both communities meet and exchange views to find common grounds before appearing in public.

This does not mean that interfaith dialogue in Rochester has overcome all obstacles and is running smoothly. There are still many challenges ahead, but there is great progress and immense hope in the future.

CONCLUSION

No religion can live in isolation in the contemporary world. It becomes essential for all faiths to open its doors for all to be studied, observed critically, and appreciated or rejected. Any religion with a universal message must accommodate its teaching to the demanding environment through interpretation, like in Islam exercising *Ijtihad* (applying scholastic judgment to the teaching of Al Qur'an and Sunnah) in light of contemporary demands or a decision made through ecclesiastical bodies to make faith understandable and applicable in the modern world. This is a natural process and has happened in the history of all major faiths. Those faiths that resisted change mostly lost their members and decayed.

Religions must demonstrate respectful tolerance for other faiths to live peacefully and even attract more members. In the modern world religion is once again emerging as a great force. It must warrant peaceful coexistence or would face violent reaction. It is in the interest of the world religions to dialogue to stay peacefully in the world and be long-lived and effective. Those religions that dialogue, provide spiritual care, and cater to the needs of humanity would be the future religions of humanity.

As said, interfaith dialogue does not mean creating a civil religion or sacrificing the fundamentals of one's faith. Rather it is an effort to respect humanity, live peacefully, and provide opportunity of freedom of worship to all. All interfaith programs that were conducted at Rochester presented in the appendixes were to bring respectful understanding between people of different faiths. It may look like having more emphasis on Islam was what the leaders of Abrahamic faiths agreed. Islam being the most misunderstood faith at present in America and the West, non-Muslims need to be familiarized with it for peaceful coexistence. The other objective through these seminars was to demonstrate publically Muslims' disassociation with violence and terrorism.

It is hoped that this chapter will provide essential guidance to Abrahamic interfaith partners and even others about the necessary tools of engagement in formal dialogue, to design programs and to execute them successfully. It will also guide the interfaith partners as to how to be respectfully engaged and avoid confusion and mismanagement. Interfaith dialogue is the demand of modern religious phenomenon in the contemporary world. Any step taken in this direction would have God's blessing.

NOTES

1. Al Qur'an, 16:125 and 29:46. Verse 16:125 says: "Call to the way of thy Lord with wisdom and goodly exhortation, and argue with them in the best manner. Surely thy Lord knows best him who strays from His path, and He knows best those who go aright." The second one more specifically addresses Muslims dealing with people of the Abrahamic faiths: "And argue not with the people of the Book except by what is best, save such of them as act unjustly. But say: we believe in that which has been revealed to us and revealed to you, and our God, and your God is One and to Him we submit."

2. The word *Lita'arafu* is used in the Qur'an, 49:13, and the word *Al Hiwar* from the Qur'anic usage *Yuhawiru* (18:34,37, and 58:1) can be used for modern interfaith dialogue.

3. Both words Al Sulh and Ta'awanu are used in the Qur'an in many places. For Al Sulh see 7:85, and for Ta'awanu 4:114 and 11:88. For more details on this topic see, Muhammad Shafiq and Mohammed Abu Nimer, *Interfaith Dialogue: A Guide for Muslims* (Herndon, Va.: IIIT, 2007).

21

Response to Part IV Chapters

David L. Johnston and Ghulam Haider Aasi

The last section of this book explores some of the issues that we feel most critically affect Muslim-Christian relations today, from the macro dimension (economic and political world order and concepts of human rights and dignity) to the micro one (motivation and strategies of Muslim and Christian peacemakers). In between, we offer case studies of interreligious initiatives in one American city, Rochester, as a sample of what is taking place in almost all major cities and towns in the United States.

Perhaps it is best to begin our response with one of the common characteristics of peacemakers, whether Muslim or Christian. Quoting from the chapter by Dueck et al., "Multilingual peacemakers are able to effectively cast a vision for peace that is comprehensible to people from widely divergent backgrounds. Praxis should emphasize this ability to speak across fences in an open-minded embrace of radical otherness." This willingness to put oneself in another's shoe might well be the prerequisite to fruitful peacebuilding, starting with American Muslims and Christians (with Evangelicals particularly in mind here) engaging in conversation.

The world seen through the eyes of Muslims from second- or third-generation immigrant families (or converts, generally) will look a great deal like the one seen by American Christians. A certain dose of patriotism and the imbibing of some aspects of American culture will lead them to at least consider the altruistic discourse of U.S. foreign policy ("fighting for freedom and democracy") and the positive spin given to the spread of "free markets" as plausible until proven otherwise. By contrast, recent

Muslim immigrants, like the people from their countries of origin, tend to consider the actions (and especially motivation) of the world's sole superpower as guilty until proven innocent. And this is despite the fact that they have immigrated, often at a great personal cost, to a land that has offered them bountiful economic opportunities and a greater measure of personal freedom. American domestic policies, after all, are quite distinct from its foreign policies.

These preliminary remarks seem necessary to us, as the chapter on human rights is likely to jar the average American evangelical Christian, who tends to assume the basic benevolence and generosity of American economic, political, and military might. Two purposes are at work in this chapter. First, by widening the notion of human rights to include economic, social, and cultural rights (as much of the world understands them) and exposing aspects of the "globalization process" that widen the gap between rich and poor and favor the interests of Western multinationals, the reader is asked to look at the world as most of the Muslims see it—a people more often poor, refugees, victims of wars and economic–political oppression, and certainly powerless. Second, with the added weight of Muslim and Christian theological notions of human equality, dignity, and responsibility before God, American Muslims and Christians are challenged to gain a fair and objective view of the world, that is, devoid of the power factor, or a perspective of humanity as a family, devoid of national, cultural, ethnic, religious, and class distinctions. Here no one is inherently superior to another. Here greater power (military or economic might) carries greater liabilities as well as responsibilities, because human beings tend naturally to be selfish and arrogant.

At the same time, dialogue between estranged parties, once the flow of conversation has brought enough trust to both sides, must at some point lead to honest truth-telling. Thus Kenneth Cragg, the veteran Christian voice in Muslim-Christian dialogue, in one of his (many) recent books, denounces the hypocrisy of American policy, eager to extend its hegemony over a whole region by dint of the military might displayed in Iraq and Afghanistan under the guise of democracy building.[1] At the same time, he points his finger to the complex issue of the inseparable relationship of Islam and politics, which continues to feed the ideology of extremists, who manage to draw significant sympathy and support from Muslim masses through their use of the Qur'an. Johnston's chapter calls both Christians and Muslims to come to common terms, to stand for global justice and peace in light of the pristine teachings of their Scriptures. Their honest and sincere dialogue will stem the schemes and activities of those extremist elements in both communities who misuse Scriptures for their worldly gains.

The chapter on interreligious activities in Rochester is heartwarming. Jews, Christians (Catholics and Protestants, including some evangelicals), and Muslims have come together not just to talk and listen to each other but also to create procedures, covenants, and institutions that will sustain and deepen the dialogue process. These initiatives and the measure of success that they have already met should encourage all of us in other cities to follow suit. As individuals or as local mosques and churches, we may feel powerless to redress inequities in the world order. But we can make a difference in our neighborhoods and cities.

Shafiq's narrative also includes the obstacles and growth pains of such bold and courageous movements. This is as it should be. Such a movement, particularly between Jews and Muslims, faces formidable obstacles and will inevitably incur fierce opposition from both sides. Redline issues such as the Israeli-Palestinian conflict will have to be shelved for a time. Evangelical churches also tend to object vociferously to "dialogue" with congregations of other faiths, fearing mostly that to engage in such an activity would be to water down their own convictions. Shafiq makes an admirable apology for all groups with such an oppositional attitude. First, he shows that the various protocols mutually agreed upon by dialogue partners ensure both the integrity of each group's faith convictions and the equality of access to the conversation, along with the opportunity to provide leadership. What is more, one of the rules clearly established from the beginning is that this cannot be a space for proselytism for any of the groups involved. Dialogue means the opportunity for mutual teaching, for a two-way conversation, including both learning and questioning in a spirit of respect. Finally, it is apparent that the leaders of the various communities have forged some lasting friendships in the process, as have many of the participants on all levels.

We strongly feel that the changes in individuals' attitudes (and worldview) as a result of deepening friendships across religious lines will translate into long-term gains in peacebuilding skills and greatly affect whole communities—one person, family, congregation at a time. This optimism is reinforced by the findings in the last chapter. The social scientists (Dueck et al.) commissioned for this study managed to leverage the synergy of a bottom–up study (profiles of exemplar peacemakers) with that of a top–down analysis based on an instrument they crafted (the Just-Peacemaking Inventory). That the descriptive study admirably corroborated the applied findings and vice versa is encouraging on at least three counts.

First, religious convictions do have a central role to play in peacebuilding activities. This was certainly true for both Muslim and Christian peace practitioners. But this truth also flowed out of the consistent discrepancies between the scoring on the JPI by the exemplars and the sample Christian population. Rather diplomatically, Dueck and colleagues note that this displayed "considerable moral ambivalence associated with peacemaking attitudes in the Protestant sample" but also considerable potential for life-changing peace education.

Second, Muslim and Christian peacemakers, while drawing on two different religious traditions, approached their task with virtually identical motivation and strategic thinking. Both groups invested personal capital in their peacebuilding ventures and took responsibility for possible repercussions in the community. Both also displayed considerable skill in their ability to use a variety of discourses in order to reach people on all sides of a conflict. And finally, both Muslim and Christian practitioners knew the importance of personal relationships and how to build on those to widen their understanding between estranged parties and reduce conflict.

The final hopeful point in the convergence of the descriptive with the applied research is that the resulting "presumption of kinship" between peacemakers, Christian and Muslims, is likely to create a growing momentum in Muslim-Christian cooperation in these areas. We have no doubt that Muslim social scientists will take up the invitation to further the scope of research on their end. We also formulate the hope that the united voices in this book, together with the exemplary peacemaking ventures of Muslims and Christians in many parts the world, will provide inspiration for evangelical Christians and American Muslims to engage in a fruitful dialogue in this country.

People of faith are already coming together in this new century like never before. So much remains to be done, yet we take heart: not only can grassroots movements of reconciliation transform local communities but in linking with others across the globe they can help shape a more just and peaceful world.

NOTE

1. Kenneth Cragg, *The Qur'an and the West* (Washington, DC: Georgetown University Press, 2005).

Conclusion

Mohammed Abu-Nimer and David Augsburger

This rich collection of chapters from the dialogue between Muslim and Evangelical Christian scholars has offered the reader a rare opportunity to learn about the differences, similarities, and the creative tension when both are faced with honesty and integrity. Each scholar from different faith groups frames and presents their views on crucial issues such as war, peace, salvation, ethics of missionary work, justice, and other issues related to internal dynamics of their own faith. And to each comes the reply from a differing frame of faith and life. Of the many fascinating issues raised, the following are, in our opinion, of special note.

- Muslim scholars viewed justice as central to their views and interpretation of peace-building and conflict resolution, and this became most visible in the opening dialogue about forgiveness. Thus Crow's response to Augsburger's chapter and Kadayifci-Orellana's chapter in the first section all clearly emphasize the centrality of the pursuit of justice as a condition for peace-building in Islamic tradition. Even in the context of the reconciliation process, a Muslim, based on his faith, would ask the perpetrator: what are you willing to do to show your accountability for the offense? Abu-Nimer notes that while Augsburger places forgiveness and reconciliation at the core of his presentation of how a Christian would view conflict resolution and peace-building, and in comparison to other Christian scholars, he has emphasized justice as essential in his views of reconciliation and forgiveness, yet he continues to place "the voluntary suffering" of Jesus as the central image in this process of reconciliation. Augsburger notes that when Muslim participants spoke of justice, they tended to refer to retributive justice (to each the equal proportion of what is deserved) and attributive justice (to each according to rank, position, or role). Christians tended to move away from both of these and spoke of redemptive justice (to each to restore what is lacking for equal well-being) and restorative justice (to each the opportunity to achieve renewed life). Crow's response identifies the need for just reparations as a major difference between Islamic and Christian interpretation for reconciliation process. Clearly this has opened an area for further and more nuanced discussion in the future.

- Stassen's chapter, reflecting his widely recognized leadership in the movement called "just peacemaking," offers ten polished and well-articulated principles of just peacemaking and presented a practical framework of peace-building that is an effective bridge between the two groups. It offers practical behavioral actions that can actually brings Muslim and Christian practitioners of peace-building closer and offer seasoned and wise guidelines as they pursue their work. In fact, when comparing Kadayifci-Orellana's principles and Stassen's Christian just-peacemaking practices, a series of striking similarities emerge in the pursuit of virtues, for example, mercy, forgiveness, justice, and advocacy for individual and collective responsibilities.
- When examined closely, Stassen's concrete examples for guiding Christian practitioners in their pursuit of peace work in reality speak to all peacemakers, of all faiths, and offer a challenge to those who work outside faith paradigms. These could as easily qualify as guiding ethical principles for consideration and action by Hindu, Muslim, Buddhist, or Jewish practitioners of peace-building as well as Christians. Practitioners from these faith groups could adopt these principles in their own faith language or adapt them to fit their theological narrative with little difficulty. In his response to the Kadayifci-Orellana chapter, Stassen illustrates how such linkages are possible in the context of Islam and Christianity.
- The section on religious diversity and identity reflects a major difference between the Muslim and Christian approach to the issue. While Shenk and Dueck offer a solid critical review of the major changes across two millennia within historic Christendom in dealing with diversity, and Rabia Harris ponders narrative vulnerability in religious identity, Riffat Hassan pursues the topic from a classic Muslim scholar's approach of explaining to Western readers the richness of the Qur'an and Hadith in promoting diversity and pluralism. Her analysis is a necessary step for Muslim scholars to begin their own critical analysis of Islamic tradition

and interpretation and the deep internal examination of Muslim civilization and history. Such narrative is not often shared in the hallways of interfaith dialogue. For Muslim participants to critically examine the exclusive and religion-centric periods of their tradition, they will have to develop a high level of trust with their Christian counterparts as well as overcome the current asymmetric power relations. Many of these scholars often argue that in these days of strong Western powers and declining Islamic political power, there is too much negative emphasis on the shortcomings of Muslim societies and even of the Muslim religion. Thus they point out deficiencies in pluralist Islam while speaking from a Western paradigm and context. The Shenk and Dueck chapter in a similar manner risked offering sharp self-criticism of the Christian alliances of religion and empire, the joining of church and state that violated the central tenets of the Christian scriptures. Not all Evangelical readers will find this analysis easy to assimilate, or appreciate its being a basis for interreligious dialogue, but the candor and confessional nature of their contribution does not go unnoticed.

- Nevertheless, the systematic examination of Islamic history and tradition by Muslim intellectuals and scholars is an inevitable step toward the indigenous framing of current Islamic perspectives on pluralism and democracy as well. In fact, such process is probably most needed for many Muslim youth or those from younger generations who are struggling to redefine their Islamic identity in a context of brutal globalization processes. In his response, James Jones captures this need: "In spite of these issues, the critically reflective, intellectually rigorous, forward looking perspective of this piece reminds us that modern American Muslim academics/theologians have still not consistently produced this type of much needed scholarship. Perhaps this will only be possible after Muslims establish their own seminaries and other institutions of higher learning in the United States."
- The need for such a complex interfaith dialogue process and the potential contribution it can make to Christian-Muslim relations is reflected in the psychological factors of fear, stereotyping, prejudice, and the defense mechanisms deployed to justify them, as identified by Evelyne Reisacher's chapter. Her analysis sheds an important light on the basic dynamics of fear experienced by people who lack basic understanding of the "other," especially among Christians in European and American contexts. Asma Afsaruddin's response attempts to provide a parallel reality of fear among Muslims in the post-9/11 policy of war. Nevertheless, the chapter illustrates how dialogue and positive exposure or encounter programs can gradually shift individuals' negative perceptions and replace fear with much needed trust and build dialogical and day-to-day interpersonal relationships.

- Osman Bakar's chapter narrates the depth and serious commitment of Muslims and their faith to interfaith dialogue. He draws heavily on the Qur'an and Hadith and historical-traditional sources to illustrate that Islam as a religion beyond any doubt supports dialogue. In arguing this perspective, he exclusively focuses on the Universalist nature of Islamic teaching and avoids the exclusivist and religiocentric interpretations. This strategy has been adopted by many Muslim scholars who offered an Islamic universal perspective.
- However a genuine interfaith conversation should not focus only on the exploration of strengths and positive images of each faith, but it should not shy away from difficult issues or hard places. Thus Woodberry and Omar offered two perspectives on the issues of conversion and the right of Muslims and Christians to engage in witness, proselytization, conversion, and apostasy.
- Although they agreed that both Muslims and Christians perceive calling others to join their faith as inherent to their respective traditions, each offered a unique way to pursue and frame such calling. Woodberry proposed mutual respectful witness—noting the parallels between the understanding and practice of Christian witness and Muslim *da'wah* and the need, recognized in former Muslim-Christian dialogues, for both communities to have freedom to convince and be convinced. Omar notes that the contextual conditions and realities of our world place many obstacles for any Muslim to practice such beliefs, especially when considering that many Christian faith-based development agencies in Africa and south Asia have great resources that have often been used historically (though to lesser extent recently) for inappropriate missionary persuasion. In addition, Omar asserts that the two faith traditions continue to misunderstand each other's perceptions of this need to convert or conduct *da'wah*. There is "a significant gap in understanding between many Christians and Muslims in the way in which they perceive of their respective missions." These differences are obviously not settled in this section; however, the depth and sensitivity of the divide in how Muslims and Christians can pursue their *da'wah* and missionary work is well articulated by Omar's contribution. Woodberry's response sharpens the issues from the Christian perspective. There he affirms that Christian aid organizations are "acutely aware" of the historical and contemporary misuse and exploitation of power in the name of Christian evangelism. Woodberry encourages a scriptural revisitation of evangelism themes and calls for a return to respectful guidelines of witness, as detailed in his chapter. The critical voice offered by Omar to the Muslim communities and scholars of theology is crucial in possibly addressing some of the current debates regarding religious freedom and Islamic laws of apostasy. He calls for honest reflec-

tion on both sides. "The case of Abdul Rahman's conversion to Christianity [in Afghanistan] has once again highlighted the urgent need for Muslims to seriously reexamine the restrictive traditional shari'ah laws on religious conversion from Islam. It is not good enough for Muslims engaged in interreligious dialogue to skirt this issue by pointing out their support for the Chambésy statement affirming 'the right to convince or to be convinced.'"

- Any effective interfaith dialogue process or design ought to be linked to the day-to-day reality experienced in communities. The last set of chapters presented three unique cases.
- First, Johnston posed a challenge to Christians and Muslims to reframe systematically the religious interpretations of their texts of scripture to emphasize the central value given to human rights. A human rights formula rooted in Christian and Muslim theological convictions can serve not only to prevent the dominance of a secular human rights, it may broaden the discussion beyond the partisanship of politicians monopolizing all discussion of human rights. It might actually deepen the understanding and appreciation of these rights among both average Muslims and Christians.
- Second, Dueck, Reimer, Morgan, and Brown provided a set of empirical data capturing the motivation and the narratives of Muslims and Christians who work for peace. Their stories and values reflect a committed group of individuals who struggle daily to maintain a vision of hope for their communities. The striking similarities shared by the Muslim and Christian peacemakers are true testimony that in the context of the harsh reality of seeking to intervene in human conflict and/or violence, many of the seemingly major theological debates disappear. Both Muslim and Christian peacemakers often adopt the similar strategies and seek the same sources for support and sustainability or empowerment. A practical follow-up for this empirical study would have been to bring these peacemakers to one setting and provide the opportunity for them to share their similar experiences and offer support for each other's struggle. Such intrafaith meetings of like-minded practitioners have often proved extremely helpful. If extended to an interfaith gathering, it could be most engaging.
- The Shafiq case of the Rochester, New York, Abrahamic Interfaith Initiative is probably the most appropriate way to end this edited volume. He lays out a set of practical instructions on how to build a solid intercommunity relationship built on genuine and open dialogical processes.
- The scholarly contribution of this volume is reflected in the diversity and critical perspectives presented by most authors as well as being the first interfaith book produced by Evangelical Christian and Muslim

> scholars. However, as editors and facilitators of the scholarly dialogue, we must relate the processes in which these chapters were produced.

The post-9/11 reality of the massive deployment of military forces and violent escalation in the exclusivist narratives, especially with the systematic violation of basic human rights on both sides of the Atlantic, forces us to seriously seek nonviolent ways to comprehend and cope. Both intra- and interfaith dialogue are identified by our authors as important, indeed crucial, modes and vehicles for sorting out political, cultural, and religious differences.

There were a variety of difficult issues raised during the discussion of these chapters, which mainly pertain to Muslim–Evangelical relations: U.S. foreign policy practices in the various Muslim worlds, current conditions and status of the Muslim community in Europe and the United States, the persecution of some Christian minorities in the Muslim and Arab world, and issues of underdevelopment and exploitation of economic resources of Muslim countries.

The group felt the tension between exploring these current issues and the academic commitment to focus on key theological differences between Islam and Christianity. Muslim scholars expressed their deep appreciation for gaining an in-depth knowledge of the Evangelical traditions in Christianity; Christian scholars marveled at the variety and complementarity of Muslims from many cultural heritages and perspectives. Nevertheless, the Muslim scholars remained motivated by the need to address the above list of difficult issues. On the other hand, the Fuller Seminary scholars emphasized their hope to deepen the theological conversation and repeatedly emphasized the limitations of Christian peacemakers to influence these issues in view of the shortcomings and failure of the popular Evangelical Christian attempts to dominate in the realm of public policy making on the above concerns.

Despite the above differences, interpersonal relationship and friendship were woven among most of the participants, and new projects and initiatives have been formed. Meals and music were shared, cultural and religious practices were explained and observed, families were affected by the dialogue process, and seeds of hope were planted in places where few if any of us had dreamed of going or working. For these opportunities we are grateful to our participants for their courage and respect in human interactions.

Appendix A

COMMISSION ON JEWISH-MUSLIM UNDERSTANDING (CJMU)

Statement of Purpose

The Commission on Jewish-Muslim Understanding of the Greater Rochester Area has the purpose of creating mutual understanding and appreciation between the Jewish and Muslim communities with a view toward broadening mutual respect and enhancing active cooperation within the Greater Rochester area.

Through educational and social opportunities, and social justice activities, the Commission encourages increased understanding and dialogue among its members, its synagogues and *masjids*, and within the community at large. One of the main purposes of the Jewish-Muslim Commission is to address educational, social, religious, and moral issues of the communities at large.

The Commission commits itself to specific steps toward implementing its purpose by:

- Fostering interaction between Jewish and Muslim communities.
- Defending the civil and human rights of members of both communities through advocacy, education, dialogue, and public relations.

- Addressing the media regarding its role in presenting accurate and fair reporting on issues of concern to Jews and Muslims and its role in fostering each other's understanding.
- Creating educational programs of common interest.
- Maintaining links with other interfaith and community groups in the area.

Signed by Jewish Members and Muslim Members

Appendix B

COMMISSION ON CHRISTIAN MUSLIM RELATIONS (CCMR)

The Commission was formed in 1993. Since its inception, the Commission has done a marvelous job in outreach programs. Its seminars and activities are attended by up to 250 people. The following are the bylaws of the Commission. These bylaws were revised and amended in 2003 and were passed unanimously on September 1, 2004.

Statement of Purpose

The Commission on Christian Muslim Relations of the Muslim Community of the Greater Rochester Area, through the Council of Masajid (GRCM) and the Greater Rochester Community of Churches (GRCC) has the purpose of deepening mutual understanding and appreciation between the Christian and Muslim communities. Our objective is to broaden mutual respect and to enhance active participation within the Greater Rochester Area. We understand one another as peoples who are grounded in Abrahamic faith traditions. Together we will address ethical, social, and moral issues.

The above stated purposes will be accomplished through

- Education
- Social interaction

- Monitor and response to media
- Advocating

Our mission is to increase understanding, improve dialogue, and dispel fear. The commission shall foster interaction, defend civil and human rights, and challenge perceived public notions of our respective faith communities.

Membership

Each community will have a minimum of six and a maximum of nine members. The Commission encourages the sponsoring bodies to strive for diversity and gender representation.

Officers

The Commission will elect a chair and vice chair alternating between Muslims and Christians. The Commission will elect a recording secretary/treasurer to record and distribute minutes and to receive, record, and distribute funds as directed. Officers will serve two-year terms beginning January 1. Officers' terms may or may not be renewable as executive and Commission members choose.

Accountability

The Commission will submit an annual report to GRCM and GRCC every December.

Finance

GRCM and GRCC, the sponsoring organizations, will provide a minimal budget. Extra funding for special events is the responsibility of the Commission.

Amendments

Amendments to these bylaws may be made by a majority vote of the Commission members following consideration at two successive meetings. At least four members of each community must be in favor of the amendment under consideration.

Honorary Life Membership

The Commission may grant, in recognition of long-time exemplary service to the cause of Christian–Muslim relations, a nonvoting honorary life membership. The Commission meets monthly. It reviews minutes, discusses any significant event occurred during the month, and plans for future activities. Below I list some of the joint seminars the Commission has organized for public education and building peaceful relations.

Appendix C

MUSLIM-CATHOLIC ALLIANCE: AN AGREEMENT OF UNDERSTANDING AND COOPERATION

The following is a solemn document of agreement between the Roman Catholic Diocese of Rochester, New York, and the Council of Masajid of Rochester, New York. Affirming our faith in only one God, and recognizing our common history and shared Abrahamic traditions, we pray to the merciful God to inspire in us respect, mutual understanding, and love and to guide us to pursue our common values for the benefit of all in our society and beyond.

Article I

In adherence to the spirit and laws of our respective religious traditions, to the principles of the Universal Declaration of Human rights, and to the Bill of Rights embodied in our American Constitution, we affirm our commitment to uphold the right of every human being to freedom of speech, thought, religion, and conscience.

Article II

We jointly declare our dedication to challenge continuously all forms of religious, ethnic intolerance, and bigotry through active promotion of mutual understanding and respect for human life and dignity.

a. By responding openly to acts of religious, racial, ethnic, or any other kind of intolerance.
b. By investing time, labor, and talents to sensitizing our own communities to the evils of such intolerance.
c. By informing and educating each other on matters of public concern.

Article III

We dedicate and commit ourselves to foster the maturing relationship of mutual respect and cooperation between our two communities, by promoting a deeper knowledge of and respect for each other's history, traditions, and sensitivities.

For us to accomplish this, our communities are seriously encouraged to discover even better ways to foster and promote:

a. A comprehensive dialogue that leads to goodwill and mutual understanding.
b. The development and dissemination of appropriate information involving each other's religious traditions for both children and adults. Combined learning experiences are especially encouraged.
c. The necessity to deepen awareness and sensitivity to issues of special contemporary concern to either community.

Article IV

In regard to community outreach, whenever possible, we are strongly encouraged to collaborate in developing mutually beneficial services while respecting the integrity and independence of each other's service organizations.

a. By supporting, whenever feasible, efforts in each other's community as well as in the general public to provide for the basic needs of all.
b. By being, whenever possible, cognizant of comprehending and being sensitive to the global needs of each tradition.

Article V

A joint committee will be formed by the Diocese and the Council to see to it that this agreement is fully and faithfully implemented.

Signed today: May 5, 2003

Signed by Representatives
The Roman Catholic Diocese of Rochester
Greater Rochester Council of Masajid

Appendix D

A PLEDGE OF REMEMBRANCE AND A COMMITMENT TO PEACE

We are people of faith fervently praying for peace in our world and in our community in this time of increasing crisis. While some may feel helpless about being able to change the course of global events, we do not believe we are spiritually or politically powerless. All of our traditions call us to value each human life and to stand up for injustice and human rights. We believe there is an important role each of us can play in peacemaking in this community—our community—with potential ripples in the world beyond Rochester.

We are a remarkable community that has been a model for interfaith cooperation. We draw strength from the experiences we have lived together. We believe we can continue to do God's will by reaching out to each other across our differences and refusing to be pitted against each other.

We Pledge to Remember we cannot expect unanimity on issues as complex and filled with pain as those currently confronting us—not across groups, nor within our groups, nor even within even our own anguished hearts and minds.

We Pledge to Remember the promises of relationships that can endure through turmoil and grief. We remember when we have stood with one another in times of distress, and we pledge to remain committed to being friends when the world would separate us from one another.

We Pledge to Remember that each act has the power to heal and bring us closer together or to sting and further divide us. When we speak or act publicly, regardless of our feelings of rage or terror or shame, we will remember that we can choose our responses, and be sensitive to not using words that are perceived as hurtful.

We Pledge to Remember that we may not be able to change others' opinions, but we can encourage a climate of openness in which we can explore, with sensitivity and with understanding, the history, points of view, and fears of others.

We Pledge to Remember to pray for the healing of our wounds. All of our hearts are breaking, and we remember that God's heart is broken too.

We Pledge to Remember that we are all children of God. As such we pledge to offer each other hope and a vision of a just world.

We Pledge to Remember that hope requires action to be fulfilled. We pledge to be bold about reaching out and *one thing each day* to open communication, to bridge differences, to offer compassion, and to bring about healing.

Appendix E

MODEL 1: ISLAM 101

Four Sessions

1. The Message and the Messenger:

   In this session you will learn about the message of Al Qur'an and the way prophet Muhammad delivered the message as a messenger and living model of the Qur'an.

2. Muslim Life around the Clock:

   This session will tell how observant Muslims actually spend their day. How their beliefs affect the way they live their lives from moment to moment. There will be a video spotlighting Muslim youth.

3. Jihad: Personal and Public:

   The news media has turned Jihad into a scary word, practically synonymous with terrorism. Actually, the concept, which means "striving," has deeply spiritual as well as political dimensions not only in Islam but also in Christianity. The session explores these dimensions, working comparatively from one religion to other.

4. Women in the Qur'an:

   Many Muslim women scholars have gone back to the words of the Qur'an to discover a clear assertion of the equality of men and women. This session will include equality of women in religious, social, and family life along with other topics.

ANOTHER ISLAM 101 SERIES

1. Faith and Worship in Islam

   How do Muslims actually spend their day? How their beliefs affect the way they live their lives.

2. Muhammad and the Qur'an

   We will learn about the message of the Qur'an and the way Prophet Muhammad delivered the message; as a messenger and a living model of the Qur'an.

3. Jihad and Extremism: Christianity and Islam

   The news media has turned *jihad* into a scary word, practically synonymous with terrorism. Actually the concept, which means "striving," has a deep spiritual as well as a political dimension not only in Islam but also in Christianity. This session explores these dimensions, working comparatively from one religion to the other.

4. Violence and Terrorism: Christianity and Islam

   The practice of violence and terrorism is alarmingly increasing in the world as a means of settling issues. What is the perspective of the two religions on violence and terrorism?

ANOTHER ISLAM 101 SERIES BETWEEN THE ISLAMIC CENTER AND THE EPISCOPAL DIOCESE

Three sessions

1. Islam: Belief and Teaching
2. Islam: Family, Social Life and Women's Issues
3. Islam: Forgiveness and Justice

MODEL 2: ISLAM 201 SESSIONS

Both sessions were free and open to those who had attended any Islam 101 classes and are members of the Muslim community.

Qur'an: The Written and the Living
Prelude: A variety of recitation styles of the Qur'an from the CD accompanying the book

Approaching the Qur'an, The Early Revelations. (ten minutes)

A. *The Written Qur'an (twenty minutes)*

1. Language: miracle, selection of words makes the Qur'anic language unique in its style (unlike the Arabic of the Hadith).
2. Composition: how it was revealed, the writing, how it was put together into book form and its preservation.
3. Structure: surahs (chapter topics), the Mecca surahs (more spiritual and belief orientated), and the Medina surahs (focused on daily life).

B. *Hadith and Sunnah: The Living Qur'an (twenty minutes)*

1. Hadith: commentary on the Qur'an, by the Prophet Muhammad, written down as a deeper explanation of the meaning of the Qur'an.
2. Sunnah: unwritten form of the life of the Prophet, what he said, did, and approved.

C. *Question and Answer (thirty minutes)*

D. *Open Discussion (thirty minutes)*

Session II: Shar'iah (Islamic Law): Its Application in Modern Times

A. *Introduction (ten minutes)*

B. *Shar'iah the Divine Law (twenty minutes)*

1. The roots of Shar'iah in the Qur'an and Sunnah.
2. Shar'iah and Capital Punishment.
3. Shar'iah and Human Rights.

C. Fatwah: Its Application and significance in Shar'iah. (twenty minutes)

D. Question and Answer (thirty minutes)

E. Open Discussion (thirty minutes)

The Greater Rochester Community of Churches (GRCC) and the Greater Rochester Council of Masajid (GRCM) sponsor the Commission on Christian Muslim Relations

MODEL 3: ISLAM IN AMERICA: MANY FACES

Content: The media often presents Islam as if it were a monolith, as if it were exactly the same in every country and at every time. Our program tonight will try to dispel this myth by describing two of the "many faces" of Islam here in the United States: the face of the Muslim immigrant community and the face of our home-grown African American Muslim community. What are the hopes and fears of these communities? How are their hopes and fears like and unlike the hopes and fears of the many other faces of Islam in other parts of the world?

Title: Extremism and Fundamentalism in Islam and Christianity

Content: How is it that Islam and Christianity, religions dedicated to peace and human flourishing, have in many instances become distorted by fundamentalism and extremism— and have even been manipulated to justify violence? Tonight's session is dedicated to addressing this controversial question in a calm, informed, and respectful way.

MODEL 4: PASSAGES OF LIFE

These were very successful series between the Catholic and Muslim communities and were well attended.

"Beginnings and Endings as Seen through Muslim and Catholic Eyes"

A. Conception and Childhood

Content: Attitudes of Islam and Catholic Christianity toward life in the womb, toward abortion, and toward children and child rearing; role of informed conscience.

B. Youth and Growing Up

Content: Attitudes of Islam and Catholic Christianity toward education of the young, balancing discipline with permissiveness, rites of passage, handling emerging sexuality and gender issues, handling conflicts with surrounding culture, handling religious education, and conscience formation.

C. Marriage

Content: Attitudes of Islam and Christianity toward the purpose and meaning of marriage, connection between marriage and the larger community, rites and their meaning, and divorce.

D. Aging, Dying, and Death

Content: Attitudes of Islam and Catholic Christianity toward the aging process, illness, loss, incapacity, end-of-life issues, funeral rites, and mourning.

E. Afterlife

Content: Beliefs of Islam and Catholic Christianity about the life to come; how those beliefs affect the present.

MODEL 5: JUDAISM AND ISLAM 101

Four Series

A. Prayers

Place: Islamic Center of Rochester, New York.

Jews pray three times a day and Muslims five. What are these prayers and what are our expectations from them? What do our faiths say about the role and impact of prayers?

The session begins with the tour of the Center and opportunity to observe daily prayers.

The number of audience was in hundreds unexpectedly. The program was shifted to the *masjid* (a Muslim place of worship) and was jam-packed with Jews and Muslims. Many Jews and Muslims wondered when they saw the conservative rabbi speaking in the *masjid*.

B. Food and Fasting

Muslims fast during Ramadan and Jews on Yom Kippur and a few other fast days. Why do we do this and how does it affect us? Both faiths are also concerned of what we eat and how the food is prepared—whether it is Kosher or Halal. What does this tell us about our attitudes toward food and the meaning of eating? Beginning with the tour of the synagogue and followed by a "tasting" of Jewish and Muslim foods.

C. Prophets, Prophecy and Prophethood

Both of our faiths recognize the existence of prophets and revere them in our respective ways. What makes a prophet and why should we care? Why haven't we seen any around lately?

D. T G I F:

Jews live Fridays with expectancy as they prepare for the oncoming Sabbath at sundown. Muslims also treat Fridays differently with extended prayers, though they do not share the concept of Sabbath. But we both thank God it's Friday.

MODEL 6

Three Sessions

These series were well attended and very appreciated.

A. Journey to America

A historical perspective of a secular history of our cultures. How we established our communities in America.

B. Overcoming Challenges and Obstacles, Islamic center

This session will cover the prejudice, racism, and discrimination and other related issues the two communities have or are been through.

C. Multiple Faces of American Jews and American Muslims

MODEL 7: CONCEPTIONS AND MISCONCEPTIONS OF WOMEN IN JUDAISM AND ISLAM

Rituals and customs, home and family

The seminar took place at Temple Sinai and many members of the Muslim and Jewish communities participated. It was quite successful.

MODEL 8: JEWISH-MUSLIM PICNIC

MODEL 9: JEWISH-MUSLIM YOUTH MEETING

Watching "Promises" documentary

MODEL 10: MUSLIM-CATHOLIC ALLIANCE (MCA)

The MCA celebrated its second anniversary.

Speakers included Dr. Sayyid M. Syeed, secretary general of the Islamic Society of North America (ISNA), and Fr. Francis V. Tiso, PhD, associate director, Secretariat for Ecumenical and Interreligious Affairs, Subcommittee on Interreligious Dialogue, United States Conference of Catholic Bishops (USCCB)

The Cathedral was packed with people and the program was well received and appreciated.

MODEL 11: COMMISSION ON CHRISTIAN MUSLIM RELATIONS (CCMR)

Presents

"Facing Our Fears about Islam"

This series will use a combination of videos and outside speakers to focus on the fears non-Muslims tend to have about Muslims and Islam. These fears are often triggered by the media's indiscriminate use of words and images. We will look at these words and images to see where the problems lie and to work out together ways of addressing them.

Dates: Monday evenings, 10/20, 10/27, 11/3
Time: 7–8:30 p.m.
Place: Islamic Center of Rochester
727 Westfall Road, Rochester, NY 14620

Monday, October 20, 2008
Program 1: "What Shapes American Views of Islam?"
Facilitator: Dr. Emil Homerin, professor, religion and classics, University of Rochester

Monday, October 27, 2008
Program 2: "Media Images of Islam: Fact and Myth"
Facilitator: Dr. Melanie May, vice president, Colgate Rochester Crozer Divinity School, Rochester

Monday, November 3, 2008
Program 3: "Overcoming Our Fears of the "Other"
Facilitator: Rev. Gordon Webster, Downtown United Presbyterian Church, Rochester

Format: Brief focusing talk, thirty minutes for break-out sessions; thirty minutes for plenary gathering.

Cosponsors: Muslim-Catholic Alliance (MCA), Nazareth College, Center for Interfaith Studies and Dialogue (CISD)

Contact for further information: Dr. George Dardess: gdardess@yahoo.com or call Islamic Center at: 442-0117

Appendix F

MODEL 12: MUSLIM LEADERSHIP TRAINING: SENSITIVITY TO CHRISTIAN BELIEFS

Surah 49:13: "O humankind, we created you from a single pair of male and female, and made you into different nations and tribes, so that you might get to know each other."

DATE: Sunday, June 6 6:30–8:30 p.m.
TIME:
Dinner 6:30–7:00 p.m.
Panel presentations and topical discussions 7:00–8:00 p.m.
Open forum 8:00–8:20 p.m.
Wrap-up/Feedback: possibility of future sessions, topics
INTRODUCTION: George Dardess (six to seven minutes)
PANELISTS:
Rev. Denise Yarbrough, Ecumenical and Interfaith Officer Episcopal Diocese of Rochester
Rev. Peter Carman, pastor, Lake Avenue Baptist Church
Fr. Joe Marcoux, Roman Catholic Diocese of Rochester
TOPICS:

1. Creation
2. Original sin
3. The Trinity
4. Jesus Christ—Who is He?
5. What unites Christians?

PLEASE NOTE: The Panel Presentations and Topical Discussions will follow the following format:

Each panelist will get two minutes for topic no. 1, and then we will have six minutes of discussion on topic no. 1. Then we will move on to topic no. 2 and so on through the five topics followed by a Q&A session.

APPENDIXES: PROCEEDINGS OF THE CONFERENCE: VARIOUS CD TRANSCRIPTIONS

Index

About the Contributors

Ghulam Haider Aasi is associate professor and chairperson of Islamic studies and history of religions at the American Islamic College, Chicago. He holds graduate degrees in Arabic and Islamic studies from the University of Punjab and in religion from Temple University, Philadelphia. Aasi has been a visiting professor at the Institute of Islamic Thought and Civilization, Malaysia, and the National Mahidol University, Thailand. His articles are published in numerous international journals. He has been an adjunct faculty in Islamic studies at the Lutheran School of Theology at Chicago since 1985 —(www.lstc.edu/ccmepj/speakers.html).

Mohammed Abu-Nimer is a professor of international peace and conflict resolution at American University's School of International Service. He is also director of the Peace-building and Development Institute at American University and director of the Salam Institute for Peace & Justice. Some of his most recent publications include *Unity in Diversity: Interfaith Dialogue in the Middle East* with Amal Khoury and Emily Welty (2007) and *Modern Islamic Thought: Dynamic, Not Static* with Abdul Aziz Said and Meena Sharify-Funk (2006).

Asma Afsaruddin is associate professor of Arabic and Islamic studies at the University of Notre Dame and chair of the board of directors of the Center for the Study of Islam & Democracy. She is the author and/or editor of four books, including the recently published *The First Muslims: History and Memory* (2008) and *Excellence and Precedence: Medieval Islamic Discourse on Legitimate Leadership* (2002). Her research interests include

Qur'an and hadith, pluralism in Islamic religious and political thought, Islamic intellectual history, and gender issues. Afsaruddin has received major grants from the Harry Frank Guggenheim Foundation and the Carnegie Corporation of New York for her current book-length project on jihad and martyrdom in Islamic thought and practice.

David Augsburger is professor of pastoral care and counseling at Fuller Theological Seminary. Author of twenty-five books, the most appropriate to this chapter are *Conflict Mediation across Cultures* (1992), *Helping People Forgive* (1996), and *Hate-work: Working through the Pain and Pleasures of Hate* (2004).

Osman Bakar, professor emeritus of philosophy and former deputy vice chancellor at the University of Malaya, is currently professor of Islamic thought and civilization at the International Institute of Islamic Thought and Civilization in Malaysia. He is also a senior fellow at the Center for Muslim-Christian Understanding, Georgetown University, Washington, DC. He was educated at London University, where he obtained his BSc and MSc in mathematics. He earned his doctorate in Islamic philosophy from Temple University, Philadelphia. A Fullbright visiting scholar, he has published 13 books and more than 150 articles on Islamic thought and civilization, particularly Islamic philosophy and science, and on contemporary Islam and interreligious and intercivilizational dialogues. The founder of the Center for Civilizational Dialogue at the University of Malaya, he has also served as advisor and consultant to various international academic and professional organizations and institutions, including UNESCO and the Qatar Foundation. He is a member of the West–Islamic World Initiative for Dialogue established by the World Economic Forum based in Switzerland (www.iiu.edu.my/istac/profile2.php).

Steve Brown is a clinical psychologist employed at Patton State Hospital. He has recently completed research on an instrument measuring attitudes toward peace.

Karim Douglas Crow earned his MA and doctor of philosophy (with honors) from the Institute of Islamic Studies, McGill University, and his BA (with distinction) from the American University of Beirut, Lebanon. Crow has lectured at the University of Maryland, University of Virginia, New York University, and Columbia University. Dr. Crow's publications include *When God Created Wisdom—The 'Aql Creation Narratives in Early Islam*. Other published articles include "Sacred Mind and Profane Mind: Two Kinds of 'Aql with al-Muhasibi and al Hakim al Tirmidhi" in the *Journal of Islamic Studies* and "Islamic Ethics and 'Changing Behavior'" in the *Interna-*

tional Journal of Nonviolence. Crow is a member of the Middle East Studies Association of North America, the Middle East Medievalists at the World Music Institute, and Minbar al-Hurr ("Pulpit of Freedom"—Beirut) (www.american.edu/cgp/scholars.htm).

Alvin C. Dueck is professor of psychology, Fuller Graduate School of Psychology. He is editor with Cameron Lee of *Why Psychology Needs Theology: A Radical-Reformation Perspective* (2005).

Rabia Terri Harris is an essayist, editor, peace activist, public intellectual, practicing chaplain, freelance theologian, sometime translator, and aspiring servant of Allah. She founded the Muslim Peace Fellowship in 1994 and serves as its executive director. As a columnist and contributing editor at *Fellowship*, the magazine of the Fellowship of Reconciliation (www.forusa.org), Rabia has spent well over a decade engaged in interreligious peace and justice work.

Riffat Hassan is a member of the Islamic Research Foundation International and is an award-winning scholar, a voice for moderate Islam and interreligious dialogue, and professor of religious studies and humanities at the University of Louisville, Kentucky. In February 1999, she founded the International Network for the Rights of Female Victims of Violence in Pakistan (INRFVVP), a nonprofit organization with a worldwide membership, which has played a noteworthy role in highlighting the issue of violence against girls and women, particularly with reference to "crimes of honor" (www.irfi.org/articles/articles_101_150/religious_conservatism.htm).

David L. Johnston worked as pastor and teacher in Algeria, Egypt, and the West Bank between 1978 and 1996. He subsequently completed a PhD in Islamic studies from Fuller Theological Seminary in Pasadena, California, and spent five years at the Religious Studies Department of Yale University as a postdoctoral fellow, parttime lecturer, and research associate. He teaches Islamic studies as an adjunct professor at the University of Pennsylvania and St. Joseph's University. His articles have appeared, among other places, in *Islamic Law and Society*, *Islamochristiana*, *The Maghreb Review*, *Die Welt des Islams*, and *The Encyclopaedia of the Qur'an*. His forthcoming book is titled *Earth, Empire and Sacred Text: Muslims and Christians as Trustees of Creation* (2008).

James (Jimmy) Jones is associate professor of world religions with a concurrent appointment in African studies at Manhattanville College (Purchase, New York). Dr. Jones is also a visiting professor of comparative religion at Cordoba University's Graduate School of Islamic and Social Science

(Ashburn, Virginia). He is currently the academic director of the Summer Arabic/Qur'an Immersion Program at Cairo's Al-Azhar University where he has served for the past four years. His most recent publication is a chapter in the book *Islamophobia and Anti-Americanism* (Mohamed Nimer, ed., 2007) titled "What Is Taking Place Is a Clash of Cousins."

S. Ayse Kadayifci-Orellana is currently assistant professor in the field of peace and conflict resolution at the School of International Service at American University, Washington, DC. She is also one of the founding members and the associate director of Salam Institute for Peace & Justice, a nonprofit organization for research, education, and practice on issues related to conflict resolution, nonviolence, and development with a focus on bridging differences between Muslim and non-Muslim communities. She received her PhD from American University's School of International Service in Washington, DC, in 2002 with a master's degree in conflict analysis from University of Kent in Canterbury, England.

Joshua P. Morgan is a doctoral student of psychology at Azusa Pacific University. He is currently completing his predoctoral internship at Loma Linda University Health Care. His primary interest is in the integration of psychology and spirituality, particularly spiritual formation.

Abdul Rashied Omar is a research scholar of Islamic studies and peace-building at the Joan B. Kroc Institute for International Peace Studies, University of Notre Dame, USA. He completed his master's degree and a PhD in religious studies from the University of Cape Town (2005). Dr. Omar's research and teaching are focused in the area of religion, violence, and peace-building, with a twin focus on the Islamic ethics of war and peace and interreligious dialogue. Currently he is completing a book manuscript on "Religion, Violence, and State Terror" and in collaboration with two international scholars he is coediting *A Dictionary of Christian-Muslim Relations.*

Kevin S. Reimer is professor of psychology at Azusa Pacific University. Educated in Canada and the United States, he holds degrees in developmental psychology, biological sciences, theology, and literature. He is widely published in behavioral science and religion. Reimer's books include *The Reciprocating Self* (2005), *A Peaceable Psychology* (2009), and *Mere Samaritans* (2009). He is ordained in the Presbyterian Church (USA).

Evelyne Reisacher, assistant professor of Islamic studies and intercultural relations, has taught at Fuller since 2001. Her current research involves exploring gender issues in Islam, Muslim–Christian relations, world religions, and right brain–to–right brain communication, as well as studying intercultural attachment. With mastery of seven languages, including French, Arabic, German, Hebrew, Greek, Latin, and English, she has also served as a translator at various conferences and talks throughout Europe and the Middle East. Reisacher recently published an article titled "Beyond the Veil" in *Christianity and Islam* (2005), a publication of the Center of Christian Ethics at Baylor University.

Muhammad Shafiq is professor and executive director at the Center for Interfaith Studies and Dialogue (www.naz.edu/dept/cisd), Nazareth College, Rochester, New York. He is also executive director and imam of the Islamic Center of Rochester. He has been an active worker and participant in several interfaith forums and dialogue groups in America and abroad for more than three decades. He has published more than forty articles and several books. Among them are *Interfaith Dialogue: A Guide for Muslims* (coauthor, 2007) and *Growth of Islamic Thought in North America* (1994).

Wilbert R. Shenk is senior professor of history and contemporary culture, Fuller Graduate School of Intercultural Studies. His most recent work is a volume he edited, *North American Foreign Missions, 1810–1914: Theology, Theory, Policy* (2004).

Glen Stassen is the author of *Living the Sermon on the Mount* (2006), *Just Peacemaking: Transforming Initiatives for Justice and Peace* (1992), and *Kingdom Ethics: Following Jesus in Contemporary Context*, with David Gushee (2003), which won the Christianity Today Award for Best Book of 2004 in Theology or Ethics. He is Lewis B. Smedes Professor of Christian ethics at Fuller Theological Seminary, where he won the All Seminary Council Faculty Award for Outstanding Community Service to Students. At Berea College, he won the Seabury Award for Excellence in Teaching.

J. Dudley Woodberry is senior professor of Islamic studies at Fuller and is considered one of the foremost Christian scholars of Islam. He has served as consultant on the Muslim world to President Carter, the State Department, USAID, and other U.S. government agencies. His newest work, *Muslim and Christian Reflections on Peace*, edited with Osman Zumrut and Mustafa Koylu, came out in 2005. Recent teaching and lecturing trips have taken him to Korea, Indonesia, Denmark, Norway, and Pakistan.